Praise for *Java to Kotlin*

Nat and Duncan open the book by saying they wish this book had existed when they adopted Kotlin. I completely agree. The book takes their experiences, their trials and errors, and helps you, the reader, to be on the right path. It definitely is a book that should be on anyone's shelf coming to Kotlin from the JVM ecosystem. An enjoyable read, and an even better reference guide!

—Hadi Hariri, JetBrains

To take familiar good old Java code and see it transform, incrementally, into concise, clear, expressive and easy to maintain Kotlin code is a wonderful way to learn the language. Benefit from the experience McGregor and Pryce have distilled in this book.

—Dr. Venkat Subramaniam, award-winning author and founder of Agile Developer, Inc.

The fastest way to upgrade your skills from Java to Kotlin. Essential reading for any professional Java developer.

—Dawn Griffiths and David Griffiths, authors of Head First Kotlin

Java to Kotlin

A Refactoring Guidebook

Duncan McGregor and Nat Pryce

Beijing • Boston • Farnham • Sebastopol • Tokyo

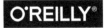

Java to Kotlin

by Duncan McGregor and Nat Pryce

Published by O'Reilly Media, Inc., 1005 Gravenstein Highway North, Sebastopol, CA 95472.

O'Reilly books may be purchased for educational, business, or sales promotional use. Online editions are also available for most titles (*http://oreilly.com*). For more information, contact our corporate/institutional sales department: 800-998-9938 or *corporate@oreilly.com*.

Acquisitions Editor: Suzanne McQuade
Development Editor: Sarah Grey
Production Editor: Kate Galloway
Copyeditor: nSight, Inc.
Proofreader: Sonia Saruba
Indexer: Judith McConville
Interior Designer: David Futato
Cover Designer: Karen Montgomery
Illustrator: Kate Dullea

August 2021: First Edition

Revision History for the First Edition
2021-08-13: First Release

See *http://oreilly.com/catalog/errata.csp?isbn=9781492082279* for release details.

978-1-492-08227-9

[LSI]

Table of Contents

Preface

Hello, this is Duncan and Nat. As you're reading this preface, you're probably trying to decide whether to invest some hours into reading the rest of this book. So let's cut to the chase:

> This book won't teach you to program computers in Kotlin.

We started writing a book that would, but it soon became clear that Kotlin is a large language, and so the book was going to take longer to write than we wanted. There are also already some great books in that space, and we don't like competing against great.

We decided instead to make our lives easier by concentrating on teaching Kotlin to Java developers, based on a workshop that we run called Refactoring to Kotlin. This teaches the Kotlin language by converting existing code and is (according to our marketing material) designed for Java teams wanting to leverage their existing knowledge to accelerate their Kotlin adoption.

We started writing *that* book, but it soon became clear that Kotlin is *still* a large language, and so we would *still* be writing for a long time. We also found that motivated and experienced Java developers can pick up most of Kotlin very quickly. It felt patronizing to plow our way through language features that our target readers will probably just appreciate and adopt as soon as they see them. So we abandoned that idea, and as a result:

> This book won't teach you the Kotlin language.

So why should you read it? Because we have written the book we wish was available when we first adopted Kotlin. We are experienced programmers who know Java and the Java ecosystem well. We hope you are too. Like us, you probably have experience in a number of other languages. You've learned the basics of Kotlin, and you recognize that to get the best out of the language you will need to design your systems differently. You have found that some things that are cumbersome in Java are much easier in Kotlin, and that some features, such as checked exceptions, are not there at all. You don't want to end up merely writing Java code in Kotlin syntax.

Perhaps you have skin in the game. Maybe you're in a technical leadership position, or have successfully convinced your team to adopt Kotlin. You might have spent some political capital to get Kotlin into the project. Now you need to ensure that the transition goes smoothly.

You may be responsible for a Java codebase and want to ensure that introducing Kotlin won't destabilize its existing, business-critical code. Or you may be starting a Kotlin project from scratch but realize your design instincts turn more readily to Java and objects than to Kotlin and functions.

If this is you, as it was us, then you've come to the right place. This book will help you adapt your thinking and designs to take advantage of Kotlin. That's not enough, though, because you have existing code that you need to maintain and enhance. So we also show how to migrate that code from Java to Kotlin syntax, and from Java to Kotlin thinking, incrementally and safely, using the automated refactoring tools built into the IntelliJ IDE.

How This Book Is Organized

This book is about how to transition from Java to Kotlin, mainly focused on code but touching on projects and organizations. Each chapter addresses an aspect of this transition, looking at some aspect of typical Java projects that can be improved on the journey. They are named in the pattern *Java Way* to *Kotlin Way*, where we recommend that you prefer the latter over the former. Maybe Kotlin makes easier an approach that was difficult in Java, or Kotlin discourages an approach that is common in Java to guide design in a direction that is less error-prone, more concise, and more tool-friendly.

We don't just *recommend* you adopt the Kotlin way though; the chapters also show how to make the transformation. Not by just rewriting the Java, but by gradually refactoring it to Kotlin it in a way that is safe and allows us to maintain a mixed language codebase.

How Did We Choose the Topics?

We began by analyzing Java and Kotlin developers' use of their respective languages and conducting interviews to identify areas of difference and confusion. This was backed by a machine learning analysis of 33,459 open source Java and Kotlin codebases. These identified candidates that we labeled in the thing-to-another-thing form before ranking them according to frequency and developer-pain-quotient in order to establish which should make the cut. Finally, we ordered the surviving topics by…

...it's no good, we can't lie to you.

The truth is that we started by choosing topics that we wanted to write about, and that we felt would be interesting and informative. Chapter 15, *Encapsulated Collections to Type Aliases*, Chapter 9, *Multi- to Single-Expression Functions*, and Chapter 20, *Performing I/O to Passing Data* are typical of these chapters. We also looked for places where the grain of Kotlin and Java differ significantly, because those were the places where we found we learned most by asking why they were different. This led to chapters like Chapter 4, *Optional to Nullable*, Chapter 6, *Java to Kotlin Collections*, and Chapter 8, *Static Methods to Top-Level Functions*.

As we wrote those chapters, other topics presented themselves and were added to the list. In particular, as we wrote the refactoring steps for a chapter, we often found ourselves making changes to code that we felt deserved their own chapter. Chapter 13, *Streams to Iterables to Sequences*, Chapter 10, *Functions to Extension Functions*, and Chapter 11, *Methods to Properties* are examples of these.

The result of this process is by no means exhaustive. If you have already skimmed the table of contents or index, you will find important topics unaddressed. Take co-routines for example: this paragraph is the only reference to this huge subject, because we have found that they haven't changed the way that we write server-side code, so we didn't want to write about them. There are also topics that we would like to have covered if only we had space and time, including: builders, domain-specific languages, reflection, dependency injection frameworks, transactions...the list goes on!

We hope that what we *have* written about is interesting to you. It is largely a book of tactics rather than strategies, concentrating on the small battles that we can win from our place in the trenches, rather than what might be achieved by directing whole divisions. As larger themes emerge, we will try to connect them, though, and to bring things together in the final chapter, Chapter 23, *Continuing the Journey*, where we talk about what we have learned during the writing process.

Complexity

How should we judge the internal quality of our software? Assuming that it does what our customers want or need it to do, how can we compare two potential implementations, or decide whether a change makes one better or worse? The answer that your authors choose is complexity. Other things being equal, we favor simple designs that yield predictable behavior.

Of course to some extent, simplicity and complexity are in the eye of the beholder. Your authors do have slightly different personal preferences and so sometimes disagree over whether one implementation or another is better. Where that happens, we sometimes explore the alternatives in the relevant chapter. However, we do both have a shared belief in the power of functional programming to reduce the complexity of our systems, especially when combined with object-oriented (OO) message passing.

Java has been moving in this direction over the years. Scala ran toward functional programming but away from OO. We find that the grain of Kotlin lets us mix functional and object programming in a way that reduces complexity and brings out the best in mere mortal developers.

Perfect Code

On the subject of mere mortals, we should address code quality. It is sorely tempting to aim for perfection when committing code to a book. We know that you will be judging us by the code here, and like many developers, a great deal of our own self-worth is tied up in the quality of the work we produce.

At the same time, we are engineers not artists. Our job is to balance scope, schedule, and cost for our customers. No one but us really cares about the quality of the code except when it affects one of these three higher values.

So in our examples, we have tried to show realistic production code. The starting points are sometimes not as good as we might like; we are, after all, trying to show ways of improving them. Often refactorings will make things worse before they get better, so definitely don't judge us by code in the middle of a chapter. By the end of a chapter, our aim is to have code that is good enough, but not so perfect that we could be accused of wasting our clients' money.

That said, we have a policy of applying cost-effective changes to tidy up, even once we have covered the topic we set out to illustrate, and more than once we have invented a topic, and written a chapter just to leave the code in a state that we're happy with. In the end, we are artists as well as engineers.

Code Formatting

Our code follows (our interpretation of) the standard coding conventions of Java and Kotlin where possible.

The practical line length for printed code samples is much shorter than the 120 characters we usually use in an IDE these days, so we have had to split lines more often than usual to make the code fit in the page width. Our production code might have four or five parameters or arguments on a line; in this book we will often only have one. Through formatting the examples for the page, we have come to like the more vertical style. We find that Kotlin naturally seems to want to take more vertical space than Java, but even Java readability seems improved by shorter lines, more breaks, and more visual alignment. Certainly scrolling sideways is almost as inconvenient in an IDE as in a book, and our pairing sessions are improved by less scrolling and more side-by-side windows. One line per parameter also greatly improves diffs between code versions. We hope that at the very least you don't find it too painful to read, and if you don't, then try it for your own code.

We will sometimes hide code that isn't relevant to the discussion. A line that starts with an ellipsis of three dots indicates that we have omitted some code for clarity or brevity. For example:

```
fun Money(amount: String, currency: Currency) =
    Money(BigDecimal(amount), currency)

... and other convenience overloads
```

Conventions Used in This Book

The following typographical conventions are used in this book:

Italic
: Indicates new terms, URLs, email addresses, filenames, and file extensions.

`Constant width`
: Used for program listings, as well as within paragraphs to refer to program elements such as variable or function names, databases, data types, environment variables, statements, and keywords.

This element signifies a tip or suggestion.

This element signifies a general note.

This element indicates a warning or caution.

Using Code Examples

Most of the code examples in the book (the ones from the refactoring sections) can be accessed online on GitHub. The reference is immediately after the code, like this:

```
class TableReaderAcceptanceTests {
    @Test
    fun test() {
    }
}
```

Example 0.1 [table-reader.1:src/test/java/travelator/tablereader/TableReaderAcceptanceTests.kt]

If you are reading this on a device, the reference should be a hyperlink to that version of the file on GitHub. On real paper, you can click all you like; nothing will happen, sorry. But if you take the example number, in this case *0.1*, and type it into a form on the book's website (*https://java-to-kotlin.dev/code.html*), it will show you links that take you to the same place.

In Git, the different code examples (these sometimes span multiple chapters) evolve in separate branches. The steps are tagged—*table-reader.1* is the tag in this case. The GitHub link is to code with that tag, so you can view the file shown (*src/test/java/travelator/tablereader/TableReaderAcceptanceTests.kt* here) and the others in the example at that version. You can also select other tags to see the different versions, and different branches to see different examples. For quicker navigation, you can clone the repository, open it in IntelliJ, and use the Git tool window to switch branches and versions.

The code examples are not real! The codebase builds and passes its tests, but it is fictional. There are places where the examples don't join up properly, and others where if you peek behind the curtain you will see us wiggling the levers. We have tried to be honest, but prefer to ship!

If you have a technical question or a problem using the code examples, visit the book's website (*https://java-to-kotlin.dev*) or email *bookquestions@oreilly.com*.

This book is here to help you get your job done. In general, if example code is offered with this book, you may use it in your programs and documentation. You do not need to contact us for permission unless you're reproducing a significant portion of the code. For example, writing a program that uses several chunks of code from this book does not require permission. Selling or distributing examples from O'Reilly books does require permission. Answering a question by citing this book and quoting example code does not require permission. Incorporating a significant amount of example code from this book into your product's documentation does require permission.

We appreciate, but generally do not require, attribution. An attribution usually includes the title, author, publisher, and ISBN. For example: "*Java to Kotlin* by Duncan McGregor and Nat Pryce (O'Reilly). Copyright 2021 Duncan McGregor and Nat Pryce, 978-1-492-08227-9."

If you feel your use of code examples falls outside fair use or the permission given above, feel free to contact us at *permissions@oreilly.com*.

O'Reilly Online Learning

For more than 40 years, *O'Reilly Media* has provided technology and business training, knowledge, and insight to help companies succeed.

Our unique network of experts and innovators share their knowledge and expertise through books, articles, conferences, and our online learning platform. O'Reilly's online learning platform gives you on-demand access to live training courses, in-depth learning paths, interactive coding environments, and a vast collection of text and video from O'Reilly and 200+ other publishers. For more information, please visit *http://oreilly.com*.

How to Contact Us

Please address comments and questions concerning this book to the publisher:

O'Reilly Media, Inc.
1005 Gravenstein Highway North
Sebastopol, CA 95472
800-998-9938 (in the United States or Canada)
707-829-0515 (international or local)
707-829-0104 (fax)

We have a web page for this book, where we list errata, examples, and any additional information. You can access this page at *https://oreil.ly/java-to-kotlin*.

Email *bookquestions@oreilly.com* to comment or ask technical questions about this book.

For news and information about our books and courses, visit *http://www.oreilly.com*.

Find us on Facebook: *http://facebook.com/oreilly*

Follow us on Twitter: *http://twitter.com/oreillymedia*

Watch us on YouTube: *http://youtube.com/oreillymedia*

Acknowledgments

Thank you to Hadi Hariri for suggesting to O'Reilly that we should write a book, and to Zan McQuade for believing him. Thank you to our editor Sarah Grey, who had to live with the consequences, and Kerin Forsyth and Kate Galloway for tidying everything up and actually getting it published.

Many friends and colleagues, and some lovely strangers, reviewed drafts ranging from early and uncoordinated to tantalizingly nearly complete. Thank you to Yana Afanasyeva, Jack Bolles, David Denton, Bruce Eckel, Dmitry Kandalov, Kevin Peel, James Richardson, Ivan Sanchez, Jordan Stewart, Robert Stoll, Christoph Sturm, Łukasz Wycisk, and Daniel Zappold and to our technical reviewers, Uberto Barbini, James Harmon, Mark Maynard, and Augusto Rodriguez. We really appreciate all your suggestions, encouragement, and candor.

Extreme Programming revolutionized the way that write software—we all owe a debt of gratitude to Ward Cunningham and Kent Beck. Thank you also to Martin Fowler, without whom this book might not have been written. In the UK the eXtreme Tuesday Club has been innovating on these ideas since 1999, and has attracted a cabal of developers. We are lucky to have worked with, and learned from, many talented members of this group. If you have a problem, if no one else can help, and if you can find them, maybe you can hire them.

Duncan's Bit

I don't think my wife will ever understand what I do for a living, and there's no chance that she will read the rest of this book, but she will probably get this far. So thank you, Jo McGregor, for putting up with me writing rather than spending time with you, and talking about writing when I was spending time with you. I couldn't have done it without your support and encouragement. Thank you also to our two wonderful sons, Callum and Alistair, who make us so proud.

Thank you to Vickie Kennish for taking a keen interest in becoming the mother of an author, checking on progress during our COVID lockdown walks. My late father, John, would I'm sure have played it more casual, but be bragging about the book to his friends. Also gone but not forgotten is our beautiful cat Sweet Pea, who kept me company through most of the writing but died just before it was finished.

The friendship and support of Robin Helliwell has been a constant throughout my adult life. Likewise, my sister Lucy Seal, and many other family members too numerous to list individually. In my professional life, in addition to those who gave feedback, thank you to Alan Dyke, Richard Care, and Gareth Sylvester-Bradley, all influential and supportive beyond the call of duty.

Nat's Bit

When I told my wife, Lamaan, that I was planning to write another book, her immediate reaction was not one of horror. For that, and for her constant encouragement, I owe her many thanks.

Hat tip to my sister, Lois Pryce, and brother-in-law, Austin Vince, whose motorcycle journeys, books, and films inspired the overland travel planning application used in the worked example code.

And thanks to Oliver and Alex. Now that the book is finished, I am once again available for consultancy in music and games programming.

CHAPTER 1

Introduction

The Grain of a Programming Language

Like wood, a programming language has a grain. In both carpentry and programming, when you work *with* the grain, things go smoothly. When you work *against* the grain, things are more difficult. When you work against the grain of a programming language, you have to write more code than necessary, performance suffers, you are more likely to introduce defects, you usually have to override convenient defaults, and you have to fight against the tooling every step of the way.

Going against the grain involves constant effort with an uncertain payoff.

For example, it has always been possible to write Java code in a functional style, but few programmers did before Java 8—for good reasons.

Here's Kotlin code that calculates the sum of a list of numbers by folding the list with the addition operator:

```
val sum = numbers.fold(0, Int::plus)
```

Let's compare that to what was required in Java 1.0 to do the same.

The mists of time will pass over you while transporting you to 1995…

Java 1.0 does not have first-class functions, so we have to implement functions as objects and define our own interfaces for different types of function. For example, the addition function takes two arguments, so we have to define the type of two-argument functions:

```
public interface Function2 {
    Object apply(Object arg1, Object arg2);
}
```

Then we have to write the fold higher-order function, hiding the iteration and mutation required by the Vector class. (The 1995 Java standard library doesn't yet include the Collections Framework.)

```
public class Vectors {
    public static Object fold(Vector l, Object initial, Function2 f) {
        Object result = initial;
        for (int i = 0; i < l.size(); i++) {
            result = f.apply(result, l.get(i));
        }
        return result;
    }

    ... and other operations on vectors
}
```

We have to define a separate class for every function we want to pass to our fold function. The addition operator can't be passed around as a value, and the language has no method references, lambdas, or closures at this time, not even inner classes. Nor does Java 1.0 have generics or autoboxing—we have to cast the arguments to the expected type and write the boxing between reference types and primitives:

```
public class AddIntegers implements Function2 {
    public Object apply(Object arg1, Object arg2) {
        int i1 = ((Integer) arg1).intValue();
        int i2 = ((Integer) arg2).intValue();
        return new Integer(i1 + i2);
    }
}
```

And, finally, we can use all that to calculate the sum:

```
int sum = ((Integer) Vectors.fold(counts, new Integer(0), new AddIntegers()))
    .intValue();
```

That's a lot of effort for what is a single expression in a mainstream language in 2020.

But that's not the end of it. Because Java doesn't have standard function types, we can't easily combine different libraries written in a functional style. We have to write adapter classes to map between the function types defined in different libraries. And, because the virtual machine has no JIT and a simple garbage collector, our functional code has worse performance than the imperative alternative:

```
int sum = 0;
for (int i = 0; i < counts.size(); i++) {
    sum += ((Integer)counts.get(i)).intValue();
}
```

In 1995, there is just not enough benefit to justify the effort of writing Java in a functional style. Java programmers found it easier to write imperative code that iterated over collections and mutated state.

Writing functional code *goes against the grain* of Java 1.0.

A language's grain forms over time as its designers and users build a common understanding of how language features interact and encode their understanding and preferences in libraries that others build upon. The grain influences the way that programmers write code in the language, which influences the evolution of the language and its libraries and programming tools, changing the grain, altering the way that programmers write code in the language, on and on in a continual cycle of mutual feedback and evolution.

For example, as we move forward through time, Java 1.1 adds anonymous inner classes to the language, and Java 2 adds the Collections Framework to the standard library. Anonymous inner classes mean that we don't need to write a named class for each function we want to pass to our `fold` function, but the resulting code is arguably harder to read:

```
int sum = ((Integer) Lists.fold(counts, new Integer(0),
    new Function2() {
        public Object apply(Object arg1, Object arg2) {
            int i1 = ((Integer) arg1).intValue();
            int i2 = ((Integer) arg2).intValue();
            return new Integer(i1 + i2);
        }
    })).intValue();
```

Functional idioms still go against the grain of Java 2.

Fast-forward to 2004, and Java 5 is the next release that significantly changes the language. It adds generics and autoboxing, which improve type safety and reduce boilerplate code:

```
public interface Function2<A, B, R> {
    R apply(A arg1, B arg2);
}

int sum = Lists.fold(counts, 0,
    new Function2<Integer, Integer, Integer>() {
        @Override
        public Integer apply(Integer arg1, Integer arg2) {
            return arg1 + arg2;
        }
    });
```

Java developers often use Google's Guava library (*https://oreil.ly/dMX73*) to add some common higher-order functions over collections (although `fold` is not among them), but even the authors of Guava recommend writing imperative code by default, because it has better performance and is usually easier to read.

Functional programming still goes largely against the grain of Java 5, but we can see the start of a trend.

Java 8 adds anonymous functions (aka lambda expressions) and method references to the language, and the Streams API to the standard library. The compiler and virtual machine optimize lambdas to avoid the performance overhead of anonymous inner classes. The Streams API fully embraces functional idioms, finally allowing:

```
int sum = counts.stream().reduce(0, Integer::sum);
```

However, it isn't entirely plain sailing. We still can't pass the addition operator as a parameter to the Streams `reduce` function, but we have the standard library function `Integer::sum` that does the same thing. Java's type system still creates awkward edge cases because of its distinction between reference and primitive types. The Streams API is missing some common higher-order functions that we would expect to find if coming from a functional language (or even Ruby). Checked exceptions don't play well with the Streams API and functional programming in general. And making immutable classes with value semantics still involves a lot of boilerplate code. But with Java 8, Java has fundamentally changed to make a functional style work, if not completely with the grain of the language, at least not against it.

The releases after Java 8 add a variety of smaller language and library features that support more functional programming idioms, but nothing that changes our sum calculation. And that brings us back to the present day.

In the case of Java, the grain of the language, and the way programmers adapted to it, evolved through several distinct programming styles.

An Opinionated History of Java Programming Style

Like ancient poets, we divide the development of Java programming style into four distinct ages: Primeval, Beans, Enterprise, and Modern.

Primeval Style

Originally intended for use in domestic appliances and interactive TV, Java only took off when Netscape adopted Java applets in its hugely popular Navigator browser. Sun released the Java development kit 1.0, Microsoft included Java in Internet Explorer, and suddenly everyone with a web browser had a Java runtime environment. Interest in Java as a programming language exploded.

The fundamentals of Java were in place by this time:

- The Java virtual machine and its bytecode and class file format
- Primitive and reference types, null references, garbage collection
- Classes and interfaces, methods and control flow statements
- Checked exceptions for error handling, the abstract windowing toolkit

- Classes for networking with internet and web protocols
- The loading and linking of code at runtime, sandboxed by a security manager

However, Java wasn't yet ready for general-purpose programming: the JVM was slow and the standard library sparse.

Java looked like a cross between C++ and Smalltalk, and those two languages influenced the Java programming style of the time. The "getFoo/setFoo" and "AbstractSingletonProxyFactoryBean" conventions that programmers of other languages poke fun at were not yet widespread.

One of Java's unsung innovations was an official coding convention that spelled out how programmers should name packages, classes, methods, and variables. C and C++ programmers followed a seemingly infinite variety of coding conventions, and code that combined multiple libraries ended up looking ~~like a right dog's dinner~~ somewhat inconsistent. Java's one true coding convention meant that Java programmers could seamlessly integrate strangers' libraries into their programs, and encouraged the growth of a vibrant open source community that continues to this day.

Bean Style

After Java's initial success, Sun set out to make it a practical tool for building applications. Java 1.1 (1996) added language features (most notably inner classes), improved the runtime (most notably just-in-time compilation and reflection), and extended the standard library. Java 1.2 (1998) added a standard collections API and the Swing cross-platform GUI framework, which ensured Java applications looked and felt equally awkward on every desktop operating system.

At this time, Sun was eying Microsoft's and Borland's domination of corporate software development. Java had the potential to be a strong competitor to Visual Basic and Delphi. Sun added a slew of APIs that were heavily inspired by Microsoft APIs: JDBC for data base access (equivalent to Microsoft's ODBC), Swing for desktop GUI programming (equivalent to Microsoft's MFC), and the framework that had the greatest influence on Java programming style, JavaBeans.

The JavaBeans API was Sun's answer to Microsoft's ActiveX component model for low-code, graphical, drag-and-drop programming. Windows programmers could use ActiveX components in their Visual Basic programs or embed them in office documents or web pages on their corporate intranet. Despite how easy it was to use ActiveX components, they were notoriously difficult to write. JavaBeans were much easier; you merely had to follow some additional coding conventions for your Java class to be considered a "bean" that could be instantiated and configured in a graphical designer. The promise of "Write once, run anywhere" meant you would also be able to use—or sell—JavaBean components on any operating system, not just Windows.

For a class to be a JavaBean, it needed to have a constructor that took no arguments, be serializable, and declare an API made up of public properties that could be read and optionally written, methods that could be invoked, and events that objects of the class would emit. The idea was that programmers would instantiate beans in a graphical application designer, configure them by setting their properties, and connect events emitted by beans to the methods of other beans. By default, the Beans API defined properties by pairs of methods whose names started with *get* and *set*. This default could be overridden, but doing so required the programmer to write more classes of boilerplate code. Programmers usually went to the effort only when retrofitting existing classes to act as JavaBeans. In new code, it was much easier to go with the grain.

The drawback of Beans style is that it relies heavily on mutable state and requires more of that state to be public than plain old Java objects do, because visual builder tools could not pass parameters to an object's constructor, but instead had to set properties. User interface components work well as beans, because they can safely be initialized with default content and styling and adjusted after construction. When we have classes that have no reasonable defaults, treating them in the same way is error-prone, because the type checker can't tell us when we have provided all the required values. The Beans conventions make writing correct code harder, and changes in dependencies can silently break client code.

In the end, graphical composition of JavaBeans did not become mainstream, but the coding conventions stuck. Java programmers followed the JavaBean conventions even when they had no intention of their class being used as a JavaBean. Beans had an enormous, lasting, and not entirely positive influence on Java programming style.

Enterprise Style

Java did eventually spread through the enterprise. It didn't replace Visual Basic on the corporate desktop as expected, but rather unseated C++ as the server-side language of choice. In 1998, Sun released Java 2 Enterprise Edition (then known as J2EE, now JakartaEE), a suite of standard APIs for programming server-side, transaction processing systems.

The J2EE APIs suffer from *abstraction inversion*. The JavaBeans and applets APIs also suffer from abstraction inversion—they both disallow passing parameters to constructors, for example—but it is far more severe in J2EE. J2EE applications don't have a single entry point. They are composed of many small components whose lifetime is managed by an application container, and are exposed to one another through a JNDI name service. Applications need a lot of boilerplate code and mutable state to look up the resources they depend on. Programmers responded by inventing *dependency injection* (DI) frameworks that did all the resource lookup and binding, and managed lifetimes. The most successful of these is Spring. It builds upon the JavaBeans coding conventions and uses reflection to compose applications from Bean-like objects.

Abstraction Inversion

Abstraction inversion is an architectural flaw in which a software platform prevents client code from using lower-level mechanisms that it requires. This forces programmers to reimplement those lower-level mechanisms using the higher-level facilities exposed by the platform's API, which in turn uses the very features being reimplemented. The result is unnecessary code, poor performance, and additional maintenance and testing costs.

Take, for example, J2EE servlets. In the Servlet API, the servlet container, not the web application, was responsible for instantiating servlet objects. In fact, the web application wasn't written in Java at all; it was an XML file that listed the classes that the servlet container would instantiate. So every servlet had to have a no-argument constructor, and the web application couldn't initialize its servlets by passing objects to their constructors.

Instead, you had to write a `ServletContextListener` that created objects required by the application's servlets and stored them as named, untyped attributes of the `ServletContext`:

```
public class ExampleServletContextListener
    implements ServletContextListener {

    public void contextInitialized(ServletContextEvent contextEvent) {
        ServletContext context = contextEvent.getServletContext();
        context.setAttribute("example.httpClient", createHttpClient());
        context.setAttribute("example.template", new URITemplate(
            context.getInitParameter("example.template")));
        ...
    }

    ...
}
```

Servlets initialized themselves by looking for the objects they needed in the context and casting them to the expected type:

```
public class ExampleServlet extends HttpServlet {
    private HttpClient httpClient;
    private URITemplate routeServiceTemplate;
    ...

    public void init(ServletConfig config) throws ServletException {
        super.init(config);
        ServletContext context = config.getServletContext();
        this.httpClient =
            (HttpClient) context.getAttribute("example.httpClient");
```

```
            this.routeServiceTemplate =
                (URITemplate) context.getAttribute("example.template");
            ...
        }

        ...
    }
```

That's a lot of effort to achieve what you could do with a constructor call if the Servlet API didn't prevent you from doing so. And the constructor call would be type checked. It's no wonder that Java programmers found dependency injection frameworks to be an improvement!

The Servlet API finally allowed web applications to instantiate servlets and pass dependencies to their constructors in version 3.0, more than *20 years* after the Servlet API was first published.

In terms of programming style, DI frameworks encourage programmers to eschew direct use of the `new` keyword and instead rely on the framework to instantiate objects. The Android APIs also exhibit abstraction inversion, and Android programmers also turn to DI frameworks to help them write to the APIs. DI frameworks' focus on mechanism over domain modeling leads to enterprisey class names such as Spring's infamous `AbstractSingletonProxyFactoryBean`.

On the plus side, though, the Enterprise Era saw the release of Java 5, which added generics and autoboxing to the language, the most significant change to date. This era also saw a massive uptake of open source libraries in the Java community, powered by the Maven packaging conventions and central package repository. The availability of top-notch open source libraries fueled the adoption of Java for business-critical application development, and led to more open source libraries, in a virtuous circle. This was followed by best-in-class development tools, including the IntelliJ IDE, which we use in this book.

Modern Style

Java 8 brought the next big change to the language—lambdas—and significant additions to the standard library to take advantage of them. The Streams API encouraged a functional programming style, in which processing is performed by transforming streams of immutable values rather than changing the state of mutable objects. A new date/time API ignored JavaBeans coding conventions for property accessors and followed coding conventions common to the Primeval Age.

The growth of the cloud platforms meant that programmers didn't need to deploy their servers into JavaEE application containers. Lightweight web application frameworks let programmers write a `main` function to compose their applications. Many server-side programmers stopped using DI frameworks—function and object composition were good enough—so DI frameworks released greatly simplified APIs to stay relevant. With no DI framework or mutable state, there's less need to follow JavaBean coding conventions. Within a single codebase, exposing fields of immutable values works fine, because the IDE can encapsulate a field behind accessors in an instant if they're needed.

Java 9 introduced modules, but so far they have not seen widespread adoption outside the JDK itself. The most exciting thing about recent Java releases has been the modularization of the JDK and removal of seldom-used modules, such as CORBA, from the JDK into optional extensions.

The Future

The future of Java promises more features to make Modern Style easier to apply: records, pattern matching, user-defined value types, and eventually the unification of primitive and reference types into a uniform type system.

However, this is a challenging effort that will take many years to complete. Java started off with some deep-seated inconsistencies and edge cases that are hard to unify into clean abstractions while staying backward compatible. Kotlin has the benefit of 25 years of hindsight, and a clean slate from which to start afresh.

The Grain of Kotlin

Kotlin is a young language, but it clearly has a different grain than Java.

When we wrote this, the "Why Kotlin" (*https://oreil.ly/pqZbu*) section of the Kotlin home page gave four design goals: concise, safe, interoperable, and tool-friendly. The designers of the language and its standard library also encoded implicit preferences that contribute to these design goals. These preferences include:

Kotlin prefers the transformation of immutable data to mutation of state.
: Data classes make it easy to define new types with value semantics. The standard library makes it easier and more concise to transform collections of immutable data than to iterate and mutate data in place.

Kotlin prefers behavior to be explicit.
: For example, there is no implicit coercion between types, even from smaller to larger range. Java implicitly converts `int` values to `long` values, because there is no loss of precision. In Kotlin, you have to call `Int.toLong()` explicitly. The preference for explicitness is especially strong when it comes to control flow. Although you can overload arithmetic and comparison operators for your own types, you cannot overload the shortcut logical operators (`&&` and `||`), because that would allow you to define different control flow.

Kotlin prefers static over dynamic binding.
Kotlin encourages a type-safe, compositional coding style. Extension functions are bound statically. By default, classes are not extensible and methods are not polymorphic. You must explicitly opt in to polymorphism and inheritance. If you want to use reflection, you have to add a platform-specific library dependency. Kotlin is designed from the outset to be used with a language-aware IDE that statically analyzes the code to guide the programmer, automate navigation, and automate program transformation.

Kotlin doesn't like special cases.
Compared to Java, Kotlin has fewer special cases that interact in unpredictable ways. There is no distinction between primitive and reference types. There is no `void` type for functions that return but do not return a value; functions in Kotlin either return a value or never return at all. Extension functions allow you to add new operations to existing types that look the same at the call point. You can write new control structures as inline functions, and the `break`, `continue`, and `return` statements act the same as they do in built-in control structures.

Kotlin breaks its own rules to make migration easier.
The Kotlin language has features to allow idiomatic Java and Kotlin code to coexist in the same codebase. Some of those features remove guarantees provided by the type checker and should *only* be used to interoperate with legacy Java. For example, `lateinit` opens a hole in the type system so that Java dependency injection frameworks that initialize objects by reflection can inject values through the encapsulation boundaries that are normally enforced by the compiler. If you declare a property as `lateinit var`, it's up to you to ensure the code initializes the property before reading it. The compiler will not catch your mistakes.

When we, Nat and Duncan, revisit the earliest code we wrote in Kotlin, it tends to look like Java dressed in Kotlin syntax. We came to Kotlin after years writing a lot of Java and had ingrained habits that affected how we wrote Kotlin code. We wrote unnecessary boilerplate, didn't make good use of the standard library, and avoided using null because we weren't yet used to the type checker enforcing null safety. The Scala programmers on our team went too far the other way—their code looked like Kotlin trying to be Scala, cosplaying as Haskell. None of us had yet found the sweet spot that comes from working with the grain of Kotlin.

The path to idiomatic Kotlin is complicated by the Java code we have to keep working along the way. In practice, it is not enough just to learn Kotlin. We have to work with the different grains of Java *and* Kotlin, being sympathetic to both as we gradually transition from one to the other.

Refactoring to Kotlin

When we started our journey to Kotlin, we were responsible for maintaining and enhancing business-critical systems. We were never able to focus *only* on converting our Java codebase to Kotlin. We always had to migrate code to Kotlin at the same time as changing the system to meet new business needs, maintaining a mixed Java/Kotlin codebase as we did so. We managed the risk by working in small changes, making each easy to understand and cheap to discard if we found out it broke something. Our process was first to convert Java code to Kotlin, giving us a Java-esque design in Kotlin syntax. We then incrementally applied Kotlin language features to make the code increasingly easy to understand, more type safe, more concise, and with a more compositional structure that is easier to change without unpleasant surprises.

Small, safe, reversible changes that improved the design: we *refactored* from idiomatic Java to idiomatic Kotlin.

Refactoring *between* languages is usually harder than refactoring *within* a single language because refactoring tools do not work well across the boundaries between the languages, if they work at all. Porting logic from one language to another must be done manually, which takes longer and introduces more risk. Once multiple languages are in use, the language boundary impedes refactoring because when you refactor code in one language, the IDE does not update dependent code written in other languages to be compatible.

What makes the combination of Java and Kotlin unique is the (relatively) seamless boundary between the two languages. Thanks to the design of the Kotlin language, the way it is mapped to the JVM platform, and JetBrains' investment in developer tooling, refactoring Java to Kotlin and refactoring a combined Java/Kotlin codebase is almost as easy as refactoring in a single codebase.

Our experience has been that we can refactor Java to Kotlin without affecting productivity, and that productivity then accelerates as we convert more of the codebase to Kotlin.

Refactoring Principles

The practice of refactoring has come a long way since its initial popularization in Martin Fowler's book, *Refactoring: Improving the Design of Existing Code* (Addison-Wesley), published in 1999. This book had to detail manual steps for even simple refactorings like renaming identifiers but notes that some state-of-the-art development environments were beginning to provide automated support to reduce such drudgery. Nowadays we expect our tools to automate even complicated scenarios such as extracting an interface or changing function signatures.

These individual refactorings rarely stand alone though. Now that the building-block refactorings can be performed automatically, we have the time and energy to combine them to make larger-scale changes to our codebase. When the IDE does not have distinct user-interface actions for a large-scale transformation we wish to do, we have to perform it as a sequence of more granular refactorings. We use the IDE's automatic refactoring whenever we can, and fall back on text editing when the IDE does not automate a transformation we need.

It's tedious and error-prone to refactor by editing text. To reduce the risk, and our boredom, we minimize the amount of text editing we have to do. If we *must* edit text, we prefer that edit to affect a single expression. So we use automatic refactorings to transform the code so that is possible, edit one expression, and then use automatic refactorings to tidy back up to the final state we're aiming for.

The first time we describe a large-scale refactoring, we'll go through it step by step and show how the code changes at each step. This takes quite a lot of space on the page and will take a bit of reading time to follow. In practice, however, these large refactorings are quick to apply. They typically take a few seconds, a few minutes at most.

We expect the refactorings published here to date quite quickly as tools improve. The individual IDE steps may be renamed, and some combinations might be implemented as single refactorings in their own right. Experiment in your context to find ways of gradually and safely transforming your code that are better than those we present, and then share them with the world too.

We Assume Good Test Coverage

As Martin Fowler says in *Refactoring: Improving the Design of Existing Code*: "[I]f you want to refactor, the essential precondition is having solid tests." Good test coverage ensures that the code transformations we want to only improve design have not inadvertently changed our system's behavior. In this book, we assume that you have good test coverage. We do not cover how to write automated tests. Other authors have addressed these topics in more detail than we could in this book, for example: *Test-Driven Development By Example* by Kent Beck (Addison-Wesley) and *Growing Object-Oriented Software Guided By Tests* by Steve Freeman and Nat Pryce (Addison-Wesley). We do, however, show how to apply Kotlin features to improve our tests.

As we walk through multistep code transformations, we won't always say when we run the tests. Assume that we run our tests after every change that we show that compiles, no matter how small.

If your system does not already have good test coverage, it can be difficult (and expensive) to retrofit tests to the code because the logic you want to test is entangled with other aspects of the system. You're in a chicken and egg situation: you have to refactor to be able to add tests so that you can safely refactor. Again, other authors have addressed these topics in more detail than we could, for example: *Working Effectively with Legacy Code* by Michael Feathers (Pearson).

We've listed more books about these topics in the Bibliography.

We Commit for Git Bisect

Just as we don't explicitly state when we run our tests, nor do we explicitly state when we commit our changes. Assume we commit our changes whenever they have added value to the code, no matter how small.

We know our test suite isn't perfect. If we accidentally break something that is not caught by our tests, we want to find the commit that introduced the fault and fix it as quickly as we can.

The `git bisect` command automates that search. We write a new test that demonstrates the error, and `git bisect` does a binary search of the history to find the first commit that makes that test fail.

If the commits in our history are large, and contain a mishmash of unrelated changes, `git bisect` won't help as much as it could. It cannot tell which of the source changes within a commit introduced the error. If commits mix refactoring *and* changes to behavior, reverting a bad refactoring step is likely to break *other* behavior in the system.

Therefore, we commit small, focused changes that separate refactorings from each other, and from changes to behavior, to make it easy to understand what changed and fix any erroneous change. For the same reason, we very rarely squash commits.

We prefer to commit changes straight onto the mainline branch—"trunk-based development"—but changing code in a sequence of small, independent commits is just as beneficial when working in branches and merging less frequently.

What Are We Working On?

In the chapters that follow, we take examples from the codebase of *Travelator*, a fictional application for planning and booking international surface travel. Our (still fictional) users plan routes by sea, rail, and road; search for places to stay and sights to see; compare their options by price, time, and spectacle; and finally book their trips, all from web and mobile frontends that invoke backend services via HTTP.

Each chapter pulls an informative example from a different part of the Travelator system, but they share common domain concepts: money, currency conversion, journeys, itineraries, bookings, and so on.

Our aim is that, like our Travelator application, this book will help you plan your journey from Java to Kotlin.

Let's Get Started!

Enough chitchat. You're probably itching to convert all that Java to Kotlin. We'll start in the next chapter by adding Kotlin support to our project's build file.

CHAPTER 2

Java to Kotlin Projects

What is the first step of the journey from pure Java to a mixed and then increasingly Kotlin codebase?

Strategy

The first time we, Nat and Duncan, introduced Kotlin to a Java codebase, we were members of a small team that included six developers, building a relatively greenfield project. We had already deployed some web applications with Kotlin, but our enterprise architects insisted that we write the new system in Java 8. This was shortly after Kotlin 1.0 had been released, but before Google announced that Kotlin was an official language for Android, so the architects were understandably wary about committing to a language with an uncertain future for a strategic system that they expected to be around for decades.

In Java, we leaned toward a functional approach, designing the core application domain model as immutable data types transformed by pipelines. However, we kept bumping into Java's limitations: the verbosity required to implement immutable value types, the distinction between primitive and reference types, null references, and Streams lacking common higher-order functions. Meanwhile, we could see Kotlin being adopted at an ever-increasing rate across the industry and even within the company. When we saw Google's announcement, we decided to start converting our Java to Kotlin.

Our judgment was that starting in the core domain model would give us the biggest bang for our buck. Kotlin's data classes shrank the code significantly, in some cases replacing hundreds of lines of code with a single declaration. We started carefully, using IntelliJ to convert a small value class that had no dependencies on other classes beyond those in the standard library, and examined how that affected the rest of our

Java codebase. It had no effect at all! Emboldened by this success, we picked up the pace. Whenever a new feature needed changes to a Java domain model class, we would first convert it to a Kotlin data class, commit the conversion, and then implement the feature.

As more of the domain model logic became pure Kotlin, we were able to make better use of Kotlin features. For example, we replaced calls to the Stream API with Kotlin's standard functions on collections and sequences. The biggest improvement though, was replacing our use of Java's Optional type with nullable references. This simplified our code and gave us greater confidence in its null safety.

Another project in the company adopted Kotlin for a different reason. They had a mature Java system that was built on a dependency injection framework. The developers found that the framework's use of reflection and annotations made the code difficult to understand and navigate in the IDE. Kotlin's lightweight syntax for closures offered a way to define the structure of their application and distinguish between object graphs instantiated for the whole application, for each HTTP request, or for each database transaction. They gradually refactored the underpinnings of their system from a framework that obscured the architecture to a style that composed functions and made the architecture visible in the code. This work became the http4k (*https://http4k.org*) web programming toolkit.

As these two examples show, your choice of starting point should depend on a number of factors, including why your team is adopting Kotlin, how large the codebase is, and how frequently it changes. You know your project and can decide what is most important to change.

If you are choosing Kotlin for its language features, it makes sense to convert the classes you are working in most frequently, as we did in our first project. If you are choosing Kotlin to use a specific library, then it makes sense to start writing Kotlin against the API, annotate it to make your Kotlin code convenient to the Java code in the rest of the app, and continue from there.

In a small team it's easy to establish the Kotlin coding style for your system (beyond the standard style guide), for instance, error handling conventions, how code is to be organized into files, what should be a top-level declaration and what should be in an object, and so on.

Above a certain size, you run the risk of Kotlin code becoming inconsistent as people establish their own conventions in different parts of the system. So it may be worth starting with a small subteam working in one area of the system, who establish conventions and build up a body of example code. Once there are some established conventions, you can expand the effort to the rest of the team and other parts of the system.

In the rest of this book, we will examine in detail how to progress, how to keep your Java code maintainable while you are introducing Kotlin that it depends upon, and how to take advantage of Kotlin's features to simplify the code further after IntelliJ has performed its conversion magic. But all that follows the first small step.

Adding Kotlin Support to a Java Build

If we want to refactor our Java to Kotlin, the first change we must make is to give ourselves the ability to write Kotlin code in our codebase. Happily, the Kotlin build tools and IDE make this very straightforward. It takes a few additional lines in our Gradle build configuration for it to compile Kotlin as well as Java. IntelliJ will pick up that configuration when we resync the build file, allowing us to navigate, autocomplete, and refactor across both languages almost seamlessly.

To add Kotlin to our Gradle build, we need to add the Kotlin plug-in. There is a different plug-in for each target that Kotlin supports (JVM, JavaScript, and native code), and a plug-in for building multiplatform projects. Because we have a Java project, we can ignore other platforms and use the Kotlin JVM plug-in.

We also need to add the Kotlin standard library to our dependencies and specify the minimum JVM version that the output bytecode will support. Our project targets JDK 11 (the latest LTS at the time of writing). At the time of writing, the Kotlin compiler can generate bytecode compatible with JDK 1.6 or JDK 1.8. JDK 1.8 bytecode is more efficient and runs fine on JDK 11, so we will pick that.

Kotlin Versions

The Kotlin language and standard library are still maturing, but JetBrains policy is to provide a clear migration path. The current version of Kotlin was 1.3 when we started writing this book. As we finish it, 1.5 has just been released, deprecating some standard APIs used in our code examples! We have chosen not to migrate to their replacements, so that the code is able to run on Kotlin 1.4 and 1.5.

Here are the relevant parts of our `build.gradle` before the changes:

```
plugins {
    id("java")
}

java.sourceCompatibility = JavaVersion.VERSION_11
java.targetCompatibility = JavaVersion.VERSION_11
... and other project settings ...

dependencies {
    implementation "com.fasterxml.jackson.core:jackson-databind:2.10.0"
    implementation "com.fasterxml.jackson.datatype:jackson-datatype-jsr310:2.10.0"
```

```
        implementation "com.fasterxml.jackson.datatype:jackson-datatype-jdk8:2.10.0"
        ... and the rest of our app's implementation dependencies

        testImplementation "org.junit.jupiter:junit-jupiter-api:5.4.2"
        testImplementation "org.junit.jupiter:junit-jupiter-params:5.4.2"
        testRuntimeOnly "org.junit.jupiter:junit-jupiter-engine:5.5.2"
        testRuntimeOnly "org.junit.platform:junit-platform-launcher:1.4.2"
        ... and the rest of our app's test dependencies
}

... and the rest of our build rules
```

Example 2.1 [projects.0:build.gradle]

After we have added the Kotlin plug-in, our build file looks like this:

```
plugins {
    id 'org.jetbrains.kotlin.jvm' version "1.5.0"
}

java.sourceCompatibility = JavaVersion.VERSION_11
java.targetCompatibility = JavaVersion.VERSION_11
... and other project settings ...

dependencies {
    implementation "org.jetbrains.kotlin:kotlin-stdlib-jdk8"
    ... and the rest of our app's dependencies
}

tasks.withType(org.jetbrains.kotlin.gradle.tasks.KotlinCompile) {
    kotlinOptions {
        jvmTarget = "11"
        javaParameters = true
        freeCompilerArgs = ["-Xjvm-default=all"]
    }
}

... and the rest of our build rules
```

Example 2.2 [projects.1:build.gradle]

Given those changes, we can rerun our build, and see that…

…the build still works!

If we resync the Gradle project in IntelliJ (this may happen automatically on saving), we can run our tests and programs within the IDE.

Our tests still pass, so we haven't broken anything, but neither have we proved that we can use Kotlin in our project. Let's test that by writing a "hello world" program. We create a file, *HelloWorld.kt*, in the root package of our Java source tree, *src/main/java*:

```
fun main() {
    println("hello, world")
}
```

Example 2.3 [projects.2:src/main/java/HelloWorld.kt]

Where to Put Kotlin Source

The Kotlin build plug-in adds additional source roots, *src/main/kotlin* and *src/test/kotlin*, and compiles Kotlin source files found in any of their subdirectories.

It will also compile Kotlin source found in Java source trees, in particular *src/main/java* and *src/test/java*. Although you can separate your source files by language, putting Java files in the *java* directories and Kotlin into *kotlin*, in practice your authors don't bother. It's nice to be able to look into a directory and see all the source for the corresponding package rather than casting around the filesystem. To make this work, though, we keep Kotlin source in directories mirroring the package structure rather than taking advantage of Kotlin's ability to have files in a single directory but multiple packages.

In a similar vein, while Kotlin does allow multiple public classes to be defined in a single class, when we are mixing Java and Kotlin in a project, we tend to stick to one class per file for consistency.

We can run that within the IDE by clicking the little green arrow in the lefthand margin next to `fun main()`.

We can run our build and then run it from the command line with the `java` command. Compiling the source file named *HelloWorld.kt* creates a Java class file named `HelloWorldKt`. We'll look into how Kotlin source gets translated into Java class files in more detail later, but for now, we can run our program with the `java` command, like so:

```
$ java -cp build/classes/kotlin/main HelloWorldKt
hello, world
```

It lives!

Let's delete *HelloWorld.kt*—it's done its job—commit and push.

We now have the *option* to use Kotlin in our project; the first part of this chapter gives some pointers to *where* to start using it.

Other Build Systems

We've chosen to show the changes necessary to add Kotlin support to a Gradle build here, but you can use Maven or Ant by following the instructions provided in the Tools section of the Kotlin documentation (*https://oreil.ly/bWi9n*). This also gives instructions for using the command-line compiler, `kotlinc`.

If you use Gradle, there is the option to use Kotlin, rather than the traditional Groovy, as the build definition language. This has the advantage of providing better tool support through strong typing, at the expense of having to translate historical Stack-Overflow answers into a new language.

As we are Java and Kotlin developers rather than Java and Groovy developers, your authors start new projects with the Kotlin DSL, but we don't feel the need to convert existing Groovy builds, at least not immediately. As with the Java and Kotlin in production code, we can mix and match Kotlin and Groovy in our build, so this is a conversion that we can take our time over. We don't recommend that you switch your build from Groovy to Kotlin as your first act of conversion, and certainly don't look to us to write a Groovy to Kotlin Gradle book!

Moving On

We expect the technical information in this chapter to date very quickly, as neither Gradle nor its plug-ins have a very stable interface. Your current Java build file is also almost certainly incompatible with our example in some crucial way. Despite this, though, adding Kotlin to a Java build is generally straightforward.

Devising a strategy for moving code from Java to Kotlin is more complicated and context specific. Or at least differently complicated and context specific. Individual projects should examine where Java is and isn't working for them, and where using Kotlin would alleviate problems and improve the code. You might choose to dive in and write some Kotlin from scratch, or to convert an existing Java class to Kotlin. In the spirit of this book, the latter is the approach we'll take in Chapter 3, *Java to Kotlin Classes*.

CHAPTER 3

Java to Kotlin Classes

The class is the basic unit of code organization in Java. How do we convert our Java classes to Kotlin, and what differences will we see when we have?

In this book, we'll work together on the code in Travelator, our fictional trip-planning web app. Imagine that we have a feature to implement, but we want to take the opportunity to make our code a little better before we do. You're pairing with one of Nat or Duncan (choose your favorite, just don't let Nat know). The pair is the *we* in our refactoring discussions; not just your author, but also you as part of the team working on Travelator. Welcome aboard!

Source Code

We have published the Travelator source code in a public Git repository. "Using Code Examples" on page xvi details how to access it.

Because this book is about refactoring, the important details are the changes, both between single commits and over longer intervals. We have tried to show everything you need to make sense of the code here in print; it helps to imagine that the last code sample shown is in the active editor pane as we talk about the changes we are about to make. If we have failed to make it make sense, or you just feel the need for more detail, then you can check out the code and follow along in IntelliJ.

A Simple Value Type

Let's jump into the deep end of the codebase and convert some of our existing Java to Kotlin, starting with `EmailAddress`. This is a value type that holds the two parts of, you guessed it, an email address:

```java
public class EmailAddress {
    private final String localPart; ❶
    private final String domain;

    public static EmailAddress parse(String value) { ❷
        var atIndex = value.lastIndexOf('@');
        if (atIndex < 1 || atIndex == value.length() - 1)
            throw new IllegalArgumentException(
                "EmailAddress must be two parts separated by @"
            );
        return new EmailAddress(
            value.substring(0, atIndex),
            value.substring(atIndex + 1)
        );
    }

    public EmailAddress(String localPart, String domain) { ❸
        this.localPart = localPart;
        this.domain = domain;
    }

    public String getLocalPart() { ❹
        return localPart;
    }

    public String getDomain() { ❹
        return domain;
    }

    @Override
    public boolean equals(Object o) { ❺
        if (this == o) return true;
        if (o == null || getClass() != o.getClass()) return false;
        EmailAddress that = (EmailAddress) o;
        return localPart.equals(that.localPart) &&
            domain.equals(that.domain);
    }

    @Override
    public int hashCode() { ❺
        return Objects.hash(localPart, domain);
    }

    @Override
    public String toString() { ❻
        return localPart + "@" + domain;
    }
}
```

Example 3.1 [classes.0:src/main/java/travelator/EmailAddress.java]

This class is very simple; it does nothing more than wrap two strings and provides no operations of its own. Even so, it has a lot of code:

1. Values are immutable, so the class declares its fields as final.
2. There is a static factory method to `parse` an `EmailAddress` from a string; this calls the primary constructor.
3. The fields are initialized in a constructor.
4. The accessor methods of its properties follow the JavaBean naming conventions.
5. The class implements the `equals` and `hashCode` methods to ensure that two `EmailAddress` values with equal fields compare as equal.
6. `toString` returns the canonical form.

Your authors come from the school of Java that assumes that everything we pass, store, or return is not null unless explicitly indicated otherwise. You can't see that convention, because it results in an absence of `@Nullable` annotations or null checks of parameters (Chapter 4 discusses nullability). What you *can* see is the amount of boilerplate code required to express a value composed of two other values. Happily, our IDE generated the `equals` and `hashCode` methods for us, but we have to remember to delete and regenerate those methods if we change the fields of the class to avoid confusing bugs.

So much for the Java; we're here for the Kotlin. How do we convert? Helpfully, IntelliJ has an action called "Convert Java File to Kotlin File". When we invoke it, IntelliJ offers to change other files if necessary to keep things consistent. Because the conversion can potentially modify files throughout the project, it's best to say yes.

Make sure you have no uncommitted changes before converting Java source to Kotlin so that you can easily see the impact of the conversion on the rest of your codebase and revert the conversion if it does something you didn't expect.

In this case, IntelliJ doesn't have to change any other files. It has replaced our *EmailAddress.java* file with *EmailAddress.kt* in the same directory, though:

```
class EmailAddress(val localPart: String, val domain: String) {
    override fun equals(o: Any?): Boolean {
        if (this === o) return true
        if (o == null || javaClass != o.javaClass) return false
        val that = o as EmailAddress
        return localPart == that.localPart && domain == that.domain
    }

    override fun hashCode(): Int {
        return Objects.hash(localPart, domain)
```

```
    }

    override fun toString(): String {
        return "$localPart@$domain"
    }

    companion object {
        @JvmStatic
        fun parse(value: String): EmailAddress {
            val atIndex = value.lastIndexOf('@')
            require(!(atIndex < 1 || atIndex == value.length - 1)) {
                "EmailAddress must be two parts separated by @"
            }
            return EmailAddress(
                value.substring(0, atIndex),
                value.substring(atIndex + 1)
            )
        }
    }
}
```

Example 3.2 [classes.2:src/main/java/travelator/EmailAddress.kt]

The Kotlin class is noticeably more succinct because it declares its properties in the primary constructor: the parameters after the class name. Parameters marked `val` are considered properties and so stand in for all this Java:

```
private final String localPart;
private final String domain;

public EmailAddress(String localPart, String domain) {
    this.localPart = localPart;
    this.domain = domain;
}

public String getLocalPart() {
    return localPart;
}

public String getDomain() {
    return domain;
}
```

Example 3.3 [classes.1:src/main/java/travelator/EmailAddress.java]

The primary constructor syntax is convenient, but it does interfere with the scanability of the class. Java classes that follow the standard coding conventions always define their elements in the same order: class name, superclass, interfaces, and then, within the class body, fields, constructors, and methods. This makes it easy to skim-read the class and quickly locate the features you're interested in.

It's not quite so easy to find the parts of a Kotlin class. A Kotlin class definition has a header part with the class name, primary constructor (which can contain parameters and/or property definitions), superclass (which may also be the call to the superclass's constructor), and interfaces. Then, within the class body, there are more properties and more constructors, methods, and companion objects.

Coming from Java, Nat and Duncan definitely found it harder to read classes at first, and although we got used to it eventually, we still find it hard at times to format classes for maximum readability, especially if there is a lot going on in the header part. One easy fix is to lay out the constructor parameter list line by line. With the cursor inside the parameter list, we can do that with Alt-Enter and "Put parameters on separate lines". Sometimes a blank line after the header part helps, too:

```
class EmailAddress(
    val localPart: String,
    val domain: String
) {

    override fun equals(o: Any?): Boolean {
        if (this === o) return true
        if (o == null || javaClass != o.javaClass) return false
        val that = o as EmailAddress
        return localPart == that.localPart && domain == that.domain
    }

    override fun hashCode(): Int {
        return Objects.hash(localPart, domain)
    }

    override fun toString(): String {
        return "$localPart@$domain"
    }

    companion object {
        @JvmStatic
        fun parse(value: String): EmailAddress {
            val atIndex = value.lastIndexOf('@')
            require(!(atIndex < 1 || atIndex == value.length - 1)) {
                "EmailAddress must be two parts separated by @"
            }
            return EmailAddress(
                value.substring(0, atIndex),
                value.substring(atIndex + 1)
            )
        }
    }
}
```

Example 3.4 [classes.3:src/main/java/travelator/EmailAddress.kt]

One place where Kotlin is noticeably less succinct than Java is where it uses companion objects to host static state and methods, in this case `parse()`. In Kotlin, we often prefer top-level state and functions to these class-scoped members. Chapter 8 discusses the pros and cons.

We currently have Java code that uses the static method, for example, the tests:

```
public class EmailAddressTests {

    @Test
    public void parsing() {
        assertEquals(
            new EmailAddress("fred", "example.com"),
            EmailAddress.parse("fred@example.com")
        );
    }

    @Test
    public void parsingFailures() {
        assertThrows(
            IllegalArgumentException.class,
            () -> EmailAddress.parse("@")
        );
        ...
    }

    ...
}
```

Example 3.5 [classes.0:src/test/java/travelator/EmailAddressTests.java]

The companion object, combined with the `@JVMStatic` annotation, means this didn't have to change when we converted the class to Kotlin, so we'll leave `parse` as it is for now. We'll discuss how to refactor to top-level functions in Chapter 8.

If you're new to Kotlin, you may wonder what happened to the `getLocalPart()` and `getDomain()` accessor methods. Declaring the `domain` property causes the compiler to generate a private `domain` field and a `getDomain()` method so that Java code can still call it. Here is a little throwaway code to support a marketing plan:

```
public class Marketing {

    public static boolean isHotmailAddress(EmailAddress address) {
        return address.getDomain().equalsIgnoreCase("hotmail.com");
    }
}
```

Example 3.6 [classes.3:src/main/java/travelator/Marketing.java]

You can see that Java is accessing the domain property through the `getDomain()` method. Conversely, when the class was Java and had an explicit `getDomain()` method, Kotlin code could have called it as `address.domain`. We'll discuss properties in more detail in Chapter 11.

So far, converting our class to Kotlin has saved us 14 lines of code, but we aren't done yet. Value types like this are so useful, but so tedious to get right and keep right, that Kotlin supports them at a language level. If we mark the class with the `data` modifier, the compiler generates any undefined `equals`, `hashCode`, and `toString` methods for us. That reduces the `EmailAddress` class to:

```
data class EmailAddress(
    val localPart: String,
    val domain: String
) {

    override fun toString(): String { ❶
        return "$localPart@$domain"
    }

    companion object {
        @JvmStatic
        fun parse(value: String): EmailAddress {
            val atIndex = value.lastIndexOf('@')
            require(!(atIndex < 1 || atIndex == value.length - 1)) {
                "EmailAddress must be two parts separated by @"
            }
            return EmailAddress(
                value.substring(0, atIndex),
                value.substring(atIndex + 1)
            )
        }
    }
}
```

Example 3.7 [classes.4:src/main/java/travelator/EmailAddress.kt]

❶ We don't want the generated `toString()` method, so we define the one we do want.

Frankly, that `parse` method still rankles; it's taking up a disproportionate amount of space for the work it is doing. We'll finally relieve this tension in Chapter 9. For now, though, we're done with converting our `EmailAddress` Java class to Kotlin.

The Limitations of Data Classes

A drawback of data classes is that they offer no encapsulation. We saw how the compiler generates `equals`, `hashCode`, and `toString` methods for data classes but didn't mention that it also generates a `copy` method that creates a new copy of the value with different values for one or more of its properties.

For example, the following code creates a copy of an `EmailAddress` with a `localPart` of "postmaster" and the same domain:

```
val postmasterEmail = customerEmail.copy(localPart = "postmaster")
```

For many types, this is very convenient. However, when a class abstracts its internal representation or maintains invariants between its properties, that `copy` method allows client code direct access to the internal state of a value, which can break its invariants.

Let's look at an abstract data type in the Travelator application, the `Money` class:

```
public class Money {
    private final BigDecimal amount;
    private final Currency currency;

    private Money(BigDecimal amount, Currency currency) { ❶
        this.amount = amount;
        this.currency = currency;
    }

    public static Money of(BigDecimal amount, Currency currency) { ❶
        return new Money(
            amount.setScale(currency.getDefaultFractionDigits()),
            currency);
    }

    ... and convenience overloads

    public BigDecimal getAmount() { ❷
        return amount;
    }

    public Currency getCurrency() { ❸
        return currency;
    }

    @Override
    public boolean equals(Object o) { ❸
        if (this == o) return true;
        if (o == null || getClass() != o.getClass()) return false;
        Money money = (Money) o;
        return amount.equals(money.amount) &&
            currency.equals(money.currency);
```

```
    }

    @Override
    public int hashCode() { ❸
        return Objects.hash(amount, currency);
    }

    @Override
    public String toString() { ❹
        return amount.toString() + " " + currency.getCurrencyCode();
    }

    public Money add(Money that) { ❺
        if (!this.currency.equals(that.currency)) {
            throw new IllegalArgumentException(
                "cannot add Money values of different currencies");
        }

        return new Money(this.amount.add(that.amount), this.currency);
    }
}
```

Example 3.8 [values.4:src/main/java/travelator/money/Money.java]

❶ The constructor is private. Other classes obtain `Money` values by calling the static `Money.of` method, which guarantees that the scale of the amount is consistent with the number of minor units of the currency. Most currencies have one hundred minor units (two digits), but some have fewer and some more. For example, the Japanese yen has no minor units, and the Jordanian dinar is made up of one thousand fils.

The `of` method follows a coding convention of Modern Java that draws a distinction in the source between objects with identity, which are constructed by the new operator, and values, which are obtained from static methods. This convention is followed by the Java time API (for example, `LocalDate.of(2020,8,17)`) and recent additions to the collections API (for example, `List.of(1,2,3)` creates an immutable list).

The class provides some convenient overloads of the `of` method for String or int amounts.

❷ A `Money` value exposes its amount and currency properties using JavaBean conventions, even though it is not actually a JavaBean.

❸ The `equals` and `hashCode` methods implement value semantics.

❹ The `toString` method returns a representation of its properties that can be shown to the user, not just for debugging.

❺ `Money` provides operations for calculating with money values. For example, you can add monetary values together. The `add` method constructs new `Money` values by calling the constructor directly (rather than using `Money.of`), because the result of `BigDecimal.add` already has the correct scale, so we can avoid the overhead of setting the scale in `Money.of`.

The method `BigDecimal.setScale` is confusing. Although named like a JavaBean setter, it does not actually mutate the BigDecimal object. Like our `EmailAddress` and `Money` classes, `BigDecimal` is an immutable value type, so `setScale` returns a new `BigDecimal` value with the specified scale.

Sun added the `BigDecimal` class to the standard library in Java 1.1. This release also included the first version of the JavaBeans API. The hype around the Beans API popularized the JavaBeans coding conventions, and they were widely adopted, even for classes that, like `BigDecimal`, were not JavaBeans (see "Bean Style" on page 5). There were no Java conventions for value types.

Today, we avoid the "set" prefix for methods that do not mutate their receiver and instead use names that emphasize when the method returns a transformation of the receiver. A common convention is to use the prefix "with" for transformations that affect a single property, which would make the code in our `Money` class read as:

```
amount.withScale(currency.getDefaultFractionDigits())
```

In Kotlin we can write extension functions to fix such historical accidents. If we were writing a lot of code that calculated with `BigDecimals`, it might be worth doing so to improve the clarity of the code:

```
fun BigDecimal.withScale(int scale, RoundingMode mode) =
    setScale(scale, mode)
```

Converting `Money` to Kotlin produces the following code:

```
class Money
private constructor(
    val amount: BigDecimal,
    val currency: Currency
) {
    override fun equals(o: Any?): Boolean {
        if (this === o) return true
        if (o == null || javaClass != o.javaClass) return false
        val money = o as Money
        return amount == money.amount && currency == money.currency
    }
```

```
    override fun hashCode(): Int {
        return Objects.hash(amount, currency)
    }

    override fun toString(): String {
        return amount.toString() + " " + currency.currencyCode
    }

    fun add(that: Money): Money {
        require(currency == that.currency) {
            "cannot add Money values of different currencies"
        }
        return Money(amount.add(that.amount), currency)
    }

    companion object {
        @JvmStatic
        fun of(amount: BigDecimal, currency: Currency): Money {
            return Money(
                amount.setScale(currency.defaultFractionDigits),
                currency
            )
        }

        ... and convenience overloads
    }
}
```

Example 3.9 [values.5:src/main/java/travelator/money/Money.kt]

The Kotlin class still has a primary constructor, but that constructor is now marked private. The syntax for this is a little clumsy: we've reformatted the code that the translator produced in an attempt to make it easier to scan. Like `EmailAddress.parse`, the static `of` factory functions are now methods on a companion object annotated as `@JvmStatic`. Overall, the code is not much more concise than the original Java.

Can we shrink it even further by making it a data class?

When we change `class` to `data class`, IntelliJ highlights the `private` keyword of the primary constructor with a warning:

```
Private data class constructor is exposed via the generated 'copy' method."
```

What's that all about?

There is a detail hiding in the implementation of `Money`. The class maintains an invariant between its properties, guaranteeing that the scale of the amount field is equal to the default number of minor currency digits of the currency field. The private constructor prevents code outside the `Money` class from creating values that violate the invariant. The `Money.of(BigDecimal,Currency)` method ensures the invariant is true for new `Money` values. The `add` method maintains the invariant because adding two

BigDecimal values with the same scale produces a BigDecimal that also has the same scale, and it can therefore call the constructor directly. The constructor, therefore, need only assign fields, safe in the knowledge that it is never called with parameters that violate the class invariant.

However, the copy method of a data class is always public and so *would* allow client code to create Money values that violate the invariant. Unlike EmailAddress, an abstract data type like the Money class cannot be implemented by a Kotlin data class.

Don't define a value type as a data class if it must maintain invariants between its properties.

We can still make the class more concise and convenient with Kotlin features that we will encounter in later chapters. So we'll leave the Money class for now and come back to it in Chapter 12 to give it a thorough makeover.

Moving On

For most classes, it is quick and easy to convert Java to Kotlin. The result is completely compatible with existing Java code.

If we want value semantics, data classes allow us to remove even more boilerplate for simple classes like EmailAddress. Because data classes are so quick and easy to create, and require no maintenance, we use them to define new value types far more frequently in Kotlin than in Java: to declare application-specific "micro-types" that wrap primitive values, to hold intermediate results of a calculation pipeline, or to pivot data into temporary structures that make it easier to write application logic.

If our value types must maintain invariants or encapsulate their representation, data classes are not suitable. In that case we have to implement value semantics ourselves.

We left both EmailAddress and Money still looking rather Java-y...Java-ish?...Javaesque?...whatever. In the following chapters, we will explore how to apply Kotlin idioms to make code more concise, more type safe, and easier to build code upon. Chapter 9, *Multi- to Single-Expression Functions*, looks at how we can make calculation functions and methods, such as the toString method of both classes, or equals and hashCode of Money, more concise by refactoring them to single expression form. In Chapter 12, *Functions to Operators*, we make the Money type more convenient to use in Kotlin by defining operators instead of methods.

Not all our Java classes are value types. The prevalent Java coding style favors mutable objects. In Chapter 5, *Beans to Values*, we look at the advantages of using value types where Java would use mutable objects, and show how to refactor code from mutating objects to transforming values.

Many classes in Java code exist to hold static utility methods. In Kotlin, functions and data are first class features. They do not need to be declared as members of classes. Chapter 8, *Static Methods to Top-Level Functions*, explores how to convert Java classes of utility methods into top-level declarations.

CHAPTER 4

Optional to Nullable

Tony Hoare may consider the invention of null references his billion dollar mistake,[1] *but we still need to represent the absence of things in our software systems. How can we use Kotlin to embrace null while still having safe software?*

Representing Absence

Perhaps Kotlin's most attractive feature for Java programmers is its representation of nullability in the type system. This is another area where the grains of Java and Kotlin are different.

Prior to Java 8, Java relied on convention, documentation, and intuition to distinguish between references that could or could not be null. We can deduce that methods that return an item from a collection must be able to return `null`, but can `addressLine3` be `null`, or do we use an empty string when there is no information?

Over the years, your authors and their colleagues settled into a convention where Java references are assumed to be nonnull unless otherwise flagged. So we might name a field `addressLine3OrNull`, or a method `previousAddressOrNull`. Within a codebase, this works well enough (even if it is a little verbose, and requires eternal vigilance to avoid the scourge of `NullPointerExceptions`).

Some codebases opted to use `@Nullable` and `@NotNullable` annotations instead, often supported by tools that would check for correctness. Java 8, released in 2014, enhanced support for annotations to the extent that tools like the Checker Framework (*https://oreil.ly/qGYlH*) could statically check much more than just null safety. More crucially, though, Java 8 also introduced a standard `Optional` type.

1 "Null References: The Billion Dollar Mistake" on YouTube (*https://oreil.ly/Ue3Ct*).

By this time, many JVM developers had dabbled in Scala. They came to appreciate the advantages of using an *Optional* type (named `Option` in Scala's standard library) when absence was possible, and plain references when it was not. Oracle muddied the waters by telling developers not to use its `Optional` for field or parameter values, but as with many features introduced in Java 8, it was good enough and was adopted into the mainstream usage of Java.

Depending on its age, your Java code may use some or all of these strategies for dealing with absence. It is certainly possible to have a codebase in which `NullPointerExceptions` are practically never seen, but the reality is that this is hard work. Java is weighed down by null and embarrassed by its halfhearted `Optional` type.

In contrast, Kotlin *embraces* null. Making optionality part of the type system rather than the standard library means that Kotlin codebases have refreshing uniformity in their treatment of missing values. It isn't all perfect: `Map<K, V>.get(key)` returns `null` if there is no value for `key`; but `List<T>.get(index)` throws `IndexOutOfBoundsException` when there is no value at `index`. Likewise, `Iterable<T>.first()` throws `NoSuchElementException` rather than returning `null`. Such imperfections are generally caused by the desire for backward compatibility with Java.

Where Kotlin has its own APIs, they are generally good examples of how to safely use null to represent optional properties, parameters, and return values, and we can learn a lot from studying them. After you've experienced first-class nullability, returning to languages without this support feels unsafe; you are acutely aware that you are always only a dereference away from a `NullPointerException`, and that you're relying on convention to find the safe path through the minefield.

Functional programmers may advise you to use an optional (also known as *Maybe*) type rather than nullability in Kotlin. We counsel against this, even though it will give you the option to use the same (monadic—there, we said it) tools to represent potential absence, errors, asynchrony, and so on. One reason not to use `Optional` in Kotlin is that you will lose access to the language features designed specifically to support nullability; in this area the grain of Kotlin is different from the grain of, say, Scala.

Another reason not to use a wrapper type to represent optionality is subtle but important. In the Kotlin type system, `T` is a subtype of `T?`. If you have a `String` that cannot be null, you can always use it where a nullable `String` is required. In contrast, `T` is not a subtype of `Optional<T>`. If you have a `String` and want to assign it to an optional variable, you first have to wrap it in an `Optional`. Worse, if you have a function that returns an `Optional<String>` and later discover a way to always return a result, changing the return type to `String` will break all your clients. Had your return type been the nullable `String?`, you could have strengthened it to `String` while maintaining compatibility. The same applies to properties of data structures: you can easily migrate from optional to nonoptional with nullability—but not, ironically, with `Optional`.

Your authors love Kotlin's support for nullability, and have learned to lean on it to solve many problems. It takes a while to wean yourself off of avoiding nulls, but once you have, there is literally a whole new dimension of expressiveness to explore and exploit.

It seems a shame not to have that facility in Travelator, so let's look at how to migrate from Java code using `Optional`, to Kotlin and nullable.

Refactoring from Optional to Nullable

Travelator trips are divided into `Legs`, where each `Leg` is an unbroken journey. Here is one of the utility functions we've found in the code:

```
public class Legs {

    public static Optional<Leg> findLongestLegOver(
        List<Leg> legs,
        Duration duration
    ) {
        Leg result = null;
        for (Leg leg : legs) {
            if (isLongerThan(leg, duration))
                if (result == null ||
                    isLongerThan(leg, result.getPlannedDuration())
                ) {
                    result = leg;
                }
        }
        return Optional.ofNullable(result);
    }

    private static boolean isLongerThan(Leg leg, Duration duration) {
        return leg.getPlannedDuration().compareTo(duration) > 0;
    }
}
```

Example 4.1 [nullability.0:src/main/java/travelator/Legs.java]

The tests check that the code works as intended, and allow us to see its behavior at a glance:

```
public class LongestLegOverTests {

    private final List<Leg> legs = List.of(
        leg("one hour", Duration.ofHours(1)),
        leg("one day", Duration.ofDays(1)),
        leg("two hours", Duration.ofHours(2))
    );
    private final Duration oneDay = Duration.ofDays(1);

    @Test
```

```
    public void is_absent_when_no_legs() {
        assertEquals(
            Optional.empty(),
            findLongestLegOver(emptyList(), Duration.ZERO)
        );
    }

    @Test
    public void is_absent_when_no_legs_long_enough() {
        assertEquals(
            Optional.empty(),
            findLongestLegOver(legs, oneDay)
        );
    }

    @Test
    public void is_longest_leg_when_one_match() {
        assertEquals(
            "one day",
            findLongestLegOver(legs, oneDay.minusMillis(1))
                .orElseThrow().getDescription()
        );
    }

    @Test
    public void is_longest_leg_when_more_than_one_match() {
        assertEquals(
            "one day",
            findLongestLegOver(legs, Duration.ofMinutes(59))
                .orElseThrow().getDescription()
        );
    }

    ...
}
```

Example 4.2 [nullability.0:src/test/java/travelator/LongestLegOverTests.java]

Let's see what we can do to make things better in Kotlin. Converting `Legs.java` to Kotlin gives us this (after a little reformatting):

```
object Legs {
    @JvmStatic
    fun findLongestLegOver(
        legs: List<Leg>,
        duration: Duration
    ): Optional<Leg> {
        var result: Leg? = null
        for (leg in legs) {
            if (isLongerThan(leg, duration))
                if (result == null ||
                    isLongerThan(leg, result.plannedDuration))
                    result = leg
```

```
        }
        return Optional.ofNullable(result)
    }

    private fun isLongerThan(leg: Leg, duration: Duration): Boolean {
        return leg.plannedDuration.compareTo(duration) > 0
    }
}
```

Example 4.3 [nullability.3:src/main/java/travelator/Legs.kt]

The method parameters are as we might expect, with Kotlin `List<Leg>` transparently accepting a `java.util.List`. (We examine Java and Kotlin collections more in Chapter 6.) It's worth mentioning here that when a Kotlin function declares a nonnullable parameter (`legs` and `duration` here), the compiler inserts a null check before the function body. That way, if Java callers sneak in a `null`, we'll know straightaway. Because of these defensive checks, Kotlin detects unexpected nulls as close as possible to their source, in contrast to Java, where a reference can be set to `null` a long way in time and space from where it finally explodes.

Returning to the example, the Kotlin `for` loop is very similar to Java's, except for the use of the `in` keyword rather than :, and similarly applies to any type that extends `Iterable`.

Iteration and the For Loop

Actually, we can use other types as well as `Iterable` in Kotlin `for` loops. The compiler will allow `for` to be used with anything:

- That extends `Iterator`
- That has a method `iterator()` that returns an `Iterator`
- That has an in-scope extension function, `operator fun T.iterator()` returning an `Iterator`

Unfortunately, this last wrinkle doesn't actually make other people's types `Iterable`; it just makes the `for` loop work. Which is a shame, because if we were to be able to retrospectively make types `Iterable` we could then apply `map`, `reduce`, and so on to them, because these are operations defined as extension functions on `Iterable<T>`.

The converted `findLongestLegOver` code is not very idiomatic Kotlin. (Arguably, since the introduction of streams, it isn't very idiomatic Java either.) Instead of a `for` loop, we should look for something more intention revealing, but let's park that for now because our primary mission is to migrate from `Optional` to nullable. We'll illustrate that by converting our tests one by one, so that we have a mix, as we would in a codebase that we were migrating. To make use of nullability in our clients, they have to be Kotlin, so let's convert the tests:

```
class LongestLegOverTests {
    ...
    @Test
    fun is_absent_when_no_legs() {
        Assertions.assertEquals(
            Optional.empty<Any>(),
            findLongestLegOver(emptyList(), Duration.ZERO)
        )
    }

    @Test
    fun is_absent_when_no_legs_long_enough() {
        Assertions.assertEquals(
            Optional.empty<Any>(),
            findLongestLegOver(legs, oneDay)
        )
    }

    @Test
    fun is_longest_leg_when_one_match() {
        Assertions.assertEquals(
            "one day",
            findLongestLegOver(legs, oneDay.minusMillis(1))
                .orElseThrow().description
        )
    }

    @Test
    fun is_longest_leg_when_more_than_one_match() {
        Assertions.assertEquals(
            "one day",
            findLongestLegOver(legs, Duration.ofMinutes(59))
                .orElseThrow().description
        )
    }

    ...
}
```

Example 4.4 [nullability.4:src/test/java/travelator/LongestLegOverTests.kt]

Now to migrate gradually, we'll need two versions of `findLongestLegOver`: the existing `Optional<Leg>`-returning one, and a new one that returns `Leg?`. We can do that by extracting the guts of the current implementation. This is currently:

```
@JvmStatic
fun findLongestLegOver(
    legs: List<Leg>,
    duration: Duration
): Optional<Leg> {
```

```
    var result: Leg? = null
    for (leg in legs) {
        if (isLongerThan(leg, duration))
            if (result == null ||
                isLongerThan(leg, result.plannedDuration))
                result = leg
    }
    return Optional.ofNullable(result)
}
```

Example 4.5 [nullability.4:src/main/java/travelator/Legs.kt]

We "Extract Function" on all but the return statement of this `findLongestLegOver`. We can't give it the same name, so we use `longestLegOver`; we make it public because this is our new interface:

```
@JvmStatic
fun findLongestLegOver(
    legs: List<Leg>,
    duration: Duration
): Optional<Leg> {
    var result: Leg? = longestLegOver(legs, duration)
    return Optional.ofNullable(result)
}

fun longestLegOver(legs: List<Leg>, duration: Duration): Leg? {
    var result: Leg? = null
    for (leg in legs) {
        if (isLongerThan(leg, duration))
            if (result == null ||
                isLongerThan(leg, result.plannedDuration))
                result = leg
    }
    return result
}
```

Example 4.6 [nullability.5:src/main/java/travelator/Legs.kt]

The refactoring has left a vestigial `result` variable in `findLongestLegOver`. We can select it and "Inline" to give:

```
@JvmStatic
fun findLongestLegOver(
    legs: List<Leg>,
    duration: Duration
): Optional<Leg> {
    return Optional.ofNullable(longestLegOver(legs, duration))
}
```

Example 4.7 [nullability.6:src/main/java/travelator/Legs.kt]

Now we have two versions of our interface, one defined in terms of the other. We can leave our Java clients consuming the `Optional` from `findLongestLegOver` and convert our Kotlin clients to call the nullable-returning `longestLegOver`. Let's show the conversion with our tests.

We'll do the absent ones first. They currently call `assertEquals(Optional.empty<Any>(), findLongestLegOver…)`:

```
@Test
fun is_absent_when_no_legs() {
    assertEquals(
        Optional.empty<Any>(),
        findLongestLegOver(emptyList(), Duration.ZERO)
    )
}

@Test
fun is_absent_when_no_legs_long_enough() {
    assertEquals(
        Optional.empty<Any>(),
        findLongestLegOver(legs, oneDay)
    )
}
```

Example 4.8 [nullability.6:src/test/java/travelator/LongestLegOverTests.kt]

So we change them to `assertNull(longestLegOver(...)`:

```
@Test
fun `is absent when no legs`() {
    assertNull(longestLegOver(emptyList(), Duration.ZERO))
}

@Test
fun `is absent when no legs long enough`() {
    assertNull(longestLegOver(legs, oneDay))
}
```

Example 4.9 [nullability.7:src/test/java/travelator/LongestLegOverTests.kt]

Note that we've changed the test names to use `backtick quoted identifiers`. IntelliJ will do this for us if we Alt-Enter on function_names with_underscores_in_tests.

Now for the calls that don't return empty:

```
@Test
fun is_longest_leg_when_one_match() {
    assertEquals(
        "one day",
        findLongestLegOver(legs, oneDay.minusMillis(1))
            .orElseThrow().description
    )
}
```

```
@Test
fun is_longest_leg_when_more_than_one_match() {
    assertEquals(
        "one day",
        findLongestLegOver(legs, Duration.ofMinutes(59))
            .orElseThrow().description
    )
}
```

Example 4.10 [nullability.6:src/test/java/travelator/LongestLegOverTests.kt]

The Kotlin equivalent of `Optional.orElseThrow()` (aka `get()` pre-Java 10) is the `!!` (bang-bang or dammit) operator. Both the Java `orElseThrow` and the Kotlin `!!` return the value or throw an exception if there isn't one. Kotlin logically throws a `NullPointerException`. Java equally logically throws a `NoSuchElementExecption`; they just think of absence in different ways! Provided we haven't relied on the type of the exception, we can replace `findLongestLegOver(...).orElseThrow()` with `longestLegOver(...)!!`:

```
@Test
fun `is longest leg when one match`() {
    assertEquals(
        "one day",
        longestLegOver(legs, oneDay.minusMillis(1))
            !!.description
    )
}

@Test
fun `is longest leg when more than one match`() {
    assertEquals(
        "one day",
        longestLegOver(legs, Duration.ofMinutes(59))
            ?.description
    )
}
```

Example 4.11 [nullability.8:src/test/java/travelator/LongestLegOverTests.kt]

We've converted the first of the nonnull-returning tests (`is longest leg when one match`) with the `!!` operator. If it were to fail (which it doesn't, but we like to plan for these things), it would fail with a thrown `NullPointerException` rather than with a nice diagnostic. In the second case, we've solved that problem with the safe call operator `?.`, which continues evaluation only if its receiver is not `null`. This means that if the leg *is* `null`, the error will read as follows, which is much nicer:

```
Expected :one day
Actual   :null
```

Tests are one of the few places we use `!!` in practice, and even here there is usually a better alternative.

We can work this refactoring through our clients, converting them to Kotlin and then to using `longestLegOver`. Once we have converted all of them, we can delete the `Optional`-returning `findLongestLegOver`.

> ### Expand-and-Contract Refactoring
>
> We will use this technique (also known as parallel change (*https://oreil.ly/jxSPE*)) for managing changes to interfaces (with a lowercase *i*) throughout this book. It's a simple concept: add the new interface, migrate uses of the old interface to the new one, and when there are no uses of the old one, delete it.
>
> In this book we will often combine the refactoring with a conversion to Kotlin. Usually, as in this chapter, we will convert the definition and implementation(s) of the interface to Kotlin, then add the new interface to it. As we convert clients to use the new interface, we take the opportunity to convert them to Kotlin as well.
>
> Although we migrate between interfaces and convert between languages as part of this process, we try not to do them both at once. Like climbers keeping three points of contact with the rock, don't let go with both hands at once! Make one move, make sure the tests pass, then go on to the next. If the change feels risky, now might be a good time to put in some protection (run the pre-commit test suite, check-in, even deploy a canary release) so that we don't fall too far if things go wrong.
>
> And finish the job. We refactor to make our code better, which almost always means simpler, and simpler rarely correlates with larger. We allow code to get worse (with two ways of doing the same thing) before it gets better (with everyone using the new interface), but don't get stuck having to maintain both versions. If we end up supporting two versions of an interface for an extended period, they might diverge, or both need testing to ensure that they don't, and the old version may gain new clients. We could mark code as deprecated, but it's better to just get on and finish the job. That said, small shims to support legacy can be allowed to live; we love Kotlin, but we want to spend our time adding value rather than converting Java code that otherwise requires no attention.

Refactoring to Idiomatic Kotlin

Now all the code in this example is Kotlin, and we've seen how to migrate from optional to nullable. We could stop there, but consistent with our policy of going the extra refactoring mile, we'll press on to see what else this code has to teach us.

Here is the current version of `Legs`:

```
object Legs {
    fun longestLegOver(
        legs: List<Leg>,
        duration: Duration
```

```
    ): Leg? {
        var result: Leg? = null
        for (leg in legs) {
            if (isLongerThan(leg, duration))
                if (result == null ||
                    isLongerThan(leg, result.plannedDuration))
                    result = leg
        }
        return result
    }

    private fun isLongerThan(leg: Leg, duration: Duration): Boolean {
        return leg.plannedDuration.compareTo(duration) > 0
    }
}
```

Example 4.12 [nullability.9:src/main/java/travelator/Legs.kt]

The functions are contained in an `object` because our Java methods were static, so the conversion needed somewhere to put them. As we'll see in Chapter 8, Kotlin doesn't need this extra level of namespace, so we can "Move to top level" on `longestLegOver`. At the time of writing, this doesn't work very well, because IntelliJ fails to bring `isLongerThan` with its calling function, leaving it in `Legs`. The breakage is easy to fix though, leaving us with a top-level function and fixed-up references in existing code:

```
fun longestLegOver(
    legs: List<Leg>,
    duration: Duration
): Leg? {
    var result: Leg? = null
    for (leg in legs) {
        if (isLongerThan(leg, duration))
            if (result == null ||
                isLongerThan(leg, result.plannedDuration))
                result = leg
    }
    return result
}

private fun isLongerThan(leg: Leg, duration: Duration) =
    leg.plannedDuration.compareTo(duration) > 0
```

Example 4.13 [nullability.10:src/main/java/travelator/Legs.kt]

You may have noticed that `isLongerThan` has lost its braces and return statement. We'll talk though the pros and cons of single-expression functions in Chapter 9.

While we're here, there's something odd about the phrase `isLongerThan(leg, ...)`. It just doesn't read right in English. You'll no doubt get bored of our infatuation with extension functions (certainly by the end of Chapter 10), but while we still have your goodwill, let's Alt-Enter on the `leg` parameter and "Convert parameter to receiver", so that we can write `leg.isLongerThan(...)`:

```kotlin
fun longestLegOver(
    legs: List<Leg>,
    duration: Duration
): Leg? {
    var result: Leg? = null
    for (leg in legs) {
        if (leg.isLongerThan(duration))
            if (result == null ||
                leg.isLongerThan(result.plannedDuration))
                result = leg
    }
    return result
}

private fun Leg.isLongerThan(duration: Duration) =
    plannedDuration.compareTo(duration) > 0
```

Example 4.14 [nullability.11:src/main/java/travelator/Legs.kt]

So far, our changes have all been structural, changing where code is defined and how we call it. Structural refactors are inherently quite (as in mostly, rather than completely) safe. They can change the behavior of code that relies on polymorphism (either through methods or functions) or reflection, but otherwise, if the code continues to compile, it probably behaves.

Now we are going to turn our attention to the *algorithm* in `longestLegOver`. Refactoring algorithms is more dangerous, especially ones like this that rely on mutation, because tool support for transforming them is not good. We have good tests though, and it's hard to work out what this does by reading it, so let's see what we can do.

The only suggestion IntelliJ gives is to replace `compareTo` with `>`, so let's do that first. At this point, Duncan at least has run out of refactoring talent (if we were actually pairing maybe you would have a suggestion?) and so decides to rewrite the function from scratch.

To reimplement the functionality, we ask ourselves, "What is the code trying to do?" The answer is, helpfully, in the name of the function: `longestLegOver`. To implement this calculation, we can find the longest leg, and if it is longer than duration, return it, otherwise `null`. After typing `legs.` at the beginning of the function, we look at the suggestions and find `maxByOrNull`. Our longest leg is going to be `legs.maxByOrNull(Leg::plannedDuration)`. This API helpfully returns `Leg?` (and includes the phrase `orNull`) to remind us that it can't give a result if `legs` is empty. Converting our algorithm "find the longest leg, and if it is longer than duration, return it, otherwise null" to code directly, we get:

```kotlin
fun longestLegOver(
    legs: List<Leg>,
    duration: Duration
): Leg? {
    val longestLeg: Leg? = legs.maxByOrNull(Leg::plannedDuration)
```

```
    if (longestLeg != null && longestLeg.plannedDuration > duration)
        return longestLeg
    else
        return null
}
```

Example 4.15 [nullability.12:src/main/java/travelator/Legs.kt]

That passes the tests, but those multiple returns are ugly. IntelliJ will helpfully offer to lift the `return` out of the `if`:

```
fun longestLegOver(
    legs: List<Leg>,
    duration: Duration
): Leg? {
    val longestLeg: Leg? = legs.maxByOrNull(Leg::plannedDuration)
    return if (longestLeg != null && longestLeg.plannedDuration > duration)
        longestLeg
    else
        null
}
```

Example 4.16 [nullability.13:src/main/java/travelator/Legs.kt]

Now, Kotlin's nullability support allows several ways to refactor this, depending on your tastes.

We can use the Elvis operator `?:`, which evaluates to its lefthand side unless that is `null`, in which case it evaluates its righthand side. This lets us return early if we have no longest leg:

```
fun longestLegOver(
    legs: List<Leg>,
    duration: Duration
): Leg? {
    val longestLeg = legs.maxByOrNull(Leg::plannedDuration) ?:
        return null
    return if (longestLeg.plannedDuration > duration)
        longestLeg
    else
        null
}
```

Example 4.17 [nullability.14:src/main/java/travelator/Legs.kt]

We could go with a single `?.let` expression. The `?.` evaluates to `null` if fed a `null`; otherwise, it pipes the longest leg into the `let` block for us:

```
fun longestLegOver(
    legs: List<Leg>,
    duration: Duration
): Leg? =
    legs.maxByOrNull(Leg::plannedDuration)?.let { longestLeg ->
        if (longestLeg.plannedDuration > duration)
```

```
            longestLeg
        else
            null
    }
```

Example 4.18 [nullability.15:src/main/java/travelator/Legs.kt]

So inside the `let`, `longestLeg` cannot be `null`. That is succinct, and it is a pleasing single expression, but it may be hard to comprehend in a single glance. Spelling out the options with a `when` is clearer:

```
fun longestLegOver(
    legs: List<Leg>,
    duration: Duration
): Leg? {
    val longestLeg = legs.maxByOrNull(Leg::plannedDuration)
    return when {
        longestLeg == null -> null
        longestLeg.plannedDuration > duration -> longestLeg
        else -> null
    }
}
```

Example 4.19 [nullability.17:src/main/java/travelator/Legs.kt]

To simplify further, we need a trick that Duncan (who is writing this) has so far failed to internalize: `takeIf` returns its receiver if a predicate is `true`; otherwise, it returns `null`. This is exactly the logic of our previous `let` block. So we can write:

```
fun longestLegOver(
    legs: List<Leg>,
    duration: Duration
): Leg? =
    legs.maxByOrNull(Leg::plannedDuration)?.takeIf { longestLeg ->
        longestLeg.plannedDuration > duration
    }
```

Example 4.20 [nullability.16:src/main/java/travelator/Legs.kt]

Depending on our team's experience with Kotlin, that may be too subtle. Nat thinks it's fine, but we're going to err on the side of explicitness, so the `when` version gets to stay, at least until the next time someone refactors here.

Finally, let's convert the `legs` parameter to the receiver in an extension function. This allows us to rename the function to something less dubious:

```
fun List<Leg>.longestOver(duration: Duration): Leg? {
    val longestLeg = maxByOrNull(Leg::plannedDuration)
    return when {
        longestLeg == null -> null
        longestLeg.plannedDuration > duration -> longestLeg
        else -> null
```

```
    }
}
```

Example 4.21 [nullability.18:src/main/java/travelator/Legs.kt]

Just before we finish this chapter, take the time to compare this version with the original. Are there any advantages to the old version?

```
public class Legs {

    public static Optional<Leg> findLongestLegOver(
        List<Leg> legs,
        Duration duration
    ) {
        Leg result = null;
        for (Leg leg : legs) {
            if (isLongerThan(leg, duration))
                if (result == null ||
                    isLongerThan(leg, result.getPlannedDuration())
                ) {
                    result = leg;
                }
        }
        return Optional.ofNullable(result);
    }

    private static boolean isLongerThan(Leg leg, Duration duration) {
        return leg.getPlannedDuration().compareTo(duration) > 0;
    }
}
```

Example 4.22 [nullability.0:src/main/java/travelator/Legs.java]

Usually we would say "it depends," but in this case we think that the new version is better on pretty much every front. It is shorter and simpler; it's easier to see how it works; and in most cases it results in fewer calls to `getPlannedDuration()`, which is a relatively expensive operation. What if we had taken the same approach in Java? A direct translation is:

```
public class Legs {

    public static Optional<Leg> findLongestLegOver(
        List<Leg> legs,
        Duration duration
    ) {
        var longestLeg = legs.stream()
            .max(Comparator.comparing(Leg::getPlannedDuration));
        if (longestLeg.isEmpty()) {
            return Optional.empty();
        } else if (isLongerThan(longestLeg.get(), duration)) {
            return longestLeg;
        } else {
            return Optional.empty();
```

```
        }
    }

    private static boolean isLongerThan(Leg leg, Duration duration) {
        return leg.getPlannedDuration().compareTo(duration) > 0;
    }
}
```

Example 4.23 [nullability.1:src/main/java/travelator/Legs.java]

Actually, that isn't bad, but compared with the Kotlin version, you can see how `Optional` adds noise to pretty much every line of the method. Because of this, a version using `Optional.filter` is probably preferable, even though it suffers from the same comprehension problems as the Kotlin `takeIf`. Which is to say, Duncan can't tell that it works without running the tests, but Nat prefers it.

```
public static Optional<Leg> findLongestLegOver(
    List<Leg> legs,
    Duration duration
) {
    return legs.stream()
        .max(Comparator.comparing(Leg::getPlannedDuration))
        .filter(leg -> isLongerThan(leg, duration));
}
```

Example 4.24 [nullability.2:src/main/java/travelator/Legs.java]

Moving On

The absence or presence of information is inescapable in our code. By raising it to first-class status, Kotlin makes sure that we take account of absence when we have to and are not overwhelmed by it when we don't. In comparison, Java's `Optional` type feels clumsy. Luckily, we can easily migrate from `Optional` to nullable and support both simultaneously when we are not ready to convert all our code to Kotlin.

In Chapter 10, *Functions to Extension Functions*, we'll see how nullable types combine with other Kotlin language features—the safe call and Elvis operators, and extension functions—to form a grain that results in designs quite different from those we write in Java.

But that's getting ahead of ourselves. In the next chapter, we'll look at a typical Java class and translate it into a typical Kotlin class. Translation from Java to Kotlin is more than syntactic: the two languages differ in their acceptance of mutable state.

CHAPTER 5

Beans to Values

Many Java projects have settled on mutable JavaBeans or POJO (plain old Java object) conventions for representing data. Mutability brings complications, though. Why are immutable values a better choice, and how can we reduce the cost of mutability in a codebase?

Beans

As we discussed in "Bean Style" on page 5, JavaBeans were introduced to allow the development of drag-and-drop GUI builders in the Visual Basic style. A developer could drop a button onto a form, change its title and icon, and then wire in an on-click handler. Behind the scenes, the GUI builder would write code to instantiate a button object and then call setters for the properties that the developer had changed.

To define a JavaBean, a class needs a default (no-argument) constructor, getters for its properties, and setters for its mutable properties. (We'll gloss over the `Serializable` requirement, because even Sun never really took this seriously.) This makes sense for objects that have a lot of properties. GUI components typically have foreground and background colors, font, label, borders, size, alignments, paddings, and so on. Mostly the defaults for these properties are fine, so calling setters for just the special values minimizes the amount of code to be generated. Even today, a mutable component model is a solid choice for GUI toolkits.

When JavaBeans were introduced, though, we thought of most objects as mutable, not just UI components. I mean, why not? The point of objects was to encapsulate properties and manage the relationships between them. They were *designed* to solve problems like updating the width of a component when its bounds are changed, or the total of a shopping cart as items are added. Objects were the solution to the problem of managing mutable state. Java was quite radical at the time in having an immutable `String` class (although it couldn't help itself and still plumped for a mutable `Date`).

As a profession, we have a more sophisticated understanding these days. We appreciate that we can use objects to represent different types of things—values, entities, services, actions, transactions, and so on. And yet the default pattern for a Java object is still the JavaBean, a mutable object with getters and setters for its properties. Although it may be appropriate for a UI toolkit, this is not a good default pattern. For most things that we want to represent with objects, a value would be better.

Values

Value is a much overloaded term in English. In computing, we say that variables, parameters, and fields have values: the primitive or reference that they are bound to. When we refer to *a value* in this book, we are referring to a specific type of primitive or reference: those with value semantics. An object has value semantics if only its value is significant in its interactions, not its identity. Java primitives all have value semantics: every `7` is equal to every other `7`. Objects may or may not have value semantics though; in particular, mutable objects do not. In later chapters we'll look at finer distinctions, but for now, let's just define a *value* to be an immutable piece of data, and a *value type* to be a type that defines the behavior of an immutable piece of data.

So `7` is a value, and the boxed `Integer` is a value type (because boxed types are immutable), `banana` is a value (because `String`s are immutable), a `URI` is a value (because `URI`s are immutable), but `java.util.Date` is not a value type (because we can call `setYear` and others on the date).

An instance of an immutable `DBConnectionInfo` is a value, but an instance of `Database` is not a value, even if all its properties are immutable. This is because it is not a piece of data; it is a means of accessing, and mutating, pieces of data.

Are JavaBeans values? UI component JavaBeans are not values because UI components aren't just data—two otherwise identical buttons have different identities. In the case of beans used to represent plain data, it will depend on whether they are immutable. It is possible to create immutable beans, but most developers would think of these more as plain old java objects.

Are POJOs values? The term was coined to refer to classes that don't have to extend from framework types to be useful. They usually represent data and conform to the JavaBeans conventions for accessor methods. Many POJOs will not have a default constructor, but instead define constructors to initialize properties that don't have sensible defaults. Because of this, immutable POJOs are common and may have value semantics. Mutable POJOs still seem to be the default though, so much so that many people consider that object-oriented programming in Java is synonymous with mutable objects. Mutable POJOs are not values.

In summary, a bean could technically be a value but rarely is. POJOs more often have value semantics, especially in the modern Java age. So whereas *Beans to Values* is snappy, in this chapter we're really looking at refactoring from mutable objects to immutable data, so maybe we should have called it *Mutable POJOs to Values*. We hope you'll forgive the sloppy title.

Why Should We Prefer Values?

A value is immutable data. Why should we prefer immutable objects to mutable objects, and objects that represent data to other types of objects? This is a theme that we will visit time and again in this book. For now, let's just say that immutable objects are easier to reason about because they don't change, and so:

- We can put them into sets or use them as map keys.
- We never have to worry about an immutable collection changing as we iterate over its contents.
- We can explore different scenarios without having to deep-copy initial states (which also makes it easy to implement undo and redo).
- We can safely share immutable objects between different threads.

Refactoring Beans to Values

Let's look at refactoring a use of a mutable bean or POJO to a value.

Travelator has a mobile app, and the Android version is written in Java. In that code, we represent user preferences with a `UserPreferences` JavaBean:

```
public class UserPreferences {

    private String greeting;
    private Locale locale;
    private Currency currency;

    public UserPreferences() {
        this("Hello", Locale.UK, Currency.getInstance(Locale.UK));
    }

    public UserPreferences(String greeting, Locale locale, Currency currency) {
        this.greeting = greeting;
        this.locale = locale;
        this.currency = currency;
    }

    public String getGreeting() {
        return greeting;
    }
```

```
    public void setGreeting(String greeting) {
        this.greeting = greeting;
    }

    ... getters and setters for locale and currency
}
```

Example 5.1 [beans-to-values.0:src/main/java/travelator/mobile/UserPreferences.java]

The `Application` has a `preferences` property, which it passes to views that need it:

```
public class Application {

    private final UserPreferences preferences;

    public Application(UserPreferences preferences) {
        this.preferences = preferences;
    }

    public void showWelcome() {
        new WelcomeView(preferences).show();
    }

    public void editPreferences() {
        new PreferencesView(preferences).show();
    }
    ...
}
```

Example 5.2 [beans-to-values.0:src/main/java/travelator/mobile/Application.java]

(Any similarity to an actual UI framework, living or dead, is purely coincidental.)

Finally, `PreferencesView` updates its `preferences` when the user makes changes. We know that there has been a change because `onThingChange()` will be called:

```
public class PreferencesView extends View {

    private final UserPreferences preferences;
    private final GreetingPicker greetingPicker = new GreetingPicker();
    private final LocalePicker localePicker = new LocalePicker();
    private final CurrencyPicker currencyPicker = new CurrencyPicker();

    public PreferencesView(UserPreferences preferences) {
        this.preferences = preferences;
    }

    public void show() {
        greetingPicker.setGreeting(preferences.getGreeting());
        localePicker.setLocale(preferences.getLocale());
        currencyPicker.setCurrency(preferences.getCurrency());
        super.show();
    }
```

```
    protected void onGreetingChange() {
        preferences.setGreeting(greetingPicker.getGreeting());
    }

    protected void onLocaleChange() {
        preferences.setLocale(localePicker.getLocale());
    }

    protected void onCurrencyChange() {
        preferences.setCurrency(currencyPicker.getCurrency());
    }
    ...
}
```

Example 5.3 [beans-to-values.0:src/main/java/travelator/mobile/PreferencesView.java]

This design, though simple, is fraught with complications typical of mutable data, such as:

- If the `PreferencesView` and `WelcomeView` are both active, the `WelcomeView` can get out of sync with the current values.
- `UserPreferences` equality and hash-code depend on the values of its properties, which may be changed. So we can't reliably use `UserPreferences` in sets or as keys in maps.
- There is nothing to indicate that the `WelcomeView` only reads from the preferences.
- If reading and writing occur on different threads, we have to manage synchronization at the preference property level.

Before we refactor to using an immutable value, let's convert `Application` and `UserPreferences` to Kotlin, which will help us see the nature of our model. `Application` is simple:

```
class Application(
    private val preferences: UserPreferences
) {
    fun showWelcome() {
        WelcomeView(preferences).show()
    }

    fun editPreferences() {
        PreferencesView(preferences).show()
    }
    ...
}
```

Example 5.4 [beans-to-values.1:src/main/java/travelator/mobile/Application.kt]

`UserPreferences` is more complicated. "Convert to Kotlin" in IntelliJ yields this:

```
class UserPreferences @JvmOverloads constructor(
    var greeting: String = "Hello",
    var locale: Locale = Locale.UK,
    var currency: Currency = Currency.getInstance(Locale.UK)
)
```

Example 5.5 [beans-to-values.1:src/main/java/travelator/mobile/UserPreferences.kt]

This is quite a sophisticated conversion. The `@JVMOverloads` annotation tells the compiler to generate multiple constructors that allow combinations of `greeting`, `locale`, or `currency` to be defaulted. This wasn't what our original Java did; it had just two constructors (one of which was the default, no-argument constructor).

At this stage we haven't changed the functioning of our application, just simplified its expression. Those `var` (as opposed to `val`) properties are the sign that we have mutable data. It's worth reminding ourselves at this point that the Kotlin compiler is going to generate a private field, a getter method, and a setter method for each property, so that our Java continues to see the data class as a bean. Kotlin embraces the beans naming convention, and `var` properties allow us to define mutable beans, for better or worse.

Assuming worse, how now do we make `UserPreferences` immutable? After all, we do need the preferences as seen in the app to reflect any changes the user makes. The answer is to move the mutation. In common with many of the refactorings in this book, we're going to move the problematic thing (in this case mutation) up. Which is to say, toward the entry point, or into the higher-level, more application-specific code.

Instead of mutating the preferences, we are going to update the reference in the `Application`. The reference we're going to use will be an updated copy returned by `PreferencesView`. In short, our strategy is to replace an immutable reference to a mutable object with a mutable reference to an immutable value. Why? Well, this reduces both the number and visibility of the potentially moving parts, and it is visibility of mutation that causes us problems.

We'll work our way there gradually, starting by converting `PreferencesView` to Kotlin:

```
class PreferencesView(
    private val preferences: UserPreferences
) : View() {
    private val greetingPicker = GreetingPicker()
    private val localePicker = LocalePicker()
    private val currencyPicker = CurrencyPicker()

    override fun show() {
        greetingPicker.greeting = preferences.greeting
        localePicker.locale = preferences.locale
        currencyPicker.currency = preferences.currency
        super.show()
    }
```

```
    protected fun onGreetingChange() {
        preferences.greeting = greetingPicker.greeting
    }

    ... onLocaleChange, onCurrencyChange
}
```

Example 5.6 [beans-to-values.3:src/main/java/travelator/mobile/PreferencesView.kt]

`show()` overrides a method in `View` that makes the view visible and blocks the calling thread until it is dismissed. To avoid mutation, we would like a version that returns a copy of the `UserPreferences` with any changes applied, but we can't add a return type to the `View` method. So instead, we'll rename `show` to `showModal`, returning the existing mutable `preferences` property once `super.show()` has returned:

```
fun showModal(): UserPreferences {
    greetingPicker.greeting = preferences.greeting
    localePicker.locale = preferences.locale
    currencyPicker.currency = preferences.currency
    show()
    return preferences
}
```

Example 5.7 [beans-to-values.4:src/main/java/travelator/mobile/PreferencesView.kt]

`Application.editPreferences()` was calling its `preferencesView.show()` and relying on the fact that it and `PreferencesView` shared a reference to a mutable object to see any edits. We'll now make `Application.preferences` a mutable property, set from the result of `showModal`:

```
class Application(
    private var preferences: UserPreferences ❶
) {
    ...

    fun editPreferences() {
        preferences = PreferencesView(preferences).showModal()
    }
    ...
}
```

Example 5.8 [beans-to-values.4:src/main/java/travelator/mobile/Application.kt]

❶ Now a `var`

The `showModal` method is currently returning the same object passed to the view in the constructor, so this doesn't change anything really. In fact, we have the worst of both worlds: a mutable reference to mutable data.

We haven't finished though; we can make things even worse by making the `preferences` property in `PreferencesView` mutable too, so that we can set it to a new `UserPreferences` object when any UI elements are updated:

```
class PreferencesView(
    private var preferences: UserPreferences
) : View() {
    private val greetingPicker = GreetingPicker()
    private val localePicker = LocalePicker()
    private val currencyPicker = CurrencyPicker()

    fun showModal(): UserPreferences {
        greetingPicker.greeting = preferences.greeting
        localePicker.locale = preferences.locale
        currencyPicker.currency = preferences.currency
        show()
        return preferences
    }

    protected fun onGreetingChange() {
        preferences = UserPreferences(
            greetingPicker.greeting,
            preferences.locale,
            preferences.currency
        )
    }

    ... onLocaleChange, onCurrencyChange
}
```

Example 5.9 [beans-to-values.5:src/main/java/travelator/mobile/PreferencesView.kt]

Actually, we say "even worse," but this has now removed all the uses of the setters on `UserPreferences`. Without setters, we can make it a proper value, initializing its properties in its constructor and never modifying them. In Kotlin this means changing the `var` properties to `val` and inlining any use of the default constructor. This allows us to reduce `UserPreferences` to:

```
data class UserPreferences(
    val greeting: String,
    val locale: Locale,
    val currency: Currency
)
```

Example 5.10 [beans-to-values.6:src/main/java/travelator/mobile/UserPreferences.kt]

The eagle-eyed reader will notice that we sneakily made `UserPreferences` a data class. We didn't do that before now, because it was mutable. While Kotlin *allows* mutable data classes, we should be even more wary of them than of other mutable classes, because data classes implement `equals` and `hashCode`.

> **Object Equality**
>
> Data classes derive `equals` and `hashCode` methods from the values of all the properties declared in their primary constructor. So two instances of the same class will be equal when (and only when) all their corresponding properties have the same values.
>
> Maps and sets call `equals` and `hashCode` when they store objects, but if we subsequently mutate those objects, strange things happen (*https://oreil.ly/keALT*).
>
> Don't rely on equality and hash-code for mutable objects, and don't define mutable data classes.

What have we achieved so far? We've replaced two immutable references to shared mutable data with two mutable references to immutable values. Now we can see at a glance which views can update the preferences, and if we had to manage updates across threads, we could do that at the application level.

Having a mutable reference in `PreferencesView` is a bit irritating though. We can fix that by not holding a reference at all, but instead passing the preferences into `showModal`. `PreferencesView` doesn't need a `UserPreferences` property; it can just distribute its values into the UI before it shows itself and gather them back in when it is done:

```
class PreferencesView : View() {
    private val greetingPicker = GreetingPicker()
    private val localePicker = LocalePicker()
    private val currencyPicker = CurrencyPicker()

    fun showModal(preferences: UserPreferences): UserPreferences {
        greetingPicker.greeting = preferences.greeting
        localePicker.locale = preferences.locale
        currencyPicker.currency = preferences.currency
        show()
        return UserPreferences(
            greeting = greetingPicker.greeting,
            locale = localePicker.locale,
            currency = currencyPicker.currency
        )
    }
}
```

Example 5.11 [beans-to-values.7:src/main/java/travelator/mobile/PreferencesView.kt]

There is still mutation here, because we are setting values into the pickers, but these are UI components and only have default constructors, so this has to happen somewhere. To finish the job, we also have to update `Application` to move the `preferences` argument from the `PreferencesView` constructor to `showModal`:

```
class Application(
    private var preferences: UserPreferences
) {
    fun showWelcome() {
        WelcomeView(preferences).show()
    }

    fun editPreferences() {
        preferences = PreferencesView().showModal(preferences)
    }
    ...
}
```

Example 5.12 [beans-to-values.7:src/main/java/travelator/mobile/Application.kt]

Now we have only one place that preferences can change, made clear by the assignment in `editPreferences`. It is also clear that `showWelcome` can only read from the object. It may seem a bit of a waste to create a new `UserPreferences` to return from `showModal` even if nothing has changed. If you're used to sharing mutable objects, it may even seem dangerous. In the world of values, though, two `UserPreferences` with the same values are to almost all intents and purposes the same object (see "Object Equality" on page 59), and you would have to be in a very constrained environment to detect the extra allocation.

Moving On

In this chapter we've seen some advantages of immutable values over mutable objects. The refactoring example showed how to migrate mutation toward our application's entry points and event handlers by replacing immutable references to mutable objects with mutable references to immutable objects. The result is that less of our code has to deal with the consequences and complications of mutability.

That said, JavaBeans were designed for use in user interface frameworks, and UIs are in many ways the last bastion of mutable objects. If we had more exacting liveness requirements—for example, updating a `WelcomeView` when the greeting preference changed—we might prefer using shared objects with change events rather than using immutable values.

Converting mutable objects to values and transformations is a repeating motif. Chapter 6, *Java to Kotlin Collections*, continues the discussion with respect to collections. Chapter 14, *Accumulating Objects to Transformations*, looks at how to translate code that uses accumulating parameters to use higher-order functions over collections instead.

CHAPTER 6

Java to Kotlin Collections

On the face of it, Java and Kotlin have very similar collections libraries; they certainly interoperate suspiciously seamlessly. What are the differences, what motivates them, and where do we have to take care as we move from Java to Kotlin collections?

Java Collections

In Chapter 5 we saw how Java grew up in the days when we saw objects as fundamentally stateful and mutable. This was particularly true for collections—I mean, what is the point of a list if you can't add to it? We build collections by creating an empty one and adding to it. Need to remove an item from a shopping cart? Mutate the list. Shuffle a pack of cards? Obviously that changes the order of the deck. We wouldn't create a new paper to-do list every time we need milk or take the cat to the vet. Mutable collections mirror our real world experience.

On its release, the quality of its built-in collections was a good reason to adopt Java. In those days many languages had no resizable collections in their standard library. Object technology allowed us to define and use mutable collections safely. It was only natural to use this superpower now that it had been given to us, so we went ahead and used `Vector` and `HashTable` as Sun intended. Which is to say, we created them and then mutated them. There was no choice, because all the constructors created empty collections.

Java 2 (which was version 1.2 until Java had to compete with C# version numbers) introduced a revised collections library. This tidied up the ad hoc `Vector`, `Stack`, and `Hashtable` classes and created a common `Collection` interface with more useful implementations, including `ArrayList` and `HashSet`. It was now possible to create a collection as a copy of another collection. The static `Collections` class provided some helpful utility operations, like `sort` and `reverse`. Java 5 introduced generics, and cleverly retrofitted them to the existing collections, so that now we could declare types like `List<Journey>`.

The Java collections remained mutable, though—very mutable. Not only are there operations to add and remove items, but also operations like sort are defined *only* as mutations; there is no standard library function to return a sorted copy of a `List`.

As we will keep on saying, mutation is the source of many of our problems with complexity, because it allows state in one place to get out of sync with respect to state in another. For example, in Travelator we can represent a route as a `List` of `Journey`. There is also the concept of a suffer-score: the lower the suffer-score, the more pleasant a route is likely to be. Here is how we calculate a suffer-score for a route:

```
public static int sufferScoreFor(List<Journey> route) {
    Location start = getDepartsFrom(route);
    List<Journey> longestJourneys = longestJourneysIn(route, 3);
    return sufferScore(longestJourneys, start);
}
```

Example 6.1 [collections.0:src/main/java/travelator/Suffering.java]

That `start` local variable doesn't add much, so we decide to inline it:

```
public static int sufferScoreFor(List<Journey> route) {
    List<Journey> longestJourneys = longestJourneysIn(route, 3);
    return sufferScore(longestJourneys, getDepartsFrom(route));
}
```

Example 6.2 [collections.1:src/main/java/travelator/Suffering.java]

Our tests pass, we push to production, but we get bug reports suggesting that all is not well. Drilling down we find:

```
public static Location getDepartsFrom(List<Journey> route) {
    return route.get(0).getDepartsFrom();
}
```

Example 6.3 [collections.0:src/main/java/travelator/Routes.java]

```
public static List<Journey> longestJourneysIn(
    List<Journey> journeys,
    int limit
) {
    journeys.sort(comparing(Journey::getDuration).reversed()); ❶
    var actualLimit = Math.min(journeys.size(), limit);
    return journeys.subList(0, actualLimit);
}
```

Example 6.4 [collections.0:src/main/java/travelator/Suffering.java]

❶ `journeys` parameter mutated by `sort`

Ah, now we can see that finding the longest journeys has changed the apparent departure `Location`. A developer called methods on a parameter (`journeys`) to solve a problem, and that turned out to break code somewhere else in the system! You only have to spend several hundred hours of your life debugging the problems caused by aliasing errors (*https://oreil.ly/PeqKs*) like this to come to the conclusion that immutable data would be a better default. For the JDK developers, this point evidently came after the introduction of Java 2, so we have forever been stuck with mutable collections interfaces.

To be fair, although Java's collections are mutable in theory, they have, over the years, become less and less so in practice. Even at the start, it was possible to wrap a collection with, for example, `Collections.unmodifiableList`. The result is still a `List`; it still has all the mutation methods, but they all throw `UnsupportedOperationException`. We could have found out about the problem of `shortestJourneyIn` mutating our list by wrapping the result from `loadJourneys` in an `UnmodifiableList`. The tests of any code that combined the two would quickly fail, albeit only when run as opposed to when compiled. It's a shame that we cannot depend on the type system to ensure correctness, but we can't go back in time, so this is a pragmatic patch.

Wrapping a list in an `UnmodifiableList` solves the problems of depended-on code mutating our collection. If it's possible for the *original list* to be modified, we can still have issues though, because the wrapper reads through to its underlying collection. So an `UnmodifiableList` doesn't guarantee that it never changes, just that it cannot be modified through the wrapper. In these cases we have to take a defensive copy of the original list if we are to be isolated from changes. `List.copyOf(collection)` was added in Java 10 to copy an underlying collection as an `AbstractImmutableList`, which is neither modifiable nor subject to changes in the original collection.

All this second-guessing of whether the source or destination of a collection is likely to modify it, and taking appropriate action, is tedious and error-prone. The problem applies to any mutable data, but changing collections is particularly pernicious, because we often derive values (such as `departsFrom`) that can get out of date if we change the collection that we extracted them from. Rather than taking defensive copies at every function boundary, many teams, your authors' included, adopted a simpler and more efficient strategy.

Don't Mutate Shared Collections

Treat any collection shared between separate pieces of code as immutable. Sharing includes references received as a parameter, returned as a result, or assigned to a shared variable. This applies even if the collection started life as mutable, and despite the mutation operations present in the Java interfaces.

When code that we don't own does not respect this convention, we can use copies to insulate our code from mutation.

This strategy doesn't stop us from creating mutable collections and populating them within a function, but code should only change a collection that it has just created. As soon as we return a reference as a result, we should treat it as immutable—*create, don't mutate*. We might occasionally enforce this immutability by wrapping with `Collections.unmodifiableList(…)` etc., but in an aligned development team this is unnecessary, because no one would treat a shared collection as mutable.

There will of course be exceptions to the rule, places where, usually for reasons of efficiency, we want to share a collection as a mutable collection. In these cases we can get dispensation by naming (`accumulator` is a good start) and by limiting the scope of the sharing as much as possible. Within a function is ideal, between private methods in a class acceptable, across module boundaries very rarely so. Chapter 14 discusses ways to avoid (visibly) mutable collections in these situations.

Project teams that adopt this convention can produce simple and reliable software in spite of collections' mutability. On the whole, the benefits of treating collections as immutable outweigh the problems of a type system that is lying to you, because values are just so valuable. The JVM's libraries may hark back to the days when mutability was the norm, but this is a case where the grain of Java is shifting to the immutable, and it's better to be ahead of this change than behind it.

Kotlin Collections

In contrast to Java, Kotlin and its standard library were designed in an age when mutability had fallen out of fashion. However, smooth interoperation with Java was a key goal, and Java has mutable collections. Scala had tried introducing its own sophisticated persistent (immutable but data-sharing) collections, but this forced developers to copy information between collections on the interop boundary, which was both inefficient and annoying. How could Kotlin square the circle and have immutable collections interoperate seamlessly with Java?

The Kotlin developers removed the mutation methods from the Jave collections interfaces and published them in the `kotlin.collections` package as `Collection<E>`, `List<E>`, and so on. These were then extended by `MutableCollection<E>`, `MutableList<E>`, etc., which add back in the Java mutation methods. So in Kotlin we have `MutableList`, which is a subtype of `List`, which is a subtype of `Collection`. `MutableList` also implements `MutableCollection`.

On the face of it, this is a simple scheme. Mutable collections have the same operations as collections that are not mutable, plus the mutation methods. It is safe to pass a `MutableList` as an argument to code that expects a `List`, because all the `List` methods will be present and can be invoked. In terms of the Liskov Substitution Principle (*https://oreil.ly/8A8KO*), we can substitute a `MutableList` for a `List` without affecting our program correctness.

A little compiler magic allows Kotlin code to accept a `java.util.List` as a `kotlin.collections.List`:

```
val aList: List<String> = SomeJavaCode.mutableListOfStrings("0", "1")
aList.removeAt(1) // doesn't compile
```

That magic also allows Kotlin to accept the Java `List` as a `kotlin.collections.MutableList`:

```
val aMutableList: MutableList<String> = SomeJavaCode.mutableListOfStrings(
    "0", "1")
aMutableList.removeAt(1)
assertEquals(listOf("0"), aMutableList)
```

In fact, because the Java `List` is actually mutable here, we could (but almost always shouldn't) downcast to Kotlin's `MutableList` and mutate:

```
val aList: List<String> = SomeJavaCode.mutableListOfStrings("0", "1")
val aMutableList: MutableList<String> = aList as MutableList<String>
aMutableList.removeAt(1)
assertEquals(listOf("0"), aMutableList)
```

In the other direction, the compiler will allow both a `kotlin.collections.MutableList` and a `kotlin.collections.List` where a `java.util.List` is needed:

```
val aMutableList: MutableList<String> = mutableListOf("0", "1")
SomeJavaCode.needsAList(aMutableList)
```

```
val aList: List<String> = listOf("0", "1")
SomeJavaCode.needsAList(aList)
```

At face value, so far everything has been very plausible. Unfortunately, when it comes to mutability, there is more to substitution than Barbara Liskov's principle. As we saw in "Java Collections" on page 61, just because we can't see mutators on our reference of type `kotlin.collections.List`, it doesn't mean that the contents cannot change. The actual type could be a `java.util.List`, which *is* mutable. In some ways it's worse in Kotlin, because we can convert a `MutableList` to a `List` in passing:

```
val aMutableList = mutableListOf("0", "1")
val aList: List<String> = aMutableList
```

Now let's say that we accept a `List<String>` somewhere, and take its immutabilty at face value:

```
class AValueType(
    val strings: List<String>
) {
    val first: String? = strings.firstOrNull()
}
```

Everything seems fine:

```
val holdsState = AValueType(aList)
assertEquals(holdsState.first, holdsState.strings.first())
```

But wait, don't we still have a reference to a `MutableList`?

```
aMutableList[0] = "banana"
assertEquals(holdsState.first, holdsState.strings.first()) ❶
```

❶ Expected "0", actual "banana"

`AValueType` turns out to be mutable after all! Because of this, `first`, which is initialized on construction, can get out of date. Having nonmutable collections interfaces has not resulted in immutable collections!

Immutable, Read-Only, Mutable

The official line is that a nonmutable Kotlin collection is not *immutable*, but rather a *read-only view* of a collection. As with the Java `UnmodifiableList`, a read-only collection can't be changed through its interface, but may be changed through some other mechanism. Only true *immutable* collections are guaranteed never to change.

It is possible to have true immutable collections on the JVM, (the result of `java.util.List.of(...)`, for example), but this is not (yet) a standard Kotlin feature.

This is the unfortunate consequence of having your mutable collections extend your otherwise nonmutable collections; the recipient of a nonmutable collection cannot modify it, but cannot know that it won't change, because a reference of type nonmutable `List` may in fact be pointing to an object of type `MutableList`.

The rigorous solution to this problem is to separate mutable from immutable collections by not having a subtype relationship. In this scheme, if we have a mutable list and want an immutable copy of it, we have to copy the data. A good analogy is a `StringBuilder`. This is effectively a mutable `String`, but is not a subtype of `String`. Once we have a result we want to publish, we need to call `.toString()`, and subsequent modifications to the `StringBuilder` will not affect previous results. Both Clojure and Scala adopted this builder approach for their mutable collections—why doesn't Kotlin?

We suspect that the answer is: because the Kotlin designers, like your authors, had adopted the convention described in "Don't Mutate Shared Collections" on page 63. If you treat any collection received as a parameter, returned as a result, or otherwise shared between code as immutable, then having mutable collections extend nonmutable collections turns out to be quite safe. Admittedly *quite* in the sense of *mainly*, rather than *completely*, but still the benefits outweigh the costs.

The Kotlin collections make this scheme even more powerful. In Java, we have the situation where we can, in theory, mutate any collections, so the type system doesn't tell us when this is safe or otherwise. In Kotlin, if we declare all normal references as the nonmutable versions, we can use a `MutableCollection` to document when we do, in fact, consider that the collection is subject to change. In return for accepting a largely theoretical risk, we reap the rewards of very simple and efficient interoperation with Java. Pragmatism is typical of the grain of Kotlin; in this case it might be expressed as "be as safe as is sensible, but no safer."

We said that another way to express the "Don't Mutate Shared Collections" is that our code should only mutate a collection that it has just created. We see this in action if we look into the Kotlin standard library. Here, for example, is (a simplified version of) the definition of `map`:

```
inline fun <T, R> Iterable<T>.map(transform: (T) -> R): List<R> {
    val result = ArrayList<R>()
    for (item in this)
        result.add(transform(item))
    return result
}
```

Here the list is built in place by mutation and then returned as read-only. This is simple *and* efficient. Technically, we *could* downcast the result to `MutableList` and change the result, but we shouldn't. Instead, we should take the result type at face value. That way, any code sharing this collection will not have to worry about it changing.

Refactoring from Java to Kotlin Collections

Because of the smooth interop between Java and Kotlin collections described earlier, converting code with collections is usually seamless, at least at the syntactic level. If our Java code relies on mutating collections, though, we may have to take extra care to avoid ending up breaking invariants in Kotlin.

A good approach is to refactor your Java code to the convention used in "Don't Mutate Shared Collections" on page 63 before converting it to Kotlin. That's what we'll do here.

Fix Up the Java

Let's have a look at the code from Travelator we saw earlier. The static methods we've been looking at are in a class called `Suffering`:

```
public class Suffering {

    public static int sufferScoreFor(List<Journey> route) {
        Location start = getDepartsFrom(route);
        List<Journey> longestJourneys = longestJourneysIn(route, 3);
        return sufferScore(longestJourneys, start);
    }
```

```
    public static List<Journey> longestJourneysIn(
        List<Journey> journeys,
        int limit
    ) {
        journeys.sort(comparing(Journey::getDuration).reversed()); ❶
        var actualLimit = Math.min(journeys.size(), limit);
        return journeys.subList(0, actualLimit);
    }

    public static List<List<Journey>> routesToShowFor(String itineraryId) {
        var routes = routesFor(itineraryId);
        removeUnbearableRoutes(routes);
        return routes;
    }

    private static void removeUnbearableRoutes(List<List<Journey>> routes) {
        routes.removeIf(route -> sufferScoreFor(route) > 10);
    }

    private static int sufferScore(
        List<Journey> longestJourneys,
        Location start
    ) {
        return SOME_COMPLICATED_RESULT();
    }
}
```

Example 6.5 [collections.0:src/main/java/travelator/Suffering.java]

❶ `longestJourneysIn` breaks our rule by mutating its parameter.

As we saw previously, because `longestJourneysIn` mutates its parameter, we can't change the order of evaluation of `getDepartsFrom`, and `longestJourneysIn` in `sufferScoreFor`. Before we can fix this, we have to be sure that no other code depends on this mutation. This can be hard, which is itself a good reason not to allow modifying collections from the outset. If we have confidence in our tests, we can try making the edit and seeing whether anything breaks. Otherwise, we may have to add tests and/or reason with our code and dependency analysis. Let's decide that it's safe to go ahead and make the change in Travelator.

We don't want to sort the collection in place, so we need a function that returns a sorted copy of a list without modifying the original. Even Java 16 doesn't seem to have a function to do this. Curiously, `List.sort` actually creates a sorted version of itself and then mutates itself to match:

```
@SuppressWarnings({"unchecked", "rawtypes"})
default void sort(Comparator<? super E> c) {
    Object[] a = this.toArray();
    Arrays.sort(a, (Comparator) c);
    ListIterator<E> i = this.listIterator();
    for (Object e : a) {
```

```
            i.next();
            i.set((E) e);
        }
    }
```

This just goes to show how mutable thinking was the grain of Java, back in the Java 8 days when this was written. There is now `Stream.sorted`, but in our experience streams rarely perform well with small collections (see Chapter 13). Maybe we shouldn't care about performance, but we can't help ourselves! We justify our indulgence by reasoning that we know of several places in the code that currently sort in place, so will have to be changed to remove the mutation of shared collections. Reasoning that the authors of `List.sort` actually knew a thing or two about Java efficiency, we copy their code and write:

```
@SuppressWarnings("unchecked")
public static <E> List<E> sorted(
    Collection<E> collection,
    Comparator<? super E> by
) {
    var result = (E[]) collection.toArray();
    Arrays.sort(result, by);
    return Arrays.asList(result);
}
```

Example 6.6 [collections.3:src/main/java/travelator/Collections.java]

Before we go on, it's worth considering how we can be confident that this code is correct. Because of mutation, it's really quite hard. We have to be sure that `Arrays.sort` won't affect the input collection, which means checking the documentation for `Collection.toArray`. When we do, we find the magic words "The caller is thus free to modify the returned array," so that's OK; we've decoupled the input from the output. This function is a classic example of accepting mutation in the scope where we create a collection, but not outside—create, don't mutate.

While we're pulling this thread, what are we returning, and is it mutable? `Arrays.asList` returns an `ArrayList`, but not the standard one. This one is private inside `Arrays` and writes through to our `result`. Because it is backed by an array, though, we cannot add or remove items. It isn't resizable. It turns out that Java collections aren't just mutable, nonmutable, or immutable; they are sometimes mutable provided that we don't change their structure! None of these distinctions are reflected in the type system, so it is possible to make type-preserving changes that break at runtime, depending on which code path yields a collection that we subsequently try to modify, and how we try to modify it. This is yet another reason to sidestep the issue altogether and just never modify a shared collection.

Returning to our refactoring, we can use our new `sorted` in `longestJourneysIn` to stop modifying the shared collection.

Using sort, we had:

```
public static List<Journey> longestJourneysIn(
    List<Journey> journeys,
    int limit
) {
    journeys.sort(comparing(Journey::getDuration).reversed());
    var actualLimit = Math.min(journeys.size(), limit);
    return journeys.subList(0, actualLimit);
}
```

Example 6.7 [collections.2:src/main/java/travelator/Suffering.java]

Our new sorted function allows us to write:

```
static List<Journey> longestJourneysIn(
    List<Journey> journeys,
    int limit
) {
    var actualLimit = Math.min(journeys.size(), limit);
    return sorted(
        journeys,
        comparing(Journey::getDuration).reversed()
    ).subList(0, actualLimit);
}
```

Example 6.8 [collections.3:src/main/java/travelator/Suffering.java]

Now that sufferScoreFor won't be subject to the side effect in longestJourneysIn, we can inline its local variables:

```
public static int sufferScoreFor(List<Journey> route) {
    return sufferScore(
        longestJourneysIn(route, 3),
        getDepartsFrom(route));
}
```

Example 6.9 [collections.4:src/main/java/travelator/Suffering.java]

Inlining local variables might not seem much of a payoff, but it's a small example of a bigger theme. In Chapter 7, we'll look at how avoiding mutation allows us to refactor code in ways that just aren't safe otherwise.

Stepping out to look at the callers of sufferScoreFor, we find:

```
public static List<List<Journey>> routesToShowFor(String itineraryId) {
    var routes = routesFor(itineraryId);
    removeUnbearableRoutes(routes);
    return routes;
}

private static void removeUnbearableRoutes(List<List<Journey>> routes) {
    routes.removeIf(route -> sufferScoreFor(route) > 10);
}
```

Example 6.10 [collections.4:src/main/java/travelator/Suffering.java]

Hmmm, that's so pathologically mutating that it might have been written as an example in a book! At least `removeUnbearableRoutes` is telling us that it must mutate something by returning `void`. We can take baby steps by changing the function to return the parameter it is mutating and using the result—another case of making something worse before making it better:

```
public static List<List<Journey>> routesToShowFor(String itineraryId) {
    var routes = routesFor(itineraryId);
    routes = removeUnbearableRoutes(routes);
    return routes;
}

private static List<List<Journey>> removeUnbearableRoutes
    (List<List<Journey>> routes
) {
    routes.removeIf(route -> sufferScoreFor(route) > 10);
    return routes;
}
```

Example 6.11 [collections.5:src/main/java/travelator/Suffering.java]

This time we'll use `Stream.filter` to replace the mutation in `removeUnbearableRoutes`. In passing, we can take the opportunity to rename it:

```
public static List<List<Journey>> routesToShowFor(String itineraryId) {
    var routes = routesFor(itineraryId);
    routes = bearable(routes);
    return routes;
}

private static List<List<Journey>> bearable
    (List<List<Journey>> routes
) {
    return routes.stream()
        .filter(route -> sufferScoreFor(route) <= 10)
        .collect(toUnmodifiableList());
}
```

Example 6.12 [collections.6:src/main/java/travelator/Suffering.java]

Note how it is now easier to find a nice short name for our function; `removeUnbearable Routes` becomes `bearable`.

The reassignment to `routes` in `routesToShowFor` is ugly, but deliberate, because it allows us to draw parallels with the refactor in Chapter 5. There, we changed mutating-some-data-in-place to replacing-the-reference-with-a-mutated-value, and that is what we have done here too. Of course, we don't need the local variable at all really, so let's get rid of it. Invoking the Inline refactoring twice does it nicely:

```
public static List<List<Journey>> routesToShowFor(String itineraryId) {
    return bearable(routesFor(itineraryId));
}
```

```
private static List<List<Journey>> bearable
    (List<List<Journey>> routes
) {
    return routes.stream()
        .filter(route -> sufferScoreFor(route) <= 10)
        .collect(toUnmodifiableList());
}
```

Example 6.13 [collections.7:src/main/java/travelator/Suffering.java]

Convert to Kotlin

Now that we've removed all the mutation from our Java collections, it's time to convert to Kotlin. "Convert Java File to Kotlin File" on our `Suffering` class does a reasonable job, but when we wrote this, it got confused, inferring the nullability of collections and their generic types. After conversion, we had to remove `?`s from some hairy types like `List<List<Journey?>>?` to have:

```
object Suffering {
    @JvmStatic
    fun sufferScoreFor(route: List<Journey>): Int {
        return sufferScore(
            longestJourneysIn(route, 3),
            Routes.getDepartsFrom(route)
        )
    }

    @JvmStatic
    fun longestJourneysIn(
        journeys: List<Journey>,
        limit: Int
    ): List<Journey> {
        val actualLimit = Math.min(journeys.size, limit)
        return sorted(
            journeys,
            comparing { obj: Journey -> obj.duration }.reversed()
        ).subList(0, actualLimit)
    }

    fun routesToShowFor(itineraryId: String?): List<List<Journey>> {
        return bearable(Other.routesFor(itineraryId))
    }

    private fun bearable(routes: List<List<Journey>>): List<List<Journey>> {
        return routes.stream()
            .filter { route -> sufferScoreFor(route) <= 10 }
            .collect(Collectors.toUnmodifiableList())
    }

    private fun sufferScore(
        longestJourneys: List<Journey>,
```

```
        start: Location
    ): Int {
        return SOME_COMPLICATED_RESULT()
    }
}
```

Example 6.14 [collections.8:src/main/java/travelator/Suffering.kt]

We have also reformatted and tidied some imports. On the plus side, the Java code calling our Kotlin hasn't had to change. Here, for example, is a test passing a plain Java `List` to the Kotlin `longestJourneyIn`:

```
@Test public void returns_limit_results() {
    assertEquals(
        List.of(longJourney, mediumJourney),
        longestJourneysIn(List.of(shortJourney, mediumJourney, longJourney), 2)
    );
}
```

Example 6.15 [collections.8:src/test/java/travelator/LongestJourneyInTests.java]

Returning to the Kotlin, we can now take advantage of the many utilities available on Kotlin collections to simplify the code. Take `longestJourneysIn`, for example. This was:

```
@JvmStatic
fun longestJourneysIn(
    journeys: List<Journey>,
    limit: Int
): List<Journey> {
    val actualLimit = Math.min(journeys.size, limit)
    return sorted(
        journeys,
        comparing { obj: Journey -> obj.duration }.reversed()
    ).subList(0, actualLimit)
}
```

Example 6.16 [collections.8:src/main/java/travelator/Suffering.kt]

Replacing `sorted` with `sortedByDescending`, and `subList` with `take` gives:

```
@JvmStatic
fun longestJourneysIn(journeys: List<Journey>, limit: Int): List<Journey> =
    journeys.sortedByDescending { it.duration }.take(limit)
```

Example 6.17 [collections.9:src/main/java/travelator/Suffering.kt]

Now if we convert `longestJourneysIn` to an extension function (see Chapter 10), we can simplify its name to `longestJourneys`:

```
@JvmStatic
fun List<Journey>.longestJourneys(limit: Int): List<Journey> =
    sortedByDescending { it.duration }.take(limit)
```

Example 6.18 [collections.10:src/main/java/travelator/Suffering.kt]

Because longestJourneys doesn't modify its parameter, we've made it a single-expression function (Chapter 9). It can still be called from Java as a static method, but reads particularly nicely when called from Kotlin, especially if we name the argument:

```
@JvmStatic
fun sufferScoreFor(route: List<Journey>): Int {
    return sufferScore(
        route.longestJourneys(limit = 3), ❶
        Routes.getDepartsFrom(route)
    )
}
```

Example 6.19 [collections.10:src/main/java/travelator/Suffering.kt]

❶ Named argument

Moving on to bearable:

```
private fun bearable(routes: List<List<Journey>>): List<List<Journey>> {
    return routes.stream()
        .filter { route -> sufferScoreFor(route) <= 10 }
        .collect(Collectors.toUnmodifiableList())
}
```

Example 6.20 [collections.10:src/main/java/travelator/Suffering.kt]

Here we can use the techniques in Chapter 13 to convert the Stream to Kotlin. We remove the call to .stream() as Kotlin makes filter available as an extension function on List. Then we don't need the terminal toUnmodifiableList, because Kotlin filter returns a List directly:

```
private fun bearable(routes: List<List<Journey>>): List<List<Journey>> =
    routes.filter { sufferScoreFor(it) <= 10 }
```

Example 6.21 [collections.11:src/main/java/travelator/Suffering.kt]

Interestingly, this is a place where the result is potentially more mutable than our Java was. In Java, we were collecting with Collectors.toUnmodifiableList(). Kotlin filter declares its return type as List (the read-only view), but the actual runtime type is the mutable ArrayList. Provided we never downcast, this shouldn't be an issue, especially because we are now treating our shared collections as immutable even in Java.

Here then is the final code:

```
object Suffering {
    @JvmStatic
    fun sufferScoreFor(route: List<Journey>): Int =
        sufferScore(
            route.longestJourneys(limit = 3),
            Routes.getDepartsFrom(route)
        )

    @JvmStatic
```

```kotlin
    fun List<Journey>.longestJourneys(limit: Int): List<Journey> =
        sortedByDescending { it.duration }.take(limit)

    fun routesToShowFor(itineraryId: String?): List<List<Journey>> =
        bearable(routesFor(itineraryId))

    private fun bearable(routes: List<List<Journey>>): List<List<Journey>> =
        routes.filter { sufferScoreFor(it) <= 10 }

    private fun sufferScore(
        longestJourneys: List<Journey>,
        start: Location
    ): Int = SOME_COMPLICATED_RESULT()
}
```

Example 6.22 [collections.11:src/main/java/travelator/Suffering.kt]

We say final, but in practice we probably wouldn't finish this refactoring at this point. Those `List<List<Journey>>` types are hinting at some type trying to get out, and in Kotlin we don't usually publish static methods in an object like this; we prefer top-level function definitions. Chapter 8 will fix the latter at least.

Moving On

Java at one time favored programming with mutability. That has fallen out of vogue, but more by convention than by enforcement. Kotlin has taken a very pragmatic approach to mutability in its collections, giving smooth operation and a simple programming model, but only where your Java conventions align with its approach.

To help your Java and Kotlin interoperate smoothly:

- Beware that Java can mutate a collection that it has passed to Kotlin.
- Beware that Java can (at least try to) mutate a collection that it has received from Kotlin.
- Remove mutation from your use of Java collections. Where you can't, take defensive copies.

We have more to say about collections in Chapter 15, *Encapsulated Collections to Type Aliases*. In terms of this code example, Chapter 8, *Static Methods to Top-Level Functions*, continues where this chapter leaves off.

CHAPTER 7

Actions to Calculations

Neither Java nor Kotlin makes any formal distinction between imperative and functional code, although Kotlin's emphasis on immutability and expressions generally leads to more functional programs. Can we improve our code by making more of it functional?

Functions

As an industry, we have invented a lot of phrases to describe callable subprograms within a larger program. We have the very generic *subroutine*. Some languages (notably Pascal) distinguish between *functions* that return a result, and *procedures*, which don't; but most developers use the terms interchangeably. Then there are *methods*, which are subroutines associated with an object (or a class, in the case of static methods).

The C language calls them all functions but has a special `void` type to represent the absence of a return value. This was carried forward into Java. Kotlin uses `Unit` in almost the same way, except that `Unit` is not the absence of a return value, but rather a singleton value that is returned instead.

In this book we use the term *function* to refer to both result-returning and non-result-returning subroutines, whether freestanding or associated with an object. Where it's significant that they are associated with an object, we'll call them as methods.

Whatever we call them, functions are one of the fundamental building blocks of our software. We define them with some sort of notation, generally the programming language we are using. They are also generally fixed during a run of the program; in static languages, at least, we don't usually redefine functions on the fly.

This is in contrast to the other fundamental building block: data. We expect data to vary as we run our program, and different data is bound to variables. Variables are called variables because they are, wait for it, variable. Even when they are `final`, or `val`, they are usually bound to different data in different invocations of a function.

We hinted earlier at a subdivision of functions into those that return a result and those that do not. This might seem like a fundamental difference, but in practice there is a more useful way to divide functions: into *calculations* and *actions*.

Actions are functions that depend on when or how many times they are run; calculations are functions that don't—they are timeless. Most functions that we write are actions, because we have to take special care to write code that doesn't depend on when it is run. How would we go about doing that?

Calculations

To be a calculation, a function must always return the same result given the same inputs. The inputs to a function are its parameters, which are bound to arguments when the function is called. So a calculation always returns the same result when called with the same arguments.

Take a `fullName` function:

```
fun fullName(customer: Customer) = "${customer.givenName} ${customer.familyName}"
```

`fullName` is a calculation: it will always return the same value when supplied the same `Customer`. This is true only if `Customer` is immutable, or at least `givenName` and `familyName` cannot change. To keep things simple, we'll say that calculations can only have parameters that are values, as defined in Chapter 5.

Methods, and the disguised methods that are member properties, can also be calculations:

```
data class Customer(
    val givenName: String,
    val familyName: String
) {
    fun upperCaseGivenName() = givenName.toUpperCase()

    val fullName get() = "$givenName $familyName"
}
```

For a method or extension, the receiver `this`, and any property accessed via `this`, is also an input. So both `upperCaseGivenName` and `fullName` are calculations because `givenName` and `familyName` are both values.

An extension function or property can also be a calculation if the data it depends on is a value:

```
fun Customer.fullName() = "$givenName $familyName"

val Customer.fullName get() = "$givenName $familyName"
```

Computed Property or Function?

You may have wondered when to define a computed property and when to have a function that returns a result. Computed properties are confusing if they return different results at different times, at least when defined on value types (and you'll be realizing by now that your authors think that most of our types should be value types). So a good rule of thumb is to reserve computed properties for calculations.

We expand on this topic in Chapter 11.

The result of a calculation may depend on data that is not passed as parameters, but only if that data does not change. Otherwise, the function's result would be different before and after the change, which would make it an action. Even if a function always returns the same result for the same parameters, it may still be an action if it mutates something (either a parameter or an external resource such as a global variable or a database). For example:

```
println("hello")
```

`println` always returns the same `Unit` result given the same `hello` input, but it is not a calculation. It is an action.

Actions

`println` is an action because it *does* depend on when and how many times it is run. If we don't call it, nothing is output, which is different from calling it once, which is different from calling it twice. The order that we call `println` with different arguments also matters to the results we see on the console.

We call `println` for its *side effect*—the effect it has on its environment. Side effect is a bit of a misleading term because, unlike drug side effects, they are often exactly the thing that we want to happen. Maybe *outside effect* would be a better name, to emphasize that they are external to a function's parameters, local variables, and return value. In any case, functions with observable side effects are actions not calculations. Functions returning `void` or `Unit` are almost always actions, because if they do anything, they have to do it by side effect.

As we saw previously, code that reads from external mutable state must also be an action (provided that anything does actually mutate the state).

Let's look at a Customers service:

```
class Customers {
    fun save(data: CustomerData): Customer {
        ...
    }
    fun find(id: String): Customer? {
        ...
    }
}
```

Both save and find are actions; save creates a new customer record in our database and returns it. This is an action because the state of our database depends on when we call it. The result of find is also time sensitive, because it depends on previous calls to save.

Functions that have no parameters (this doesn't include methods or extension functions, which can have implicit parameters accessed via this) must either be returning a constant or be reading from some other source and so be categorized as actions. Without looking at its source, we can deduce that a top-level function requestRate is almost certainly an action, reading from some global mutable state:

```
fun requestRate(): Double {
    ...
}
```

If a function with the same apparent signature is defined as a method, it is probably a calculation that depends on properties of Metrics (provided Metrics is immutable):

```
class Metrics(
    ...
) {

    fun requestRate(): Double {
        ...
    }
}
```

We say *probably* because in languages like Java or Kotlin that allow input, output, or accessing global mutable data from any code, there is no way to be sure whether a function represents a calculation or action short of examining it and all the functions that it calls. We'll return to that problem soon.

Why Should We Care?

We should obviously pay special attention to some actions in our software. Sending the same email to every user twice is a bug, as is not sending it at all. We care exactly how many times it is sent. We may even care that it is sent at exactly 8:07 a.m., so that our offer for a free first-class upgrade is at the top of our customer's inbox when they read their email over breakfast.

Other seemingly innocuous actions may be more nocuous than we think. Changing the order of read and write actions causes concurrency bugs. Error handling is much more complicated if the second of two sequential actions fails after the first succeeded. Actions prevent us from having free rein to refactor our code, because doing so may change when or whether they are invoked.

Calculations, on the other hand, can be invoked at any time, with no consequences for calling them again and again with the same arguments except a waste of time and energy. If we are refactoring code and find that we don't need the result of a calculation, we can safely not invoke it. If it is an expensive calculation, we can safely cache its result; if it is inexpensive, we can safely recalculate it on demand if that simplifies things. It is this feeling of safety that puts the smug smile on the faces of functional programmers (well, that and knowing that a monad is just a monoid in the category of endofunctors). Those functional programmers also have a term for the property of a function that makes it a calculation: *referential transparency*. If a function is referentially transparent, we can replace its call with its result, and we can only do that if it doesn't matter when or if we call it.

Procedural Code

Nat and Duncan are both old enough to have learned to program in Sinclair BASIC on the ZX81. This dialect had no immutable data, and no support for subroutines, parameters, or local variables. It requires real discipline to program in such a system, because practically every line of code is an action and so potentially affects the functioning of every other statement.

This is in fact very close to the way that our computers actually work, with mutable values held in registers and global memory, manipulated by machine-code actions. The evolution of programming languages has been a process of restricting the ultimate flexibility of this model, so that humans can better reason with the code that they create.

Why Prefer Calculations?

We like calculations because they are so much easier to work with, but ultimately our software needs to have an effect on the world, which is an action. There is no overlap though; code can't be an action and a calculation, both timeless and time-dependent. If we take some code that is a calculation and have it invoke an action, then it becomes an action, because it will now depend on when or whether it is called. We can think of calculations as the purer code, where code inherits the most tainted level of all of its dependencies. We see the same thing with susceptibility to errors in Chapter 19. If we value purity (which in all these cases brings ease of reasoning and refactoring), we must strive to pull the boundary between impure and pure code to the outer layers of our system—those closest to the entry points. If we succeed, then a significant proportion of our code can be calculations and, hence, easily tested, reasoned with, and refactored.

What if we don't succeed in keeping actions at the bottom of our call stack? Then we can fix things with refactoring!

Refactoring Actions to Calculations

Let's have a look at recognizing and refactoring actions in existing code.

Existing Code

There is an HTTP endpoint in Travelator that allows the client app to fetch information about the customer's current trip:

```
public class CurrentTripsHandler {

    private final ITrackTrips tracking;
    private final ObjectMapper objectMapper = new ObjectMapper();

    public CurrentTripsHandler(ITrackTrips tracking) {
        this.tracking = tracking;
    }

    public Response handle(Request request) {
        try {
            var customerId = request.getQueryParam("customerId").stream()
                .findFirst();
            if (customerId.isEmpty())
                return new Response(HTTP_BAD_REQUEST);
            var currentTrip = tracking.currentTripFor(customerId.get());
            return currentTrip.isPresent() ?
                new Response(HTTP_OK,
                    objectMapper.writeValueAsString(currentTrip)) :
                new Response(HTTP_NOT_FOUND);
        } catch (Exception x) {
            return new Response(HTTP_INTERNAL_ERROR);
        }
    }
}
```

Example 7.1 [actions.0:src/main/java/travelator/handlers/CurrentTripsHandler.java]

Actions are code that is sensitive to time, so words like *current* in `CurrentTripsHandler` are a dead giveaway. The `handle` method is an action, and that's OK: things on the edge of our systems often are.

The handler delegates to some business logic, implemented in `Tracking`:

```java
class Tracking implements ITrackTrips {

    private final Trips trips;

    public Tracking(Trips trips) {
        this.trips = trips;
    }

    @Override
    public Optional<Trip> currentTripFor(String customerId) {
        var candidates = trips.currentTripsFor(customerId).stream()
            .filter((trip) -> trip.getBookingStatus() == BOOKED)
            .collect(toList());
        if (candidates.size() == 1)
            return Optional.of(candidates.get(0));
        else if (candidates.size() == 0)
            return Optional.empty();
        else
            throw new IllegalStateException(
                "Unexpectedly more than one current trip for " + customerId
            );
    }
}
```

Example 7.2 [actions.0:src/main/java/travelator/Tracking.java]

Using the *current* rule, `Tracking.currentTripFor` is evidently an action too, as is `Trips.currentTripsFor`. Here is its implementation in `InMemoryTrips`, which is used for testing in place of a version implemented with database queries:

```java
public class InMemoryTrips implements Trips {

    ...
    @Override
    public Set<Trip> currentTripsFor(String customerId) {
        return tripsFor(customerId).stream()
            .filter(trip -> trip.isPlannedToBeActiveAt(clock.instant()))
            .collect(toSet());
    }
}
```

Example 7.3 [actions.0:src/test/java/travelator/InMemoryTrips.java]

The conversions from `Set<Trip>` (the result of `Trips.currentTripsFor`) and to `Optional<Trip>` (returned from `Tracking.currentTripFor`) seem to be because there is some business rule around there being only one active trip at any time—a rule that is not enforced in the persistence layer.

Until we got here, we were relying on our knowledge of the meanings of words (in particular *current*) to deduce that Java methods represent actions rather than calculations. Here, though, there is a smoking gun. Can you spot it?

Yes: clock.instant(). That definitely depends on when we call it. (If you found another action, well done, but keep it to yourself for now. We'll come back to it.)

Even if we chose not go on with the rest of this refactoring, there is one change that we should make now. We have discussed calculations and actions as applying to named blocks of code, but they also apply at the expression level. Once you start to differentiate actions from calculations, it makes sense not to throw a random action into an otherwise pure calculation. Let's pull the action out so that the remainder of the expression is pure: select clock.instant() and "Introduce Variable", calling it now:

```
@Override
public Set<Trip> currentTripsFor(String customerId) {
    return tripsFor(customerId).stream()
        .filter(trip -> {
            Instant now = clock.instant();
            return trip.isPlannedToBeActiveAt(now);
        })
        .collect(toSet());
}
```

Example 7.4 [actions.1:src/test/java/travelator/InMemoryTrips.java]

That's still in the middle of the expression, so let's move it up (and convert to a var on the way):

```
@Override
public Set<Trip> currentTripsFor(String customerId) {
    var now = clock.instant();
    return tripsFor(customerId).stream()
        .filter(trip -> trip.isPlannedToBeActiveAt(now))
        .collect(toSet());
}
```

Example 7.5 [actions.2:src/test/java/travelator/InMemoryTrips.java]

This simple act has allowed us to realize that we were previously comparing every trip against a slightly different time! Was that a problem? Probably not here, but you may have worked on systems where it would be. Duncan, for one, has recently finished diagnosing an issue where half of a banking transaction could be accounted for in one day, and the other half in the next.

As well as making it harder to refactor our code, actions make it harder to test too. Let's see how that is manifested:

```
public class TrackingTests {

    final StoppedClock clock = new StoppedClock();

    final InMemoryTrips trips = new InMemoryTrips(clock);
    final Tracking tracking = new Tracking(trips);

    @Test
```

```
    public void returns_empty_when_no_trip_planned_to_happen_now() {
        clock.now = anInstant();
        assertEquals(
            Optional.empty(),
            tracking.currentTripFor("aCustomer")
        );
    }

    @Test
    public void returns_single_active_booked_trip() {
        var diwaliTrip = givenATrip("cust1", "Diwali",
            "2020-11-13", "2020-11-15", BOOKED);
        givenATrip("cust1", "Christmas",
            "2020-12-24", "2020-11-26", BOOKED);

        clock.now = diwaliTrip.getPlannedStartTime().toInstant();
        assertEquals(
            Optional.of(diwaliTrip),
            tracking.currentTripFor("cust1")
        );
    }

    ...
}
```

Example 7.6 [actions.0:src/test/java/travelator/TrackingTests.java]

To give predictable results, we have had to use a fake clock, injected into `InMemoryTrips`. Having previously said that `clock.instant()` depends on when we call it; in our tests it doesn't (at least, not in the same way). We could instead have set up trips relative to the time that the tests are being run, but this would make our tests harder to understand, and subject to failure if you run them around midnight.

2015 Was the End of Time

Duncan and Nat returned to work after the Christmas holidays at the beginning of 2015 to find a slew of previously passing unit tests now failing. It turns out that 2015-01-01T00:00:00 had been used as a time that would always be in the future. When 2015 arrived, all the tests that relied on before and after relationships began failing.

They fixed the tests with the refactoring in this chapter.

Is having to inject a clock test-induced design damage (*https://oreil.ly/YZx1T*)? In this case it is. The fake clock has allowed us to solve a testing problem, but at the expense of making the code more complicated. It has also allowed us to avoid a rethink that might lead to…

A Better Design

What would a better design look like here?

To make this code less time dependant, we can supply the time as an argument to the method. Although this forces the *caller* to know the time, it is as easy for our caller to ask the time as it is for this method. This is a special case of the way that we refactor to avoid dependencies on other global state; instead of reading a value within a function, we pass the value into it.

The function we want to pass the time into overrides `Trips.currentTripsFor`, so we start by adding an `Instant` parameter to that. Before, this was:

```
public interface Trips {
    ...
    Set<Trip> currentTripsFor(String customerId);
}
```

Example 7.7 [actions.0:src/main/java/travelator/Trips.java]

We use IntelliJ's "Change Signature" refactoring to add the parameter, calling it `at`. When we add a parameter, we need to tell IntelliJ what value it should use when updating the callers of our function. Because we aren't using the value in the method yet (and this is Java), we should be able to use `null` without breaking anything. Running the tests shows that we are right—they still pass.

`Trips` now looks like this:

```
public interface Trips {
    ...
    Set<Trip> currentTripsFor(String customerId, Instant at);
}
```

Example 7.8 [actions.3:src/main/java/travelator/Trips.java]

Here is the method being called:

```
class Tracking implements ITrackTrips {
    ...

    @Override
    public Optional<Trip> currentTripFor(String customerId) {
        var candidates = trips.currentTripsFor(customerId, null) ❶
            .stream()
            .filter((trip) -> trip.getBookingStatus() == BOOKED)
            .collect(toList());
        if (candidates.size() == 1)
            return Optional.of(candidates.get(0));
        else if (candidates.size() == 0)
            return Optional.empty();
        else
            throw new IllegalStateException(
                "Unexpectedly more than one current trip for " + customerId
```

```
        );
    }
}
```

Example 7.9 [actions.3:src/main/java/travelator/Tracking.java]

❶ IntelliJ introduced `null` as the argument value

Remember that we aren't using the value of the time in our implementations of `Trips` yet; we're just trying to supply it on the outside of our system to convert as much code as possible to calculations. `Tracking` isn't the outside of our interaction, so we select the `null` `Instant` and "Introduce Parameter" to add it to the signature of `Tracking.currentTripFor`:

```
@Override
public Optional<Trip> currentTripFor(String customerId, Instant at) { ❶
    var candidates = trips.currentTripsFor(customerId, at) ❶
        .stream()
        .filter((trip) -> trip.getBookingStatus() == BOOKED)
        .collect(toList());
        ...
}
```

Example 7.10 [actions.4:src/main/java/travelator/Tracking.java]

❶ Our new `Instant` parameter

When we "Introduce Parameter", IntelliJ moves the expression (`null` in this case) from the body of the method to the callers, so `CurrentTripsHandler` still compiles:

```
public Response handle(Request request) {
    try {
        var customerId = request.getQueryParam("customerId").stream()
            .findFirst();
        if (customerId.isEmpty())
            return new Response(HTTP_BAD_REQUEST);
        var currentTrip = tracking.currentTripFor(customerId.get(), null); ❶
        return currentTrip.isPresent() ?
            new Response(HTTP_OK,
                objectMapper.writeValueAsString(currentTrip)) :
            new Response(HTTP_NOT_FOUND);
    } catch (Exception x) {
        return new Response(HTTP_INTERNAL_ERROR);
    }
}
```

Example 7.11 [actions.4:src/main/java/travelator/handlers/CurrentTripsHandler.java]

❶ `null` argument value

`TrackingTests` is similarly fixed up:

```
@Test
public void returns_empty_when_no_trip_planned_to_happen_now() {
    clock.now = anInstant();
    assertEquals(
        Optional.empty(),
        tracking.currentTripFor("cust1", null) ❶
    );
}

@Test
public void returns_single_active_booked_trip() {
    var diwaliTrip = givenATrip("cust1", "Diwali",
        "2020-11-13", "2020-11-15", BOOKED);
    givenATrip("cust1", "Christmas",
        "2020-12-24", "2020-11-26", BOOKED);

    clock.now = diwaliTrip.getPlannedStartTime().toInstant();
    assertEquals(
        Optional.of(diwaliTrip),
        tracking.currentTripFor("cust1", null) ❶
    );
}
```

Example 7.12 [actions.4:src/test/java/travelator/TrackingTests.java]

❶ `null` argument value

At this point everything compiles and passes the tests, but we aren't actually using the (`null`) time that we are passing down from our handler. Let's fix that in `InMemoryTrips`, where we started. We did have:

```
public class InMemoryTrips implements Trips {

    ...
    @Override
    public Set<Trip> currentTripsFor(String customerId, Instant at) {
        var now = clock.instant();
        return tripsFor(customerId).stream()
            .filter(trip -> trip.isPlannedToBeActiveAt(now))
            .collect(toSet());
    }
}
```

Example 7.13 [actions.4:src/test/java/travelator/InMemoryTrips.java]

Now that we have the time as a parameter, we can use that rather than asking the `clock`:

```
public class InMemoryTrips implements Trips {

    ...
    @Override
    public Set<Trip> currentTripsFor(String customerId, Instant at) {
```

```
        return tripsFor(customerId).stream()
            .filter(trip -> trip.isPlannedToBeActiveAt(at))
            .collect(toSet());
    }
}
```

Example 7.14 [actions.5:src/test/java/travelator/InMemoryTrips.java]

This causes the tests that use `InMemoryTrips` to fail with a `NullPointerException`, because the method is now using the value of the parameter, and the tests are passing in `null`:

```
@Test
public void returns_empty_when_no_trip_planned_to_happen_now() {
    clock.now = anInstant();
    assertEquals(
        Optional.empty(),
        tracking.currentTripFor("cust1", null) ❶
    );
}

@Test
public void returns_single_active_booked_trip() {
    var diwaliTrip = givenATrip("cust1", "Diwali",
        "2020-11-13", "2020-11-15", BOOKED);
    givenATrip("cust1", "Christmas",
        "2020-12-24", "2020-11-26", BOOKED);

    clock.now = diwaliTrip.getPlannedStartTime().toInstant();
    assertEquals(
        Optional.of(diwaliTrip),
        tracking.currentTripFor("cust1", null) ❶
    );
}
```

Example 7.15 [actions.5:src/test/java/travelator/TrackingTests.java]

❶ These `null`s are now being dereferenced inside `InMemoryTrips`.

Instead of `null`, we need to pass the value that the tests were setting into the `clock`. A cunning refactor is to replace the `null`s with `clock.now`:

```
@Test
public void returns_empty_when_no_trip_planned_to_happen_now() {
    clock.now = anInstant();
    assertEquals(
        Optional.empty(),
        tracking.currentTripFor("cust1", clock.now)
    );
}

@Test
public void returns_single_active_booked_trip() {
```

```
    var diwaliTrip = givenATrip("cust1", "Diwali",
        "2020-11-13", "2020-11-15", BOOKED);
    givenATrip("cust1", "Christmas",
        "2020-12-24", "2020-11-26", BOOKED);

    clock.now = diwaliTrip.getPlannedStartTime().toInstant();
    assertEquals(
        Optional.of(diwaliTrip),
        tracking.currentTripFor("cust1", clock.now)
    );
}
```

Example 7.16 [actions.6:src/test/java/travelator/TrackingTests.java]

This gets our tests to pass, because we are now passing the correct time as the argument, albeit via setting and immediately reading a field in the `StoppedClock`. To fix that, we replace the `clock.now` reads with the values from the `clock.now` writes. Then the `clock` is unused, and we can delete it:

```
public class TrackingTests {

    final InMemoryTrips trips = new InMemoryTrips();
    final Tracking tracking = new Tracking(trips);

    @Test
    public void returns_empty_when_no_trip_planned_to_happen_now() {
        assertEquals(
            Optional.empty(),
            tracking.currentTripFor("cust1", anInstant())
        );
    }

    @Test
    public void returns_single_active_booked_trip() {
        var diwaliTrip = givenATrip("cust1", "Diwali",
            "2020-11-13", "2020-11-15", BOOKED);
        givenATrip("cust1", "Christmas",
            "2020-12-24", "2020-11-26", BOOKED);

        assertEquals(
            Optional.of(diwaliTrip),
            tracking.currentTripFor("cust1",
                diwaliTrip.getPlannedStartTime().toInstant())
        );
    }

    ...
}
```

Example 7.17 [actions.8:src/test/java/travelator/TrackingTests.java]

This is a pattern we often see as we refactor toward more functional code. As we reduce the scope of actions, our tests become simpler, because they can express more of their variation in parameters rather than preparing test state. We'll see this again in Chapter 17.

End Game

We're almost done now. (Refactoring is never completely done.)

With all this focus on the tests, we were about to check in before we realized that we haven't completed our refactor in `CurrentTripsHandler`:

```
public Response handle(Request request) {
    try {
        var customerId = request.getQueryParam("customerId").stream()
            .findFirst();
        if (customerId.isEmpty())
            return new Response(HTTP_BAD_REQUEST);
        var currentTrip = tracking.currentTripFor(customerId.get(), null); ❶
        return currentTrip.isPresent() ?
            new Response(HTTP_OK,
                objectMapper.writeValueAsString(currentTrip)) :
            new Response(HTTP_NOT_FOUND);
    } catch (Exception x) {
        return new Response(HTTP_INTERNAL_ERROR);
    }
}
```

Example 7.18 [actions.8:src/main/java/travelator/handlers/CurrentTripsHandler.java]

❶ We're still passing `null`

Now that neither of our `currentTripFor` methods fetch the time, `CurrentTripHandler` is the only action—the place that we need to call `Instant.now()`. We can fix things by inserting the call, leaving us with:

```
public class CurrentTripsHandler {
    private final ITrackTrips tracking;
    private final ObjectMapper objectMapper = new ObjectMapper();

    public CurrentTripsHandler(ITrackTrips tracking) {
        this.tracking = tracking;
    }

    public Response handle(Request request) {
        try {
            var customerId = request.getQueryParam("customerId").stream()
                .findFirst();
            if (customerId.isEmpty())
                return new Response(HTTP_BAD_REQUEST);
            var currentTrip = tracking.currentTripFor(
                customerId.get(),
                Instant.now() ❶
            );
```

```
            return currentTrip.isPresent() ?
                new Response(HTTP_OK,
                    objectMapper.writeValueAsString(currentTrip)) :
                new Response(HTTP_NOT_FOUND);
        } catch (Exception x) {
            return new Response(HTTP_INTERNAL_ERROR);
        }
    }
}
```

Example 7.19 [actions.9:src/main/java/travelator/handlers/CurrentTripsHandler.java]

❶ Now our action is at the application entry point.

Looking through our code, we find (scream) that we don't have any unit tests for the handler. If we want to add them, this is the level at which we would now inject a `Clock`, rather than into the individual services. Mocks or stubs allow us to test actions, but are rarely required to test calculations.

We won't show it, but we also have to consider the production implementation of `Trips`, the one that reads from our database. We are lucky and find that this passes the current time into its SQL query, so now we can just use the value of the `at` parameter in `Trips.currentTripsFor(String customerId, Instant at)` instead. It would have been more complicated if the SQL query was using the current time of the database server from a database-specific expression such as `CURRENT_TIMESTAMP` or `NOW`. As with non-SQL code, actions are so pervasive that this is a common practice even though it makes testing more complicated and the code itself less versatile. If our query had used the database time, we would have to rewrite it to receive the time from our function as a parameter, and make a mental note not to make the same mistake again.

With that done, we review our changes and find that we haven't converted any code to Kotlin!

This is significant. This way of thinking about calculations and actions doesn't depend on our implementation language, and the grain of Java is becoming more functional with time. We find, though, that Kotlin's more natural support for immutable data and other functional constructs means that the costs of making the distinction are lower, and so the cost/benefit ratio looks more favorable. Note also that a lot of the refactoring steps taken in this chapter (and others) are safe only because we are moving around the invocation of calculations and not actions.

Before we finish this chapter, what about the other action we hinted at? Here is the implementation of `InMemoryTrips`, now converted to Kotlin:

```
class InMemoryTrips : Trips {
    private val trips: MutableMap<String, MutableSet<Trip>> = mutableMapOf()

    fun addTrip(trip: Trip) {
        val existingTrips = trips.getOrDefault(trip.customerId, mutableSetOf())
```

```
            existingTrips.add(trip)
            trips[trip.customerId] = existingTrips
        }

        override fun tripsFor(customerId: String) =
            trips.getOrDefault(customerId, emptySet<Trip>())

        override fun currentTripsFor(customerId: String, at: Instant): Set<Trip> =
            tripsFor(customerId)
                .filter { it.isPlannedToBeActiveAt(at) }
                .toSet()
    }
```

Example 7.20 [actions.10:src/test/java/travelator/InMemoryTrips.kt]

That `MutableMap` of `MutableSets` is a sign that something can change over time. If they have the same customer, the result of `tripsFor` will be different after we have called `addTrip`. So `tripsFor` is an action, not a calculation. If `tripsFor` is an action, then anything that calls it is an action, including our `currentTripsFor`. The same will obviously be true of the production version of `Trips` that reads and writes to the database. After all this work, we haven't actually promoted our action to a calculation after all!

Should we be downhearted? No. Despite our previous assertion that functions are either calculations *or* actions, the truth is that in practice actionness is graduated, and actions can be more or less susceptible to time. In this case, unless other code *in this interaction* is also going to fetch the trips for a customer and find an inconsistency, we can treat `Trips` as effectively immutable. So `tripsFor`, and by extension `currentTripsFor`, are effectively calculations. In this respect our `InMemoryTrips` is less safe than our database implementation because, if accessed on multiple threads, it can mutate the collection returned by `tripsFor`, leading to potential `ConcurrentModificationExceptions` in the `filter` implementation. Categorizing our code into calculations and actions has helped us see these issues and given us a framework for deciding whether they are important in context.

Lastly, note that Kotlin's preference for immutable data makes this categorization easier. For example, when you see `List` in Java, you have to find the places in which it is created or referenced to establish its mutability and, hence, the likelihood that code accessing it can be an action. In Kotlin, when you see `MutableList` you can infer an action, although as we have seen with `InMemoryTrips`, exposing a mutable collection with a read-only alias can lead to actions pretending to be calculations.

Moving On

Categorizing code into calculations and actions (along with data) is a formalism introduced by Eric Normand in his book, *Grokking Simplicity: Taming Complex Software with Functional Thinking* (Manning Publications). As developers, we intuit the difference and soon learn to rely on our intuition, but often without realizing how or why. Giving names to the categories, and studying their qualities, allows us to reason at a more conscious and effective level.

In Chapter 5, *Beans to Values*, we refactored from a mutable bean to an immutable value. Similarly, in Chapter 6, *Java to Kotlin Collections*, we refactored from mutable to immutable collections. In both cases, we trade mutating an object for returning an amended copy, converting an action into a calculation. In doing so, we gain the advantages we've seen in this chapter: better comprehension, easier testing, and predictable refactoring. The more of our code that is calculations, the better off we are.

We will return to the topic of moving from actions to calculations in Chapter 14, *Accumulating Objects to Transformations*. In Chapter 15, *Encapsulated Collections to Type Aliases*, we'll see how immutable data combines with Kotlin's extension functions and type aliases and lets us organize our code in ways not possible in Java.

CHAPTER 8

Static Methods to Top-Level Functions

Standalone functions are one of the fundamental building blocks of software. They have to be declared as methods on a class in Java, but in Kotlin we can declare them as top-level entities. When should we prefer top-level functions, and how do we refactor our way there from Java?

Java Statics

All values and functions in a Java program have to belong to a class: they are *members* of that class. Java calls member-values *fields*, and member-functions *methods*. By default, fields values are per-instance of the class: different instances have different values. Methods are also per-instance in that they have access to the state of the instance that they are invoked on. If we mark fields as `static`, though, they are shared between all instances of the class. Static methods only have access to this shared state (and visible static fields in other classes), but in return for this restriction, we can invoke them without needing an instance of the class.

To simplify Java, the language designers tied all code and data to classes. We have class-scoped static state, so we need class-scoped static methods. They could have added freestanding data and functions, but static fields and methods will do. If the language had options, then developers would have to choose between them, and less choice is often better. The designers then carried this language design decision forward to the Java Virtual Machine, which in turn has no way to express top-level code or data.

> ### Static State
>
> In the early days of Java, static state was a lot more common than it is today. We wrote singletons and argued about how to initialize them in a lazy but safe way. We used static fields to implement per-class caches of instances. Then the new millennium fad for testing code all but killed static state. That's because it's very difficult to isolate one test from another when they are coupled by state, and very hard to uncouple them when that state is static and so shared between all tests in a JVM. (Note that *state* here refers to mutable data. Immutable data—constants—are less of a problem.)
>
> So we learned to keep otherwise static state in object fields and used dependency injection to arrange for there to be only one shared instance of the object in our application. (When we say "dependency injection" here, your authors mean "passing an object to a constructor" rather than the use of a framework.)
>
> In this chapter, we'll focus on code rather than state.

Sometimes we have a class with both nonstatic and static methods acting on the same type—for example, the email class with a static parsing method we saw in Chapter 3. Often, though, we end up with a class composed of only static methods. When there is no static state for them to share, these methods are really just stand-alone functions grouped together and called via their class name, like the methods from the `java.util.Collections` class, for example:

```
var max = Collections.max(list);
```

Amazingly, the industry didn't really notice how much of a pain that `Collections.` prefix was for a while. This was because we wrote our programs by adding more and more methods to types that we owned, so we rarely needed static functions. Static functions are useful when we want to add functionality *without* adding a method to the type that they act on. This might be because our classes are already sagging under the weight of all the methods that we have already added to them, or because we don't own the class and so can't add the method to it. Another reason for using static functions rather than methods is because the functionality only applies to some instantiations of a generic type, so it cannot be declared as a member of the generic. That `Collections.max`, for example, only applies to a collection with comparable elements.

Over time, we began to appreciate the advantages of using standard interfaces, like the Java collections, instead of working with our own abstractions. Java 5 (with its generics) was the first release that allowed us to use collections directly rather than wrapping them with our own classes. It's no accident then that Java 5 also brought the ability to `import static java.util.Collections.max` so that we could then write:

```
var m = max(list);
```

Note that this is really only a convenience provided by the compiler, because the JVM still only actually supports static methods rather than true top-level functions.

Kotlin Top-Level Functions, Objects, and Companions

Kotlin allows functions (and properties and constants) to be declared outside of classes. In this case, because the JVM has nowhere else for them to go, the compiler generates a class with static members for these top-level declarations. By default, it derives the name of the class from the name of the file defining the functions. For example, functions defined in `top-level.kt` end up as static methods on a class called `Top_levelKt`. If we know the name of the class, we can reference it from Java by either static importing `Top_LevelKt.foo` or directly invoking `Top_levelKt.foo()`. If we don't like the ugliness of `Top_LevelKt`, we can explicitly name the generated class by adding an annotation, `@file:JvmName`, to the top of the file, as we'll see later in this chapter.

As well as these top-level functions, Kotlin also allows us to define properties and functions scoped, like Java statics, to a class rather than an instance. Instead of just marking these as `static`, Kotlin borrows from Scala and collects them into `object` declarations. This type of `object` declaration (as opposed to the `object` expression that creates anonymous types) defines a singleton: a type with only one instance that provides a global point of access to that instance. All the members of an `object` will be compiled to members of a class with the name of the object. They won't actually be static methods unless specifically marked with `@JvmStatic`, though. This is because Kotlin allows these objects to extend classes and implement interfaces, and that is incompatible with static declarations.

When we need to group static and nonstatic members in the same class, we can declare the static parts in a `companion object` inside the (otherwise nonstatic) class declaration. This groups them in the file, and code in a companion object can access private state in instances of its containing class. Companion objects can also extend another class and implement interfaces—something that Java statics cannot do. Compared to Java statics though, companion objects are cumbersome if we just want to define one or two static methods.

In Kotlin, then, we can write non-instance-scoped functions as either top-level functions or methods on a singleton object, and this object may be a companion object or not scoped to a type.

Of these, all things being equal, we should default to top-level functions. They are the simplest to declare and reference, and can be moved from file to file within a package without affecting Kotlin client code (but see the caveat in "Moving Top-Level Functions" on page 104). We reserve declaring functions as methods on a singleton object instead of top-level functions for when we need the ability to implement an interface, or otherwise group functions more tightly. We use a companion object when we need to mix static and nonstatic behavior within a class, or to write factory methods with names like `MyType.of(...)`.

As with many aspects of programming, we start with the simplest thing that could work, which is usually a top-level function, and refactor to a more complicated solution only when it brings benefits, such as a more expressive API for our clients, or better maintainability for us.

Refactoring from Static Methods to Top-Level Functions

While we prefer to use top-level declarations, the Java to Kotlin conversion built into IntelliJ doesn't. It converts our Java statics into object methods. Let's see how to refactor from Java, through object declarations, to top-level functions.

At Travelator, we allow our customers to build shortlists, such as a shortlist of routes when planning their trip, or a shortlist of hotel rooms on those routes. The user can rank items in a shortlist by different criteria and discard items to narrow down the results to a final choice. Following the guidance in "Don't Mutate Shared Collections" on page 63, a shortlist is stored as an immutable list. The functions for manipulating a shortlist (returning a modified copy rather than mutating the list) are implemented as static methods of the `Shortlists` class:

```
public class Shortlists {
    public static <T> List<T> sorted(
        List<T> shortlist,
        Comparator<? super T> ordering
    ) {
        return shortlist.stream()
            .sorted(ordering)
            .collect(toUnmodifiableList());
    }

    public static <T> List<T> removeItemAt(List<T> shortlist, int index) {
        return Stream.concat(
            shortlist.stream().limit(index),
            shortlist.stream().skip(index + 1)
        ).collect(toUnmodifiableList());
    }

    public static Comparator<HasRating> byRating() {
        return comparingDouble(HasRating::getRating).reversed();
    }

    public static Comparator<HasPrice> byPriceLowToHigh() {
        return comparing(HasPrice::getPrice);
    }
```

```
    ... and other comparators
}
```

Example 8.1 [static-to-top-level.0:src/main/java/travelator/Shortlists.java]

> ### Convenience Functions
>
> `sorted` and `removeItemAt` are complicated for what they do. Nat discovered Kotlin after watching Duncan try to use the Java Streams API to analyze some publishing data. He was so horrified at the difficulty of performing basic operations that he went looking for a JVM language that would ease the pain. It certainly seems that although the Java APIs have improved recently, for many years the designers seemed to have had a policy of never knowingly adding a convenience function.
>
> In contrast, the Kotlin standard library seems to go out of its way to provide functionality just where and when we need it, often in the form of extension functions (Chapter 10) on existing types.

The functions in `Shortlists` are static methods, and have to be referenced as such. Spelled out longhand, this looks like:

```
var reordered = Shortlists.sorted(items, Shortlists.byValue());
```

Example 8.2 [static-to-top-level.5:src/test/java/travelator/ShortlistsTest.java]

We usually `static import` the methods though, and they are named to read better that way:

```
var reordered = sorted(items, byPriceLowToHigh());
```

Example 8.3 [static-to-top-level.5:src/test/java/travelator/ShortlistsTest.java]

Converting the Java to Kotlin with IntelliJ we get:

```
object Shortlists {
    @JvmStatic
    fun <T> sorted(shortlist: List<T>, ordering: Comparator<in T>): List<T> {
        return shortlist.stream().sorted(ordering)
            .collect(toUnmodifiableList())
    }

    @JvmStatic
    fun <T> removeItemAt(shortlist: List<T>, index: Int): List<T> {
        return Stream.concat(
            shortlist.stream().limit(index.toLong()),
            shortlist.stream().skip((index + 1).toLong())
        ).collect(toUnmodifiableList())
    }

    @JvmStatic
    fun byRating(): Comparator<HasRating> {
        return comparingDouble(HasRating::rating).reversed()
```

```
    }

    @JvmStatic
    fun byPriceLowToHigh(): Comparator<HasPrice> {
        return comparing(HasPrice::price)
    }

    ... and other comparators
}
```

Example 8.4 [static-to-top-level.5:src/main/java/travelator/Shortlists.kt]

Actually, that isn't quite true. At the time of writing, the converter added some spurious nullability to types, undid static imports (leaving us with `Collectors.toUnmodifiableList()`, for example), and managed to create an imports list that didn't compile. Fixing up the file manually gives us confidence that the machines won't take our jobs for a few years yet.

In Chapter 3, we saw that converting a Java class with static *and* nonstatic methods produced a Kotlin class with a companion object. Here the conversion has produced only a top-level object. Because this Java class had no nonstatic methods or state, there is no need for the Kotlin translation to include an instantiable class. Classes with both static and nonstatic methods are less suitable for conversion to top-level functions.

While the conversion didn't go completely smoothly at the Kotlin level, on the plus side, no Java code was harmed in the process. The client code remains unchanged, because the `@JvmStatic` annotations allow Java code to see the methods as static methods on a `Shortlists` class, as they were before the conversion.

We want to convert the methods to be top-level functions, but we can't just move them, because Java only understands methods, not functions. If these functions were compiled to methods on a class called `Shortlists`, Java would be happy, and that is the job of the `@file:JvmName` annotation we mentioned earlier. We can manually add the annotation at the top of the file, and remove the `object` scope and `@JvmStatic` annotations to get:

```
@file:JvmName("Shortlists")
package travelator

...

fun <T> sorted(shortlist: List<T>, ordering: Comparator<in T>): List<T> {
    return shortlist.stream().sorted(ordering)
        .collect(toUnmodifiableList())
}

fun <T> removeItemAt(shortlist: List<T>, index: Int): List<T> {
    return Stream.concat(
        shortlist.stream().limit(index.toLong()),
```

```
        shortlist.stream().skip((index + 1).toLong())
    ).collect(toUnmodifiableList())
}

... etc.
```

Example 8.5 [static-to-top-level.6:src/main/java/travelator/Shortlists.kt]

This keeps our Java happy, but irritatingly, it breaks some Kotlin code that was calling the methods. Here, for example, are the imports for a test:

```
import org.junit.jupiter.api.Test
import travelator.Shortlists.byPriceLowToHigh
import travelator.Shortlists.byRating
import travelator.Shortlists.byRelevance
import travelator.Shortlists.byValue
import travelator.Shortlists.removeItemAt
import travelator.Shortlists.sorted
```

Example 8.6 [static-to-top-level.6:src/test/java/travelator/hotels/ShortlistScenarioTest.kt]

These were importing the static Java methods, but Kotlin can't import its own top-level functions in the same way, so these lines fail with `Unresolved reference: Shortlists`. As far as Kotlin is concerned, the functions are defined in the scope of the package, not in a class in that package. The compiler may compile them to static methods of a JVM class called `ShortlistsKt`, but that class is an implementation detail of how the compiler maps Kotlin language concepts to the JVM platform and is not visible to our Kotlin code at compile time.

We could go through all the compilation errors and manually fix the imports to refer to the function at package scope. For example, we would have to change `import travelator.Shortlists.sorted` to `import travelator.sorted`. This is easy enough if the change affects a few files, but if the change has had a wide impact, fixing all the imports is a tedious job, albeit one that *might* be achieved with a single global search and replace.

Luckily, while we were writing this book, IntelliJ gained a "Move to top level" refactoring. Let's revert the last Kotlin change, back to the object declaration, and try again.

Move to Top Level

As we write this, the refactoring is so new that it isn't available on the refactoring menu, but Alt-Enter on an object method name gives the option "Move to top level". We'll do `sorted` first. IntelliJ moves the method out of the object scope to the file level:

```
@JvmStatic
fun <T> sorted(shortlist: List<T>, ordering: Comparator<in T>): List<T> {
    return shortlist.stream().sorted(ordering)
```

```
            .collect(toUnmodifiableList())
}
```

Example 8.7 [static-to-top-level.7:src/main/java/travelator/Shortlists.kt]

Unfortunately, it failed to remove the `@JvmStatic` annotation, so we have to delete that ourselves to get the code to compile. Once we do, we find that it has at least fixed up the callers, which was the problem we had when we just moved the method ourselves. Where we explicitly referenced the method in Java as `ShortLists.sorted`, we now have:

```
var reordered = ShortlistsKt.sorted(items, Shortlists.byValue());
```

Example 8.8 [static-to-top-level.8:src/test/java/travelator/ShortlistsTest.java]

For some reason, where we had a static import, things have become worse:

```
var reordered = travelator.ShortlistsKt.sorted(items, byPriceLowToHigh());
```

Example 8.9 [static-to-top-level.8:src/test/java/travelator/ShortlistsTest.java]

We can fix that with Alt-Enter and "Add on demand static import...". We have to do that once in each affected file; we should have checked in before the refactor so that we could easily see which files it changed:

```
var reordered = sorted(items, byPriceLowToHigh());
```

Example 8.10 [static-to-top-level.9:src/test/java/travelator/ShortlistsTest.java]

Compared to our previous manual approach of adding an `@file:JvmName("Shortlists")` annotation, our Java clients are now exposed to that icky `ShortlistsKt` name. Because the methods names were designed to be used with static imports though, it is almost always hidden in the imports block where no one ever looks, so we're prepared to put up with this. In return for this sacrifice, the conversion has also fixed up the Kotlin callers of `sorted`. It is now referenced in Kotlin as `travelator.sorted` rather than `travalator.Shortlists.sorted`, which was the point.

We can now move the rest of the methods on `Shortlists` in the same way. It's a little tedious, but at least when it moves the last method, IntelliJ deletes the empty object, leaving us:

```
fun <T> sorted(shortlist: List<T>, ordering: Comparator<in T>): List<T> {
    return shortlist.stream().sorted(ordering)
        .collect(toUnmodifiableList())
}

fun <T> removeItemAt(shortlist: List<T>, index: Int): List<T> {
    return Stream.concat(
        shortlist.stream().limit(index.toLong()),
        shortlist.stream().skip((index + 1).toLong())
    ).collect(toUnmodifiableList())
}
```

```
fun byRating(): Comparator<HasRating> {
    return comparingDouble(HasRating::rating).reversed()
}

fun byPriceLowToHigh(): Comparator<HasPrice> {
    return comparing(HasPrice::price)
}

... and other comparators
```

Example 8.11 [static-to-top-level.10:src/main/java/travelator/Shortlists.kt]

As we write this, the "Move to top level" refactor is limited to a single method at a time. If methods depend on each other, this can lead to some problems, as we will see in Chapter 10.

Kotlinify

Of course, we didn't move our methods to top-level functions just for the sake of it. Well, not *just* for the sake of it anyway. Now that our functions are in the idiomatic Kotlin place, let's finish the idiomatic Kotlin job.

Chapter 13 gives guidance on converting Java streams to Kotlin; in the case of `sorted`, we can just use the Kotlin `sortedWith` extension function:

```
fun <T> sorted(shortlist: List<T>, ordering: Comparator<in T>): List<T> {
    return shortlist.sortedWith(ordering)
}
```

Example 8.12 [static-to-top-level.11:src/main/java/travelator/Shortlists.kt]

This makes a very logical extension function (Chapter 10):

```
fun <T> List<T>.sorted(ordering: Comparator<in T>): List<T> {
    return sortedWith(ordering)
}
```

Example 8.13 [static-to-top-level.12:src/main/java/travelator/Shortlists.kt]

Java still calls this as a static method:

```
var reordered = sorted(items, byPriceLowToHigh());
```

Example 8.14 [static-to-top-level.12:src/test/java/travelator/ShortlistsTest.java]

Calling from Kotlin reads nicely too:

```
val hotelsByPrice = hotels.sorted(byPriceLowToHigh())
```

Example 8.15 [static-to-top-level.12:src/test/java/travelator/hotels/ShortlistScenarioTest.kt]

These Kotlin usages really aren't gaining us anything over the raw Kotlin API, so we can just inline them:

```
val hotelsByPrice = hotels.sortedWith(byPriceLowToHigh())
```

Example 8.16 [static-to-top-level.13:src/test/java/travelator/hotels/ShortlistScenarioTest.kt]

This leaves the `sorted` function for Java to call. Looking at it, it really has nothing to do with shortlists anymore. Should we move it to a more generic namespace? Maybe later; for now we'll just follow through on the rest of the file to give:

```
fun <T> Iterable<T>.sorted(ordering: Comparator<in T>): List<T> =
    sortedWith(ordering)

fun <T> Iterable<T>.withoutItemAt(index: Int): List<T> =
    take(index) + drop(index + 1)

fun byRating(): Comparator<HasRating> =
    comparingDouble(HasRating::rating).reversed()

fun byPriceLowToHigh(): Comparator<HasPrice> =
    comparing(HasPrice::price)

... and other comparators
```

Example 8.17 [static-to-top-level.14:src/main/java/travelator/Shortlists.kt]

You may have noticed that we have renamed `removeItemAt` to `withoutItemAt`. Prepositions like *with* and *without* are a useful device to let the reader know that we are not mutating an object but returning a copy.

Moving Top-Level Functions

The `withoutItemAt` Kotlin function looks to be useful, and we wonder why we can't find a version in the standard library. Now that it is a top-level function, we can move it out of `Shortlists.kt` to a different file in the same package without changing the Kotlin source that calls it. If we do though, that function will now be defined as a static method of a different JVM class in the compiled output.

If we publish Kotlin library code in a JAR file, all is fine provided dependent code is recompiled against the new version. The Kotlin compiler generates class files with metadata sections that let it map Kotlin names to JVM classes and methods. All may *not* be fine if dependent code uses our JAR as a binary dependency, and upgrades without recompiling. The JVM doesn't use the metadata that the Kotlin compiler generated. If a top-level function has moved from one class to another between versions of a binary dependency, dependent code can find a `NoSuchMethodError` thrown at runtime.

We can use the `@JvmMultifileClass` and `@JvmName` annotations to control how our top-level declarations appear in JVM class files, so that moving declarations between source files won't break binary compatibility. However, none of our Kotlin test or example code will have changed, so we can't rely on them to warn us about this kind of breakage. We just have to take extra care if we move top-level functions published in a library, or use tools to check binary compatibility for us.

Moving On

Static functions are the bread and butter of our programs. In Java these have to be static methods on a class, but in Kotlin we can and should default to defining them as top-level functions.

Automatically converting a Java class of static methods to Kotlin will create an `object` declaration, accessible from both Java and Kotlin. We can then move the methods on the object to the top level individually, remaining accessible to both languages, before applying other refactorings to take advantage of more Kotliny goodness.

The most likely next refactor is to refactor our top-level functions into extension functions, the subject of Chapter 10, *Functions to Extension Functions*.

CHAPTER 9

Multi- to Single-Expression Functions

Nat and Duncan both love Kotlin's single-expression function definitions. When should we use this form, why might we prefer it, and what Kotlin features can we use to make more functions single expressions?

As with Java, the code in a Kotlin function is usually { defined inside braces } and uses `return` to define the result of the function (unless it is `Unit`, Kotlin's alias for `void`):

```
fun add(a: Int, b: Int): Int {
    return a + b
}
```

If the top level of the code is a single expression though, we can optionally drop the result type, and define the code with an expression after an equals sign:

```
fun addToo(a: Int, b: Int): Int = a + b
```

We can read this as: the result of function `add` equals `a + b`. Which makes sense for a single expression, and can also read nicely when that expression is itself composed of subexpressions:

```
fun max(a: Int, b: Int): Int =
    when {
        a > b -> a
        else -> b
    }
```

This interpretation makes less sense for functions that have side effects, especially those that perform I/O or write to mutable state. For instance:

```
fun printTwice(s: String): Unit = println("$s\n$s")
```

We can't read this as the result of `printTwice` equals `println(..)`, because `println` doesn't have a result, or at least it doesn't return one. Its function is entirely side effects, as we explored in Chapter 7.

Reserve Single-Expression Functions for Calculations

If we adopt a convention of reserving single-expression functions for calculations ("Calculations" on page 78), then we have a way of communicating our intent when we use them. When we see a single-expression function, we will know that it isn't an action ("Actions" on page 79), and so is much safer to refactor.

In practice this means that single-expression functions shouldn't return `Unit`, or read or write from mutable state, including performing I/O.

Your authors have found that attempting to make as many functions as possible into single expressions improves our software. For one thing, if we reserve the single-expression form for calculations, then this will decrease the proportion of our code that is actions, making it easier to understand and modify. Single expressions will also tend to be shorter than the alternative, limiting the complexity of each function. When a function does get too large to be easily understood, single-expression style lets us more easily refactor for clarity, because there is less risk of breaking logic that depends on side effects and the order in which actions are performed.

We also prefer expressions as opposed to statements. Expressions are *declarative*: we declare *what* we want the function to calculate and let the Kotlin compiler and runtime decide *how* to compute that calculation. We don't have to run the code in a simulated computer in our heads to figure out what the function does.

For example, at the end of Chapter 3 we were left with this code for `EmailAddress`:

```
data class EmailAddress(
    val localPart: String,
    val domain: String
) {

    override fun toString() = "$localPart@$domain"

    companion object {
        @JvmStatic
        fun parse(value: String): EmailAddress {
            val atIndex = value.lastIndexOf('@')
            require(!(atIndex < 1 || atIndex == value.length - 1)) {
                "EmailAddress must be two parts separated by @"
            }
            return EmailAddress(
                value.substring(0, atIndex),
                value.substring(atIndex + 1)
            )
        }
    }
}
```

Example 9.1 [single-expressions.0:src/main/java/travelator/EmailAddress.kt]

The toString method is already a nice simple single expression. As we said at the time though, the amount of code required in the parse method adds insult to the injury of having to declare static methods in a companion object. Maybe focusing on making the function into a simple single expression would help?

Before we go on, we should say that lots of the refactoring sequences presented in this book are of the form "Here's one I prepared earlier." We show you the successful take. Real-life refactorings, like writing code from scratch, aren't like that. We try things that don't work at all, or we take a much more circuitous route than we show in the final edit. Because this is an otherwise small example, we've taken this opportunity to show what actually happened when we tried to convert parse to a single expression. We think that there are valuable lessons in the journey, but if you just want the destination, you should skip ahead to "Take 4: Stepping Back" on page 116.

Take 1: Inlining

Let's analyze the code and see what is preventing this function from being a nice single expression:

```
fun parse(value: String): EmailAddress {
    val atIndex = value.lastIndexOf('@') ❶
    require(!(atIndex < 1 || atIndex == value.length - 1)) { ❷
        "EmailAddress must be two parts separated by @"
    }
    return EmailAddress( ❸
        value.substring(0, atIndex),
        value.substring(atIndex + 1)
    )
}
```

Example 9.2 [single-expressions.1:src/main/java/travelator/EmailAddress.kt]

❶ Assigning to atIndex is a statement.

❷ The call to require is a statement.

❸ Creating the EmailAddress is a single expression, depending on value and atIndex.

The first statement is the assignment to atIndex. In Kotlin, assignment is a statement, not an expression (unlike Java, where we can chain assignments). Its position in the code also matters—it has to happen here in the code for the value of atIndex to be available to compile the rest of the function. The expression bound to the variable, value.lastIndexOf(Char), is a calculation though, meaning that it will always return the same result for the same arguments (this is considered an argument when we call methods). As a result, we can inline the variable atIndex without changing the result of the function, giving:

```
fun parse(value: String): EmailAddress {
    require(!(
        value.lastIndexOf('@') < 1 ||
            value.lastIndexOf('@') == value.length - 1)) {
        "EmailAddress must be two parts separated by @"
    }
    return EmailAddress(
        value.substring(0, value.lastIndexOf('@')),
        value.substring(value.lastIndexOf('@') + 1)
    )
}
```

Example 9.3 [single-expressions.2:src/main/java/travelator/EmailAddress.kt]

This version won't produce the same bytecode, nor run as fast (probably, it's notoriously difficult to second-guess HotSpot), but it will return the same result. We still have that `require` call to deal with, though, and we seem to have made everything a bit less understandable already, so let's revert the change and try another tack.

Take 2: Introduce a Function

Another way to remove the assignment statement is to have a scope where `atIndex` is always defined. We could use a function as such a scope, because a function binds a single evaluation of its arguments to its parameters. We can see this by selecting all but the code before the assignment and extracting a function `emailAddress`:

```
fun parse(value: String): EmailAddress {
    val atIndex = value.lastIndexOf('@')
    return emailAddress(value, atIndex)
}

private fun emailAddress(value: String, atIndex: Int): EmailAddress {
    require(!(atIndex < 1 || atIndex == value.length - 1)) {
        "EmailAddress must be two parts separated by @"
    }
    return EmailAddress(
        value.substring(0, atIndex),
        value.substring(atIndex + 1)
    )
}
```

Example 9.4 [single-expressions.3:src/main/java/travelator/EmailAddress.kt]

Now we can inline the `atIndex` variable in `parse`, because the `atIndex` parameter has captured its value for us:

```
fun parse(value: String): EmailAddress {
    return emailAddress(value, value.lastIndexOf('@'))
}

private fun emailAddress(value: String, atIndex: Int): EmailAddress {
    require(!(atIndex < 1 || atIndex == value.length - 1)) {
```

```
            "EmailAddress must be two parts separated by @"
        }
        return EmailAddress(
            value.substring(0, atIndex),
            value.substring(atIndex + 1)
        )
    }
```

Example 9.5 [single-expressions.4:src/main/java/travelator/EmailAddress.kt]

Now `parse` is a single expression, but `emailAddress(...)` isn't, so we can't declare victory just yet. That `require` is always going to cause us some problems, because its job is to prevent evaluation from proceeding. This is the opposite of an expression, which needs to evaluate to a value.

Often when we reach this sort of impasse when refactoring, inlining the cause of the problem will let us see the way ahead. So let's inline `require`. (Suspend disbelief for now; things are going to get worse before they get better.)

```
private fun emailAddress(value: String, atIndex: Int): EmailAddress {
    if (!!(atIndex < 1 || atIndex == value.length - 1)) {
        val message = "EmailAddress must be two parts separated by @"
        throw IllegalArgumentException(message.toString())
    }
    return EmailAddress(
        value.substring(0, atIndex),
        value.substring(atIndex + 1)
    )
}
```

Example 9.6 [single-expressions.5:src/main/java/travelator/EmailAddress.kt]

There's an awful lot of redundancy that we can remove here. Alt-Enter on the `if` condition will remove the double-negation `!!`, and then Alt-Enter on the redundant `toString` will remove it. This allows us to inline `message`, yielding:

```
private fun emailAddress(value: String, atIndex: Int): EmailAddress {
    if ((atIndex < 1 || atIndex == value.length - 1)) {
        throw IllegalArgumentException(
            "EmailAddress must be two parts separated by @"
        )
    }
    return EmailAddress(
        value.substring(0, atIndex),
        value.substring(atIndex + 1)
    )
}
```

Example 9.7 [single-expressions.6:src/main/java/travelator/EmailAddress.kt]

Now we can introduce an `else` to see the structure:

```
private fun emailAddress(value: String, atIndex: Int): EmailAddress {
    if ((atIndex < 1 || atIndex == value.length - 1)) {
        throw IllegalArgumentException(
            "EmailAddress must be two parts separated by @"
        )
    } else {
        return EmailAddress(
            value.substring(0, atIndex),
            value.substring(atIndex + 1)
        )
    }
}
```

Example 9.8 [single-expressions.7:src/main/java/travelator/EmailAddress.kt]

At this point we have a function with two statements chosen by an `if`. This is so tantalizingly close to a single expression that even the IDE can feel it: Alt-Enter on the `if`, and IntelliJ offers to "Lift return out of 'if'":

```
private fun emailAddress(value: String, atIndex: Int): EmailAddress {
    return if ((atIndex < 1 || atIndex == value.length - 1)) {
        throw IllegalArgumentException(
            "EmailAddress must be two parts separated by @"
        )
    } else {
        EmailAddress(
            value.substring(0, atIndex),
            value.substring(atIndex + 1)
        )
    }
}
```

Example 9.9 [single-expressions.8:src/main/java/travelator/EmailAddress.kt]

There it is—our single expression. Alt-Enter on the `return` offers "Convert to expression body":

```
private fun emailAddress(value: String, atIndex: Int): EmailAddress =
    if ((atIndex < 1 || atIndex == value.length - 1)) {
        throw IllegalArgumentException(
            "EmailAddress must be two parts separated by @"
        )
    } else {
        EmailAddress(
            value.substring(0, atIndex),
            value.substring(atIndex + 1)
        )
    }
```

Example 9.10 [single-expressions.9:src/main/java/travelator/EmailAddress.kt]

When we're defining a function as a single expression, `when` is often clearer than `if`. IntelliJ will do this for us if we Alt-Enter on the `if`. Here we've also removed unnecessary braces, inlined `message`, and finally converted `parse` to a single expression too:

```
fun parse(value: String) =
    emailAddress(value, value.lastIndexOf('@'))

private fun emailAddress(value: String, atIndex: Int): EmailAddress =
    when {
        atIndex < 1 || atIndex == value.length - 1 ->
            throw IllegalArgumentException(
                "EmailAddress must be two parts separated by @"
            )
        else -> EmailAddress(
            value.substring(0, atIndex),
            value.substring(atIndex + 1)
        )
    }
```

Example 9.11 [single-expressions.10:src/main/java/travelator/EmailAddress.kt]

For comparison, here is the original:

```
fun parse(value: String): EmailAddress {
    val atIndex = value.lastIndexOf('@')
    require(!(atIndex < 1 || atIndex == value.length - 1)) {
        "EmailAddress must be two parts separated by @"
    }
    return EmailAddress(
        value.substring(0, atIndex),
        value.substring(atIndex + 1)
    )
}
```

Example 9.12 [single-expressions.11:src/main/java/travelator/EmailAddress.kt]

Are we happy with the result?

Not really. We now have *more* code, and that `emailAddress` function doesn't feel like it's adding any value except for capturing `atIndex`.

Refactoring is often a process of exploration. We have a goal in mind, but don't always know how it will turn out. It's our (your authors') experience that trying to find a single-expression form of a function often improves our code, but we can't look you in the eye and say that has happened here.

We could give up on the idea, or we could push on and try to get there from here. Instead though, let's revert and try a third approach, informed by the experience we've just gained.

Take 3: Let

The reason we extracted the `emailAddress` function was to give us a scope where the `atIndex` value is defined throughout the block; rather than having to be assigned to a local variable. Where we only have one variable we need to replace, a `let` block gives us this facility without having to define a function. We can get there in baby steps by first surrounding the code after the assignment with a `let`:

```
fun parse(value: String): EmailAddress {
    val atIndex = value.lastIndexOf('@')
    atIndex.let {
        require(!(atIndex < 1 || atIndex == value.length - 1)) {
            "EmailAddress must be two parts separated by @"
        }
        return EmailAddress(
            value.substring(0, atIndex),
            value.substring(atIndex + 1)
        )
    }
}
```

Example 9.13 [single-expressions.12:src/main/java/travelator/EmailAddress.kt]

Now we can lift the return out of the `let`; unfortunately IntelliJ doesn't offer to help us this time:

```
fun parse(value: String): EmailAddress {
    val atIndex = value.lastIndexOf('@')
    return atIndex.let {
        require(!(atIndex < 1 || atIndex == value.length - 1)) {
            "EmailAddress must be two parts separated by @"
        }
        EmailAddress(
            value.substring(0, atIndex),
            value.substring(atIndex + 1)
        )
    }
}
```

Example 9.14 [single-expressions.13:src/main/java/travelator/EmailAddress.kt]

Currently, `atIndex` in the `let` block refers to the local that we are trying to remove. If we add a lambda parameter with the same name, it will bind to that instead:

```
fun parse(value: String): EmailAddress {
    val atIndex = value.lastIndexOf('@')
    return atIndex.let { atIndex -> ❶
        require(!(atIndex < 1 || atIndex == value.length - 1)) {
            "EmailAddress must be two parts separated by @"
        }
        EmailAddress(
            value.substring(0, atIndex),
            value.substring(atIndex + 1)
```

```
        )
    }
}
```

Example 9.15 [single-expressions.14:src/main/java/travelator/EmailAddress.kt]

❶ `Warning Name shadowed: atIndex`, which is the point

Inline the `atIndex` variable and we have our single expression:

```
fun parse(value: String): EmailAddress {
    return value.lastIndexOf('@').let { atIndex ->
        require(!(atIndex < 1 || atIndex == value.length - 1)) {
            "EmailAddress must be two parts separated by @"
        }
        EmailAddress(
            value.substring(0, atIndex),
            value.substring(atIndex + 1)
        )
    }
}
```

Example 9.16 [single-expressions.15:src/main/java/travelator/EmailAddress.kt]

Now Alt-Enter on the return lets us "Convert to expression body":

```
fun parse(value: String): EmailAddress =
    value.lastIndexOf('@').let { atIndex ->
        require(!(atIndex < 1 || atIndex == value.length - 1)) {
            "EmailAddress must be two parts separated by @"
        }
        EmailAddress(
            value.substring(0, atIndex),
            value.substring(atIndex + 1)
        )
    }
```

Example 9.17 [single-expressions.16:src/main/java/travelator/EmailAddress.kt]

We've reached the point of no return! Are we happy with the result?

Duncan is writing this, and he *is* pretty relieved to have made it here after 15 refactoring steps. The example has certainly served its purpose of showing some tricks to allow us to get to single-expression functions. Nevertheless, he isn't convinced that it has demonstrated that seeking single expressions has a significant payoff. This still seems to be a lot of code, and none of it feels like it is earning its keep.

Can we make this better by raising the level of abstraction? Let's try a fourth tack.

Take 4: Stepping Back

If we step out from the mechanical refactorings, we can see that what we are doing is creating an `EmailAddress` from two nonempty strings separated by a particular character, `@` in this case. Finding two nonempty strings separated by a character sounds like a higher-level concept that we could refactor toward.

One last revert, then, back to:

```
fun parse(value: String): EmailAddress {
    val atIndex = value.lastIndexOf('@')
    require(!(atIndex < 1 || atIndex == value.length - 1)) {
        "EmailAddress must be two parts separated by @"
    }
    return EmailAddress(
        value.substring(0, atIndex),
        value.substring(atIndex + 1)
    )
}
```

Example 9.18 [single-expressions.17:src/main/java/travelator/EmailAddress.kt]

This time we'll concentrate not on `atIndex`, but on those `substring` calls. We'll pull them out into variables:

```
fun parse(value: String): EmailAddress {
    val atIndex = value.lastIndexOf('@')
    require(!(atIndex < 1 || atIndex == value.length - 1)) {
        "EmailAddress must be two parts separated by @"
    }
    val leftPart = value.substring(0, atIndex)
    val rightPart = value.substring(atIndex + 1)
    return EmailAddress(
        leftPart,
        rightPart
    )
}
```

Example 9.19 [single-expressions.18:src/main/java/travelator/EmailAddress.kt]

Now, one more time with feeling. We can extract a function of all but the return statement:

```
fun parse(value: String): EmailAddress {
    val (leftPart, rightPart) = split(value)
    return EmailAddress(
        leftPart,
        rightPart
    )
}

private fun split(value: String): Pair<String, String> {
    val atIndex = value.lastIndexOf('@')
```

```
        require(!(atIndex < 1 || atIndex == value.length - 1)) {
            "EmailAddress must be two parts separated by @"
        }
        val leftPart = value.substring(0, atIndex)
        val rightPart = value.substring(atIndex + 1)
        return Pair(leftPart, rightPart)
    }
```

Example 9.20 [single-expressions.19:src/main/java/travelator/EmailAddress.kt]

IntelliJ turns out to be really quite clever here, making the result a `Pair` because it has two values to return.

This `split` would be a nice generic function that we might use in other places if it was parameterized with the character. "Introduce Parameter" on the `'@'` makes that so. We "Convert parameter to receiver" on `value` while we're there to get a little local extension function:

```
fun parse(value: String): EmailAddress {
    val (leftPart, rightPart) = value.split('@')
    return EmailAddress(
        leftPart,
        rightPart
    )
}

private fun String.split(divider: Char): Pair<String, String> {
    val atIndex = lastIndexOf(divider)
    require(!(atIndex < 1 || atIndex == length - 1)) {
        "EmailAddress must be two parts separated by @"
    }
    val leftPart = substring(0, atIndex)
    val rightPart = substring(atIndex + 1)
    return Pair(leftPart, rightPart)
}
```

Example 9.21 [single-expressions.20:src/main/java/travelator/EmailAddress.kt]

Now we can introduce a `let`, as we did previously, to get:

```
fun parse(value: String): EmailAddress =
    value.split('@').let { (leftPart, rightPart) ->
        EmailAddress(leftPart, rightPart)
    }
```

Example 9.22 [single-expressions.21:src/main/java/travelator/EmailAddress.kt]

This, finally, is a single-expression function that feels worth the effort!

To finish, we can apply the techniques from this chapter to `split` to make it a single expression, too. Here then is the final `EmailAddress.kt`:

```
data class EmailAddress(
    val localPart: String,
```

```
        val domain: String
) {

    override fun toString() = "$localPart@$domain"

    companion object {
        @JvmStatic
        fun parse(value: String): EmailAddress =
            value.splitAroundLast('@').let { (leftPart, rightPart) ->
                EmailAddress(leftPart, rightPart)
            }
    }
}

private fun String.splitAroundLast(divider: Char): Pair<String, String> =
    lastIndexOf(divider).let { index ->
        require(index >= 1 && index != length - 1) {
            "string must be two non-empty parts separated by $divider"
        }
        substring(0, index) to substring(index + 1)
    }
```

Example 9.23 [single-expressions.22:src/main/java/travelator/EmailAddress.kt]

`splitAroundLast` felt like a better name that doesn't clash with the standard `String.split`, and hints that both sides of the split must be nonempty. Words like *around*, which are unusual in identifiers, should prompt readers of the code to suspend their assumptions about what a function does and actually look it up.

Although `splitAroundLast` does feel like a generally applicable utility function, if we want to promote it to be public, we should probably write some unit tests for it. We've spent enough time for today though, so we'll make a mental note that we have a `String.splitAroundLast` lying around if we ever need one, and finally commit the change.

What Should Parse Return?

Before we leave this example, note that this refactoring would have been easier had `parse` not thrown an exception on error. `throw` is an expression that returns `Nothing`—it doesn't complete—and so doesn't sit well when we are trying to decompose into expressions. Chapter 19 talks about this in detail, but had we written `EmailAddress` from scratch in Kotlin, we would probably have returned `EmailAddress?` from `parse`, with `null` on failure. That doesn't sit well with Java clients, where the type system doesn't warn about nullability. So we would probably end up with two parsing methods, one for legacy code and one for Kotlin, removing the exception version when there were no Java clients left. We explore how to support both languages' conventions during a gradual conversion from Kotlin to Java in Chapter 12.

Moving On

Defining our calculations as single-expression functions lets us communicate that they are different from side-effecting actions. Trying to express functions as a simple single expression is a useful discipline that can lead to well-factored, clean code. To achieve single-expression form, we usually have to factor out subexpressions into their own functions.

Single-expression form is declarative: the expression describes the function's result in terms of its parameters rather than the actions that the computer must perform to compute the result. Factoring subexpressions into their own functions prompts us to think about what those subexpressions should be denoting, and so guides us to write clearer code. For example, `String.splitAroundLast('@')` better described what we wanted to calculate than `emailAddress(value: String, atIndex: Int)`.

At a deeper level, this chapter is about more than single expressions; it's about how we can rearrange our code without changing its behavior. Many different arrangements of statements and expressions will have the same behavior; refactoring is the art of finding a better one, and getting there safely. The more arrangements we can visualize, and the more safe routes we can plan, the more options we have to make our code better.

Refactorings don't always succeed the first, second, or even third time we try them. As developers, we don't always have the luxury of repeated attempts, but the more we practice improving our communication in code, the more often we'll get there before we have to give up and move on.

CHAPTER 10

Functions to Extension Functions

Kotlin has a special kind of procedure called an extension function, that is called like a method but is in fact (usually) a top-level function. It's easy to convert from a normal function to an extension function and back. When should we prefer one to the other?

Functions and Methods

Object-oriented programming is the art of solving problems by sending messages to objects. Want to know the length of `myString`? Ask it by sending it a message `myString.length()`. Want to print that string to the console? Put the string in a message and ask another object representing the console to print it for you: `System.out.println(myString)`. In classic OO languages, we define how an object reacts to a message by defining methods on classes. Methods are bound to their class and have access to the members (fields and other methods) associated with a particular instance. When we invoke a method, the runtime arranges for the correct version to be called (depending on the runtime type of the object), and for it to have access to instance state.

In contrast, in functional programming, we solve problems by calling functions with values. We find the length of `myString` by passing it to a function: `length(myString)`. We print to the console with `println(myString)`, and if we wanted to print somewhere else, we would pass that to the function: `println(myString, System.err)`. Functions are not defined *on* a type; function parameters and results *have* a type.

The paradigms have pros and cons, but for now let's just consider discoverability and extensibility.

Here is a `Customer` type:

```
data class Customer(
    val id: String,
    val givenName: String,
    val familyName: String
) {
    ...
}
```

This is a class, so straightaway we know that we can send messages to ask for the `id`, `givenName`, and `familyName`. What about other operations? In a class-based system, we only have to scroll down to see another message that we can send:

```
data class Customer(
    val id: String,
    val givenName: String,
    val familyName: String
) {
    val fullName get() = "$givenName $familyName"
}
```

Often we don't even get as far as looking at the definition. If we have a variable `val customer: Customer`, we can type `customer.` and our IDE will eagerly tell us that we can call `id`, `givenName`, `familyName`, or `fullName`. In fact, this auto-complete is in many ways better than looking at the class definition, because it also shows us other operations (`equals`, `copy`, and so on) that are defined in supertypes or implicit in the language.

In a functional decomposition, `fullName` would be a function, and, if we suspect it exists, we would have to search our codebase for it. In this case it will be a function where the only argument is of type `Customer`. It's surprisingly hard to get IntelliJ to help us. "Find Usages" grouped by parameter type will do the job, but it's hardly convenient. In practice, we expect to find the definition of `Customer` and its fundamental operations close together in the source, perhaps in the same file or at least namespace, so we might navigate there and find the functions where we expect them, but our tools haven't been very helpful.

Score one to OO for discoverability then. What about extensibility? What happens when we want to add an operation to `Customer`? Marketing would like to render the name reversed with the `familyName` in uppercase for some report or other. (You may notice that whenever we need a simple but arbitrary example, we blame marketing.)

If we own the code, we can just add a method:

```
data class Customer(
    val id: String,
    val givenName: String,
    val familyName: String
) {
    val fullName get() = "$givenName $familyName"
    fun nameForMarketing() = "${familyName.uppercase()}, $givenName}"
}
```

If we don't own the code, then we can't add a method, so we have to fall back on a function. In Java we might have a collection of these static functions in a class called `Marketing`, or `CustomerUtils`. In Kotlin we can make them top-level functions (see Chapter 8), but the principle is the same:

```
fun nameForMarketing(customer: Customer) =
    "${customer.familyName.uppercase()}, $customer.givenName}"
```

What of the functional solution? Well, this is the functional solution, too. So the functional solution is arguably better for extensibility, because extension operations are indistinguishable from those (like `fullName`) provided by the original authors, whereas the OO solution makes us look for two different types of implementation: methods and functions.

Even if we *do* own the code for the `Customer` class, we should be wary of adding methods like `nameForMarketing`. If the class `Customer` is a fundamental domain class in our application, lots of other code will depend on it. Adding a report for marketing shouldn't force us to recompile and retest everything, but it will if we add a method. So it's better that we keep `Customer` as small as possible and have noncore operations as external functions, even if this means they are not as discoverable as methods.

In Kotlin, those functions don't have to be as hard to find as we've made out, though; they can be extension functions.

Extension Functions

Kotlin's extension functions look like methods, but are in fact just functions. (As we saw in Chapter 8, technically they are *also* methods, because on the JVM all code has to be defined in a method. In "Extension Functions as Methods" on page 131, we'll see that extension functions can in fact also be nonstatic methods of another class.)

As their name implies, extension functions give us the ability to *extend* the operations available on a type. They do this while supporting the intuitive, dot-means-send-a-message calling convention of methods, which allows them to be discoverable in the same Ctrl-Space way.

So we can define an extension function:

```
fun Customer.nameForMarketing() = "${familyName.uppercase()}, $givenName}"
```

Then we can call it as if it is a method:

```
val s = customer.nameForMarketing()
```

IntelliJ will auto-suggest extension functions along with the actual methods, even if they need to be imported to bring them into scope.

Java isn't quite so helpful—it just sees the extension function as a static function:

```
var s = MarketingStuffKt.nameForMarketing(customer);
```

`MarketingStuffKt` is the name of the class containing our top-level declarations as static methods; see Chapter 8.

Interestingly, we can't call the function in the same way from Kotlin:

```
nameForMarketing(customer) // doesn't compile
```

This fails to compile, with the error:

```
Unresolved reference. None of the following candidates is applicable
because of receiver type mismatch: public fun Customer.nameForMarket
ing(): String ....
```

Receiver, by the way, is the term that Kotlin uses for the object named `this` in an extension function (or normal method): the object that receives messages.

Note that extension functions don't have any special access to the private members of the class that they are extending; they only have the same privileges as normal functions in their scope.

Extensions and Function Types

Although we can't call extension functions as normal functions in Kotlin, we can assign them to normal function references. So the following compiles:

```
val methodReference: (Customer.() -> String) =
    Customer::fullName
val extensionFunctionReference: (Customer.() -> String) =
    Customer::nameForMarketing

val methodAsFunctionReference: (Customer) -> String =
    methodReference
val extensionAsFunctionReference: (Customer) -> String =
    extensionFunctionReference
```

We can invoke these as expected:

```
customer.methodReference()
customer.extensionFunctionReference()

methodAsFunctionReference(customer)
extensionAsFunctionReference(customer)
```

We can also use the *with-receiver* references as if they took the receiver as the first argument:

```
methodReference(customer)
extensionFunctionReference(customer)
```

We cannot, however, call the plain references as if they had a receiver. Both of these lines fail to compile, with an `Unresolved reference` error:

```
customer.methodAsFunctionReference()
customer.extensionAsFunctionReference()
```

Extension Properties

Kotlin also supports extension properties. As we discuss in Chapter 11, Kotlin property accessors are actually method calls. In the same way that extension functions are static functions that are called like methods, extension properties are static functions that are called like properties, which are in turn methods. Extension properties can't store any data because they don't really add fields to their class—their value can only be computed.

The `nameForMarketing` function could have been defined as an extension *property*:

```
val Customer.nameForMarketing get() = "${familyName.uppercase()}, $givenName}"
```

In fact, it probably *should* be a property, as we will discuss in Chapter 11.

Most of what we have to say about extension functions applies to extension properties unless we specifically distinguish between them.

Extensions Are Not Polymorphic

Although invoking an extension function looks like a method call, it is not, in fact, sending a message to an object. For polymorphic method calls, Kotlin uses the dynamic type of the receiver at runtime to select the method to execute. For extensions, Kotlin uses the static type of the receiver at compile time to select the function to call.

If we need to use extensions in a polymorphic way, we can often achieve this by calling polymorphic methods from our extension functions.

Conversions

So far, we have seen extension functions adding operations to a type. Conversions from one type to another are a common case. Travelator needs to convert customer details to and from JSON and XML. How should we convert from `JsonNode` to `Customer`?

We could add a constructor: `Customer(JsonNode)` that knows how to extract the relevant data, but it really doesn't feel right to pollute our `Customer` class with dependencies on a specific JSON library, and then maybe an XML parser, and then what? The same argument applies to adding conversions to the `JsonNode` class. Even if we *could* change its code, pretty soon it would be unmanageable with all the `JsonNode.toMyDomainType()` methods.

In Java, we would write a class of utility functions of the form:

```
static Customer toCustomer(JsonNode node) {
        ...
}
```

Or with Nat and Duncan's preferred naming convention:

```
static Customer customerFrom(JsonNode node) {
        ...
}
```

How to Name Conversions

A function converting a `JsonNode` to a `Customer` might be called `nodeToCustomer`, `createCustomer`, `toCustomer`, `customerFrom`, or `customerFor`. Why should we pick `customerFrom`? Let's examine the alternatives where they are invoked.

`nodeToCustomer` is OK, but the repetition of `node` is irritating when called:

```
var customer = nodeToCustomer(node)
```

`createCustomer` is OK, but doesn't hint at the relationship between `node` and `customer`:

```
var customer = createCustomer(node)
```

`toCustomer` lets us know that `node` contains everything we need to create a `Customer`, but doesn't flow in English:

```
var customer = toCustomer(node)
```

Our preferred `customerFrom` flows, and hints that we are extracting the data for `customer` from `node`:

```
var customer = customerFrom(node)
```

We could also try `customerFor`, which also flows:

```
var customer = customerFor(node)
```

But `customerFor` suggests a different relationship than parsing. *For* implies a lookup operation: `phoneNumberFor(customer)`, or composition: `wheelFor(bicycle)`.

Do these distinctions actually matter? Mostly no, and we should be wary of leaning on the subtleties of English when our teammates and clients may not be native speakers. But there is no point in not using the bestest words that we can. Compared to `createCustomer(node)`, the use of `customerFrom(node)` may help a reader understand what is happening in one pass rather than two, or prevent an incorrect assumption that leads to an error. We can make small but significant improvements by optimizing how our code reads in context.

Calling the conversions individually isn't too horrible:

```
var customer = customerFrom(node);
var marketingName = nameForMarketing(customer);
```

If we need to combine functions, though, things start to go awry:

```
var marketingLength = nameForMarketing(customerFrom(node)).length();
```

We're all developers here, and used to reading function invocations. So it's easy to underestimate the cognitive load of searching for the innermost call and working your way out through function and method calls to compute how an expression evaluates. Not what it evaluates to, just the order in which it evaluates. In Kotlin, we can write the conversion as an extension on `JsonNode` and enjoy a soothing flow from left to right:

```
fun JsonNode.toCustomer(): Customer = ...

val marketingLength = jsonNode.toCustomer().nameForMarketing().length
```

Ahh...that's much more readable.

Nullable Parameters

Extensions really come into their own when we work with optional data. When we are sending messages to a potentially `null` object, we can use the safe-call operator `?.` that we saw in Chapter 4. That doesn't help with parameters though; to pass a nullable reference as an argument to a function that takes a nonnull parameter, we have to wrap the call in conditional logic:

```
val customer: Customer? = loggedInCustomer()
val greeting: String? = when (customer) {
    null -> null
    else -> greetingForCustomer(customer)
}
```

Kotlin's *scoping functions*, such as `let`, `apply`, and `also`, can help here. In particular, `let` converts its receiver into a lambda parameter:

```
val customer: Customer? = loggedInCustomer()
val greeting: String? = customer?.let { greetingForCustomer(it) }
```

Here the `?.` ensures that `let` is only called when the customer is not `null`, meaning that the lambda parameter, `it`, is never null, and can be passed to the function within the lambda body. You can think of `?.let` as a safe-call operator for (single) arguments.

If a function returns a nullable result, and we must pass that result to another function that expects a nonnull parameter, the scoping functions start to get cumbersome:

```
val customer: Customer? = loggedInCustomer()

val reminder: String? = customer?.let {
```

```
        nextTripForCustomer(it)?.let {
            timeUntilDepartureOfTrip(it, currentTime)?.let {
                durationToUserFriendlyText(it) + " until your next trip!"
            }
        }
    }
```

Even when we can flatten nested null checks into a pipeline of calls to `let`, all this additional mechanism adds syntactic noise and obscures the *intent* of the code:

```
val reminder: String? = customer
    ?.let { nextTripForCustomer(it) }
    ?.let { timeUntilDepartureOfTrip(it, currentTime) }
    ?.let { durationToUserFriendlyText(it) }
    ?.let { it + " until your next trip!" }
```

If we convert the problematic parameters to extension function receivers, we can chain calls directly, bringing the application logic to the fore:

```
val reminder: String? = customer
    ?.nextTrip()
    ?.timeUntilDeparture(currentTime)
    ?.toUserFriendlyText()
    ?.plus(" until your next trip!")
```

When Nat and Duncan first adopted Kotlin, they soon found that extensions and nullability form a virtuous circle. It was easier to process optional data with extension functions, so they extracted extensions private to the file or refactored functions into extensions where it made logic easier to write. They found that the names of these extensions could be more concise than that of an equivalent function without obscuring intent. As a result, they wrote more extensions to make their application logic concise. Private extensions often proved to be useful elsewhere, so they moved them into common modules where they could easily be shared. This made it easier to use optional data in other parts of the application, which led them to write more extensions, which made application logic more concise…and so on.

Although extensions are promoted as a way to extend third-party types, the concise naming they allow, and nullability in the type system, encourage us to define extensions on our own types as well. Part of the grain of Kotlin is the way these features interact to smooth our way.

Nullable Receivers

One major difference between invoking a method and calling a function is in the treatment of `null` references. If we have a reference that is `null`, we can't send a message to it, because there is nothing to send a message to—the JVM throws a `NullPointerException` if we try. In contrast, we are able to have `null` *parameters*. We may not know what to do with them, but they don't prevent the runtime from finding code to invoke.

Because the receiver in an extension function is actually a parameter, it *can* be `null`. So while `anObject.method()` and `anObject.extensionFunction()` look like equivalent calls, `method` can never be called if `anObject` is `null`, whereas `extensionFunction` can be called with `null`, if the receiver is nullable.

We could use this to extract out the steps that generate the reminder in the previous pipeline, into an extension on `Trip?`:

```
fun Trip?.reminderAt(currentTime: ZonedDateTime): String? =
    this?.timeUntilDeparture(currentTime)
        ?.toUserFriendlyText()
        ?.plus(" until your next trip!")
```

Note that we have to use the safe-call operator to dereference `this` inside the extension. Although `this` is never `null` inside a method, it can be inside an extension of a nullable type. A `null` `this` can be surprising if you're coming from Java, where it can never happen, but for extensions, Kotlin treats `this` as just another nullable parameter.

We can call this function on a nullable `Trip` without the noise of the `?.`:

```
val reminder: String? = customer.nextTrip().reminderAt(currentTime)
```

On the other hand, we've made the flow of nullability in the calling function harder to understand, because although type-checked, it is not visible in the code of the pipelines that calls the extension.

`Trip?.reminderAt` has another, more obtrusive, drawback: the return type is always the nullable `String?` even if called on a nonnullable `Trip`. In that case we will find ourselves writing code like:

```
val trip: Trip = ...
val reminder: String = trip.reminderAt(currentTime) ?: error("Should never happen")
```

This a bug waiting to happen when code around it changes, because we've made it impossible for the type checker to detect an incompatible change.

Don't write extensions on nullable types that return `null` if the receiver is `null`. Write an extension on the nonnullable type and use the safe-call operator to invoke it.

Extensions on nullable types can be useful though, when they return a nonnullable result. They act as an escape route from the realm of nullable values back to the realm of nonnullable values, terminating a pipeline of safe calls. For example, we can make the reminderAt extension return some meaningful text even when the customer doesn't have a next trip:

```
fun Trip?.reminderAt(currentTime: ZonedDateTime): String =
    this?.timeUntilDeparture(currentTime)
        ?.toUserFriendlyText()
        ?.plus(" until your next trip!")
        ?: "Start planning your next trip.  The world's your oyster!"
```

Similarly, here are two extension functions that we probably should have introduced in Chapter 4. The first is defined on any nullable type, but always returns a nonnull result:

```
fun <T : Any> T?.asOptional(): Optional<T> = Optional.ofNullable(this)
fun <T : Any> Optional<T>.asNullable(): T? = this.orElse(null)
```

This neatly brings up the subject of generic extensions.

Generics

Just as with normal functions, extensions can have generic parameters, and things become really interesting when the receiver is generic.

Here's a useful extension function that for some reason isn't part of the standard library. It is defined as an extension on any type, including null references:

```
fun <T> T.printed(): T = this.also(::println)
```

We can use this when we want to debug the value of an expression in place. For example, remember this:

```
val marketingLength = jsonNode.toCustomer().nameForMarketing().length
```

If we need to see the value of the customer for debugging, we would normally need to pull out a variable:

```
val customer = jsonNode.toCustomer()
println(customer)
val marketingLength = customer.nameForMarketing().length
```

With printed, we have a function that prints the value of the receiver and returns it unchanged, so that we can write:

```
val marketingLength = jsonNode.toCustomer().printed().nameForMarketing().length
```

which is much less disruption and easy to search for before we check in.

Note that even if we had been able to add a method to Any?, there is no way for a method to say that it returns the same type as its receiver. Had we written:

```
class Any {
    fun printed() = this.also(::println)
}
```

the return type would have been `Any`, so we could not then invoke `nameForMarketing()` etc. on the result.

We can also define extension functions for specialized generic types, for example, `Iterable<Customer>`:

```
fun Iterable<Customer>.familyNames(): Set<String> =
    this.map(Customer::familyName).toSet()
```

This extension function is applicable to any `Collection<Customer>` but not to collections of other types. This allows us to use collections to represent domain concepts rather than defining our own types, as we will see in Chapter 15. We can also extract parts of collections pipelines into named operations; see "Extracting Part of a Pipeline" on page 188.

Extension Functions as Methods

We normally define extension functions as top-level functions. They can, though, be defined *inside* a class definition. In this case they can access the members of their own class and *extend* another type:

```
class JsonWriter(
    private val objectMapper: ObjectMapper,
) {
    fun Customer.toJson(): JsonNode = objectMapper.valueToTree(this)
}
```

Here `Customer.toJson` has access to two values of `this`. It can refer to the `Customer` receiver of the extension function or the `JsonWriter` instance of the method. In longhand, the function is:

```
fun Customer.toJson(): JsonNode =
    this@JsonWriter.objectMapper.valueToTree(this@toJson)
```

This isn't a technique that we should use too often (it can be hard to interpret which receiver applies without IDE assistance), but it can simplify code by allowing the simple left-to-right reading of extension functions while hiding details that would complicate things. In particular, it allows DSLs to hide details (like the `ObjectMapper`) that clients shouldn't be bothered by.

Refactoring to Extension Functions

The actual mechanics of converting a static method to an extension function are simple, but we have to hone a sense for where an extension function will make things better. Let's work our way through a part of Travelator and see how we do.

Those clever people in marketing have come up with a spreadsheet that gives customers a score according to how valuable they are to the company: their expected future spending. They're constantly tweaking the algorithm, so they don't want us to automate that. Instead, they export a tab-separated file of customer data, score, and spend, and we produce a summary report from that file. Here are our tests:

```
class HighValueCustomersReportTests {

    @Test
    public void test() throws IOException {
        List<String> input = List.of(
            "ID\tFirstName\tLastName\tScore\tSpend",
            "1\tFred\tFlintstone\t11\t1000.00",
            "4\tBetty\tRubble\t10\t2000.00",
            "2\tBarney\tRubble\t0\t20.00",
            "3\tWilma\tFlintstone\t9\t0.00"
        );
        List<String> expected = List.of(
            "ID\tName\tSpend",
            "4\tRUBBLE, Betty\t2000.00",
            "1\tFLINTSTONE, Fred\t1000.00",
            "\tTOTAL\t3000.00"
        );
        check(input, expected);
    }

    @Test
    public void emptyTest() throws IOException {
        List<String> input = List.of(
            "ID\tFirstName\tLastName\tScore\tSpend"
        );
        List<String> expected = List.of(
            "ID\tName\tSpend",
            "\tTOTAL\t0.00"
        );
        check(input, expected);
    }

    @Test
    public void emptySpendIs0() {
        assertEquals(
            new CustomerData("1", "Fred", "Flintstone", 0, 0D),
            HighValueCustomersReport.customerDataFrom("1\tFred\tFlintstone\t0")
        );
    }

    private void check(
        List<String> inputLines,
        List<String> expectedLines
    ) throws IOException {
        var output = new StringWriter();
        HighValueCustomersReport.generate(
            new StringReader(String.join("\n", inputLines)),
            output
```

```
        );
        assertEquals(String.join("\n", expectedLines), output.toString());
    }
}
```

Example 10.1 [extensions.0:src/test/java/travelator/marketing/HighValueCustomersReportTests.java]

You can see that we haven't gone to town on these, because the people in marketing do have a habit of changing their minds, but in essence the report needs to list the customers who have a score of 10 or more, sorted by spend, with a final total line.

Here is the code:

```
public class HighValueCustomersReport {

    public static void generate(Reader reader, Writer writer) throws IOException {
        List<CustomerData> valuableCustomers = new BufferedReader(reader).lines()
            .skip(1) // header
            .map(line -> customerDataFrom(line))
            .filter(customerData -> customerData.score >= 10)
            .sorted(comparing(customerData -> customerData.score))
            .collect(toList());

        writer.append("ID\tName\tSpend\n");
        for (var customerData: valuableCustomers) {
            writer.append(lineFor(customerData)).append("\n");
        }
        writer.append(summaryFor(valuableCustomers));
    }

    private static String summaryFor(List<CustomerData> valuableCustomers) {
        var total = valuableCustomers.stream()
            .mapToDouble(customerData -> customerData.spend)
            .sum();
        return "\tTOTAL\t" + formatMoney(total);
    }

    static CustomerData customerDataFrom(String line) {
        var parts = line.split("\t");
        double spend = parts.length == 4 ? 0 :
            Double.parseDouble(parts[4]);
        return new CustomerData(
            parts[0],
            parts[1],
            parts[2],
            Integer.parseInt(parts[3]),
            spend
        );
    }

    private static String lineFor(CustomerData customer) {
        return customer.id + "\t" + marketingNameFor(customer) + "\t" +
            formatMoney(customer.spend);
```

```
    }

    private static String formatMoney(double money) {
        return String.format("%#.2f", money);
    }

    private static String marketingNameFor(CustomerData customer) {
        return customer.familyName.toUpperCase() + ", " + customer.givenName;
    }
}
```

Example 10.2 [extensions.0:src/main/java/travelator/marketing/HighValueCustomersReport.java]

You can see that this is already quite a functional (as opposed to object-oriented) expression of the solution. This will make it easy to convert to top-level functions, and top-level functions are easy to convert to extension functions.

But first, here is `CustomerData`:

```
public class CustomerData {
    public final String id;
    public final String givenName;
    public final String familyName;
    public final int score;
    public final double spend;

    public CustomerData(
        String id,
        String givenName,
        String familyName,
        int score,
        double spend
    ) {
        this.id = id;
        this.givenName = givenName;
        this.familyName = familyName;
        this.score = score;
        this.spend = spend;
    }

    ... and equals and hashcode
}
```

Example 10.3 [extensions.0:src/main/java/travelator/marketing/CustomerData.java]

This isn't trying to represent everything about a customer, just the data we care about for this report, which is why whoever wrote it just used fields. (Chapter 11 discusses this trade-off.) I doubt we (erm, whoever wrote it) would even have bothered with `equals` and `hashCode` had it not been for the `emptySpendIs0` test. That `double` for spend looks suspicious too, but it hasn't caused us any problems yet, so we'll suspend our disbelief and just convert the whole thing to a Kotlin data class (see Chapter 5) before we go on.

Normally, that would be a really simple job because of the excellent interop, but it turns out that (at the time of writing) the converter cannot believe that anyone would stoop to raw field access. So it doesn't update Java that accesses, for example, `customerData.score` to call `customerData.getScore()` (the Kotlin property), resulting in a slew of compile failures. Rather than fixing those, we revert, and use the "Encapsulate Fields" refactor to convert all the fields and field accesses in `Customer` to getters:

```
public class CustomerData {
    private final String id;
    private final String givenName;
    private final String familyName;
    private final int score;
    private final double spend;

    ...

    public String getId() {
        return id;
    }

    public String getGivenName() {
        return givenName;
    }
    ...
}
```

Example 10.4 [extensions.1:src/main/java/travelator/marketing/CustomerData.java]

The refactoring has also updated the client code to call the getters:

```
private static String lineFor(CustomerData customer) {
    return customer.getId() + "\t" + marketingNameFor(customer) + "\t" +
        formatMoney(customer.getSpend());
}
```

Example 10.5 [extensions.1:src/main/java/travelator/marketing/HighValueCustomersReport.java]

The getters allow us to convert `CustomerData` to a Kotlin data class without breaking the Java. "Convert Java File to Kotlin File", followed by adding the `data` modifier and deleting the `equals` and `hashCode` overrides, gives us:

```
data class CustomerData(
    val id: String,
    val givenName: String,
    val familyName: String,
    val score: Int,
    val spend: Double
)
```

Example 10.6 [extensions.2:src/main/java/travelator/marketing/CustomerData.kt]

Now we can go ahead and convert `HighValueCustomerReport` to Kotlin, too; it's entirely self-contained. That doesn't go brilliantly, because `customerDataFrom` doesn't compile after the conversion:

```
object HighValueCustomersReport {
    ...
    @JvmStatic
    fun customerDataFrom(line: String): CustomerData {
        val parts = line.split("\t".toRegex()).toTypedArray()
        val spend: Double = if (parts.size == 4) 0 else parts[4].toDouble() ❶
        return CustomerData(
            parts[0],
            parts[1],
            parts[2], parts[3].toInt(), ❷
            spend
        )
    }
    ...
}
```

Example 10.7 [extensions.3:src/main/java/travelator/marketing/HighValueCustomersReport.kt]

❶ `The integer literal does not conform to the expected type Double.`

❷ Odd formatting.

The converter hasn't been smart enough to know that Kotlin doesn't coerce the integer 0 to double, leading to a compile error. Let's help IntelliJ out by clicking the error and Alt-Entering to fix it, in the hope that it will return the favor when the machines rule the world. After a reformat, this gives us:

```
object HighValueCustomersReport {
    ...
    @JvmStatic
    fun customerDataFrom(line: String): CustomerData {
        val parts = line.split("\t".toRegex()).toTypedArray()
        val spend: Double = if (parts.size == 4) 0.0 else parts[4].toDouble()
        return CustomerData(
            parts[0],
            parts[1],
            parts[2],
            parts[3].toInt(),
            spend
        )
    }
    ...
}
```

Example 10.8 [extensions.4:src/main/java/travelator/marketing/HighValueCustomersReport.kt]

As we discussed in Chapter 8, the conversion has placed the functions into an `object HighValueCustomersReport` so that Java code can still find them. If we try to convert them to top-level functions using the techniques in that chapter, we find that dependencies between the methods mean that the code doesn't compile at times. We can solve the problem either by moving the private methods first or by just ignoring the compiler until the `HighValueCustomersReport` is emptied and removed.

```
package travelator.marketing

...

@Throws(IOException::class)
fun generate(reader: Reader?, writer: Writer) {
    val valuableCustomers = BufferedReader(reader).lines()
        .skip(1) // header
        .map { line: String -> customerDataFrom(line) }
        .filter { (_, _, _, score) -> score >= 10 }
        .sorted(Comparator.comparing { (_, _, _, score) -> score })
        .collect(Collectors.toList())
    writer.append("ID\tName\tSpend\n")
    for (customerData in valuableCustomers) {
        writer.append(lineFor(customerData)).append("\n")
    }
    writer.append(summaryFor(valuableCustomers))
}

private fun summaryFor(valuableCustomers: List<CustomerData>): String {
    val total = valuableCustomers.stream()
        .mapToDouble { (_, _, _, _, spend) -> spend }
        .sum()
    return "\tTOTAL\t" + formatMoney(total)
}

fun customerDataFrom(line: String): CustomerData {
    val parts = line.split("\t".toRegex()).toTypedArray()
    val spend: Double = if (parts.size == 4) 0.0 else parts[4].toDouble()
    return CustomerData(
        parts[0],
        parts[1],
        parts[2],
        parts[3].toInt(),
        spend
    )
}

private fun lineFor(customer: CustomerData): String {
    return customer.id + "\t" + marketingNameFor(customer) + "\t" +
        formatMoney(customer.spend)
}

private fun formatMoney(money: Double): String {
    return String.format("%#.2f", money)
}
```

```
private fun marketingNameFor(customer: CustomerData): String {
    return customer.familyName.toUpperCase() + ", " + customer.givenName
}
```

Example 10.9 [extensions.5:src/main/java/travelator/marketing/HighValueCustomersReport.kt]

OK, it's time to look for places where extension functions can improve the code. At the end is the `marketingNameFor` that we saw (a slightly different version of) earlier. If we Alt-Enter on the `customer` parameter, IntelliJ will offer to "Convert parameter to receiver". This gives:

```
private fun lineFor(customer: CustomerData): String {
    return customer.id + "\t" + customer.marketingNameFor() + "\t" +
        formatMoney(customer.spend)
}

...
private fun CustomerData.marketingNameFor(): String {
    return familyName.toUpperCase() + ", " + givenName
}
```

Example 10.10 [extensions.6:src/main/java/travelator/marketing/HighValueCustomersReport.kt]

That `For` in `marketingNameFor` is confusing now that we've moved the parameter to be the receiver, because the `For` doesn't have a subject. Let's "Convert function to property" named `marketingName` (Chapter 11 explains how and why) and then "Convert to expression body". Oh, and "Convert concatenation to template" on both strings! Phew, that flurry of Alt-Entering gives:

```
private fun lineFor(customer: CustomerData): String =
    "${customer.id}\t${customer.marketingName}\t${formatMoney(customer.spend)}"

private fun formatMoney(money: Double): String {
    return String.format("%#.2f", money)
}

private val CustomerData.marketingName: String
    get() = "${familyName.toUpperCase()}, $givenName"
```

Example 10.11 [extensions.7:src/main/java/travelator/marketing/HighValueCustomersReport.kt]

Now `formatMoney` is letting us down, so again we can "Convert parameter to receiver", rename to `toMoneyString`, and "Convert to expression body":

```
private fun lineFor(customer: CustomerData): String =
    "${customer.id}\t${customer.marketingName}\t${customer.spend.toMoneyString()}"

private fun Double.toMoneyString() = String.format("%#.2f", this)
```

Example 10.12 [extensions.8:src/main/java/travelator/marketing/HighValueCustomersReport.kt]

The `String.format` rankles a bit. Kotlin would allow us to write `"%#.2f".format(this)`, but we prefer swapping the parameter and receiver to give:

```
private fun Double.toMoneyString() = this.formattedAs("%#.2f")

private fun Double.formattedAs(format: String) = String.format(format, this)
```

Example 10.13 [extensions.9:src/main/java/travelator/marketing/HighValueCustomersReport.kt]

`Double.formattedAs` is the first extension function we've written that had a parameter as well as its receiver. That's because the others have been very specific conversions, but this one is more general. While we're thinking general, `formattedAs` can equally well apply to any type, including `null`, so we can upgrade it to:

```
private fun Any?.formattedAs(format: String) = String.format(format, this)
```

Example 10.14 [extensions.10:src/main/java/travelator/marketing/HighValueCustomersReport.kt]

It now feels like a good candidate for moving into our library of generally useful Kotlin functions.

Next, `customerDataFrom` is in our sights. It is currently:

```
fun customerDataFrom(line: String): CustomerData {
    val parts = line.split("\t".toRegex()).toTypedArray()
    val spend: Double = if (parts.size == 4) 0.0 else parts[4].toDouble()
    return CustomerData(
        parts[0],
        parts[1],
        parts[2],
        parts[3].toInt(),
        spend
    )
}
```

Example 10.15 [extensions.11:src/main/java/travelator/marketing/HighValueCustomersReport.kt]

Before we go on, let's observe that `CharSequence.split()`, `String.toRegex()`, `Collection<T>.toTypedArray()`, `String.toDouble()`, and `String.toInt()` are all extension functions provided by the Kotlin standard library.

There's a lot we can tidy up before we address the signature of `customerDataFrom`. Kotlin has a `CharSequence.split(delimiters)` that we can use in place of the regex. Then we can inline `spend`, followed by Alt-Enter and "Add names to call arguments" to help make sense of the constructor call:

```
fun customerDataFrom(line: String): CustomerData {
    val parts = line.split("\t")
    return CustomerData(
        id = parts[0],
        givenName = parts[1],
        familyName = parts[2],
        score = parts[3].toInt(),
        spend = if (parts.size == 4) 0.0 else parts[4].toDouble()
    )
}
```

Example 10.16 [extensions.12:src/main/java/travelator/marketing/HighValueCustomersReport.kt]

Chapter 9 argues in favor of single-expression functions. This certainly doesn't *need* to be a single expression, but let's practice anyway:

```
fun customerDataFrom(line: String): CustomerData =
    line.split("\t").let { parts ->
        CustomerData(
            id = parts[0],
            givenName = parts[1],
            familyName = parts[2],
            score = parts[3].toInt(),
            spend = if (parts.size == 4) 0.0 else parts[4].toDouble()
        )
    }
```

Example 10.17 [extensions.13:src/main/java/travelator/marketing/HighValueCustomersReport.kt]

At last, we can get around to converting to an extension function. Again we change the name (to `toCustomerData`) to make sense at the call site:

```
fun String.toCustomerData(): CustomerData =
    split("\t").let { parts ->
        CustomerData(
            id = parts[0],
            givenName = parts[1],
            familyName = parts[2],
            score = parts[3].toInt(),
            spend = if (parts.size == 4) 0.0 else parts[4].toDouble()
        )
    }
```

Example 10.18 [extensions.14:src/main/java/travelator/marketing/HighValueCustomersReport.kt]

Note that the Java in our tests can still call this as a static method:

```
@Test
public void emptySpendIs0() {
    assertEquals(
        new CustomerData("1", "Fred", "Flintstone", 0, 0D),
        HighValueCustomersReportKt.toCustomerData("1\tFred\tFlintstone\t0")
    );
}
```

Example 10.19 [extensions.14:src/test/java/travelator/marketing/HighValueCustomersReportTests.java]

Now let's address `summaryFor`:

```
private fun summaryFor(valuableCustomers: List<CustomerData>): String {
    val total = valuableCustomers.stream()
        .mapToDouble { (_, _, _, _, spend) -> spend }
        .sum()
    return "\tTOTAL\t" + total.toMoneyString()
}
```

Example 10.20 [extensions.15:src/main/java/travelator/marketing/HighValueCustomersReport.kt]

That destructuring is odd, but we can get rid of it by hand-converting the stream to Kotlin. This isn't a thing IntelliJ can do when we wrote this, but we give guidance in Chapter 13. We'll remove the string concatenation while we're there:

```
private fun summaryFor(valuableCustomers: List<CustomerData>): String {
    val total = valuableCustomers.sumByDouble { it.spend }
    return "\tTOTAL\t${total.toMoneyString()}"
}
```

Example 10.21 [extensions.16:src/main/java/travelator/marketing/HighValueCustomersReport.kt]

Now the familiar combination of converting to an appropriately named single-expression extension function:

```
private fun List<CustomerData>.summarised(): String =
    sumByDouble { it.spend }.let { total ->
        "\tTOTAL\t${total.toMoneyString()}"
    }
```

Example 10.22 [extensions.17:src/main/java/travelator/marketing/HighValueCustomersReport.kt]

At this stage, only `generate` is left unimproved:

```
@Throws(IOException::class)
fun generate(reader: Reader?, writer: Writer) {
    val valuableCustomers = BufferedReader(reader).lines()
        .skip(1) // header
        .map { line: String -> line.toCustomerData() }
        .filter { (_, _, _, score) -> score >= 10 }
        .sorted(Comparator.comparing { (_, _, _, score) -> score })
        .collect(Collectors.toList())
    writer.append("ID\tName\tSpend\n")
    for (customerData in valuableCustomers) {
        writer.append(lineFor(customerData)).append("\n")
    }
    writer.append(valuableCustomers.summarised())
}
```

Example 10.23 [extensions.18:src/main/java/travelator/marketing/HighValueCustomersReport.kt]

Again, we currently have to convert Java streams to Kotlin list operations by hand:

```
@Throws(IOException::class)
fun generate(reader: Reader, writer: Writer) {
    val valuableCustomers = reader.readLines()
        .drop(1) // header
        .map(String::toCustomerData)
        .filter { it.score >= 10 }
        .sortedBy(CustomerData::score)
    writer.append("ID\tName\tSpend\n")
    for (customerData in valuableCustomers) {
        writer.append(lineFor(customerData)).append("\n")
    }
```

```
        writer.append(valuableCustomers.summarised())
    }
```

Example 10.24 [extensions.19:src/main/java/travelator/marketing/HighValueCustomersReport.kt]

`Appendable.appendLine()` is another extension function that allows us to simplify the output stage:

```
@Throws(IOException::class)
fun generate(reader: Reader, writer: Writer) {
    val valuableCustomers = reader.readLines()
        .drop(1) // header
        .map(String::toCustomerData)
        .filter { it.score >= 10 }
        .sortedBy(CustomerData::score)
    writer.appendLine("ID\tName\tSpend")
    for (customerData in valuableCustomers) {
        writer.appendLine(lineFor(customerData))
    }
    writer.append(valuableCustomers.summarised())
}
```

Example 10.25 [extensions.20:src/main/java/travelator/marketing/HighValueCustomersReport.kt]

It feels like we should be able to remove that `// header` comment by extracting a function. "Extracting Part of a Pipeline" on page 188 details how to extract a function from a chain, but look at what happens when we try that technique but don't convert `withoutHeader` to an extension function:

```
@Throws(IOException::class)
fun generate(reader: Reader, writer: Writer) {
    val valuableCustomers = withoutHeader(reader.readLines())
        .map(String::toCustomerData)
        .filter { it.score >= 10 }
        .sortedBy(CustomerData::score)
    writer.appendLine("ID\tName\tSpend")
    for (customerData in valuableCustomers) {
        writer.appendLine(lineFor(customerData))
    }
    writer.append(valuableCustomers.summarised())
}

private fun withoutHeader(list: List<String>) = list.drop(1)
```

Example 10.26 [extensions.21:src/main/java/travelator/marketing/HighValueCustomersReport.kt]

We've lost the nice pipeline flow from left to right, top to bottom: `withoutHeader` comes before the `readLines` in the text but after it in execution order. Alt-Enter on the `list` parameter in `withoutHeader` and "Convert Parameter to Receiver" restores the flow:

```
@Throws(IOException::class)
fun generate(reader: Reader, writer: Writer) {
    val valuableCustomers = reader.readLines()
```

```
            .withoutHeader()
            .map(String::toCustomerData)
            .filter { it.score >= 10 }
            .sortedBy(CustomerData::score)
        writer.appendLine("ID\tName\tSpend")
        for (customerData in valuableCustomers) {
            writer.appendLine(lineFor(customerData))
        }
        writer.append(valuableCustomers.summarised())
}

private fun List<String>.withoutHeader() = drop(1)
```

Example 10.27 [extensions.22:src/main/java/travelator/marketing/HighValueCustomersReport.kt]

We can make this even more expressive with two more extensions, `List<String>.toValuableCustomers()` and `CustomerData.outputLine`:

```
@Throws(IOException::class)
fun generate(reader: Reader, writer: Writer) {
    val valuableCustomers = reader
        .readLines()
        .toValuableCustomers()
        .sortedBy(CustomerData::score)
    writer.appendLine("ID\tName\tSpend")
    for (customerData in valuableCustomers) {
        writer.appendLine(customerData.outputLine)
    }
    writer.append(valuableCustomers.summarised())
}

private fun List<String>.toValuableCustomers() = withoutHeader()
    .map(String::toCustomerData)
    .filter { it.score >= 10 }
...

private val CustomerData.outputLine: String
    get() = "$id\t$marketingName\t${spend.toMoneyString()}"
```

Example 10.28 [extensions.23:src/main/java/travelator/marketing/HighValueCustomersReport.kt]

This still isn't quite as sweet as we might like, but we've proved the point of extension functions. Chapters 20 and 21 will complete this refactoring. In the meantime, here's the whole file:

```
@Throws(IOException::class)
fun generate(reader: Reader, writer: Writer) {
    val valuableCustomers = reader
        .readLines()
        .toValuableCustomers()
        .sortedBy(CustomerData::score)
    writer.appendLine("ID\tName\tSpend")
    for (customerData in valuableCustomers) {
        writer.appendLine(customerData.outputLine)
```

```
    }
    writer.append(valuableCustomers.summarised())
}

private fun List<String>.toValuableCustomers() = withoutHeader()
    .map(String::toCustomerData)
    .filter { it.score >= 10 }

private fun List<String>.withoutHeader() = drop(1)

private fun List<CustomerData>.summarised(): String =
    sumByDouble { it.spend }.let { total ->
        "\tTOTAL\t${total.toMoneyString()}"
    }

internal fun String.toCustomerData(): CustomerData =
    split("\t").let { parts ->
        CustomerData(
            id = parts[0],
            givenName = parts[1],
            familyName = parts[2],
            score = parts[3].toInt(),
            spend = if (parts.size == 4) 0.0 else parts[4].toDouble()
        )
    }


private val CustomerData.outputLine: String
    get() = "$id\t$marketingName\t${spend.toMoneyString()}"

private fun Double.toMoneyString() = this.formattedAs("%#.2f")

private fun Any?.formattedAs(format: String) = String.format(format, this)

private val CustomerData.marketingName: String
    get() = "${familyName.toUpperCase()}, $givenName"
```

Example 10.29 [extensions.23:src/main/java/travelator/marketing/HighValueCustomersReport.kt]

Note that every function except the entry point is a single-expression extension function. We haven't made `generate` an extension function because there isn't a natural parameter to make the receiver; it doesn't feel like a natural operation on `Reader` or `Writer`. That may change when we continue refactoring this code in Chapter 20. Let's see, shall we?

Moving On

Extension functions and properties are the unsung heroes of the Kotlin language. Their canonical use is to add operations to types we cannot modify ourselves.

However, Kotlin language features and tooling combine to encourage us—quite insistently—to write extension functions for our *own* types as well. Kotlin's safe call operator makes it more convenient to call an extension function through a potentially null reference than to pass the reference to a function as a parameter when it is non-null. The type of a freestanding generic extension can express relationships between the receiver and its result that cannot be expressed by open methods. Autocompletion in IntelliJ includes extension functions along with the methods that can call on a value, but it does not show you functions that you can pass the value to as a parameter.

As a result, extension functions allow us to write code that is more easily discovered, understood, and maintained. Many of the other techniques presented in this book build on extension functions, as we will see in Chapter 15, *Encapsulated Collections to Type Aliases*, Chapter 18, *Open to Sealed Classes*, and others.

CHAPTER 11
Methods to Properties

Java does not distinguish between property access methods and other types. Kotlin, on the other hand, treats properties differently than member functions. When should we prefer a computed property to a function returning a result?

Fields, Accessors, and Properties

Most programming languages allow us to group data together in some way, giving names (and often types) to the properties of a composite.

Here, for example, is a *record*, composed of three *fields*, in ALGOL W, one of the first general-purpose languages to support record types. (ALGOL W was also the language in which Tony Hoare introduced null references.)

```
RECORD PERSON (
    STRING(20) NAME;
    INTEGER AGE;
    LOGICAL MALE;
);
```

Things were different then: real programmers only had CAPITAL LETTERS, and gender was a Boolean.

In ALGOL W, we can (well OK, could) update the age held in a `PERSON` record:

```
AGE(WILMA) := AGE(WILMA) + 1;
```

In this case the compiler will emit the instructions to reach into the memory of the record, find the bytes representing Wilma's age, and increment it. Records, also known as *structs* (for structure) in other languages, are a convenience for grouping related data. There is no information hiding here, just composition.

Most early object-oriented systems (C++ in particular) were based on this record mechanism. Instance variables were simply record fields, and methods (aka member functions) were fields holding pointers to functions. Smalltalk was different. Smalltalk objects can have instance variables, but access to this state is by sending a message to the object asking for the value. Messages, not fields, is the fundamental abstraction.

The Java implementers took a little of each approach. Objects can have public fields, but clients can't just reach into their memory to retrieve them; they have to call bytecode instructions to access their values. This allows us to treat classes as records while allowing the runtime to enforce private field access.

Although direct access to fields was *permitted*, from the outset it was discouraged. We can't change the internal representation of data if clients access fields directly, at least not without changing those clients too. We also cannot maintain any invariant relationships between fields if clients can mutate them directly, and as we've seen in Chapter 5, in those days objects were all about mutation. Fields access is also not polymorphic, so subclasses cannot change their implementation. In those days, objects were all about the subclassing too.

So instead of direct field access in Java, we usually write *accessor* methods: getters and (if need be) setters. Getters usually do nothing except return the value of a field, but they may instead compute a value from other fields. Setters may maintain invariants or fire events as well as update a field or, perhaps, more than one field.

Sometimes, though, data is just data. When it is, then direct access to public fields may be fine, especially when we have immutable values (which is to say, final fields of immutable types). For more complicated models, polymorphic behavior and/or a uniform way of accessing values from either a field or a calculation become useful, and accessor methods come into their own.

The Kotlin designers choose to take the decision away from us and only support accessor methods. The language doesn't support giving direct access to fields. Kotlin will generate code to access public fields of Java classes but does not define public fields itself. (A special annotation, `@JvmField`, provides a back door if you really need it.) They did this to encourage us to use accessors so that we can change representations without affecting clients.

To encourage accessors further, Kotlin allows us to generate both a private member-variable and an accessor in a single *property* declaration.

So in Java we can give access to a field directly:

```
public class PersonWithPublicFields {
    public final String givenName;
    public final String familyName;
    public final LocalDate dateOfBirth;
```

```
    public PersonWithPublicFields(
        String givenName,
        String familyName,
        LocalDate dateOfBirth
    ) {
        this.givenName = givenName;
        this.familyName = familyName;
        this.dateOfBirth = dateOfBirth;
    }
}
```

Or, we can write our own accessor:

```
public class PersonWithAccessors {
    private final String givenName;
    private final String familyName;
    private final LocalDate dateOfBirth;


    public PersonWithAccessors(
        ...
    }

    public String getGivenName() {
        return givenName;
    }

    public String getFamilyName() {
        return familyName;
    }

    ...
}
```

In Kotlin, we only have properties:

```
data class PersonWithProperties(
    val givenName: String,
    val familyName: String,
    val dateOfBirth: LocalDate
) {
}
```

This declaration will generate private fields: `givenName`, `familyName`, and `dateOfBirth`, accessor methods `getGivenName()` and so on, and a constructor to initialize all the fields.

In Java, we can access (visible) fields directly or call accessors:

```
public static String accessField(PersonWithPublicFields person) {
    return person.givenName;
}
```

```
public static String callAccessor(PersonWithAccessors person) {
    return person.getGivenName();
}

public static String callKotlinAccessor(PersonWithProperties person) {
    return person.getGivenName();
}
```

In Kotlin, we can access visible fields (from Java classes) directly or call accessors as if they were fields:

```
fun accessField(person: PersonWithPublicFields): String =
    person.givenName

fun callAccessor(person: PersonWithAccessors): String =
    person.givenName

fun callKotlinAccessor(person: PersonWithProperties): String =
    person.givenName
```

Properties are a convenience backed by some compiler magic. They make it as simple to use fields and accessors in Kotlin as plain old fields in Java, so we will naturally write code that can take advantage of encapsulation. For example, we might find that we want to define a property in an interface or compute a property that we previously stored.

Computed properties are those not backed by a field. If we have `givenName` and `familyName` backed by fields, there is no need to store `fullName`; we can compute it when we need it:

```
public class PersonWithPublicFields {
    public final String givenName;
    public final String familyName;
    public final LocalDate dateOfBirth;

    public PersonWithPublicFields(
        ...
    }

    public String getFullName() {
        return givenName + " " + familyName;
    }
}
```

If we use direct-field access in Java, there is now a difference between the way we access the stored and computed properties:

```
public static String fieldAndAccessor(PersonWithPublicFields person) {
    return
        person.givenName + " " +
        person.getFullName();
}
```

This isn't the case in Kotlin, even when accessing the Java fields and methods, which is nice:

```
fun fieldAndAccessor(person: PersonWithPublicFields) =
    person.givenName + " " +
    person.fullName
```

In Kotlin, we define computed properties outside the constructor:

```
data class PersonWithProperties(
    val givenName: String,
    val familyName: String,
    val dateOfBirth: LocalDate
) {
    val fullName get() = "$givenName $familyName"
}
```

So, in Java, we *can* define classes that give direct access to fields, but *should* generally use accessors, which are just methods named (by convention but not always) with a `get` or `set` prefix. In Kotlin, we cannot define fields and accessors separately. When we define a property in Kotlin, the compiler generates a field and accessors that follow the Java naming convention. When we refer to a property in Kotlin, the syntax is the same as Java's syntax for field access, but the compiler generates a call to the accessor. This even applies across the interop boundary: when we refer to properties of Java objects, the compiler will generate a call to the accessor if one exists and follows the Java naming convention.

How to Choose

Returning to the question at the beginning of the chapter: given that computed properties are just methods with sugar on top, when should we choose a computed property, and when should we choose a method?

A good rule of thumb is to use a property when it depends only on other properties on the type and is cheap to compute. This applies to `fullName`, so that is a good computed property. What about a person's age?

We can compute age easily (ignoring time zones) from the `dateOfBirth` property, so we might be tempted in Java to write `fred.getAge()`. But this doesn't depend only on other properties, it also depends on when we call it. Unlikely though it is, `fred.age == fred.age` can return `false`.

Age is an action ("Actions" on page 79); its result depends on when it is called. Properties should be calculations ("Calculations" on page 78), timeless and dependent only on their inputs, in this case the `dateOfBirth` property. Hence `age()` should be a function, not a property:

```
data class PersonWithProperties(
    val givenName: String,
```

```
    val familyName: String,
    val dateOfBirth: LocalDate
) {
    fun age() = Period.between(dateOfBirth, LocalDate.now()).years
}
```

What about a cryptographic hash of all the other properties of the object? This is a calculation (for immutable objects), but if it is expensive to compute, it should be a method `hash()` not a property `hash`. We might even want to hint at the cost of the method in its name:

```
data class PersonWithProperties(
    val givenName: String,
    val familyName: String,
    val dateOfBirth: LocalDate
) {
    fun computeHash(): ByteArray =
        someSlowHashOf(givenName, familyName, dateOfBirth.toString())
}
```

We could make a property by calculating it up front and storing it in a field:

```
data class PersonWithProperties(
    val givenName: String,
    val familyName: String,
    val dateOfBirth: LocalDate
) {
    val hash: ByteArray =
        someSlowHashOf(givenName, familyName, dateOfBirth.toString())
}
```

This has the disadvantage of making every instance slow to create, whether or not its `hash` is ever accessed. We might split the difference with a lazy property:

```
data class PersonWithProperties(
    val givenName: String,
    val familyName: String,
    val dateOfBirth: LocalDate
) {
    val hash: ByteArray by lazy {
        someSlowHashOf(givenName, familyName, dateOfBirth.toString())
    }
}
```

In a limited scope this would be fine, but if the class was more widely used, we should at least hint at the potential first-invocation performance issue by hiding the computed property behind a function:

```
data class PersonWithProperties(
    val givenName: String,
    val familyName: String,
    val dateOfBirth: LocalDate
) {
```

```
        private val hash: ByteArray by lazy {
            someSlowHashOf(givenName, familyName, dateOfBirth.toString())
        }
        fun hash() = hash
    }
```

In this case, we might consider an extension property. As we saw in Chapter 10, though, extension properties can only be computed rather than backed by a field and so cannot be lazy. Apart from that, most of the discussion here also applies to extension functions versus extension properties.

Mutable Properties

So what of mutable properties? Kotlin allows us to define properties as `var`, for variable.

If you've read this far, you'll know that your authors like to keep their data (Chapter 5) and collections (Chapter 6) immutable. We can *imagine* using Kotlin to define a mutable property to integrate with some Java code that required it, but very, very rarely use mutable public properties in practice. We might occasionally define a property that will change over time (to give access to a count, for example), but almost never one that clients can set. In practice, we find that data classes with copy methods work better in almost all situations that might have called for a setter; in fact, we would go as far as to say that allowing `var` properties in data classes was a language design mistake.

Refactoring to Properties

IntelliJ provides excellent refactoring support for converting between Kotlin methods and properties. This is on the one hand simple, because both are simply method calls, and on the other complicated, because Java interop relies on naming conventions to identify accessors. Let's look at an example from Travelator.

Some of our hardier clients like to camp, so we list campsites in the application:

```
public class CampSite {
    private final String id;
    private final String name;
    private final Address address;
    ...

    public CampSite(
        String id,
        String name,
        Address address
        ...
    ) {
        this.id = id;
```

```
        this.name = name;
        this.address = address;
        ...
    }

    public String getId() {
        return id;
    }

    public String getName() {
        return name;
    }

    public String getCountryCode() {
        return address.getCountryCode();
    }

    public String region() {
        return address.getRegion();
    }

    ...
}
```

Example 11.1 [methods-to-properties.0:src/main/java/travelator/CampSite.java]

This is typical of a domain class that has grown over the years. It has lots of properties, some backed by fields like `id` and `name`, and some computed (for low values of compute) like `countryCode` and `region`. Someone ignored bean conventions by naming an accessor `region` rather than `getRegion`, but it is clear to us what they meant.

Here's some code that uses the accessors:

```
public class CampSites {

    public static Set<CampSite> sitesInRegion(
        Set<CampSite> sites,
        String countryISO,
        String region
    ) {
        return sites.stream()
            .filter( campSite ->
                campSite.getCountryCode().equals(countryISO) &&
                    campSite.region().equalsIgnoreCase(region)
            )
            .collect(toUnmodifiableSet());
    }
}
```

Example 11.2 [methods-to-properties.0:src/main/java/travelator/CampSites.java]

Let's convert `Campsite` to Kotlin with IntelliJ (and then make it a data class):

```
data class CampSite(
    val id: String,
    val name: String,
    val address: Address,
    ...
) {
    val countryCode: String
        get() = address.countryCode

    fun region(): String {
        return address.region
    }

    ...
}
```

Example 11.3 [methods-to-properties.1:src/main/java/travelator/CampSite.kt]

Our field-backed properties have become constructor properties, and the computed `countryCode` a computed property. However, IntelliJ has not realized that `region` is a property, because it didn't obey getter naming conventions and has simply converted the method. The net result is that client code doesn't need to change. If we want to correct the oversight, we can Alt-Enter on `region` and "Convert function to property", yielding:

```
val region: String
    get() {
        return address.region
    }
```

Example 11.4 [methods-to-properties.2:src/main/java/travelator/CampSite.kt]

As with most computed properties, this is better as a single expression (see Chapter 9):

```
val region: String get() = address.region
```

Example 11.5 [methods-to-properties.3:src/main/java/travelator/CampSite.kt]

Changing the Kotlin `region` method to a property means that the accessor method will now be named `getRegion`; thankfully, IntelliJ is smart enough to fix up our clients for us:

```
public static Set<CampSite> sitesInRegion(
    Set<CampSite> sites,
    String countryISO,
    String region
) {
    return sites.stream()
        .filter( campSite ->
            campSite.getCountryCode().equals(countryISO) &&
                campSite.getRegion().equalsIgnoreCase(region) ❶
        )
```

```
        .collect(toUnmodifiableSet());
}
```

Example 11.6 [methods-to-properties.3:src/main/java/travelator/CampSites.java]

❶ `campsite.region()` has been replaced by `campsite.getRegion()`.

If we now convert `sitesInRegion` to Kotlin, we get the following:

```
object CampSites {
    fun sitesInRegion(
        sites: Set<CampSite>,
        countryISO: String,
        region: String?
    ): Set<CampSite> {
        return sites.stream()
            .filter { campSite: CampSite ->
                campSite.countryCode == countryISO &&
                    campSite.region.equals(region, ignoreCase = true) ❶
            }
            .collect(Collectors.toUnmodifiableSet())
    }
}
```

Example 11.7 [methods-to-properties.4:src/main/java/travelator/CampSites.kt]

❶ `campsite.getRegion()` is now invoked by `campsite.region`.

We saw how to move `sitesInRegion` to the top level in Chapter 8, and to an extension function in Chapter 10:

```
fun Set<CampSite>.sitesInRegion(
    countryISO: String,
    region: String
): Set<CampSite> {
    return stream()
        .filter { campSite: CampSite ->
            campSite.countryCode == countryISO &&
                campSite.region.equals(region, ignoreCase = true)
        }
        .collect(Collectors.toUnmodifiableSet())
}
```

Example 11.8 [methods-to-properties.5:src/main/java/travelator/CampSites.kt]

Streams to Iterables to Sequences (Chapter 13) and *Multi- to Single-Expression Functions* (Chapter 9) show how to finish the job to:

```
fun Iterable<CampSite>.sitesInRegion(
    countryISO: String,
    region: String
): Set<CampSite> =
    filter { site ->
        site.countryCode == countryISO &&
```

```
            site.region.equals(region, ignoreCase = true)
    }.toSet()
```

Example 11.9 [methods-to-properties.6:src/main/java/travelator/CampSites.kt]

Due to the excellent tooling and interop around methods, accessors, and properties, this has been a mercifully short refactor. So we crave your indulgence while we add just one more tweak.

`sitesInRegion` is a bit of an odd method. It is making up for a deficiency in our modeling, which is that regions are just strings not entities. Without the country code, if we filter just on region name "Hampshire," we risk returning a set of sites, most of which are in an English county, but where one (Moonlight Camping—it sounds lovely) is on a Canadian island. Until we can fix that, what if we pull the filter predicate out into its own method?

```
fun Iterable<CampSite>.sitesInRegion(
    countryISO: String,
    region: String
): Set<CampSite> =
    filter { site ->
        site.isIn(countryISO, region)
    }.toSet()

fun CampSite.isIn(countryISO: String, region: String) =
    countryCode == countryISO &&
        this.region.equals(region, ignoreCase = true)
```

Example 11.10 [methods-to-properties.7:src/main/java/travelator/CampSites.kt]

Now that we have `Campsite.isIn(...)`, maybe `sitesInRegion` could be inlined into the places that call it, because the code is now really quite self-explanatory. We prefer to find and publish the fundamental operations that clients can build on, rather than hiding them inside functions. Pulling on this thread, we might expand the functionality of `isIn` by making `region` optional:

```
fun CampSite.isIn(countryISO: String, region: String? = null) =
    when (region) {
        null -> countryCode == countryISO
        else -> countryCode == countryISO &&
            region.equals(this.region, ignoreCase = true)
    }
```

Example 11.11 [methods-to-properties.8:src/main/java/travelator/CampSites.kt]

Nat prefers the same, but with an Elvis operator:

```
fun CampSite.isIn(countryISO: String, region: String? = null) =
    countryCode == countryISO &&
        region?.equals(this.region, ignoreCase = true) ?: true
```

Example 11.12 [methods-to-properties.9:src/main/java/travelator/CampSites.kt]

Duncan likes a good Elvis but thinks the code is clearer his way. Your team will probably have these little battles (choose Duncan's way).

A fundamental operation like `isIn` might now be promoted to a method (as opposed to an extension function) on `Campsite` or, even better, `Address`. This way, the problem of regions not being entities is confined to the type closest to the problem, and fixing it there will have the least effect on the rest of the codebase.

Moving On

Kotlin provides a convenient syntax for both field-backed and computed properties that allows us to express the difference between accessing a property and calling a function, even if they are the same message-passing mechanism under the hood.

We should prefer a property to a method when it applies to a value type, depends only on the value, and is not expensive to compute. In these cases, refactoring from a method to a property is simple and makes our code easier to understand.

CHAPTER 12
Functions to Operators

If we have a large Java codebase, our Java and Kotlin will have to coexist for some time. What can we do to support the conventions of both languages as we gradually translate the system to Kotlin?

So far, we have shown the translation of code from Java to Kotlin happening all in one go. We have used automatic refactorings to perform the translation safely, but by the end, all the affected code has been converted to idiomatic Kotlin.

In large codebases, this is not always possible. We must continue to evolve features in Java while we are introducing Kotlin. Where there is a boundary between the two, we want to use conventional Java on one side and conventional Kotlin on the other. This is especially true when we convert foundational classes that support a lot of our system's functionality.

A Foundational Class: Money

Every system contains some foundational classes that many parts of the codebase use. An example in Travelator is the `Money` class, which we first saw in Chapter 3. Travelers need to budget for their trips. They want to compare costs of different travel options, see those costs converted to the their preferred currency, book things, pay for things, and so on. The `Money` class is so widely used that we cannot convert it and all the code that depends on it to idiomatic Kotlin in one fell swoop. We have to continue working on features that use `Money` in both Java and Kotlin while the conversion is ongoing.

This leaves us between Scylla and Charybdis. Do we leave `Money` as a Java class while we convert code that depends on it to Kotlin, but in the meantime limit the Kotlin features we can use in that dependent code? Or do we convert the `Money` class to Kotlin while we still have Java code using it, allowing us to use Kotlin features in dependent code but leaving the remaining Java code inconsistent and unconventional?

The fact that we even have these options is a testament to how well Kotlin/Java interop works in both directions. In practice, we don't have to choose. With some cunning refactoring tactics and a few annotations to control how the Kotlin compiler generates code for the JVM, we can get the best of both worlds. We can define `Money` in Kotlin, allowing us to take advantage of Kotlin's features, and still provide an idiomatic API for Java code that we are maintaining.

We converted the `Money` class to Kotlin in Chapter 3. Since we left it at the end of that chapter, we have (without you, sorry) been able to make the code more concise without affecting Java code that depends on it. We refactored most of the methods to single-expression form (Chapter 9), and we took advantage of Kotlin's flow-sensitive type inference to simplify the `equals` method greatly.

Here is `Money` now. It isn't significantly different but has a lot less syntactic noise:

```
class Money private constructor(
    val amount: BigDecimal,
    val currency: Currency
) {
    override fun equals(other: Any?) =
        this === other ||
            other is Money &&
            amount == other.amount &&
            currency == other.currency

    override fun hashCode() =
        Objects.hash(amount, currency)

    override fun toString() =
        amount.toString() + " " + currency.currencyCode

    fun add(that: Money): Money {
        require(currency == that.currency) {
            "cannot add Money values of different currencies"
        }
        return Money(amount.add(that.amount), currency)
    }

    companion object {
        @JvmStatic
        fun of(amount: BigDecimal, currency: Currency) = Money(
            amount.setScale(currency.defaultFractionDigits),
            currency
        )

        ... and convenience overloads
    }
}
```

Example 12.1 [operators.0:src/main/java/travelator/money/Money.kt]

However, it still retains the grain of Java, as does the Kotlin code that uses it. The `Money` class follows conventions for value types that are common in Modern Java, but are not the way things are usually done in Kotlin. In particular, it uses methods of a companion object to create values, and it uses methods rather than operators for arithmetic.

In a monolingual codebase, it would be pretty straightforward to address those issues. However, we still have plenty of Java code that uses the `Money` class. We'll continue to make changes in Java *and* Kotlin, until Kotlin has edged Java out altogether. In the meantime, we want to ensure that code that uses `Money` in either language is conventional enough not to frighten the horses.

Adding a User-Defined Operator

Kotlin code that calculates with `Money` values is still rather clumsy:

```
val grossPrice = netPrice.add(netPrice.mul(taxRate))
```

It is not significantly different from the equivalent Java:

```
final var grossPrice = netPrice.add(netPrice.mul(taxRate));
```

Using methods for arithmetic operations makes the calculation harder to read. It's the best we can do in Java, but in Kotlin we can define arithmetic operators for our own classes, allowing us to write that calculation as:

```
val grossPrice = netPrice + netPrice * taxRate
```

Taking addition as an example, let's take a look at how we can give our `Money` class arithmetic operators.

We give a class the `+` operator by writing an operator method or extension function called `plus`. For our `Money` class, we can rename the existing `add` method to `plus` and add the `operator` modifier:

```
class Money private constructor(
    val amount: BigDecimal,
    val currency: Currency
) {
    ...

    operator fun plus(that: Money): Money {
        require(currency == that.currency) {
            "cannot add Money values of different currencies"
        }
        return Money(amount.add(that.amount), currency)
    }

    ...
}
```

Example 12.2 [operators.2:src/main/java/travelator/money/Money.kt]

With this change, our Kotlin code can add `Money` values with the + operator, whereas the Java code calls `plus` as a method.

When we go to check in, though, we find that our rename has rippled across hundreds of files of Java code, introducing a name that doesn't follow Java conventions. Java classes in the standard library with arithmetic operations, such as `BigDecimal` and `BigInteger`, all use the name `add`, not `plus`.

We can make a function appear to have different names in Java and Kotlin by annotating its definition with the `@JvmName` annotation. Let's revert the change we just made and take another run at it, starting by annotating the method with `@JvmName("add")`:

```
@JvmName("add")
fun add(that: Money): Money {
    require(currency == that.currency) {
        "cannot add Money values of different currencies"
    }
    return Money(amount.add(that.amount), currency)
}
```

Example 12.3 [operators.3:src/main/java/travelator/money/Money.kt]

Now when we rename the method to `plus`, our Java code is unchanged, and marking it as an operator allows both Java and Kotlin code to call the method according to their respective language conventions:

```
@JvmName("add")
operator fun plus(that: Money): Money {
    require(currency == that.currency) {
        "cannot add Money values of different currencies"
    }
    return Money(amount.add(that.amount), currency)
}
```

Example 12.4 [operators.4:src/main/java/travelator/money/Money.kt]

Is this desirable? It can be quite confusing to have the same method appear under different names in different parts of the same codebase. On the other hand, because it's an operator method, the name `plus` should only appear in the definition of the method, and all uses of the method from Kotlin should be via the + operator. The phrase `operator fun plus` is more like a language keyword than a method name. IntelliJ navigates seamlessly between calls to `add` in Java and the definition of `operator plus` in Kotlin. On balance, your authors think it's worth using the `@JvmName` annotation in this case, but in general you will need to come to an agreement within your team about how you use the `@JvmName` annotation to adjust Kotlin classes to Java clients.

Calling Our Operator from Existing Kotlin Code

Looking at our Kotlin client code, we find we still have a problem. At the time of writing, IntelliJ does not have an automated refactoring to replace all direct calls to an operator method with use of the respective operator. Any of our Kotlin code that had been calling the `Money.add` method before we turned it into an operator will be left calling `Money.plus` as a method instead of using the + operator. IntelliJ can automatically refactor each of those call sites from a method call to an operator, but we would have to go through them one by one, invoking the refactoring individually.

To address this problem, we can use a sequence of refactoring steps to switch *all* our Kotlin code over to use the + operator at once, and leave in the code the capability to replay the steps as we convert more Java classes to Kotlin. So let's re-revert our change and take yet another run at the conversion.

This time, we'll extract the entire body of the `add` method as a method called `plus` and make it a public, operator method:

```
fun add(that: Money): Money {
    return plus(that)
}

operator fun plus(that: Money): Money {
    require(currency == that.currency) {
        "cannot add Money values of different currencies"
    }
    return Money(amount.add(that.amount), currency)
}
```

Example 12.5 [operators.6:src/main/java/travelator/money/Money.kt]

Using IntelliJ's automatic refactoring, we make `this` explicit in the call to `plus`:

```
fun add(that: Money): Money {
    return this.plus(that)
}
```

Example 12.6 [operators.7:src/main/java/travelator/money/Money.kt]

From this form, IntelliJ lets us automatically refactor from method call to operator:

```
fun add(that: Money): Money {
    return this + that
}
```

Example 12.7 [operators.8:src/main/java/travelator/money/Money.kt]

Finally we can transform the `add` method to single-expression form:

```
fun add(that: Money) = this + that

operator fun plus(that: Money): Money {
    require(currency == that.currency) {
```

```
            "cannot add Money values of different currencies"
        }
        return Money(amount.add(that.amount), currency)
    }
```

Example 12.8 [operators.9:src/main/java/travelator/money/Money.kt]

We now have two methods for addition. The `plus` operator implements the addition logic and is what we'd like all our Kotlin code to use in the future, but nothing calls it directly yet. The `add` method will remain for use by our Java code, while it exists, and its body contains the ideal syntax we would like to use in our Kotlin code.

We can convert all our Kotlin code that adds `Money` values to use the operator syntax by inlining the `Money.add` method. When we do, IntelliJ reports that it was unable to inline all the uses of `add`. That's just what we want! We can't inline Kotlin code into Java, so IntelliJ has inlined the body of the `add` method only into the Kotlin call sites and has kept its definition in the `Money` class because it is still called by Java. All our Kotlin code is now using the `+` operator, and our Java code is unchanged.

In the future, when we translate more Java classes that add `Money` values to Kotlin, we can inline the `add` method again to make the converted Kotlin class use the `+` operator instead of method call syntax. As long as there is Java code in our codebase that calls it, IntelliJ will preserve the `add` method. After we've converted the last Java class that adds `Money`, IntelliJ will remove the now unused `add` method as part of the inline refactoring. Our codebase will then only use the `+` operator.

Operators for Existing Java Classes

While we're working on the `plus` method, we can also take the opportunity to use the `+` operator *inside* the method. The `Money` class represents its `amount` property as a `BigDecimal`, a class from the Java standard library. We can replace the call to the `BigDecimal.add` method with the `+` operator:

```
operator fun plus(that: Money): Money {
    require(currency == that.currency) {
        "cannot add Money values of different currencies"
    }
    return Money(this.amount + that.amount, currency)
}
```

Example 12.9 [operators.11:src/main/java/travelator/money/Money.kt]

Our code continues to compile. How is that possible?

The Kotlin standard library includes extension functions that define operators for classes in the Java standard library: mathematical classes, such as `BigInteger` and `BigDecimal`, and collections, such as `List<T>` or `Set<T>`. Because these extension functions are defined in the `kotlin` package, they are available to any package automatically: we don't need to import them.

Conventions for Denoting Values

The static `of` functions on the companion object, used to denote `Money` values, also break Kotlin conventions.

Java syntax distinguishes between instantiating a class with the `new` operator and obtaining an object as the result of a method call. A Modern Java convention is that stateful objects, for which identity is significant, are constructed with the new operator, and values are denoted by calls to static factory functions. For example, the expression `new ArrayList<>()` constructs a new mutable list distinct from any other mutable list, while the expression `List.of("a","b","c")` denotes an immutable list value.

Kotlin does not draw a distinction between constructing objects and calling functions: the syntax for instantiating a class is the same as that for calling a function. Nor are there coding conventions to distinguish between constructing a new stateful object that has a distinct identity and denoting values that do not.

Although the Kotlin code for calling a function and instantiating a class look the same, they are implemented by different JVM bytecode. A source-compatible change between calling a constructor and a function will not be binary compatible.

Where a class needs multiple factory functions, as does our `Money` class, they are usually defined as top-level functions, not on the companion object of the class. IntelliJ does its bit to nudge one toward this style: it is much better at autosuggesting top-level functions than methods on a companion object.

So, it would be more conventional if we created `Money` instances with expressions like `Money(...)` or, alternatively, `moneyOf(...)`, rather than `Money.of(...)`.

As we saw in Chapter 3, `Money` has a private constructor (and isn't a data class) to preserve the relationship between its currency and the precision of its `amount`. So it looks like the easiest option would be to define top-level `moneyOf` functions in the same source file as the `Money` class. However, those `moneyOf` functions would have to call the `Money` class's constructor. They can't call it if it is still declared as `private`, but could if we change the constructor to `internal`.

Internal visibility would make the constructor visible to any Kotlin code in the same compilation unit (Gradle subproject or IntelliJ module) but prevent it from being called by Kotlin code in other compilation units. The compilation unit, rather than the class, would be responsible for guaranteeing the invariants of the `Money` class by never calling its constructor inappropriately. That would be safe enough if it wasn't for those Java parts of our system that we will continue to maintain during our system's transition to Kotlin.

Java and the JVM do not have the concept of internal visibility. The Kotlin compiler translates internal features of a class to a public feature in the JVM class files it generates, and records the internal visibility as additional metadata that is processed by the Kotlin compiler but ignored by the Java compiler. As a result, Kotlin features declared as internal appear to be public to the Java compiler and JVM, allowing us to create invalid `Money` values accidentally when we're working in the Java code of our project. That makes top-level `moneyOf` functions an unattractive option.

Instead, we can lean on Kotlin's operator overloading again. If we define a function call operator for the `Money` class's companion object, Kotlin code can create `Money` values by using the same syntax as if they were directly calling the constructor:

```
val currently = Money.of(BigDecimal("9.99"), GBP))

val proposal = Money(BigDecimal("9.99"), GBP))
```

It won't actually be a constructor call, though; in longhand it is:

```
val proposal = Money.Companion.invoke(BigDecimal("9.99", GBP))
```

Just as we found when renaming the `add` method to `plus`, if we try to achieve this by merely renaming `of` to `invoke`, we will have a knock-on effect on our Java code. Java code that creates `Money` values changes from reading as `Money.of(BigDecimal(100), EUR)` to `Money.invoke(BigDecimal(100), EUR)`. The `of` methods had *two* responsibilities: to enforce the class invariants when constructing `Money` values, and to provide syntactic sugar in the caller that conforms to Modern Java conventions for denoting values. Renaming from `of` to `invoke` doesn't affect the former but messes up the latter.

We can use the same combination of extract method and refactor the call to the extracted method and inline method to avoid any negative effects on our Java code as we refactor our Kotlin code to follow Kotlin conventions.

First, extract the `of` method's entire body as a method called `invoke`:

```
class Money private constructor(
    val amount: BigDecimal,
    val currency: Currency
) {
    ...

    companion object {
        @JvmStatic
        fun of(amount: BigDecimal, currency: Currency) =
            invoke(amount, currency)

        private fun invoke(amount: BigDecimal, currency: Currency) =
            Money(
                amount.setScale(currency.defaultFractionDigits),
                currency
            )
```

```
        ... and convenience overloads
    }
}
```

Example 12.10 [operators.12:src/main/java/travelator/money/Money.kt]

Then make invoke a public operator method:

```
@JvmStatic
fun of(amount: BigDecimal, currency: Currency) =
    invoke(amount, currency)

operator fun invoke(amount: BigDecimal, currency: Currency) =
    Money(
        amount.setScale(currency.defaultFractionDigits),
        currency
    )
```

Example 12.11 [operators.13:src/main/java/travelator/money/Money.kt]

We can now call the Money companion object as a function that looks like a constructor. So how come the call to Money(...) in the body of the invoke method does not overflow the call stack? Inside the invoke method, the call to Money(...) is not a recursive call to invoke but actually calls the private Money constructor. Outside the class, a call to Money(...) calls the companion object's invoke method, because the private constructor is not visible. We have the best of both worlds: conventional syntax for creating instances of the class, and an encapsulation boundary that guarantees the class's invariants.

To make existing Kotlin code use the new syntax, we need to first make the companion object's of method call itself as a function:

```
@JvmStatic
fun of(amount: BigDecimal, currency: Currency) =
    this(amount, currency)
```

Example 12.12 [operators.14:src/main/java/travelator/money/Money.kt]

Then, we inline the of method into our Kotlin code. Again, Java code will not be affected, and when no Java code is calling the of method, the IDE will remove it for us.

Before the inline refactoring, Kotlin code that creates Money values looks like this:

```
interface ExchangeRates {
    fun rate(fromCurrency: Currency, toCurrency: Currency): BigDecimal

    @JvmDefault
    fun convert(fromMoney: Money, toCurrency: Currency): CurrencyConversion {
        val rate = rate(fromMoney.currency, toCurrency)
        val toAmount = fromMoney.amount * rate
        val toMoney = Money.of(toAmount, toCurrency)
```

```
        return CurrencyConversion(fromMoney, toMoney)
    }
}
```

Example 12.13 [operators.16:src/main/java/travelator/money/ExchangeRates.kt]

After the inline refactoring, it looks like this:

```
interface ExchangeRates {
    fun rate(fromCurrency: Currency, toCurrency: Currency): BigDecimal

    @JvmDefault
    fun convert(fromMoney: Money, toCurrency: Currency): CurrencyConversion {
        val rate = rate(fromMoney.currency, toCurrency)
        val toAmount = fromMoney.amount * rate
        val toMoney = Money(toAmount, toCurrency)
        return CurrencyConversion(fromMoney, toMoney)
    }
}
```

Example 12.14 [operators.17:src/main/java/travelator/money/ExchangeRates.kt]

We're left with a class that is conventional and convenient, whether we're using it from Kotlin or Java.

Moving On

Java and Kotlin have different conventions that work with the different grains of the two languages.

We don't want our use of Kotlin to have a negative effect on our Java or leave our Kotlin code as mere Java in Kotlin syntax.

Using annotations and delegation, we can ensure that both Kotlin and Java code follow their respective language conventions during the transition to Kotlin. The extract-and-inline refactoring combination makes this easy to add to our codebase, and to remove when no longer needed.

CHAPTER 13

Streams to Iterables to Sequences

Java and Kotlin both allow us to transform and reduce collections. They have different design goals and implementations, though. What does Kotlin use instead of Java streams, when should we convert, and how?

Java Streams

Java 8 introduced streams in 2014, making good use of the new lambdas. Say we want to work out the average length of some strings, except that blank strings (those with only whitespace characters) should be treated as if they are empty. Previously we might have written:

```
public static double averageNonBlankLength(List<String> strings) {
    var sum = 0;
    for (var s : strings) {
        if (!s.isBlank())
            sum += s.length();
    }
    return sum / (double) strings.size();
}
```

With Java streams, we can express this algorithm as `filter`, `map`, and `reduce` by first converting the `List` to a `Stream` and applying transformations:

```
public static double averageNonBlankLength(List<String> strings) {
    return strings
        .stream()
        .filter(s -> !s.isBlank())
        .mapToInt(String::length)
        .sum()
        / (double) strings.size();
}
```

Rather than having to run the for-loop in our heads to see what this code is doing, we can see the steps of the algorithm declared line by line and rely on the runtime to implement those steps for us.

If we are really in a hurry for those results, we can even write:

```
public static double averageNonBlankLength(List<String> strings) {
    return strings
        .parallelStream() ❶
        .filter(s -> !s.isBlank())
        .mapToInt(String::length)
        .sum()
        / (double) strings.size();
}
```

❶ `parallelStream` will divide the work across multiple threads.

There are different types of fundamental operations going on here: `map` changes the type of items, not their number; `filter` keeps or rejects items depending on some property, but keeps their type the same; and `sum` is a reduction of the collection to a single property. Not shown in this example are the operations `skip(n)` and `limit(n)`. These return streams without the first and last `n` elements, respectively.

Java streams are lazy: `strings.filter(...).mapToInt(...)` does nothing but set up a pipeline for some terminal operation, `sum` in this case, to suck values through. Laziness means that later pipeline stages can limit the amount of work earlier stages have to perform. Consider translating a list of words until we see the word `STOP`. The loop version might look like this:

```
public static List<String> translatedWordsUntilSTOP(List<String> strings) {
    var result = new ArrayList<String>();
    for (var word: strings) {
        String translation = translate(word);
        if (translation.equalsIgnoreCase("STOP"))
            break;
        else
            result.add(translation);
    }
    return result;
}
```

By breaking out of the loop, we don't translate all the words, only the minimum we need. Java 9 introduced `dropWhile` and `takeWhile`, which allow us to express this as:

```
public static List<String> translatedWordsUntilSTOP(List<String> strings) {
    return strings
        .stream()
        .map(word -> translate(word))
        .takeWhile(translation -> !translation.equalsIgnoreCase("STOP"))
        .collect(toList());
}
```

This works because the `collect` causes values to be sucked through the pipeline, and `takeWhile` stops sucking from its predecessor when its predicate returns `false`.

On the subject of sucking, streams can be surprisingly slow for small collections. They are great for large-scale data crunching where we want to throw all available cores at a problem—not so great for summing the cost of five items in a shopping cart. The problem is that Java streams were designed to provide general collection transformations, lazy evaluation, *and* parallel processing, and these have different demands. Kotlin doesn't try to implement parallel operations, leaving two abstractions; iterables are good for transforming and reducing collections, whereas sequences give lazy evaluation.

Kotlin Iterables

Instead of creating a new interface to define collections operations, Kotlin provides extension functions on `Iterable`. The simplest Kotlin expression of the same algorithm is:

```
fun averageNonBlankLength(strings: List<String>): Double =
    (strings
        .filter { it.isNotBlank() }
        .map(String::length)
        .sum()
        / strings.size.toDouble())
```

Here `filter` is an extension function on `Iterable`. Unlike the `Stream.filter`, though, which returns another `Stream`, the Kotlin `filter` returns a `List` (which is `Iterable`, so we can continue the chain); `map` returns a `List`, too, so this single expression creates two additional lists in memory.

The first is a `List` of the nonblank strings, the second is a `List` of the lengths of those strings. When (if) we care about performance, this can be a problem, because both of those lists will take time to populate and memory to support.

The `List` of lengths is a particular issue, because the integers will have been *boxed* (wrapped in an `Integer` object) to fit in the list. The Java streams example used `mapToInt(String::length)` to avoid this problem. `IntStream` (and `LongStream` and `DoubleStream`, but curiously not `BooleanStream` or `CharStream`) were created to prevent streams having to box and unbox, but you have to remember to use them, and `IntStream` is not a `Stream<Integer>`.

Should we care about performance? Mostly no—this Kotlin will be fast *unless* we have large collections, the opposite of streams, which are only fast *if* we have large collections. When we do have large collections, we can switch over to sequences.

Kotlin Sequences

The Kotlin `Sequence` abstraction offers the same lazy evaluation as Java streams. The `map` operation on a `Sequence` returns another `Sequence`: the operations in the chain are only performed when some terminal operation requires their evaluation. If we have a `Collection`, `Iterable`, or even an `Iterator`, there are `asSequence()` extension functions to convert. After that the API is suspiciously familiar:

```
fun averageNonBlankLength(strings: List<String>): Double =
    (strings
        .asSequence()
        .filter { it.isNotBlank() }
        .map(String::length)
        .sum()
        / strings.size.toDouble())
```

The familiarity is suspicious because all those operations (`filter`, `map`, `sum`) are now extensions not on `Iterable` but `Sequence`, and they don't return a `List`; they return another `Sequence`. Except, that is, for `sum`, which can't even pretend to do its job without reading all the data, so it is a terminal operation. This code reads the same as the iterable version, but each of the functions is actually different.

Swapping Iterables and Sequences

`Iterable<T>` and `Sequence<T>` have the same single method signature: `public operator fun iterator(): Iterator<T>`. They both also have extension functions for `map`, `filter`, `reduce`, and so on, which take the same parameters. But they are not the same type, because their semantics are very different. The operations on `Iterable` are eager, whereas those on `Sequence` are lazy, so we cannot swap one for the other with impunity (as we will see later in this chapter).

Nevertheless, the fact that they have such similar APIs means that in situations like this, we can often change very little (source) code when we do want to swap between them.

The sequence version of `averageNonBlankLength` won't pay the price of creating the intermediate lists to hold the results of each stage, but for small numbers of items, the cost of setting up and executing the pipeline may be higher than creating the lists. In this case the `Int` lengths will still be boxed as `Integer`, albeit one at a time rather than creating a whole list of them. In many cases, the API designers will have provided a clever solution to remove boxing. In this case, it is `sumBy`:

```
fun averageNonBlankLength(strings: List<String>): Double =
    (strings
        .asSequence()
        .filter { it.isNotBlank() }
```

```
        .sumBy(String::length)
        / strings.size.toDouble())
```

sumBy (also available as an extension on Iterable) avoids boxing by taking a function that returns an Int. It can do this because it is a terminal operation, so it doesn't return another sequence or collection.

Multiple Iterations

If you use Java streams, you have probably tried to do something like this:

```
public static double averageNonBlankLength(List<String> strings) {
    return averageNonBlankLength(strings.stream());
}

public static double averageNonBlankLength(Stream<String> strings) {
    return strings
        .filter(s -> !s.isBlank())
        .mapToInt(String::length)
        .sum()
        / (double) strings.count();
}
```

This looks very plausible: we've just extracted a function, taking a Stream parameter rather than the List. There is no size property on Stream, but count() gives the same result, so we use that. When we run it, though, we get java.lang.IllegalStateException: stream has already been operated upon or closed.

The problem is that a Stream has hidden state. Once we have consumed all its items (and sum does just that), we can't go around again to count them. Even though sum is actually a method on IntStream, each stream in the pipeline consumes its predecessor, so the input strings is consumed by the sum.

In Java this is enough to put you off extracting Stream operations into functions. Let's try the same thing with a Kotlin Sequence:

```
fun averageNonBlankLength(strings: List<String>): Double =
    averageNonBlankLength(strings.asSequence())

fun averageNonBlankLength(strings: Sequence<String>): Double =
    (strings
        .filter { it.isNotBlank() }
        .sumBy(String::length)
        / strings.count().toDouble())
```

In Kotlin, we can call the Sequence version from the List version and all is fine…for now.

We are storing up trouble though. To see why, let's step out another layer and add a function that takes an Iterator:

```
fun averageNonBlankLength(strings: Iterator<String>): Double =
    averageNonBlankLength(strings.asSequence())
```

If we call this function, we now get `java.lang.IllegalStateException: This sequence can be consumed only once`. (Comparing this to the streams error, we see that the Kotlin developers seem to be more grammatically pedantic than the JVM developers.) Now the `Sequence` is acting like a Java `Stream`, but previously it wasn't. What changed?

It turns out that some sequences can safely be iterated over multiple times: those backed by a collection that is held in memory, for example. Others cannot. Now that our `Sequence` is provided by an `Iterator`, the first run through (to calculate the `sum`) continued until `Iterator.hasNext()` returned `false`. If we were to try to run through the `Sequence` again (to `count`), the `Iterator` state would not have changed, so `hasNext()` would immediately return `false`. This would lead `strings.count()` to return `0`, resulting in `averageNonBlankLength` always returning `Infinity` (if there was any input).

This sort of behavior is, erm, *undesirable*, so sequences wrapping iterators are deliberately hobbled with `Sequence.constrainOnce()` to prevent this. It is `constrainOnce()` that throws the `IllegalStateException` if we try to consume twice.

The other canonical example of a `Sequence` that cannot be consumed more than once is one backed by reading from an external resource, such as a file or network socket. In such cases we can't in general just go back and replay input to iterate again.

Unfortunately, the difference between the two types of `Sequence` is not reflected in the type system, so we will only discover any incompatibility between our algorithm and our input at runtime. As we will see in Chapter 20, this is exacerbated by the common technique of using `sequenceOf(...)` or `List.asSequence()` as our test data; these sequences *do* support multiple iterations and won't warn us of the problem.

In practice, this problem is usually only an irritation, causing some wasted time and reworking. It will tend not to happen if you are converting from streams code, because that will not have had the issue in the first place, but rather when applying a `Sequence` from scratch or converting from an `Iterable`.

In this particular case, we can make things work by keeping count of items as they whiz past in the first iteration, rather than counting again at the end:

```
fun averageNonBlankLength(strings: Sequence<String>): Double {
    var count = 0
    return (strings
        .onEach { count++ }
        .filter { it.isNotBlank() }
        .sumBy(String::length)
        / count.toDouble())
}
```

This is the first problem that we have solved in this book with a mutable local variable! We can hide our shame inside a more generally useful utility class: `CountingSequence`:

```
class CountingSequence<T>(
    private val wrapped: Sequence<T>
) : Sequence<T> {
    var count = 0
    override fun iterator() =
        wrapped.onEach { count++ }.iterator()
}

fun averageNonBlankLength(strings: Sequence<String>): Double {
    val countingSequence = CountingSequence(strings)
    return (countingSequence
            .filter { it.isNotBlank() }
            .sumBy(String::length)
            / countingSequence.count.toDouble())
}
```

This a recurrent theme in Kotlin algorithms: we might occasionally need to stoop to mutation to implement something in a sensible or efficient way, but we can usually hide the mutation in a way that both reduces its visibility and makes for a useful abstraction. In this case, this is aided by the fact that `Sequence` is an interface with just one method, making it very easy to implement it ourselves. Java's `Stream` is also an interface, but with 42 methods and no `AbstractStream` class to provide default implementations!

Before we leave this section, you may have been silently fuming ever since we introduced `Stream.count()`. If not, can you see what the issue is?

One of the points of `Stream` and `Sequence` is that they allow us to work on arbitrarily large datasets, and finding the size of these datasets by counting them individually is not very efficient, even if it can sometimes be done. In general, even if we can, in practice, iterate over a `Sequence` more than once, it is likely to be inefficient in the use cases that caused us to use `Sequence` in the first place.

Only Iterate Over a Sequence Once

As a rule of thumb, if they operate on a `Sequence`, our algorithms should complete in a single pass. This way, they will be able to work with sequences that do not support multiple iteration and can be efficient with large numbers of items.

We can use `Sequence.constrainOnce()` in our tests to make sure that we don't accidentally go around again.

Choosing Between Streams, Iterables, and Sequences

If we already have code using Java streams, it will continue to run just fine on the JVM, even when converted to Kotlin. It will even look a little nicer, since Kotlin can move the lambda outside the method and allow the use of the implicit `it` lambda parameter:

```
fun averageNonBlankLength(strings: List<String>): Double =
    (strings
        .stream()
        .filter { it.isNotBlank() }
        .mapToInt(String::length)
        .sum()
        / strings.size.toDouble())
```

In addition, we can use extension functions to *add* operations to streams, in the same way as Kotlin defines its `Sequence` operations.

If our code is working on large collections, and in particular using `parallelStream()`, then the default should be to leave the streams alone, because in these cases they are well optimized by the JVM. The Kotlin standard library even provides extensions `Stream<T>.asSequence()` and `Sequence<T>.asStream()` that allow us to swap horses mid, erm, `Stream`.

If we decide to convert to a Kotlin abstraction, then we can choose `Iterable` or `Sequence`, depending on whether the streams code takes advantage of lazy evaluation.

Lazy evaluation is required if:

- We need to produce results before we have finished reading the input.
- We need to process more data than we can fit into memory (including intermediate results).

Lazy evaluation may give better performance for:

- Large collections with many pipeline stages, where building intermediate collections may be slow.
- Pipelines where early stages could be skipped, depending on information only available in later stages.

We can illustrate the last point with the same translation example we saw with streams:

```
public static List<String> translatedWordsUntilSTOP(List<String> strings) {
    return strings
        .stream()
        .map(word -> translate(word))
        .takeWhile(translation -> !translation.equalsIgnoreCase("STOP"))
```

```
            .collect(toList());
    }
```

We can convert this to the equivalent iterable expression:

```
fun translatedWordsUntilSTOP(strings: List<String>): List<String> =
    strings
        .map { translate(it) }
        .takeWhile { !it.equals("STOP", ignoreCase = true) }
```

But then *all* words in the input `List` will be translated to another `List` by `map`, even those after `STOP`. Using a `Sequence` avoids translating words we aren't going to return:

```
fun translatedWordsUntilSTOP(strings: List<String>): List<String> =
    strings
        .asSequence()
        .map { translate(it) }
        .takeWhile { !it.equals("STOP", ignoreCase = true) }
        .toList()
```

If we don't need lazy evaluation, and for smaller collections, or when writing from scratch in Kotlin, `Iterable` pipelines are simple, generally quick, and easy to reason with. Your authors will often convert streams to iterables to take advantage of the far richer API that Kotlin provides. If iterables prove too slow (or sometimes too greedy for memory) with large collections, then we can convert to sequences. If that still isn't enough, we can move (hopefully not back) to streams, and maybe even take advantage of parallelism.

Algebraic Transformation

Laziness and parallelism will of course affect *when* the stages of our pipeline are invoked. If any of our algorithm depends on the order of operations, it may be broken if we swap between streams, iterables, and sequences. What we want is code with a predictable *algebra*: a set of rules for manipulating operations while preserving behavior.

We saw in Chapter 7 that we can categorize functions (actually any code, including lambdas) according to whether they depend on when they are run. Calculations ("Calculations" on page 78) are safe to refactor because we can move their invocations around without affecting their result or the result of any other code. In contrast, moving an action ("Actions" on page 79) from an iterable to a sequence, or vice versa, may change when it is invoked, and hence the outcome of our program. The more of our code that is expressed as calculations, the more we can treat its representation as something that we can transform according to rules.

We can also apply another algebra—arithmetic—to simplify our definition of `averageNonBlankLength`. This is currently:

```
class CountingSequence<T>(
    private val wrapped: Sequence<T>
) : Sequence<T> {
    var count = 0
    override fun iterator() =
        wrapped.onEach { count++ }.iterator()
}

fun averageNonBlankLength(strings: Sequence<String>): Double {
    val countingSequence = CountingSequence(strings)
    return (countingSequence
            .filter { it.isNotBlank() }
            .sumBy(String::length)
            / countingSequence.count.toDouble())
}
```

All that complication arises because we don't want the simple average, but the average where blank strings are counted as if empty. Filtering the blanks from the sum, but not the count, is one way to do this. Mathematically, though, it is equivalent to the following:

```
fun averageNonBlankLength(strings: Sequence<String>): Double =
    strings
        .map { if (it.isBlank()) 0 else it.length }
        .average()
```

This is a mathematical rearrangement, and, as with our code refactoring, works only if all the operations are calculations. It is also dangerously seductive, because we have slipped back to boxing our integers to pass them to `average`.

What we need is an `averageBy` analog of `sumBy`. We can do that by mating the Kotlin runtime definitions of `Sequence.sumBy` with `Sequence.average` to give:

```
inline fun <T> Sequence<T>.averageBy(selector: (T) -> Int): Double {
    var sum: Double = 0.0
    var count: Int = 0
    for (element in this) {
        sum += selector(element)
        checkCountOverflow(++count)
    }
    return if (count == 0) Double.NaN else sum / count
}
```

This again stoops to mutation in the name of efficiency, and finally allows us to write:

```
fun averageNonBlankLength(strings: Sequence<String>): Double =
    strings.averageBy {
        if (it.isBlank()) 0 else it.length
    }
```

Why did we not just write it that way in the first place? Well, sometimes we see these equivalences, sometimes we don't! Remember that we started here:

```java
public static double averageNonBlankLength(List<String> strings) {
    var sum = 0;
    for (var s : strings) {
        if (!s.isBlank())
            sum += s.length();
    }
    return sum / (double) strings.size();
}
```

Given this code, it is natural to translate the `if` statement to a `filter`:

```java
public static double averageNonBlankLength(List<String> strings) {
    return strings
        .stream()
        .filter(s -> !s.isBlank())
        .mapToInt(String::length)
        .sum()
        / (double) strings.size();
}
```

What if our original code had been more functional? Rather than using an `if` statement to decide *whether* to add, it might have used a ternary expression to calculate *the amount* to add:

```java
public static double averageNonBlankLength(List<String> strings) {
    var sum = 0;
    for (var s : strings) {
        sum += s.isBlank() ? 0 : s.length();
    }
    return sum / (double) strings.size();
}
```

Ah—then our initial translation would probably have been:

```java
public static double averageNonBlankLength(List<String> strings) {
    return strings
        .stream()
        .mapToInt(s -> s.isBlank() ? 0 : s.length())
        .average()
        .orElse(Double.NaN);
}
```

In that case, we would have had a shorter chapter but learned less.

Refactoring from Streams to Iterables and Sequences

Travelator logs operational events as it runs, so we know that it is working as we expect. These are sent as JSON to an indexing server, which can generate pretty graphs and alerts specified with its own query language. Somehow, though, those nice people in marketing are always asking questions that we can't write queries for.

In these cases, we fetch events from the server and process them locally. The querying, marshaling, and paging of the events is hidden behind a simple `EventStore` interface that returns an `Iterator<Map<String, Object>>`, where `Map<String, Object>` represents JSON objects:

```
public interface EventStore {

    Iterator<Map<String, Object>> query(String query);

    default Stream<Map<String, Object>> queryAsStream(String query) {
        Iterable<Map<String, Object>> iterable = () -> query(query);
        return StreamSupport.stream(iterable.spliterator(), false);
    }
}
```

Example 13.1 [streams-to-sequences.0:src/main/java/travelator/analytics/EventStore.java]

The interface contains its own conversion of the `Iterator` to a `Stream` for our happy convenience. (Amazingly, no conversion function is built into the JDK.)

Here is the sort of thing that we haven't been able to write in the indexing server's query language. It calculates the average number of interactions customers make to complete a booking successfully:

```
public double averageNumberOfEventsPerCompletedBooking(
    String timeRange
) {
    Stream<Map<String, Object>> eventsForSuccessfulBookings =
        eventStore
            .queryAsStream("type=CompletedBooking&timerange=" + timeRange)
            .flatMap(event -> {
                String interactionId = (String) event.get("interactionId");
                return eventStore.queryAsStream("interactionId=" + interactionId);
            });
    Map<String, List<Map<String, Object>>> bookingEventsByInteractionId =
        eventsForSuccessfulBookings.collect(groupingBy(
            event -> (String) event.get("interactionId"))
        );
    var averageNumberOfEventsPerCompletedBooking =
        bookingEventsByInteractionId
            .values()
            .stream()
            .mapToInt(List::size)
            .average();
    return averageNumberOfEventsPerCompletedBooking.orElse(Double.NaN);
}
```

Example 13.2 [streams-to-sequences.0:src/main/java/travelator/analytics/MarketingAnalytics.java]

We did our best when we wrote this to make it understandable. We named intermediate variables, and specified their types when and only when it seemed to help, and formatted carefully—and it still looks like someone knocked the code onto the floor and tried to put it back together in the hope that we didn't notice. We sometimes end up in a losing battle like this: we could extract a function to simplify code at the call site, but if we can't give that function a good name, we have just kicked the can down the source file.

Implicit or Explicit Types

Sometimes a variable's type is essential to understanding how code works; other times it just clutters an already wordy block. In this respect, explicit types are like comments, but they have the added advantage of being checked and enforced by the compiler. As with comments, we should try to write code that doesn't need explicit variable types. Good naming can help, as can refactoring into functions where the return type can be shown.

If these fail though, there is no shame in showing a variables type if it improves the readability of the code, and we should certainly prefer to communicate in types rather than comments.

We're going to convert this code to Kotlin in the fervent hope that our favorite language will allow us to do a better job. Here is the result of the automated conversion:

```
fun averageNumberOfEventsPerCompletedBooking(
    timeRange: String
): Double {
    val eventsForSuccessfulBookings = eventStore
        .queryAsStream("type=CompletedBooking&timerange=$timeRange")
        .flatMap { event: Map<String?, Any?> ->
            val interactionId = event["interactionId"] as String?
            eventStore.queryAsStream("interactionId=$interactionId")
        }
    val bookingEventsByInteractionId = eventsForSuccessfulBookings.collect(
        Collectors.groupingBy(
            Function { event: Map<String, Any> ->
                event["interactionId"] as String?
            }
        )
    )
    val averageNumberOfEventsPerCompletedBooking = bookingEventsByInteractionId
        .values
        .stream()
        .mapToInt { obj: List<Map<String, Any>> -> obj.size }
        .average()
    return averageNumberOfEventsPerCompletedBooking.orElse(Double.NaN)
}
```

Example 13.3 [streams-to-sequences.1:src/main/java/travelator/analytics/MarketingAnalytics.kt]

At the time of writing, the Java to Kotlin converter is not as clever as it might be mapping between lambdas in the two languages. This is particularly noticeable in streams code, because that is where most Java lambdas are to be found. Most of the issues can be fixed with Alt-Enter on the odd code and accepting a quick fix. Let's start by tidying up nullability, removing the vestigial `Function`, and simplifying that ugly `mapToInt` lambda:

```
fun averageNumberOfEventsPerCompletedBooking(
    timeRange: String
): Double {
    val eventsForSuccessfulBookings = eventStore
        .queryAsStream("type=CompletedBooking&timerange=$timeRange")
        .flatMap { event ->
            val interactionId = event["interactionId"] as String
            eventStore.queryAsStream("interactionId=$interactionId")
        }
    val bookingEventsByInteractionId = eventsForSuccessfulBookings.collect(
        groupingBy { event -> event["interactionId"] as String }
    )
    val averageNumberOfEventsPerCompletedBooking = bookingEventsByInteractionId
        .values
        .stream()
        .mapToInt { it.size }
        .average()
    return averageNumberOfEventsPerCompletedBooking.orElse(Double.NaN)
}
```

Example 13.4 [streams-to-sequences.2:src/main/java/travelator/analytics/MarketingAnalytics.kt]

The Java code before conversion mixed some old-style explicitly typed variables: `Stream<Map<String, Object>>`, for example, with the implicit `var averageNumberOfEventsPerCompletedBooking`. The conversion has dropped the explicit types. It is certainly less intimidating this way, but also less comprehensible if we actually care how it is doing whatever it is doing. We'll leave it this way for now but review our decision before we finish.

At this point, we have Kotlin code using Java streams that runs just fine. We could leave it alone. Travelator is a huge success, with many thousands of completed bookings a day, and streams are a good choice for throughput, so why convert to Kotlin? You didn't buy this book for that sort of attitude though, so we'll push on under the pretense that we are measuring performance at every stage and will stop if we see it degrade significantly.

Iterables First

Looking at the code, we see that it has two stages. The first stage processes an input of indeterminate length, producing a collection in memory:

```
val eventsForSuccessfulBookings = eventStore
    .queryAsStream("type=CompletedBooking&timerange=$timeRange")
    .flatMap { event ->
        val interactionId = event["interactionId"] as String
```

```
        eventStore.queryAsStream("interactionId=$interactionId")
    }
val bookingEventsByInteractionId = eventsForSuccessfulBookings.collect(
    groupingBy { event -> event["interactionId"] as String }
)
```

Example 13.5 [streams-to-sequences.2:src/main/java/travelator/analytics/MarketingAnalytics.kt]

The second processes that collection:

```
val averageNumberOfEventsPerCompletedBooking = bookingEventsByInteractionId
    .values
    .stream()
    .mapToInt { it.size }
    .average()
return averageNumberOfEventsPerCompletedBooking.orElse(Double.NaN)
```

Example 13.6 [streams-to-sequences.2:src/main/java/travelator/analytics/MarketingAnalytics.kt]

As we saw earlier, Java uses streams for both these cases, whereas in Kotlin we would tend to use a `Sequence` to process input of unknown length and an `Iterable` to process data in memory. Acting on in-memory data is easier to reason with, so we'll convert `averageNumberOfEventsPerCompletedBooking` first.

Until IntelliJ comes up with automated refactoring, we are left having to do this by hand. Usually, we would have tests to make this safer, but this is fast-moving and arbitrary analytics code, so it turns out we cut corners. Before we begin refactoring proper, we write a quick test that talks to production and shows that the result for yesterday was 7.44; now we can keep running that to check that it doesn't change.

We know that we can apply collection operations directly to `Map.values` in Kotlin (those on `Iterable`), so we can remove the `.stream()`; `average()` is an operation on `IntStream` in Java, but Kotlin conveniently declares `Iterable<Int>.average()`, so we don't have to `mapToInt`, just `map`. Finally, where `IntStream.average()` returns an empty `OptionalDouble` if the stream has no elements, Kotlin's `Iterable<Int>.average()` returns `NaN` (not a number), which means we can use the result directly:

```
val averageNumberOfEventsPerCompletedBooking = bookingEventsByInteractionId
    .values
    .map { it.size }
    .average()
return averageNumberOfEventsPerCompletedBooking
```

Example 13.7 [streams-to-sequences.3:src/main/java/travelator/analytics/MarketingAnalytics.kt]

Has this been a good change though?

Looking at the code, we are now creating an intermediate `List<Int>` on which to call `average()`. This will result in boxing each value, and this time there is no `averageBy()` (as there was `sumBy()` in the previous example) to prevent this.

Whether this code performs better or worse than the stream version will depend on the number of values in the `Map`, how our particular JVM optimizes boxing, and how heavily HotSpot has optimized this path; only measuring in real conditions will tell. If we have to choose a generic solution, we should probably write our own `Collection.averageBy`. That way we can leverage knowing the size of a `Collection`. We could use the one we prepared earlier in the chapter (albeit for `Sequence`) or refactor from here. We can refactor from here by extracting `values` and using `sumBy()`:

```
val values = bookingEventsByInteractionId.values
return values.sumBy { it.size } / values.size.toDouble()
```

Example 13.8 [streams-to-sequences.4:src/main/java/travelator/analytics/MarketingAnalytics.kt]

Now "Extract Function" `averageBy` on the returned expression:

```
val values = bookingEventsByInteractionId.values
return averageBy(values)
```

Example 13.9 [streams-to-sequences.5:src/main/java/travelator/analytics/MarketingAnalytics.kt]

```
private fun averageBy(
    values: MutableCollection<MutableList<MutableMap<String, Any>>>
): Double {
    return values.sumBy { it.size } / values.size.toDouble()
}
```

Example 13.10 [streams-to-sequences.5:src/main/java/travelator/analytics/MarketingAnalytics.kt]

Eeek! It turns out that the type of `bookingEventsByInteractionId` was a lot more mutable than we wanted. It came from `Collectors.groupingBy`, a stream operation that only has Java collections to return after all. We'll change it to use `Collection` in place of the `MutableCollection` for now, and then "Introduce Parameter" named `selector` on the lambda:

```
private fun averageBy(
    values: Collection<MutableList<MutableMap<String, Any>>>,
    selector: (MutableList<MutableMap<String, Any>>) -> Int
): Double {
    return values.sumBy(selector) / values.size.toDouble()
}
```

Example 13.11 [streams-to-sequences.6:src/main/java/travelator/analytics/MarketingAnalytics.kt]

Now we don't want to care about the actual type of items in the `Collection`. If we select the `MutableList<MutableMap<String, Any>>`, and "Extract/Introduce Type Parameter", we get the following:

```
private fun <T : MutableList<MutableMap<String, Any>>> averageBy(
    values: Collection<T>,
    selector: (T) -> Int
): Double {
    return values.sumBy(selector) / values.size.toDouble()
}
```

Example 13.12 [streams-to-sequences.7:src/main/java/travelator/analytics/MarketingAnalytics.kt]

That refactoring is clever enough that we don't begrudge having to tell IntelliJ that T can be anything really (by removing the MutableList<MutableMap<String, Any>> type restriction):

```
private fun <T> averageBy(
    values: Collection<T>,
    selector: (T) -> Int
): Double {
    return values.sumBy(selector) / values.size.toDouble()
}
```

Example 13.13 [streams-to-sequences.8:src/main/java/travelator/analytics/MarketingAnalytics.kt]

IntelliJ also added the type to the call for some reason:

```
val values = bookingEventsByInteractionId.values
return averageBy<MutableList<MutableMap<String, Any>>>(values) { it.size }
```

Example 13.14 [streams-to-sequences.7:src/main/java/travelator/analytics/MarketingAnalytics.kt]

So we remove the MutableList<MutableMap<String, Any>> from there too.

Finally, we can make averageBy the tiny single-expression inline extension function it was born to be (see Chapters 9 and 10):

```
inline fun <T> Collection<T>.averageBy(selector: (T) -> Int): Double =
    sumBy(selector) / size.toDouble()
```

Example 13.15 [streams-to-sequences.9:src/main/java/travelator/analytics/MarketingAnalytics.kt]

This version doesn't box integers nor iterate more than once, so it is probably as efficient as we are going to get. But again, only measuring in our specific circumstances will tell for sure.

Note that when we wrote Sequence.averageNonBlankLength earlier, we had to count the number of items. By defining averageBy as an extension on Collection rather than on Iterable, we can use the fact that we can ask the size of in-memory collections to avoid the tedious bookkeeping.

Then Sequences

So far, we have converted the in-memory pipeline. Now we are left with the code that reads an unknown number of events from the eventStore. We will want to keep this code lazy.

Returning to the entry point, we now have:

```
fun averageNumberOfEventsPerCompletedBooking(
    timeRange: String
): Double {
    val eventsForSuccessfulBookings = eventStore
        .queryAsStream("type=CompletedBooking&timerange=$timeRange")
        .flatMap { event ->
```

```
            val interactionId = event["interactionId"] as String
            eventStore.queryAsStream("interactionId=$interactionId")
        }
    val bookingEventsByInteractionId = eventsForSuccessfulBookings.collect(
        groupingBy { event -> event["interactionId"] as String }
    )
    return bookingEventsByInteractionId.values.averageBy { it.size }
}
```

Example 13.16 [streams-to-sequences.9:src/main/java/travelator/analytics/MarketingAnalytics.kt]

Now the variable `bookingEventsByInteractionId` is only really there to give a checkpoint in the algorithm: it names an intermediate in the hope that it aids understanding. Moving up the function, `eventsForSuccessfulBookings` is a `Stream`, so we can convert the `collect(groupingBy(...))` to Kotlin with `asSequence().groupBy {...}`; the lambda remains unchanged:

```
val bookingEventsByInteractionId = eventsForSuccessfulBookings
    .asSequence()
    .groupBy { event ->
        event["interactionId"] as String
    }
```

Example 13.17 [streams-to-sequences.10:src/main/java/travelator/analytics/MarketingAnalytics.kt]

Swapping out one method for another method (or extension function) with a similar name that takes a compatible lambda is a good sign that we are on the right track.

Now for that `flatMap`, used to fetch all the events for any interaction that had a completed booking:

```
val eventsForSuccessfulBookings = eventStore
    .queryAsStream("type=CompletedBooking&timerange=$timeRange")
    .flatMap { event ->
        val interactionId = event["interactionId"] as String
        eventStore.queryAsStream("interactionId=$interactionId")
    }
```

Example 13.18 [streams-to-sequences.10:src/main/java/travelator/analytics/MarketingAnalytics.kt]

This would also *probably just work*™ if we had sequences rather than streams. Thankfully, we know how to convert from the `Stream` to a `Sequence`: it's the `.asSequence()` extension provided by the Kotlin JDK interop. We need to apply it to both streams:

```
val eventsForSuccessfulBookings = eventStore
    .queryAsStream("type=CompletedBooking&timerange=$timeRange")
    .asSequence()
    .flatMap { event ->
        val interactionId = event["interactionId"] as String
        eventStore
            .queryAsStream("interactionId=$interactionId")
            .asSequence()
    }
```

Example 13.19 [streams-to-sequences.11:src/main/java/travelator/analytics/MarketingAnalytics.kt]

Awesomely, this continues to compile and pass our (cursory) test! It compiles because, although we have changed the type of `eventsForSuccessfulBookings` from `Stream` to `Sequence`, we then call `eventsForSuccessfulBookings.asSequence()`:

```
val bookingEventsByInteractionId = eventsForSuccessfulBookings
    .asSequence()
    .groupBy { event ->
        event["interactionId"] as String
    }
```

Example 13.20 [streams-to-sequences.11:src/main/java/travelator/analytics/MarketingAnalytics.kt]

This resolves to `Sequence.asSequence()`, which is a no-op. We can inline `asSequence` to prove it:

```
val bookingEventsByInteractionId = eventsForSuccessfulBookings
    .groupBy { event ->
        event["interactionId"] as String
    }
```

Example 13.21 [streams-to-sequences.12:src/main/java/travelator/analytics/MarketingAnalytics.kt]

Returning to `eventsForSuccessfulBookings`, we now have:

```
val eventsForSuccessfulBookings = eventStore
    .queryAsStream("type=CompletedBooking&timerange=$timeRange")
    .asSequence()
    .flatMap { event ->
        val interactionId = event["interactionId"] as String
        eventStore
            .queryAsStream("interactionId=$interactionId")
            .asSequence()
    }
```

Example 13.22 [streams-to-sequences.11:src/main/java/travelator/analytics/MarketingAnalytics.kt]

What we really wanted was for `EventStore` to support `queryAsSequence`. We can do this without modifying it by introducing an extension function:

```
fun EventStore.queryAsSequence(query: String) =
    this.queryAsStream(query).asSequence()
```

Example 13.23 [streams-to-sequences.12:src/main/java/travelator/analytics/MarketingAnalytics.kt]

This allows us to remove the `asSequence` calls from the calling function:

```
fun averageNumberOfEventsPerCompletedBooking(
    timeRange: String
): Double {
    val eventsForSuccessfulBookings = eventStore
        .queryAsSequence("type=CompletedBooking&timerange=$timeRange")
        .flatMap { event ->
            val interactionId = event["interactionId"] as String
            eventStore
                .queryAsSequence("interactionId=$interactionId")
```

```
        }
    val bookingEventsByInteractionId = eventsForSuccessfulBookings
        .groupBy { event ->
            event["interactionId"] as String
        }
    return bookingEventsByInteractionId.values.averageBy { it.size }
}
```

Example 13.24 [streams-to-sequences.12:src/main/java/travelator/analytics/MarketingAnalytics.kt]

OK, time to review. We've converted our Java to Kotlin, and are using iterables to process the in-memory operations, and sequences (backed by streams in `EventStore`) to process the unbounded operations. We really can't claim, though, that the structure of the algorithm has become much clearer. A little less noisy, yes, but hardly expressive.

The function is currently divided into three parts, and if we're honest, they are pretty arbitrary. Sometimes we can gain greater insight by inlining everything and seeing what we have, so let's do that:

```
fun averageNumberOfEventsPerCompletedBooking(
    timeRange: String
): Double {
    return eventStore
        .queryAsSequence("type=CompletedBooking&timerange=$timeRange")
        .flatMap { event ->
            val interactionId = event["interactionId"] as String
            eventStore
                .queryAsSequence("interactionId=$interactionId")
        }.groupBy { event ->
            event["interactionId"] as String
        }.values
        .averageBy { it.size }
}
```

Example 13.25 [streams-to-sequences.13:src/main/java/travelator/analytics/MarketingAnalytics.kt]

It looks like the part starting with `flatMap` and ending before `groupBy` might standalone. Let's see how to extract part of a pipeline into its own function.

Extracting Part of a Pipeline

First we select from the start of the pipeline to the last stage we want to include, so from `eventStore` up to but not including `.groupBy`. "Extract Function", calling it (in this case) `allEventsInSameInteractions`:

```
fun averageNumberOfEventsPerCompletedBooking(
    timeRange: String
): Double {
    return allEventsInSameInteractions(timeRange)
        .groupBy { event ->
            event["interactionId"] as String
        }.values
```

```
        .averageBy { it.size }
}

private fun allEventsInSameInteractions(timeRange: String) = eventStore
    .queryAsSequence("type=CompletedBooking&timerange=$timeRange")
    .flatMap { event ->
        val interactionId = event["interactionId"] as String
        eventStore
            .queryAsSequence("interactionId=$interactionId")
    }
```

Example 13.26 [streams-to-sequences.14:src/main/java/travelator/analytics/MarketingAnalytics.kt]

Now we select the bits of the pipeline that we don't want in the new function, so `event Store` to before `.flatMap`, and "Introduce Parameter". Accept any name that IntelliJ chooses—it won't live long:

```
fun averageNumberOfEventsPerCompletedBooking(
    timeRange: String
): Double {
    return allEventsInSameInteractions(
        eventStore
            .queryAsSequence("type=CompletedBooking&timerange=$timeRange")
    )
        .groupBy { event ->
            event["interactionId"] as String
        }.values
        .averageBy { it.size }
}

private fun allEventsInSameInteractions(
    sequence: Sequence<MutableMap<String, Any?>>
) = sequence
    .flatMap { event ->
        val interactionId = event["interactionId"] as String
        eventStore
            .queryAsSequence("interactionId=$interactionId")
    }
```

Example 13.27 [streams-to-sequences.15:src/main/java/travelator/analytics/MarketingAnalytics.kt]

That's really ugly, but once we convert the `sequence` parameter of `allEventsInSame Interactions` to a receiver and reformat, we have:

```
fun averageNumberOfEventsPerCompletedBooking(
    timeRange: String
): Double {
    return eventStore
        .queryAsSequence("type=CompletedBooking&timerange=$timeRange")
        .allEventsInSameInteractions()
        .groupBy { event ->
            event["interactionId"] as String
        }.values
        .averageBy { it.size }
```

```
}

fun Sequence<Map<String, Any?>>.allEventsInSameInteractions() =
    flatMap { event ->
        val interactionId = event["interactionId"] as String
        eventStore
            .queryAsSequence("interactionId=$interactionId")
    }
```

Example 13.28 [streams-to-sequences.16:src/main/java/travelator/analytics/MarketingAnalytics.kt]

As we discussed in Chapter 10, extension functions really come into their own when we are chaining operations. In Java, we couldn't extend the Streams API with `allEventsInSameInteractions()`, so we ended up breaking the chain, either by calling a function or by introducing an explaining variable.

Final Tidy

This is still a little clunky, and we could probably make it more efficient by not creating lists in the grouping, but that will do. Oh, except for a wafer-thin type alias and extension property:

```
typealias Event = Map<String, Any?>

val Event.interactionId: String? get() =
    this["interactionId"] as? String
```

Example 13.29 [streams-to-sequences.17:src/main/java/travelator/analytics/MarketingAnalytics.kt]

This lets us concentrate on the hard stuff when we read the code:

```
class MarketingAnalytics(
    private val eventStore: EventStore
) {
    fun averageNumberOfEventsPerCompletedBooking(
        timeRange: String
    ): Double = eventStore
        .queryAsSequence("type=CompletedBooking&timerange=$timeRange")
        .allEventsInSameInteractions()
        .groupBy(Event::interactionId)
        .values
        .averageBy { it.size }

    private fun Sequence<Event>.allEventsInSameInteractions() =
        flatMap { event ->
            eventStore.queryAsSequence(
                "interactionId=${event.interactionId}"
            )
        }
}

inline fun <T> Collection<T>.averageBy(selector: (T) -> Int): Double =
    sumBy(selector) / size.toDouble()
```

```
fun EventStore.queryAsSequence(query: String) =
    this.queryAsStream(query).asSequence()
```

Example 13.30 [streams-to-sequences.17:src/main/java/travelator/analytics/MarketingAnalytics.kt]

In passing, note that `allEventsInSameInteractions` is an example of an extension function as method that we discussed in Chapter 10. It has access to both `this` from `MarketingAnalytics` (to access `eventStore`) and `this` from `Sequence<Event>`.

Moving On

We aren't going to claim that the refactored Kotlin code in this example is beautiful, but we do think that it is a significant improvement on the original Java. Extension functions, Kotlin's lambda syntax, and improved type inference combine to reduce a lot of the noise associated with Java streams. When we have in-memory collections, using iterables rather than streams can also be more efficient as well as cleaner.

CHAPTER 14

Accumulating Objects to Transformations

Java programs usually rely heavily on mutable state because it is so arduous in Java to define value types and transform values, even with the Streams API. What is the best way to translate Java code that relies upon mutable objects and side effects to Kotlin code that transforms immutable values?

Calculating with Accumulator Parameters

One of the most important things our travelers want to know is how much their adventures will cost. International travel makes this rather complicated. A trip will incur costs in multiple currencies as it wends its way across borders, but the traveler wants to be able to compare overall costs to make decisions about routes and where to stay. So Travelator summarizes costs by local currency *and* the traveler's preferred currency, and then shows the overall total in the preferred currency. It does this using the `CostSummary` and `CostSummaryCalculator` classes. Let's take a look at how they are used, and then we'll look at their implementation.

The `Itinerary` class has an operation for summarizing its costs with a `CostSummaryCalculator`. It is used like this:

```
val fx: ExchangeRates = ...
val userCurrency = ...
val calculator = CostSummaryCalculator(userCurrency, fx) ❶

fun costSummary(i: Itinerary): CostSummary {
    i.addCostsTo(calculator) ❷
    return calculator.summarise() ❸
}
```

Example 14.1 [accumulator.0:src/test/java/travelator/itinerary/Itinerary_CostTest.kt]

❶ Here the code creates a `CostSummaryCalculator` with the traveler's preferred currency and a source of currency exchange rates.

❷ This tells the `Itinerary` to add its costs to the calculator. In response, the `Itinerary` adds the cost of its elements: the journeys along the route, accommodation, and other chargeable services.

❸ This calls the calculator's `summarise` method to obtain the `CostSummary` after all the costs have been collected.

Someone has already converted the `Itinerary` class to Kotlin, but the implementations of `addCostsTo` still have a Java flavor:

```
data class Itinerary(
    val id: Id<Itinerary>,
    val route: Route,
    val accommodations: List<Accommodation> = emptyList()
) {
    ...

    fun addCostsTo(calculator: CostSummaryCalculator) {
        route.addCostsTo(calculator)
        accommodations.addCostsTo(calculator)
    }

    ...
}

fun Iterable<Accommodation>.addCostsTo(calculator: CostSummaryCalculator) {
    forEach { a ->
        a.addCostsTo(calculator)
    }
}
```

Example 14.2 [accumulator.0:src/main/java/travelator/itinerary/Itinerary.kt]

The logic relies upon side effects to accumulate costs in the mutable state of the `CostSummaryCalculator`.

The benefit of this design is that we can use the calculator to summarize the costs of any object in our domain model, without knowing the structure of that object. The object is responsible for adding its costs to the calculator and passing the calculator to its children so that they can add *their* costs. This decouples the code that needs the costs from the code that provides the costs, allowing us to evolve them independently.

For example, a `Route` contains a list of `Journey`, each of which has a cost, and `Accommodation` has a room rate, a number of nights, and additional costs such as meals and hotel services. The `Itinerary` doesn't have to know or care how these objects are structured, or how to collect their respective costs. That knowledge is encapsulated in the `Route` and `Accommodation` classes.

However, our use of mutable state has two significant disadvantages.

First, it introduces the possibility of aliasing errors (*https://oreil.ly/PeqKs*). Aliasing errors create "spooky action at a distance" (as Einstein famously described quantum entanglement) that is not immediately obvious from the source code. We saw an example in Chapter 6, when a function sorted a mutable list parameter and broke its caller.

In the case of the `CostSummaryCalculator`, if we reuse a calculator to summarize the costs of multiple entities, we have to reset its state between each calculation. If we do not reset the calculator state, costs collected during one calculation will be included in the next. The type system cannot help us avoid this mistake.

The example at the start of this chapter *may* make this error. The calculator is not local to the `costSummary` method, and `costSummary` does not reset the calculator before each calculation. We can't tell whether this is a problem merely by looking at the `costSummary` method. We have to understand how that method is used in its wider context, and as we make changes in that context, we have to make sure those changes do not break our assumptions about how the `costSummary` method is used.

The second problem with mutable state is that it scatters the implementation of our algorithms across the code. We'll return to this later in this chapter.

Before we look at `CostSummaryCalculator`, let's have a look at the `CostSummary` that it computes. It uses `CurrencyConversion` (thankfully already Kotlin):

```
data class CurrencyConversion(
    val fromMoney: Money,
    val toMoney: Money
)
```

Example 14.3 [accumulator.0:src/main/java/travelator/money/CurrencyConversion.kt]

A `CostSummary` is a mutable POJO (as described in Chapter 5) that holds a list of `CurrencyConversion`, from local currencies to the traveler's preferred currency:

```
public class CostSummary {
    private final List<CurrencyConversion> lines = new ArrayList<>();
    private Money total;

    public CostSummary(Currency userCurrency) {
        this.total = Money.of(0, userCurrency);
    }

    public void addLine(CurrencyConversion line) {
        lines.add(line);
        total = total.add(line.getToMoney());
    }
```

```java
    public List<CurrencyConversion> getLines() {
        return List.copyOf(lines);
    }

    public Money getTotal() {
        return total;
    }
}
```

Example 14.4 [accumulator.0:src/main/java/travelator/itinerary/CostSummary.java]

`CostSummary` also reports the total cost in the preferred currency. It stores the total cost in a field rather than calculating it in `getTotal` because the application often sorts items by their `CostSummary.total`, and recalculating every time we make a comparison turned out to be a bottleneck. This means that a `CostSummary` has to update `total` whenever a `CurrencyConversion` is added.

`CostSummary` is also effectively a shared mutable collection. Because this breaks our rule of thumb in "Don't Mutate Shared Collections" on page 63, it performs a copy in `getLines` to limit the damage.

Now to `CostSummaryCalculator`. It keeps a running total for each `Currency` in a `currencyTotals` field when `addCost` is called. The `summarise` method constructs a `CostSummary` using a source of exchange rates to convert local costs to the traveler's preferred currency:

```java
public class CostSummaryCalculator {
    private final Currency userCurrency;
    private final ExchangeRates exchangeRates;
    private final Map<Currency, Money> currencyTotals = new HashMap<>();

    public CostSummaryCalculator(
        Currency userCurrency,
        ExchangeRates exchangeRates
    ) {
        this.userCurrency = userCurrency;
        this.exchangeRates = exchangeRates;
    }

    public void addCost(Money cost) {
        currencyTotals.merge(cost.getCurrency(), cost, Money::add);
    }

    public CostSummary summarise() {
        var totals = new ArrayList<>(currencyTotals.values());
        totals.sort(comparing(m -> m.getCurrency().getCurrencyCode()));

        CostSummary summary = new CostSummary(userCurrency);
        for (var total : totals) {
            summary.addLine(exchangeRates.convert(total, userCurrency));
        }
```

```
        return summary;
    }

    public void reset() {
        currencyTotals.clear();
    }
}
```

Example 14.5 [accumulator.0:src/main/java/travelator/itinerary/CostSummaryCalculator.java]

Thus, the calculation of a `CostSummary` is spread between two classes that intertwine the following responsibilities:

- Hold information from the context of the calculation that is needed to compute the summary.
- Calculate per-currency totals, so the calculation doesn't accumulate rounding errors.
- Convert costs to the traveler's preferred currency.
- Calculate the grand total in the traveler's preferred currency.
- Sort the currency conversions in alphabetical order of the original currency code.
- Store the currency conversions and grand total so they can be displayed to the traveler.

Such smearing of responsibilities across classes is common when we compute by mutating shared state. We'd like to disentangle the responsibilities and simplify the implementation. What final structure we should we aim for?

One clue is in the name of the `CostCurrencyCalculator` class. In linguistic jargon, the `CostCurrencyCalculator` is an *agent noun*: a noun derived from a verb that means no more than a thing that performs the action identified by the verb, like *driver* or *baker* or *calculator*. `CostCurrencyCalculator` is a so-called "doer class."

Another clue is in the data that the class holds. The traveler's preferred currency and source of exchange rates are the context for the calculation. They are managed elsewhere in the application and held by `CostCurrencyCalculator` so that they are close at hand for its calculations. The map of totals by currency (`currencyTotals`) contains transient, intermediate results of the calculation that are irrelevant after the calculation is complete and, in fact, should be discarded to avoid aliasing errors. The class doesn't *own* any data, only holds it temporarily for operational reasons.

The `CostCurrencyCalculator` class doesn't represent a *concept* in our application domain model, but a *function* that we perform upon elements of that domain model. In Kotlin, we usually implement functions not with objects but with, well, functions.

Let's refactor the calculation from mutable classes to functions that work with immutable data.

Refactoring to Functions over Immutable Data

Converting the two classes to Kotlin leaves us with Java in Kotlin syntax. Here is `CostSummary` after a little tidying and rearranging:

```
class CostSummary(userCurrency: Currency) {
    private val _lines = mutableListOf<CurrencyConversion>()

    var total: Money = Money.of(0, userCurrency)
        private set

    val lines: List<CurrencyConversion>
        get() = _lines.toList()

    fun addLine(line: CurrencyConversion) {
        _lines.add(line)
        total += line.toMoney
    }
}
```

Example 14.6 [accumulator.1:src/main/java/travelator/itinerary/CostSummary.kt]

The automatic conversion of `CostSummaryCalculator` needs less tidying:

```
class CostSummaryCalculator(
    private val userCurrency: Currency,
    private val exchangeRates: ExchangeRates
) {
    private val currencyTotals = mutableMapOf<Currency, Money>()

    fun addCost(cost: Money) {
        currencyTotals.merge(cost.currency, cost, Money::add)
    }

    fun summarise(): CostSummary {
        val totals = ArrayList(currencyTotals.values)
        totals.sortWith(comparing { m: Money -> m.currency.currencyCode })

        val summary = CostSummary(userCurrency)
        for (total in totals) {
            summary.addLine(exchangeRates.convert(total, userCurrency))
        }
        return summary
    }

    fun reset() {
        currencyTotals.clear()
```

```
    }
}
```

Example 14.7 [accumulator.1:src/main/java/travelator/itinerary/CostSummaryCalculator.kt]

We can start from here and refactor away the mutability. We'll work from the inside, making `CostSummary` an immutable value type, and gradually push immutability outward through the `CostSummaryCalculator`. Before we do though, we've been stung by Java's obsession with sorting collections in place before now, so we fix that first:

```
fun summarise(): CostSummary {
    val totals = currencyTotals.values.sortedBy {
        it.currency.currencyCode
    }
    val summary = CostSummary(userCurrency)
    for (total in totals) {
        summary.addLine(exchangeRates.convert(total, userCurrency))
    }
    return summary
}
```

Example 14.8 [accumulator.2:src/main/java/travelator/itinerary/CostSummaryCalculator.kt]

Now we see a pattern that is common in mutating code: create an object (`CostSummary` in this case), call some initialization steps, and then return it. Whenever we see initialization steps like this, we should reach for `apply`:

```
fun summarise(): CostSummary {
    val totals = currencyTotals.values.sortedBy {
        it.currency.currencyCode
    }
    val summary = CostSummary(userCurrency).apply {
        for (total in totals) {
            addLine(exchangeRates.convert(total, userCurrency))
        }
    }
    return summary
}
```

Example 14.9 [accumulator.3:src/main/java/travelator/itinerary/CostSummaryCalculator.kt]

Using `apply` allows us to group the initialization steps into a block to better express our intent. It's like a mini builder: the `summarise` function never sees a reference to a partially initialized `CostSummary`, only the completed object.

This is small-scale functional thinking—trying to limit the scope of mutation even within a function. Functional thinking also helps us see that looping over `totals`, creating a `CurrencyConversion` for each, and calling `addLine` with it, is the same as creating a `conversions` list and looping over that:

```
fun summarise(): CostSummary {
    val conversions = currencyTotals.values.sortedBy {
        it.currency.currencyCode
```

```
    }.map { exchangeRates.convert(it, userCurrency) }

    return CostSummary(userCurrency).apply {
        conversions.forEach(this::addLine)
    }
}
```

Example 14.10 [accumulator.4:src/main/java/travelator/itinerary/CostSummaryCalculator.kt]

Why make this change? Well, we want to strip a `CostSummary` down to its immutable essence. If `CostSummary` was immutable, client code would have to pass the list of lines to its constructor instead of calling its `addLine` method. `CostSummary` shouldn't be responsible for currency conversion, so we're making the `apply` block look like we want its constructor to look. From here we add a secondary constructor that duplicates this initialization logic:

```
class CostSummary(userCurrency: Currency) {
    private val _lines = mutableListOf<CurrencyConversion>()

    var total: Money = Money.of(0, userCurrency)
        private set

    val lines: List<CurrencyConversion>
        get() = _lines.toList()

    constructor(
        userCurrency: Currency,
        lines: List<CurrencyConversion>
    ): this(userCurrency) {
        lines.forEach(::addLine)
    }

    fun addLine(line: CurrencyConversion) {
        _lines.add(line)
        total += line.toMoney
    }
}
```

Example 14.11 [accumulator.5:src/main/java/travelator/itinerary/CostSummary.kt]

Now we can change the `CostSummaryCalculator.summarise` method to call the new constructor, treating the `CostSummary` class as if it was an immutable value type:

```
fun summarise(): CostSummary {
    val conversions = currencyTotals.values.sortedBy {
        it.currency.currencyCode
    }.map { exchangeRates.convert(it, userCurrency) }

    return CostSummary(userCurrency, conversions)
}
```

Example 14.12 [accumulator.5:src/main/java/travelator/itinerary/CostSummaryCalculator.kt]

This in turn allows us to make the `CostSummary` class actually immutable, at least from outside:

```
class CostSummary(
    userCurrency: Currency,
    val lines: List<CurrencyConversion>
) {

    var total: Money = Money.of(0, userCurrency)
        private set

    init {
        lines.forEach {
            total += it.toMoney
        }
    }
}
```

Example 14.13 [accumulator.6:src/main/java/travelator/itinerary/CostSummary.kt]

As we can see from that nasty `var` and `init`, it's sometimes hard to get away from mutation once it has set in, especially for accumulators like this; `fold` is our friend here. We had a series of actions ("Actions" on page 79) acting on the mutable variable `total`, and `fold` converts the actions to a single calculation ("Calculations" on page 78) that we can use to initialize an immutable variable:

```
class CostSummary(
    userCurrency: Currency,
    val lines: List<CurrencyConversion>
) {
    val total = lines
        .map { it.toMoney }
        .fold(Money.of(0, userCurrency), Money::add)
}
```

Example 14.14 [accumulator.7:src/main/java/travelator/itinerary/CostSummary.kt]

Now that it is fully immutable, we can make `CostSummary` a data class if we can make `total` a primary constructor parameter. We could do this by converting the current constructor to a secondary constructor, but instead we are going to move all the calculation into the `CostSummaryCalculator`, leaving the `CostSummary` merely to hold the results of that calculation.

To do this, we first select the expression to the right of the equals sign in the definition of the `total` property and use the IDE's "Introduce Parameter" refactoring to push the expression out as a constructor parameter:

```
class CostSummary(
    val lines: List<CurrencyConversion>,
    total: Money
) {
```

```
        val total = total
    }
```

Example 14.15 [accumulator.8:src/main/java/travelator/itinerary/CostSummary.kt]

The `total` property is now highlighted as a style warning: the IDE detected that the property can be declared in the constructor parameter. A quick Alt-Enter on the warning leaves the class declaration as:

```
class CostSummary(
    val lines: List<CurrencyConversion>,
    val total: Money
)
```

Example 14.16 [accumulator.9:src/main/java/travelator/itinerary/CostSummary.kt]

Meanwhile, back at the `CostSummaryCalculator`, IntelliJ has pulled the calculation into `summarise`, leaving it looking like this:

```
fun summarise(): CostSummary {
    val lines = currencyTotals.values
        .sortedBy { it.currency.currencyCode }
        .map { exchangeRates.convert(it, userCurrency) }

    val total = lines
        .map { it.toMoney }
        .fold(Money.of(0, userCurrency), Money::add)

    return CostSummary(lines, total)
}
```

Example 14.17 [accumulator.9:src/main/java/travelator/itinerary/CostSummaryCalculator.kt]

Now we can make `CostSummary` a data class. Its sole responsibility is to hold the results of the calculation for filtering, sorting, and display:

```
data class CostSummary(
    val lines: List<CurrencyConversion>,
    val total: Money
)
```

Example 14.18 [accumulator.10:src/main/java/travelator/itinerary/CostSummary.kt]

We said previously that mutable state can obscure algorithms by smearing them through the code. We can now look back and see that was the case with `CostSummary`. When we arrived, calculating the total was split into initializing a mutable `total` property and updating it in the `addLine` method:

```
class CostSummary(userCurrency: Currency) {
    private val _lines = mutableListOf<CurrencyConversion>()

    var total: Money = Money.of(0, userCurrency)
        private set

    val lines: List<CurrencyConversion>
```

```
        get() = _lines.toList()

    fun addLine(line: CurrencyConversion) {
        _lines.add(line)
        total += line.toMoney
    }
}
```

Example 14.19 [accumulator.1:src/main/java/travelator/itinerary/CostSummary.kt]

Now the calculation is a single expression in `summarise`:

```
val total = lines
    .map { it.toMoney }
    .fold(Money.of(0, userCurrency), Money::add)
```

Example 14.20 [accumulator.9:src/main/java/travelator/itinerary/CostSummaryCalculator.kt]

Let's Do That Again

Similarly, whatever is happening with currencies is still hidden in the remaining mutations in `CostSummaryCalculator`:

```
class CostSummaryCalculator(
    private val userCurrency: Currency,
    private val exchangeRates: ExchangeRates
) {
    private val currencyTotals = mutableMapOf<Currency, Money>()

    fun addCost(cost: Money) {
        currencyTotals.merge(cost.currency, cost, Money::add)
    }

    fun summarise(): CostSummary {
        val lines = currencyTotals.values
            .sortedBy { it.currency.currencyCode }
            .map { exchangeRates.convert(it, userCurrency) }

        val total = lines
            .map { it.toMoney }
            .fold(Money.of(0, userCurrency), Money::add)

        return CostSummary(lines, total)
    }

    fun reset() {
        currencyTotals.clear()
    }
}
```

Example 14.21 [accumulator.9:src/main/java/travelator/itinerary/CostSummaryCalculator.kt]

We can apply a similar process to eliminate these, but this time we won't add a secondary constructor. Instead, we will apply "Expand-and-Contract Refactoring" on page 44 by adding an overload of the `summarise` method that takes the costs:

```
fun summarise(costs: Iterable<Money>): CostSummary {
    val delegate = CostSummaryCalculator(userCurrency, exchangeRates)
    costs.forEach(delegate::addCost)
    return delegate.summarise()
}
```

Example 14.22 [accumulator.11:src/main/java/travelator/itinerary/CostSummaryCalculator.kt]

This is quite sneaky. The old `summarise` method is an action: its result depends on the past history of calling `addCost` and `reset`. This new `summarise` is a calculation: its result depends only on the values of its inputs (the `costs` parameter plus the `userCurrency` and `exchangeRates` properties it accesses). And yet the new `summarise` uses the old one; it just limits the scope of mutation to a local variable, converting it to a calculation.

When we use this version of `summarise`, we have drawn a distinction between the *context* of cost-summary calculations, which we pass to the constructor as `userCurrency` and `exchangeRates`, and the parameters of a *specific* calculation (the `costs` that we pass to the `summarise` method). This will be significant later ("Enriching the Abstraction We Discovered" on page 207).

Now that we have two `summarise` methods, we can move our callers to the new one. To switch over to using the new `summarise`, we'll have to extract the costs from the entities we want to summarize, rather than telling them to add their costs to a mutable calculator that we pass in. Instead of asking children to add their costs to the `CostSummaryCalculator`, parents will ask their children for their costs and combine them.

We'll end up using the calculator like this:

```
val fx: ExchangeRates = ...
val userCurrency = ...
val calculator = CostSummaryCalculator(userCurrency, fx)

fun costSummary(i: Itinerary) =
    calculator.summarise(i.costs())
```

Example 14.23 [accumulator.12:src/test/java/travelator/itinerary/Itinerary_CostTest.kt]

And we'll report the costs from our domain models like this:

```
data class Itinerary(
    val id: Id<Itinerary>,
    val route: Route,
    val accommodations: List<Accommodation> = emptyList()
) {
    ...
```

```
    fun costs(): List<Money> = route.costs() + accommodations.costs()
    ...
}

fun Iterable<Accommodation>.costs(): List<Money> = flatMap { it.costs() }
```

Example 14.24 [accumulator.12:src/main/java/travelator/itinerary/Itinerary.kt]

When all uses of `CostSummaryCalculator` in the application are using our new `summarise` method, we can flatten the calculation of the `currencyTotals` and `CostSummary` into that method, the one that currently uses a local to do the job:

```
fun summarise(costs: Iterable<Money>): CostSummary {
    val delegate = CostSummaryCalculator(userCurrency, exchangeRates)
    costs.forEach(delegate::addCost)
    return delegate.summarise()
}
```

Example 14.25 [accumulator.11:src/main/java/travelator/itinerary/CostSummaryCalculator.kt]

We can effectively inline the entire class into this method using local variables instead:

```
fun summarise(costs: Iterable<Money>): CostSummary {
    val currencyTotals = mutableMapOf<Currency, Money>()
    costs.forEach {
        currencyTotals.merge(it.currency, it, Money::plus)
    }
    val lines = currencyTotals.values
        .sortedBy { it.currency.currencyCode }
        .map { exchangeRates.convert(it, userCurrency) }
    val total = lines
        .map { it.toMoney }
        .fold(Money(0, userCurrency), Money::add)
    return CostSummary(lines, total)
}
```

Example 14.26 [accumulator.13:src/main/java/travelator/itinerary/CostSummaryCalculator.kt]

Our tests still pass, and IntelliJ tells us that all the other methods of `CostSummary Calculator` are now unused, as is the `currencyTotals` field, so by deleting them all we have finally succeeded in removing all the mutable state from the class. Not from that method though—we still have a mutable map! This is the last remnant of the smearing out of the algorithm that we mentioned earlier. We have finally brought all the logic into this one method, and because all our logic is in one place, we know that it happens at one time and is safe to refactor to any equivalent form.

What is that form? We have to think about that, but come to the conclusion that the `MutableMap.merge` is accumulating a total per currency. When we have all the data at once, as we do now, we can perform the same calculation by grouping by currency and summing the lists:

```
class CostSummaryCalculator(
    private val userCurrency: Currency,
    private val exchangeRates: ExchangeRates
) {
    fun summarise(costs: Iterable<Money>): CostSummary {
        val currencyTotals: List<Money> = costs
            .groupBy { it.currency }
            .values
            .map { moneys -> moneys.reduce(Money::add) }
        val lines: List<CurrencyConversion> = currencyTotals
            .sortedBy { it.currency.currencyCode }
            .map { exchangeRates.convert(it, userCurrency) }
        val total = lines
            .map { it.toMoney }
            .fold(Money(0, userCurrency), Money::add)
        return CostSummary(lines, total)
    }
}
```

Example 14.27 [accumulator.14:src/main/java/travelator/itinerary/CostSummaryCalculator.kt]

It is a bit irritating that we have to use `reduce` to sum monies instead of having a nice `Iterable<Money>.sum()` extension function. We should probably fix that. And now that the calculation is all in one place, we might ponder whether there is meaning in the fact that we use `reduce` in one expression and `fold` in another (hint, there is), but these are thoughts that we can have only because the code is now set out in one place.

The key thing is that we can see the shape of the `summarise` calculation more clearly now. It is a pure function that is applied to a collection of costs and is evaluated in the context of some exchange rates and the traveler's preferred currency. The function transforms the nested entities of our domain model into a flat collection of costs and then transforms the costs into a map of the total for each currency, transforms the totals for each `Currency` into a list of `CurrencyConversion`, and finally transforms the list of currency conversions into a `CostSummary`.

A functional program transforms its inputs into outputs.

If you can't write that easily in one step, transform the inputs into an intermediate representation that is easy to transform into the outputs.

Introduce intermediate forms and transformations until you have a pipeline of simple transformations between intermediate forms that compose to transform the inputs that you *have* to the outputs that you *want*.

We will look more at pure functions evaluated in context in Chapter 16.

Enriching the Abstraction We Discovered

Travelator does more with exchange rates and the traveler's preferred currency than summarize costs. For example, while the user is browsing hotel rooms, it shows the cost of each room in both local and preferred currencies. That is, the hotel room browser performs a currency conversion on an individual cost. The `CostSummaryCalculator` also has to perform currency conversions on individual costs to calculate a summary. If we extract that functionality as a public method, which we can call `toUserCurrency`, we can initialize the hotel room browser with a `CostSummaryCalculator` instead of passing it both the exchange rates and preferred currency. We can also remove the currency conversion calculation—that we now see is duplicated code—from the hotel room browser.

At that point, the class is no longer a calculator of cost summaries. It holds the context for any pricing we do for an individual traveler. So let's rename it to reflect its newfound responsibility. At the moment, we can't think of a better name than `PricingContext`, which leaves our class looking like this:

```
class PricingContext(
    private val userCurrency: Currency,
    private val exchangeRates: ExchangeRates
) {
    fun toUserCurrency(money: Money) =
        exchangeRates.convert(money, userCurrency)

    fun summarise(costs: Iterable<Money>): CostSummary {
        val currencyTotals: List<Money> = costs
            .groupBy { it.currency }
            .values
            .map {
                it.sumOrNull() ?: error("Unexpected empty list")
            }
        val lines: List<CurrencyConversion> = currencyTotals
            .sortedBy { it.currency.currencyCode }
            .map(::toUserCurrency)
        val total = lines
            .map { it.toMoney }
            .sum(userCurrency)
        return CostSummary(lines, total)
    }
}
```

Example 14.28 [accumulator.16:src/main/java/travelator/itinerary/PricingContext.kt]

> **Naming**
>
> The name is a bit too generic for our tastes, but will do until we think of something better. At least it's not misleading. Renames are cheap, even in a mixed Java/Kotlin codebase, so a small incremental improvement is better than no improvement.

This leaves the code that used to use the `CostSummaryCalculator` looking like this:

```
val fx: ExchangeRates = ...
val userCurrency = ...
val pricing = PricingContext(userCurrency, fx)

fun costSummary(i: Itinerary) = pricing.summarise(i.costs())
```

Example 14.29 [accumulator.16:src/test/java/travelator/itinerary/Itinerary_CostTest.kt]

Now that we have this concept in our codebase, we can identify other parts of our application that can use it. We can move logic from those parts onto the `PricingContext`, making it a one-stop shop for operations that need to convert monetary amounts into the traveler's preferred currency. And should it end up full of disparate methods for different use cases, then we can move the operations from methods to extension functions to keep them closer to where they are needed (see Chapter 10).

Moving On

We started this chapter with a calculation that relied on shared, mutable state. It duplicated logic from the standard library and introduced the risk of aliasing errors. By the end of the chapter, we had refactored the same calculation to a transformation of immutable data.

To do so, we moved mutation out of our code in two directions, outward and inward. Outward was obvious: we made the `CostSummaryCalculator` treat the `CostSummary` class as an immutable value type and then made `CostSummary` immutable. Then we made users of `CostSummaryCalculator` treat it as an immutable context to a calculation and then made `CostSummaryCalculator` immutable. But inward? We replaced the imperative code that mutated collections and fields with calls to standard higher-order functions, like `groupingBy`, `fold`, and `reduce`. Under the hood, those functions may mutate state, but they hide that mutation from their callers. From outside, the functions are calculations.

We can use the same approach in our own code when we need to. Sometimes mutating a collection is the easiest thing to do. The standard library does not always have a higher-order function that transforms data the way we want. If we do need a mutable collection, we can hide that mutation inside a calculation to limit the blast radius of any potential aliasing errors. However, every release adds more functions to the standard library, so the need diminishes over time.

Functional programming does not eliminate mutable state but instead *makes it the responsibility of the runtime.* A functional program declares what the runtime should calculate and lets the runtime be responsible for computing that calculation. Kotlin is not a pure functional language, but we benefit by following that principle where we can.

CHAPTER 15
Encapsulated Collections to Type Aliases

In Java, we encapsulate collections of objects in classes to control mutation and add operations. Controlling mutation is less of a concern in Kotlin, and we can use extension functions to add operations. How would our designs be better without the encapsulation, and how do we get there?

In Chapter 6 we looked at the differences between the grains of Java and Kotlin when it comes to collections. Java's collection interfaces, in keeping with its object-oriented roots, are fundamentally mutable, whereas Kotlin treats collections as value types. As we saw, if we mutate shared collections, we can run into all sorts of trouble. We *could* avoid that trouble by not mutating shared collections ("Don't Mutate Shared Collections" on page 63), but in Java that's hard to do when those `add` and `set` methods are just an autocomplete away. Instead of convention and discipline, most Java code sensibly opts for the safer approach of simply not sharing raw collections. Instead, collections are hidden inside another object.

Here, for example, is a `Route` in Travelator:

```
public class Route {
    private final List<Journey> journeys; ❶

    public Route(List<Journey> journeys) {
        this.journeys = journeys; ❷
    }

    public int size() { ❸
        return journeys.size();
    }

    public Journey get(int index) { ❸
        return journeys.get(index);
    }
```

```
    public Location getDepartsFrom() { ❹
        return get(0).getDepartsFrom();
    }

    public Location getArrivesAt() { ❹
        return get(size() - 1).getArrivesAt();
    }

    public Duration getDuration() { ❹
        return Duration.between(
            get(0).getDepartureTime(),
            get(size() - 1).getArrivalTime());
    }

    ...
}
```

Example 15.1 [encapsulated-collections.0:src/main/java/travelator/itinerary/Route.java]

❶ A `Route` encapsulates a `List` of `Journey`.

❷ The raw data is passed in the constructor.

❸ Access to the data, for example for displaying in the UI, is provided by `size` and `get` methods.

❹ The `Route` class implements application logic that uses the contents of the encapsulated list.

Defensive Copies

To fully encapsulate the list, the `Route` constructor could take a defensive copy of the `journeys` parameter. However, we "know" that our system only creates `Route` objects in the JSON deserializer or in tests, neither of which holds onto the list of journeys after creating the `Route` that uses it. There is, therefore, no risk of aliasing errors (*https://oreil.ly/PeqKs*), and we can save the cost of a copy whenever we create a `Route`.

If someone comes along and creates a `Route` with a collection that they later modify, we may come to regret this optimization. This is the problem with using conventions that are not underwritten by the type system.

Once we have a `Route` class, it is a convenient namespace to host operations on routes, like `getDepartsFrom` and `getDuration`. In this case, all the methods shown only use other public methods, and there is no polymorphic behavior, so these operations *could* be defined as static methods taking a `Route` parameter. We can view `Route` as more of a namespace than a class: the operations don't *have* to be methods; it's just more convenient that they are, at least in Java, where static functions are so much less discoverable than methods. In Kotlin, as we saw in Chapter 10, making the operations into extension functions would let us find and call them as if they were methods. `Route` as a class would then be adding no value to `List` of `Journey`, just preventing people from changing it. And in an all-Kotlin codebase, that `List` would be effectively immutable anyway.

In fact, `Route` is doing worse than adding no value to `List<Journey>`—it is removing value. If we had a `List<Journey>`, our frontend code could use its `Iterator` when rendering:

```
public void render(Iterable<Journey> route) {
    for (var journey : route) {
        render(journey);
    }
}
```

Example 15.2 [encapsulated-collections.0:src/main/java/travelator/UI.java]

With a `Route`, we're back to programming in the 1980s:

```
public void render(Route route) {
    for (int i = 0; i < route.size(); i++) {
        var journey = route.get(i);
        render(journey);
    }
}
```

Example 15.3 [encapsulated-collections.0:src/main/java/travelator/UI.java]

If we encapsulate a collection, we *reduce* the operations available for us to work with its contents to only those defined by the encapsulating class. When we want to process that data in a new way, the path of least resistance is to add new methods to the class. The more methods we add to the class, the more the class *increases* the coupling between different parts of our application. Before we know it, adding an operation to support a new UI function ends up recompiling our data-access layer.

Composing Domain Collections

If we don't encapsulate the collection—if we make our domain model *be* the appropriate data structure, rather than hiding it inside another class boundary—we *extend* the operations available for us to work with the data. Then we have our application-specific operations *and* all the operations defined for the collection. Client code can define the operations it needs in terms of the rich Collections API without having to add them to the class.

Rather than a `Route` class accreting all the route functionality and in turn coupling all the parts of our application together, we can view functionality as operations to be composed by importing extension functions. The UI can define functions that render

List<Journey>, which in turn import functions that transform Iterable<Journey>. The persistence layer can transform database responses into List<Journey> and have no particular concept of "routyness" at all.

We can program like this in Java, but the poor discoverability of static functions, combined with mutable collections, goes against the grain of the language. Kotlin has extension functions to make static functions more discoverable, and immutable collections, so that breaking our domain model into collection types and separate operations becomes the happy path.

If we don't need to control access to a collection to prevent embarrassing mutation, and we don't need to write a class to host operations on collections of a type, then is our Route class doing anything for us? Well, it is giving a name to List<Journey>, and it is also giving a type to this List<Journey> that might distinguish it from another List<Journey>—those in reports about all the journeys our travelers have booked this week, for example. Apart from that, though, in some ways it actually gets in our way, as we will see in "Substitute a Type Alias" on page 218.

Where differentiating between different types of lists of journeys is *not* critical, Kotlin allows us to use type aliases to associate the name Route with List<Journey> rather than having to use a class to do this:

```
typealias Route = List<Journey>
```

In Kotlin, then, the obstacles to using collections as domain types have been removed. Encapsulating immutable collections should be the exception rather than the rule.

Collections with Other Properties

Of course, we can't always just substitute type aliases for classes. Take our Itinerary class, for example:

```
class Itinerary(
    val id: Id<Itinerary>,
    val route: Route
) {
    ...
}
```

Example 15.4 [encapsulated-collections.0:src/main/java/travelator/itinerary/Itinerary.kt]

In addition to the Journeys currently hidden in its route, Itinerary has an Id that allows us to address it as an entity. In these cases, we can't just replace the class with its collection.

In these cases, we can gain many of the advantages of unencapsulated collections by making Itinerary implement List<Journey>. That's hard to do right now, because Route doesn't implement that interface itself, but this is a good strategy as more of our domain is expressed as complete collections. We'll get to it in "Refactoring Collections with Other Properties" on page 222.

Refactoring Encapsulated Collections

One of the core services of our Travelator application is route planning.

The `Route` that we saw earlier is a sequence of journeys that can take the traveler from one location to another. We'd like to add some functionality that will allow us to sell accommodation where a `Route` is split over days, but as a key domain abstraction, `Route` is collapsing under the weight of all the operations that we have already added to it and coupling disparate parts of the codebase together. Let's see if we can refactor `Route` to make some room before we start work on the new feature.

Here again is the Java `Route` class:

```
public class Route {
    private final List<Journey> journeys;

    public Route(List<Journey> journeys) {
        this.journeys = journeys;
    }

    public int size() {
        return journeys.size();
    }

    public Journey get(int index) {
        return journeys.get(index);
    }

    public Location getDepartsFrom() {
        return get(0).getDepartsFrom();
    }

    ... many methods
}
```

Example 15.5 [encapsulated-collections.1:src/main/java/travelator/itinerary/Route.java]

Convert Operations to Extensions

We're going to make `Route` less unwieldy (maybe even more wieldy) by moving its operations from methods to functions. Extension functions make this a reasonable strategy, but only from Kotlin, where they are much more discoverable. So we're only going to attempt this stunt once the majority of our uses of `Route` are Kotlin. Luckily, our team really likes converting Java to Kotlin and has been beavering away as they work through the chapters of this book, so we're ready to try this refactoring.

Ultimately, we want to unencapsulate the collection so that our clients work in terms of `List<Journey>` rather than using `Route`, and operations are provided by extension functions on that `List<Journey>`.

We'll start by converting `Route` to Kotlin, which after some tidying yields:

```
class Route(
    private val journeys: List<Journey>
) {
    fun size(): Int = journeys.size

    operator fun get(index: Int) = journeys[index]

    val departsFrom: Location
        get() = get(0).departsFrom

    ... many methods
}
```

Example 15.6 [encapsulated-collections.2:src/main/java/travelator/itinerary/Route.kt]

As usual, you should assume that we are running our tests between refactors to make sure that we haven't broken anything. All is fine at the moment.

Once a class is in Kotlin, IntelliJ can convert methods into extension methods. Let's try out this refactoring on the `departsFrom` property: select it, press Alt-Enter, and choose "Convert member to extension". The method disappears and reappears at the top level of the file:

```
val Route.departsFrom: Location
    get() = get(0).departsFrom
```

Example 15.7 [encapsulated-collections.3:src/main/java/travelator/itinerary/Route.kt]

Kotlin code will continue to be able to access `route.departsFrom` as a property, but Java code can't. IntelliJ has helpfully fixed up the one Java usage to see the property as a static method:

```
public void renderWithHeader(Route route) {
    renderHeader(
        RouteKt.getDepartsFrom(route), ❶
        route.getArrivesAt(),
        route.getDuration()
    );
    for (int i = 0; i < route.size(); i++) {
        var journey = route.get(i);
        render(journey);
    }
}
```

Example 15.8 [encapsulated-collections.3:src/main/java/travelator/UI.java]

❶ Call of static method in `Route.kt`

"Convert member to extension" works well for methods that only call `Route`'s public API. It will fail if we try it on, for example, `withJourneyAt`:

```
fun withJourneyAt(index: Int, replacedBy: Journey): Route {
    val newJourneys = ArrayList(journeys)
    newJourneys[index] = replacedBy
    return Route(newJourneys)
}
```

Example 15.9 [encapsulated-collections.3:src/main/java/travelator/itinerary/Route.kt]

This references the `journeys` property, which is currently private and so not visible to an extension function. At this point we can make the property public (provided that we don't abuse it by mutating the `List` from Java code). This fixes the extension function:

```
fun Route.withJourneyAt(index: Int, replacedBy: Journey): Route {
    val newJourneys = ArrayList(journeys)
    newJourneys[index] = replacedBy
    return Route(newJourneys)
}
```

Example 15.10 [encapsulated-collections.4:src/main/java/travelator/itinerary/Route.kt]

We can continue the process of converting members to extensions until there are no members left; even `size` and `get` can be moved out, provided we are happy to use them statically in any remaining Java clients:

```
public void render(Route route) {
    for (int i = 0; i < RouteKt.getSize(route); i++) {
        var journey = RouteKt.get(route, i);
        render(journey);
    }
}
```

Example 15.11 [encapsulated-collections.5:src/main/java/travelator/UI.java]

(Note that as we have converted the `size` method to a `size` extension property, Java sees a `getSize` function.)

Here then is all that is left of the once-bloated `Route` class:

```
class Route(
    val journeys: List<Journey>
)

val Route.size: Int
    get() = journeys.size

operator fun Route.get(index: Int) = journeys[index]

...
```

Example 15.12 [encapsulated-collections.5:src/main/java/travelator/itinerary/Route.kt]

All its operations (bar accessing the `journeys`) are now extensions, albeit in the same file. But now that they *are* extensions, we can move them from this file to others, even in different modules, to better decouple our dependencies.

Substitute a Type Alias

Now that we've achieved our goal of decoupling the `Route` functionality from the class, is that class superfluous? Actually, wrapping the `List` is worse than superfluous: it prevents us from easily using all the useful extension functions in Kotlin's standard library to construct, transform, and process routes. To quote one of Alan Perlis's Epigrams of Programming (*https://oreil.ly/QDOJz*): "It is better to have 100 functions operate on one data structure than 10 functions on 10 data structures." We don't want a `Route` to *have* a `List` of `Journey`; we want it to *be* a `List` of `Journey`. This is very easy to achieve in Kotlin with delegation:

```
class Route(
    val journeys: List<Journey>
) : List<Journey> by journeys
```

Example 15.13 [encapsulated-collections.6:src/main/java/travelator/itinerary/Route.kt]

In fact, though, we may want more than for a `Route` to be a `List` of `Journey`; we may want a `List` of `Journey` to be a `Route`. To see why, let's look at that `withJourneyAt` function that we glossed over earlier.

When a traveler decides that they would rather not travel by camel, we can't just replace a `Journey`, because `Route` is immutable. Instead, we return a new `Route` where `journeys` is a copy with the relevant `Journey` replaced:

```
@Test
fun replaceJourney() {
    val journey1 = Journey(waterloo, alton, someTime(), someTime(), RAIL)
    val journey2 = Journey(alton, alresford, someTime(), someTime(), CAMEL)
    val journey3 = Journey(alresford, winchester, someTime(), someTime(), BUS)
    val route = Route(listOf(journey1, journey2, journey3))

    val replacement = Journey(alton, alresford, someTime(), someTime(), RAIL)
    val replaced = route.withJourneyAt(1, replacement)

    assertEquals(journey1, replaced.get(0))
    assertEquals(replacement, replaced.get(1))
    assertEquals(journey3, replaced.get(2))
}
```

Example 15.14 [encapsulated-collections.5:src/test/java/travelator/itinerary/RouteTests.kt]

(In passing, note that this test was made more complicated by only having `get` to access the components of a `route`. We can fix that now that we can access the `journeys` property directly.)

Here's the implementation again:

```
fun Route.withJourneyAt(index: Int, replacedBy: Journey): Route {
    val newJourneys = ArrayList(journeys)
    newJourneys[index] = replacedBy
    return Route(newJourneys)
}
```

Example 15.15 [encapsulated-collections.4:src/main/java/travelator/itinerary/Route.kt]

Because `Route` wraps `journeys`, we can't just operate on `journeys`; we have to unwrap, operate, and then wrap back up again. If a `List<Journey>` was a `Route`, then we could use a nice generic function like:

```
fun <T> Iterable<T>.withItemAt(index: Int, replacedBy: T): List<T> =
    this.toMutableList().apply {
        this[index] = replacedBy
    }
```

Example 15.16 [encapsulated-collections.7:src/main/java/travelator/itinerary/Route.kt]

As it is, even using `withItemAt`, we still have to deal with the wrapper:

```
fun Route.withJourneyAt(index: Int, replacedBy: Journey): Route =
    Route(journeys.withItemAt(index, replacedBy))
```

Example 15.17 [encapsulated-collections.7:src/main/java/travelator/itinerary/Route.kt]

Any operation that transforms `Routes` will have this problem—a problem that wouldn't exist if we just used a type alias to say that a `Route` and `List<Journey>` are the same type.

To get there, we will have to remove all the calls to the `Route` constructor and the accesses of the `journeys` property, effectively unwrapping our carefully crafted encapsulation. There is a trick to do this automagically, but it relies on having converted all clients of `Route` to Kotlin. So does using a type alias though, so if we have any remaining Java clients, we have to resign ourselves to some manual editing.

What we're going to do is replace the class with a type alias and, at the same time, add temporary definitions that emulate the API of the class. That API is currently:

```
class Route(
    val journeys: List<Journey>
) : List<Journey> by journeys
```

Example 15.18 [encapsulated-collections.6:src/main/java/travelator/itinerary/Route.kt]

We emulate it with:

```
typealias Route = List<Journey>

fun Route(journeys: List<Journey>) = journeys

val Route.journeys get() = this
```

Example 15.19 [encapsulated-collections.8:src/main/java/travelator/itinerary/Route.kt]

Because there is no `new` keyword in Kotlin, we can emulate the constructor call `Route(...)` with a function of the same name. Similarly, we replace the `journeys` property with an extension property that returns the receiver itself. The net result is that our Kotlin clients continue to compile against this new API:

```
val route = Route(listOf(journey1, journey2, journey3)) ❶

val replacement = Journey(alton, alresford, someTime(), someTime(), RAIL)

assertEquals(
    listOf(journey1, replacement, journey3),
    route.withJourneyAt(1, replacement).journeys ❷
)
```

Example 15.20 [encapsulated-collections.8:src/test/java/travelator/itinerary/RouteTests.kt]

❶ Our new function, not the constructor

❷ Extension property, not the class property

Inlining both function and property completes the refactor. The encapsulated collection is now just a collection:

```
val route = listOf(journey1, journey2, journey3) ❶

val replacement = Journey(alton, alresford, someTime(), someTime(), RAIL)

assertEquals(
    listOf(journey1, replacement, journey3),
    route.withJourneyAt(1, replacement) ❷
)
```

Example 15.21 [encapsulated-collections.9:src/test/java/travelator/itinerary/RouteTests.kt]

❶ `Route` was a no-op

❷ As was `journeys`

Any remaining Java clients will have been broken when we replaced the `Route` class with a type alias, because Java doesn't understand type aliases. We fixed those by hand, replacing `Route` with `List<Journey>`:

```
public void render(List<Journey> route) {
    for (int i = 0; i < RouteKt.getSize(route); i++) {
        var journey = RouteKt.get(route, i);
        render(journey);
    }
}
```

Example 15.22 [encapsulated-collections.8:src/main/java/travelator/UI.java]

Our transformation is almost complete. We still have `size` and `get` functions:

```
val Route.size: Int
    get() = this.size

operator fun Route.get(index: Int) = this[index]
```

Example 15.23 [encapsulated-collections.9:src/main/java/travelator/itinerary/Route.kt]

Because these have the same signature as their method counterparts on `List`, the compiler warns us that they are shadowed; our Kotlin will be calling the methods, not the extensions. That means that if we didn't have any Java client code invoking the extensions as statics, we could delete them.

We do have a Java client, though—that pesky rendering code, which is still calling the extensions as `getSize` and `get` in `RouteKt`. Those extensions are calling the methods that we want to use, but we can't inline code from Kotlin to Java, so we'll just delete the extensions anyway. Now the compiler will tell us where we need to fix the Java, and we can do that by hand:

```
public void render(List<Journey> route) {
    for (int i = 0; i < route.size(); i++) {
        var journey = route.get(i);
        render(journey);
    }
}
```

Example 15.24 [encapsulated-collections.10:src/main/java/travelator/UI.java]

In reality, of course, we would replace this with:

```
public void render(Iterable<Journey> route) {
    for (var journey : route) {
        render(journey);
    }
}
```

Example 15.25 [encapsulated-collections.10:src/main/java/travelator/UI.java]

The Kotlin clients are unphased by deleting the extensions, because they were always calling the methods on `List`, so the transformation is almost complete. We can also now inline `withJourneyAt`, because it too is a no-op. This leaves us with `Route` like this:

```
typealias Route = List<Journey>

val Route.departsFrom: Location
    get() = first().departsFrom

val Route.arrivesAt: Location
    get() = last().arrivesAt

val Route.duration: Duration
    get() = Duration.between(
```

```
            first().departureTime,
            last().arrivalTime
        )
    ... other operations moved
```

Example 15.26 [encapsulated-collections.10:src/main/java/travelator/itinerary/Route.kt]

Our Kotlin usages are just `List` operations:

```
val route = listOf(journey1, journey2, journey3)
assertEquals(
    listOf(journey1, replacement, journey3),
    route.withItemAt(1, replacement)
)
```

Example 15.27 [encapsulated-collections.10:src/test/java/travelator/itinerary/RouteTests.kt]

Any residual Java is readable, if a little ugly:

```
public void renderWithHeader(List<Journey> route) {
    renderHeader(
        RouteKt.getDepartsFrom(route),
        RouteKt.getArrivesAt(route),
        RouteKt.getDuration(route)
    );
    for (var journey : route) {
        render(journey);
    }
}
```

Example 15.28 [encapsulated-collections.10:src/main/java/travelator/UI.java]

Refactoring Collections with Other Properties

As we saw previously, we can't use type aliases when our types have collections with other attributes. We looked at `Itinerary`, which combines an `id` with a `Route`:

```
class Itinerary(
    val id: Id<Itinerary>,
    val route: Route
) {

    fun hasJourneyLongerThan(duration: Duration) =
        route.any { it.duration > duration }

    ...
}
```

Example 15.29 [encapsulated-collections.11:src/main/java/travelator/itinerary/Itinerary.kt]

We can get the advantages of being able to query `Journeys` directly by implementing `Route` with delegation:

```
class Itinerary(
    val id: Id<Itinerary>,
    val route: Route
```

```
) : Route by route { ❶

    fun hasJourneyLongerThan(duration: Duration) =
        any { it.duration > duration }

    ...
}
```

Example 15.30 [encapsulated-collections.12:src/main/java/travelator/itinerary/Itinerary.kt]

❶ The `by route` clause declares that the `Itinerary` object will delegate all methods on the `Route` interface to the `route` parameter passed to its constructor. A class can override this behavior by providing its own implementation of methods of the delegated interface, but we don't want to do this for `Itinerary`.

Now that we can treat `Itinerary` as a `Route`, we can move `hasJourneyLongerThan` out as an extension and have it available to any `Route`, not just to `Itinerary`:

```
fun Route.hasJourneyLongerThan(duration: Duration) =
    any { it.duration > duration }
```

Example 15.31 [encapsulated-collections.13:src/main/java/travelator/itinerary/Itinerary.kt]

All those extensions to `Route` (aka `List<Journey>`) that we moved from methods to extensions are also now applicable to `Itinerary` as well:

```
fun Iterable<Itinerary>.shortest() =
    minByOrNull {
        it.duration ❶
    }
```

Example 15.32 [encapsulated-collections.13:src/main/java/travelator/itinerary/itineraries.kt]

❶ This is `Route.duration`, aka `List<Journey>.duration`

What we can't do as easily is create a new `Itinerary` from an existing one. This is now easy for `Route`, because standard API operations on `List<Journey>` (actually, usually `Iterable<Journey>`, as we saw in Chapter 6) return `List<Journey>`, which is the other name for `Route`:

```
fun Route.withoutJourneysBy(travelMethod: TravelMethod) =
    this.filterNot { it.method == travelMethod }
```

Example 15.33 [encapsulated-collections.13:src/main/java/travelator/itinerary/itineraries.kt]

For `Itinerary`, we have to create a new `Itinerary` to rewrap the result:

```
fun Itinerary.withoutJourneysBy(travelMethod: TravelMethod) =
    Itinerary(
        id,
        this.filterNot { it.method == travelMethod }
    )
```

Example 15.34 [encapsulated-collections.13:src/main/java/travelator/itinerary/itineraries.kt]

This is yet another place where data classes come to the rescue:

```
data class Itinerary(
    val id: Id<Itinerary>,
    val route: Route
) : Route by route {

    ...
}
```

Example 15.35 [encapsulated-collections.14:src/main/java/travelator/itinerary/Itinerary.kt]

Making `Itinerary` a data class means that we can make a copy with just a revised route, no matter how many other properties it has:

```
fun Itinerary.withoutJourneysBy(travelMethod: TravelMethod) =
    copy(route = filterNot { it.method == travelMethod } )
```

Example 15.36 [encapsulated-collections.14:src/main/java/travelator/itinerary/itineraries.kt]

Better still, we can add a method `withTransformedRoute`:

```
data class Itinerary(
    val id: Id<Itinerary>,
    val route: Route
) : Route by route {

    fun withTransformedRoute(transform: (Route).() -> Route) =
        copy(route = transform(route))

    ...
}
```

Example 15.37 [encapsulated-collections.15:src/main/java/travelator/itinerary/Itinerary.kt]

This allows us to create a transformed `Itinerary` almost as easily as we could create a transformed `Route`:

```
fun Itinerary.withoutJourneysBy(travelMethod: TravelMethod) =
    withTransformedRoute {
        filterNot { it.method == travelMethod }
    }

fun Itinerary.withoutLastJourney() =
    withTransformedRoute { dropLast(1) }
```

Example 15.38 [encapsulated-collections.15:src/main/java/travelator/itinerary/itineraries.kt]

Moving On

We started this chapter with a Java class that encapsulated a mutable collection to guarantee value semantics. As we translated more of our code to Kotlin, we could rely on Kotlin's type system to prevent the collection from being modified, and no longer needed to encapsulate it within the class. That allowed us to convert operations from methods to extensions, and move their definitions close to where they are used. Because our class encapsulated a single collection, we were able to eliminate the class altogether and replace it with a type alias.

Immutable collections and extensions allow us to organize our code in ways that are not available in Java. We can group all the logic required by a particular feature of the application in the same module, regardless of the domain classes the logic applies to. However, if we wanted methods of those domain classes to be polymorphic methods, we would have to define them on those classes and not in our feature module. In Chapter 18, *Open to Sealed Classes*, we look at sealed classes, an alternative to object-oriented polymorphism that is more convenient when we define type hierarchies in one part of the code and operations on those types in another.

Finally, note that reusing built-in types like `List` rather than defining a specific type is not without cost. We might be storing items in a `List` as an implementation detail rather than a modeling choice. It's also a lot easier to "Find usages" of a specific wrapper class than a generic specialization. Nevertheless, the standard collection types are pervasive because they are such good abstractions—so good that we generally shouldn't hide them. Chapter 22, *Classes to Functions*, looks at what happens if we take this idea and run with it.

CHAPTER 16

Interfaces to Functions

In Java, we use interfaces to specify a contract between code that defines some functionality and code that needs it. Those interfaces couple the two parties together, which can make our software harder to maintain. How do function types help solve this problem?

Imagine, if you can, that you need to send email from some code that you are writing. Just that for now—not receive mail, or list sent messages—just fire and forget.

The code that describes the email is simple enough:

```
data class Email(
    val to: EmailAddress,
    val from: EmailAddress,
    val subject: String,
    val body: String
)
```

Given an `Email`, client code would *like* to call the simplest possible function to send it, which is:

```
fun send(email: Email) {
    ...
}
```

Of course when we come to implement this function, we discover that to actually send email, we require all sorts of other information. Not information about the email itself but, rather, configuration about how to send it. Things like the sending server's hostname and security credentials—all the things that your nontechnical relative doesn't know, but you need to set up their new computer. We'll add three extra parameters to `sendEmail` to stand in for all this configuration:

```
fun sendEmail(
    email: Email,
```

```
    serverAddress: InetAddress,
    username: String,
    password: String
) {
    ...
}
```

As a client, things have just become a lot less convenient. Everywhere we want to send email has to know this configuration; we'll be passing it around from the top to the bottom of the codebase. Solving that problem by hiding the details in global variables works fine until we discover that every run of the unit test suite now sends 50 emails! There must be a better way of hiding these petty details.

Object-Oriented Encapsulation

Object-oriented languages have a ready-made solution to this problem—objects can encapsulate the data:

```
class EmailSender(
    private val serverAddress: InetAddress,
    private val username: String,
    private val password: String
) {
    fun send(email: Email) {
        sendEmail(
            email,
            serverAddress,
            username,
            password
        )
    }
}
```

Now when we want to send email, we need access to an `EmailSender` (rather than the static function). Once we have an `EmailSender`, instead of calling a function, we invoke a method, and we don't need to tell the method all the petty details because it already knows them; they are the fields of its class:

```
// Where we know the configuration
val sender: EmailSender = EmailSender(
    inetAddress("smtp.travelator.com"),
    "username",
    "password"
)

// Where we send the message
fun sendThanks() {
    sender.send(
        Email(
            to = parse("support@internationalrescue.org"),
            from = parse("support@travelator.com"),
```

```
                subject = "Thanks for your help",
                body = "..."
            )
        )
    }
```

In general, the place where we know the configuration and the place where we want to send an email will be separated in our code, often by many layers. Usually in OO, the sender will be captured as a property of a class and used by its methods:

```
// Where we know the configuration
val subsystem = Rescuing(
    EmailSender(
        inetAddress("smtp.travelator.com"),
        "username",
        "password"
    )
)

// Where we send the message
class Rescuing(
    private val emailSender: EmailSender
) {
    fun sendThanks() {
        emailSender.send(
            Email(
                to = parse("support@internationalrescue.org"),
                from = parse("support@travelator.com"),
                subject = "Thanks for your help",
                body = "..."
            )
        )
    }
}
```

Often we will extract an interface:

```
interface ISendEmail {
    fun send(email: Email)
}

class EmailSender(
    ...
) : ISendEmail {
    override fun send(email: Email) {
        sendEmail(
            email,
            serverAddress,
            username,
            password
        )
    }
}
```

If our client code depends on the ISendEmail interface rather than the EmailSender class, we can configure our tests to use a fake implementation of ISendEmail, which doesn't actually send emails but instead allows us to check what would be sent if it did. Not only can we provide fakes that don't send emails at all, but also different genuine implementations like SmtpEmailSender and X400EmailSender, each of which hides both its configuration and implementation from its clients. We came for the information hiding but stayed for the implementation hiding.

When we say *hiding*, it sounds a bit pejorative, but the concealment is useful to both client and implementor. The former doesn't have the problem of having to supply the configuration details at the point of use; the latter is able to evolve separately from its users (provided it doesn't change API, expressed in the interface).

Before we leave the object-oriented realm, note that we don't have to create a named class to implement ISendEmail; we can do it anonymously:

```
fun createEmailSender(
    serverAddress: InetAddress,
    username: String,
    password: String
): ISendEmail =
    object : ISendEmail {
        override fun send(email: Email) =
            sendEmail(
                email,
                serverAddress,
                username,
                password
            )
    }
```

Why might we want to do this? Well, when we don't control all the clients of our code (we are publishing a library external to our organization, for example), this gives us flexibility to change our implementation, safe in the knowledge that clients cannot depend on a specific implementation class by downcasting to it and calling other methods. We call the object that we return here a *closure*, because it closes over values that it requires from its enclosing context (the function call), capturing them for later reference.

In Kotlin 1.4, we can declare our ISendEmail interface as a fun interface (one with only one abstract method). This way, we can define the implementation of the single operation with a lambda rather than with an object with a single method:

```
fun interface ISendEmail {
    fun send(email: Email)
}

fun createEmailSender(
    serverAddress: InetAddress,
```

```
    username: String,
    password: String
) = ISendEmail { email ->
    sendEmail(
        email,
        serverAddress,
        username,
        password
    )
}
```

Again, the lambda here is a closure, capturing the values of the parameters of its enclosing function.

Functional Encapsulation

Having seen how an OO programmer solves the problem of encapsulating pesky details so clients don't have to supply them at the point of use, how would a functional programmer approach the same problem?

Remember that we're trying to get to a function with this signature:

```
fun send(email: Email) {
    ...
}
```

But we actually need all this information to send the message:

```
fun sendEmail(
    email: Email,
    serverAddress: InetAddress,
    username: String,
    password: String
) {
    ...
}
```

In functional terms, this is an example of *partial application* (*https://oreil.ly/V1KOm*): fixing some of the arguments to a function to yield a function with fewer arguments. Although some languages provide built-in support for this, in Kotlin the easiest approach is to write a function to partially apply our configuration.

What we want is a function that takes the configuration and returns a function that knows how to send an email:

```
fun createEmailSender(
    serverAddress: InetAddress,
    username: String,
    password: String
): (Email) -> Unit { ❶
    ...
}
```

❶ The return type of our function is itself a function that takes an `Email` and returns `Unit`.

Thus, `createEmailSender` is a constructor. Not a class constructor, but a function taking the same role. Both `createEmailSender` and `::EmailSender` are functions that return an object that knows how to send a message.

To see how this works in functions, we can write this in longhand first by defining an inner function that captures the arguments it requires from the parent:

```
fun createEmailSender(
    serverAddress: InetAddress,
    username: String,
    password: String
): (Email) -> Unit {

    fun result(email: Email) {
        sendEmail(
            email,
            serverAddress,
            username,
            password
        )
    }
    return ::result
}
```

We can then make the result a lambda expression:

```
fun createEmailSender(
    serverAddress: InetAddress,
    username: String,
    password: String
): (Email) -> Unit {

    val result: (Email) -> Unit =
        { email ->
            sendEmail(
                email,
                serverAddress,
                username,
                password
            )
        }
    return result
}
```

If we inline `result` and convert the whole function to a single expression, we are left with this functional definition:

```
fun createEmailSender(
    serverAddress: InetAddress,
```

```
        username: String,
        password: String
    ): (Email) -> Unit =
        { email ->
            sendEmail(
                email,
                serverAddress,
                username,
                password
            )
        }
```

So createEmailSender is a function that returns a lambda that calls sendEmail, combining the lambda's single Email argument with the configuration from its own parameters. This is a closure in functional land, and it's not a coincidence that it is very similar to the OO versions with a `fun interface` or `object` definition.

To use this function, we can create it in one place and invoke it in another, very much as we did with the object solution:

```
// Where we know the configuration
val sender: (Email) -> Unit = createEmailSender(
    inetAddress("smtp.travelator.com"),
    "username",
    "password"
)

// Where we send the message
fun sendThanks() {
    sender( ❶
        Email(
            to = parse("support@internationalrescue.org"),
            from = parse("support@travelator.com"),
            subject = "Thanks for your help",
            body = "..."
        )
    )
}
```

❶ An implicit invoke call is hidden here.

This is the same shape as the OO case (if we replace the hidden invoke with send):

```
fun sendThanks() {
    sender.send(
        Email(
            to = parse("support@internationalrescue.org"),
            from = parse("support@travelator.com"),
            subject = "Thanks for your help",
            body = "..."
        )
```

```
    )
}
```

In the unlikely event that you're joining us from JavaScript or Clojure, the functional form will be familiar, but if you came to Kotlin from Java, this solution probably feels quite alien.

Function Types in Java

Both the object and functional forms have allowed us to encapsulate things (in this case configuration, but it could equally well have been collaborators) to transport them from the place where they are known to the place where they are used. Any data structure could have done that, but because the object and the function both have an operation that can be run (`send` and `invoke`, respectively), the client can remain oblivious to the details of the configuration and just pass the information that is specific to each invocation (the `Email`).

One way of unifying the functional and OO solutions is to view a function as an object with a single `invoke` method. This is exactly what Java 8 did when it introduced lambdas. To refer to a function type, Java uses interfaces with a *Single Abstract Method* (SAM) that has the desired signature. Lambdas in Java are a special syntax to implement a SAM interface. The Java runtime defines SAM interfaces named by role: `Consumer`, `Supplier`, `Function`, `BiFunction`, `Predicate`, and so on for us. It also provides primitive specializations, like `DoublePredicate`, to avoid boxing issues.

Expressed in Java, our functional solution is:

```
// Where we know the configuration
Consumer<Email> sender = createEmailSender(
    inetAddress("example.com"),
    "username",
    "password"
);

// Where we send the message
public void sendThanks() {
    sender.accept( ❶
        new Email(
            parse("support@internationalrescue.org"),
            parse("support@travelator.com"),
            "Thanks for your help",
            "..."
        )
    );
}
```

❶ `accept` is the name of the single abstract method on the `Consumer` interface.

`createEmailSender` can be implemented with a lambda:

```
static Consumer<Email> createEmailSender(
    InetAddress serverAddress,
    String username,
    String password
) {
    return email -> sendEmail(
        email,
        serverAddress,
        username,
        password
    );
}
```

This is equivalent to creating an anonymous implementation of the interface, a technique that will be very familiar to those of us who programmed in Java before Java 8:

```
static Consumer<Email> createEmailSender(
    InetAddress serverAddress,
    String username,
    String password
) {
    return new Consumer<Email>() {
        @Override
        public void accept(Email email) {
            sendEmail(
                email,
                serverAddress,
                username,
                password
            );
        }
    };
}
```

We say "equivalent to creating an anonymous implementation of the interface," but under the hood, the implementation is more complex to avoid unnecessarily defining classes and instantiating objects.

Note that we can't assign the `(Email) -> Unit` result of the Kotlin `createEmailSender` to a variable of type `Consumer<Email>`. This is because the Kotlin runtime uses its own function types, and the compiler compiles `(Email) -> Unit` into `Function1<Email, Unit>`. There are a whole series of Kotlin `FunctionN` interfaces for the different numbers of parameters.

Because the interfaces are not compatible, to mix Java and Kotlin at this functional level, we will have to thunk sometimes. Given a Kotlin function type `(Email) -> Unit`:

```
// Kotlin function type
val sender: (Email) -> Unit = createEmailSender(
    inetAddress("smtp.travelator.com"),
    "username",
    "password"
)
```

We can't just assign `sender` to `Consumer<Email>`:

```
val consumer: Consumer<Email> = sender // Doesn't compile ❶
```

❶ `Type mismatch. Required: Consumer<Email> Found:(Email) -> Unit`

We can, though, convert with a lambda:

```
val consumer: Consumer<Email> = Consumer<Email> { email ->
    sender(email)
}
```

There is a situation where we don't have to convert, which is calling a Java method that takes a SAM parameter, for example, this constructor:

```
class Rescuing {
    private final Consumer<Email> emailSender;

    Rescuing(Consumer<Email> emailSender) {
        this.emailSender = emailSender;
    }
    ...
}
```

Here, the compiler *is* able to convert `(Email) -> Unit` to `Consumer<Email>`, because Kotlin will convert parameters automatically, so that we can say:

```
Rescuing(sender)
```

Mix and Match

There are two sides to an abstraction, the client code and the implementation code. So far, both client and implementor have either been object-oriented or functional. In the OO case, fields carry configuration, and the client invokes a method. In the functional scheme, a function closes over the configuration, and the client invokes the function.

Can we unify these approaches, passing an OO implementation to a function-expecting client or vice versa? Or, in Kotlin terms, can we convert `ISendEmail` to `(Email) -> Unit` and the inverse? Why yes we can!

Remember that in Java and Kotlin, function types are just interfaces. Because of this, `EmailSender` can implement the type `Consumer<Email>` or `(Email) -> Unit`, respectively, by defining a method with the signature of the function type.

So in Java, we can write:

```
public class EmailSender
    implements ISendEmail,
        Consumer<Email> ❶
{
        ...
    @Override
    public void accept(Email email) { ❷
        send(email);
    }

    @Override
    public void send(Email email) {
        sendEmail(email, serverAddress, username, password);
    }
}
```

❶ Declare

❷ Implement

This is the Kotlin equivalent:

```
class EmailSender(
        ...
) : ISendEmail,
    (Email) -> Unit ❶
{
    override operator fun invoke(email: Email) =
        send(email) ❷

    override fun send(email: Email) {
        sendEmail(
            email,
            serverAddress,
            username,
            password
        )
    }
}
```

❶ Declare

❷ Implement

If we do this, we can use our class-based sender in place of our functional one. We'll stick with Kotlin now:

```
// Where we know the configuration
val sender: (Email) -> Unit = EmailSender(
    inetAddress("smtp.travelator.com"),
```

```
        "username",
        "password"
    )

    // Where we send the message
    fun sendThanks() {
        sender( ❶
            Email(
                to = parse("support@internationalrescue.org"),
                from = parse("support@travelator.com"),
                subject = "Thanks for your help",
                body = "..."
            )
        )
    }
```

❶ There is an implicit `invoke` here.

Now our object-oriented implementation has gained an `invoke` method to fit in with the functional approach. This calls into question the usefulness of our `ISendEmail` interface. We can see that it is equivalent to the function type `(Email) -> Unit`. All it does is give the name `send` to what happens when you invoke it. Maybe we could just use the type `(Email) -> Unit` everywhere in place of `ISendEmail`?

If you think that isn't expressive enough, then maybe you aren't a functional programmer. Luckily, there is a middle ground: we can use a type alias to give a name to the functional type, thus communicating our intent:

```
typealias EmailSenderFunction = (Email) -> Unit

class EmailSender(
    ...
) : EmailSenderFunction {
    override fun invoke(email: Email) {
        sendEmail(
            email,
            serverAddress,
            username,
            password
        )
    }
}
```

In reality, we would probably call `EmailSenderFunction`, `EmailSender`. Here we've given it a different name to avoid confusion with the OO version, but the fact that we want to call them the same thing shows that they serve the same purpose from the client's perspective.

Expressive Function Types

Once we have our head in the functional mindset, the type `(Email) -> Unit` may be expressive enough to tell us the role of the function, especially when bound to a variable named `sender`. What can you do with an email that doesn't return a result? Well, if it doesn't return a result, it must be an action ("Actions" on page 79), but deleting an email might also have a similar signature. Objects have that advantage over functions—they get to name their methods (`send(email)` is obviously different than `delete(email)`)—at the expense of also having to name the type of the object or interface.

Kotlin has a feature that can help make function types more expressive: we can name the parameters. So if it helps, we could write `(toSend: Email) -> Unit`. It doesn't make a great difference here but can be very useful in situations with parameters of the same type, for example `(username: String, password: String) -> AuthenticatedUser`. If we use this form, IntelliJ will even helpfully name the parameters when we implement the function with a lambda or a class.

There is another way of bridging the OO–FP gap that doesn't involve making our classes implement function types: create a function reference at the point of translation. Here is our old class-based solution:

```
class EmailSender(
    private val serverAddress: InetAddress,
    private val username: String,
    private val password: String
) {
    fun send(email: Email) {
        sendEmail(
            email,
            serverAddress,
            username,
            password
        )
    }
}
```

We can convert an instance of `EmailSender` to a function type with a lambda:

```
val instance = EmailSender(
    inetAddress("smtp.travelator.com"),
    "username",
    "password"
)
val sender: (Email) -> Unit = { instance.send(it) }
```

or just use a method reference:

```
val sender: (Email) -> Unit = instance::send
```

Although we've shown these conversions in Kotlin, they also work in Java (with a slightly different syntax). They work with the `send` method on the `ISendEmail` interface too, although it's not clear that the interface is doing much for us if we are using the function type.

Can we do the opposite and pass our functional sender into something that expects an `ISendEmail`? This requires more ceremony, because we have to create an anonymous object implementing `ISendEmail` to perform the thunk:

```
val function: (Email) -> Unit = createEmailSender(
    inetAddress("smtp.travelator.com"),
    "username",
    "password"
)

val sender: ISendEmail = object : ISendEmail {
    override fun send(email: Email) {
        function(email)
    }
}
```

If we had used a Kotlin 1.4 `fun interface`, we could again remove some boilerplate:

```
fun interface ISendEmail {
    fun send(email: Email)
}

val sender = ISendEmail { function(it) }
```

Comparing the Approaches

Let's remind ourselves of the OO approach.

First we define a type:

```
class EmailSender(
    private val serverAddress: InetAddress,
    private val username: String,
    private val password: String
) {
    fun send(email: Email) {
        sendEmail(
            email,
            serverAddress,
            username,
            password
        )
    }
}
```

Then we create instances and call methods:

```
// Where we know the configuration
val sender: EmailSender = EmailSender(
    inetAddress("smtp.travelator.com"),
    "username",
    "password"
)

// Where we send the message
fun sendThanks() {
    sender.send(
        Email(
            to = parse("support@internationalrescue.org"),
            from = parse("support@travelator.com"),
            subject = "Thanks for your help",
            body = "..."
        )
    )
}
```

In functional land, we don't have to define a type, because `(Email) -> Unit` just exists (which is to say, is provided by the runtime), so we can just say:

```
// Where we know the configuration
val sender: (Email) -> Unit = createEmailSender(
    inetAddress("smtp.travelator.com"),
    "username",
    "password"
)

// Where we send the message
fun sendThanks() {
    sender( ❶
        Email(
            to = parse("support@internationalrescue.org"),
            from = parse("support@travelator.com"),
            subject = "Thanks for your help",
            body = "..."
        )
    )
}
```

❶ With or without the `invoke`

Clients using the *object* have to know to call the `send` method to send email; in contrast, clients using the *function* just have to invoke it, but they only know that the function sends email because it has been assigned the name `sender`. If that name got lost in the call hierarchy, we are left to guess what happens from the function signature.

The quid pro quo of the OO clients having to know to call the send method is that we could package up a number of email-related operations into an EmailSystem, with methods like send, list, and delete, and pass all this functionality to clients in one go. Clients can then choose which they need in which context:

```
interface EmailSystem {
    fun send(email: Email)
    fun delete(email: Email)
    fun list(folder: Folder): List<Email>
    fun move(email: Email, to: Folder)
}
```

To achieve this functionally would require either passing individual functions around or some sort of map of name to function, maybe an instance of a class itself:

```
class EmailSystem(
    val send: (Email) -> Unit,
    val delete: (Email) -> Unit,
    val list: (folder: Folder) -> List<Email>,
    val move: (email: Email, to: Folder) ->  Unit
)
```

Given such an object, clients could treat it very much like an implementation of the interface:

```
fun sendThanks(sender: EmailSystem) {
    sender.send(
        Email(
            to = parse("support@internationalrescue.org"),
            from = parse("support@travelator.com"),
            subject = "Thanks for your help",
            body = "..."
        )
    )
}
```

But this is not the same as the OO code. Instead of invoking a send *method*, what is actually happening here is that we are calling getSender to access a property of function type, and then calling invoke on that function:

```
fun sendThanks(sender: EmailSystem) {
    sender.send.invoke(
        Email(
            to = parse("support@internationalrescue.org"),
            from = parse("support@travelator.com"),
            subject = "Thanks for your help",
            body = "..."
        )
    )
}
```

The code may read the same, but it generates very different, and fundamentally incompatible, bytecode.

Coupling

A subtle difference between expressing a dependency as either an implementation of `ISendEmail`, or as an implementation of the function type `(Email) -> Unit`, is the coupling between the client and the implementation, in particular when they are in different code modules.

`ISendEmail` has to be defined somewhere. The client can't define it, because the implementor will depend on the interface, and the client on the implementation, leading to a circular dependency. So the interface has to be defined either with the implementation, or in a separate place (package or JAR file) depended on by both implementation and its clients. The latter (an application of the dependency inversion principle (*https://oreil.ly/AcrWj*)) is in theory preferable but in practice more work and thus often neglected.

With or without dependency inversion, the result is the client and implementation being coupled by the interface in ways that can make systems hard to reason with and refactor. Any change to methods on `EmailSystem` might affect all code that depends on the interface.

In contrast, in the functional world, the runtime defines all the function types, so they don't introduce a compile-time dependency between the client and an implementation. Unlike `ISendEmail`, which we have to define somewhere, `(Email) -> Unit` (or in Java, `Consumer<Email>`) is part of the language. Of course, there will be a runtime dependency—the constructor code needs to be visible where the dependency is created, and the client has to be able to invoke the implementation code—but these cause less coupling. For example, when a dependency is expressed as a function type, we can rename `EmailSystem.send`, and the only change in our client code will be to use a different method reference; the internals of `sendThanks` are unaffected.

Only Pass Types That You Own or That the Runtime Defines

An early rule of thumb for OO systems was that, on the inside of our systems, we should program in terms of types that we own rather than those supplied by libraries. That way we are insulated from changes that we don't control and are more likely to write code that can be reused with different implementations.

An exception to this rule is taking a dependency on types provided by the runtime; these are very unlikely to change. Function types allow us to easily convert from unstable to stable interfaces, allowing parts of our systems to evolve at different rates.

Object-Oriented or Functional?

Both the object-oriented and functional approaches can achieve the same goals, and with similar levels of expressiveness. Which should we choose?

Let's consider this from the context of the client code. If our client only needs to list email, it should have a dependency on a single `(Folder) -> List<Email>` function. This way it is not coupled to an implementation, and the dependency can be satisfied by anything implementing the function type, including:

- A plain function
- An object implementing the function type
- Method reference selecting a method with the desired signature
- A lambda with the desired signature

Even if we already happen to have an interface, let's say `EmailSystem`, which defines the desired method along with `send`, `move`, and `delete`:

```
interface EmailSystem {
    fun send(email: Email)
    fun delete(email: Email)
    fun list(folder: Folder): List<Email>
    fun move(email: Email, to: Folder)
}
```

we shouldn't needlessly couple our client to this interface when the function type will do:

```
class Organiser(
    private val listing: (Folder) -> List<Email>
) {
    fun subjectsIn(folder: Folder): List<String> {
        return listing(folder).map { it.subject }
    }
}

val emailSystem: EmailSystem = ...
val organiser = Organiser(emailSystem::list)
```

Depending on the wider interface misses the opportunity to communicate precisely which operations we require and forces clients to provide an implementation of the whole interface. This is particularly irritating in tests, where we will have to introduce fake objects just to get our test code to compile.

The drives of communication and reduced coupling are so strong that even if our client needs to send and delete email, and in practice these will be supplied by a single `EmailSystem`, the client should probably depend on two functions rather than the interface:

```
class Organiser(
    private val listing: (Folder) -> List<Email>,
    private val deleting: (Email) -> Unit
) {
    fun deleteInternal(folder: Folder) {
        listing(rootFolder).forEach {
            if (it.to.isInternal()) {
                deleting.invoke(it)
            }
        }
    }
}

val organiser = Organiser(
    emailSystem::list,
    emailSystem::delete
)
```

Only when the client requires three related operations does it feel like a multimethod interface should be the default:

```
class Organiser(
    private val emails: EmailSystem
) {
    fun organise() {
        emails.list(rootFolder).forEach {
            if (it.to.isInternal()) {
                emails.delete(it)
            } else {
                emails.move(it, archiveFolder)
            }
        }
    }
}

val organiser = Organiser(emailSystem)
```

Even here, it might be better for the client to accept an object that only supports the desired operations. We can do that with a new interface (`Dependencies` here), implemented with an `object`:

```
class Organiser(
    private val emails: Dependencies
) {
    interface Dependencies {
        fun delete(email: Email)
        fun list(folder: Folder): List<Email>
        fun move(email: Email, to: Folder)
    }

    fun organise() {
        emails.list(rootFolder).forEach {
            if (it.to.isInternal()) {
```

```
                    emails.delete(it)
                } else {
                    emails.move(it, archiveFolder)
                }
            }
        }
    }

val organiser = Organiser(object : Organiser.Dependencies {
    override fun delete(email: Email) {
        emailSystem.delete(email)
    }

    override fun list(folder: Folder): List<Email> {
        return emailSystem.list(folder)
    }

    override fun move(email: Email, to: Folder) {
        emailSystem.move(email, to)
    }
})
```

That's pretty irritating though; maybe this is a place where a class of functions would be better:

```
class Organiser(
    private val emails: Dependencies
) {
    class Dependencies(
        val delete: (Email) -> Unit,
        val list: (folder: Folder) -> List<Email>,
        val move: (email: Email, to: Folder) -> Unit
    )

    fun organise() {
        emails.list(rootFolder).forEach {
            if (it.to.isInternal()) {
                emails.delete(it)
            } else {
                emails.move(it, archiveFolder)
            }
        }
    }
}

val organiser = Organiser(
    Organiser.Dependencies(
        delete = emailSystem::delete,
        list = emailSystem::list,
        move = emailSystem::move
    )
)
```

So, until it becomes hard work, we should default to expressing our client's needs as function types. Our implementation then can be just a function, or something implementing the function type, or a method converted to the function type through method references or lambdas, whichever makes most sense in context.

The Legacy of Java

Although we said earlier that "our runtime defines all the functions types," that wasn't true of Java until Java 8 introduced `Supplier`, `Consumer`, `Predicate`, and so on, and the ability to implement them with method references or lambdas.

Because of this, legacy Java code usually expresses dependencies with the same multimethod interfaces that we would use to group them by subsystem (like `EmailSystem`), even when only one of those methods is required to implement the functionality. This leads to the coupling problems described earlier. It also leads to a need for mocking (or, more pedantically, faking) frameworks to create test implementations of broad interfaces where in practice only one method will be called. These fakes then sprout the functionality to fail early if you call a method that you didn't mean to call, a problem that would be solved at compile time if a single function expressed the dependency.

Once we have introduced a mocking framework into our codebase (or, more usually, two or three mocking frameworks to cater to different tastes), they allow us to solve problems, like generating implementations for unused methods and stubbing out interactions with external systems. Usually, though, our code would be improved by restructuring to avoid the need for mocks. Expressing dependencies as function types is one example; another is moving the interaction with external systems to the outer layers of our code, as we will see in Chapter 20. Chapter 17 looks at how to reduce mock use by refactoring our tests to a more functional form.

Traceability

There is a downside to expressing dependencies with function types, and it is a common issue with adding a layer of indirection. If we use IntelliJ to find the callers of `EmailSystem.send`, the trail goes cold at the point where `EmailSystem::send` is converted to `(Email) -> Unit`. The IDE doesn't know that invocations of the function are actually calling the method. It's like our hero enters a river, and the posse tracking them has to scour both banks upstream and downstream to find where they get out.

This is a price we pay for indirection with method calls too, but our tooling is wise to these and can at least find all places where a particular method is implemented, and where an implementation is called through an interface. As with using unencapsulated collections (Chapter 15), the price that we pay for decoupling and generality is that tooling, and developers, have less context to hang analysis on. We trust that IDE support will improve its functional analysis, and in the meantime, we can help by not passing function types too far from where they are initialized to where they are used.

Refactoring from Interfaces to Functions

Travelator is quite well-designed in the Java fashion, with interfaces expressing the relations between components. For example, the `Recommendations` engine depends on `FeaturedDestinations` and a `DistanceCalculator`:

```
public class Recommendations {
    private final FeaturedDestinations featuredDestinations;
    private final DistanceCalculator distanceCalculator;

    public Recommendations(
        FeaturedDestinations featuredDestinations,
        DistanceCalculator distanceCalculator
    ) {
        this.featuredDestinations = featuredDestinations;
        this.distanceCalculator = distanceCalculator;
    }
    ...
}
```

Example 16.1 [interfaces-to-funs.0:src/main/java/travelator/recommendations/Recommendations.java]

The `FeaturedDestinations` interface has a few methods, grouping functionality that accesses a remote service:

```
public interface FeaturedDestinations {
    List<FeaturedDestination> findCloseTo(Location location);
    FeaturedDestination findClosest(Location location);

    FeaturedDestination add(FeaturedDestinationData destination);
    void remove(FeaturedDestination destination);
    void update(FeaturedDestination destination);
}
```

Example 16.2 [interfaces-to-funs.0:src/main/java/travelator/destinations/FeaturedDestinations.java]

It looks like we've already converted the `DistanceCalculator` interface to Kotlin. It too has more than one method, and hides another external service:

```
interface DistanceCalculator {
    fun distanceInMetersBetween(
        start: Location,
        end: Location
    ): Int

    fun travelTimeInSecondsBetween(
        start: Location,
        end: Location
```

```
    ): Int
}
```

Example 16.3 [interfaces-to-funs.0:src/main/java/travelator/domain/DistanceCalculator.kt]

Despite taking a dependency on a total of seven methods, `Recommendations` only actually uses two of them in its implementation:

```
public List<FeaturedDestinationSuggestion> recommendationsFor(
    Set<Location> journey
) {
    var results = removeDuplicates(
        journey.stream()
            .flatMap(location ->
                recommendationsFor(location).stream()
            )
    );
    results.sort(distanceComparator);
    return results;
}

public List<FeaturedDestinationSuggestion> recommendationsFor(
    Location location
) {
    return featuredDestinations
        .findCloseTo(location) ❶
        .stream()
        .map(featuredDestination ->
            new FeaturedDestinationSuggestion(
                location,
                featuredDestination,
                distanceCalculator.distanceInMetersBetween( ❷
                    location,
                    featuredDestination.getLocation()
                )
            )
        ).collect(toList());
}
```

Example 16.4 [interfaces-to-funs.0:src/main/java/travelator/recommendations/Recommendations.java]

❶ Method on `FeaturedDestinations`

❷ Method on `DistanceCalculator`

`RecommendationsTests` uses mocks to provide implementations of its `DistanceCalculator` and `FeaturedDestinations`, which are passed to the instance of `Recommendations` under test:

```
public class RecommendationsTests {

    private final DistanceCalculator distanceCalculator =
        mock(DistanceCalculator.class);
```

```
    private final FeaturedDestinations featuredDestinations =
        mock(FeaturedDestinations.class);
    private final Recommendations recommendations = new Recommendations(
        featuredDestinations,
        distanceCalculator
    );
    ...
}
```

Example 16.5 [interfaces-to-funs.0:src/test/java/travelator/recommendations/RecommendationsTests.java]

The tests specify that the expected interactions with the mocks are using two methods: `givenFeaturedDestinationsFor` and `givenADistanceBetween`, which we won't bore you with:

```
@Test
public void returns_recommendations_for_multi_location() {
    givenFeaturedDestinationsFor(paris,
        List.of(
            eiffelTower,
            louvre
        ));
    givenADistanceBetween(paris, eiffelTower, 5000);
    givenADistanceBetween(paris, louvre, 1000);

    givenFeaturedDestinationsFor(alton,
        List.of(
            flowerFarm,
            watercressLine
        ));
    givenADistanceBetween(alton, flowerFarm, 5300);
    givenADistanceBetween(alton, watercressLine, 320);

    assertEquals(
        List.of(
            new FeaturedDestinationSuggestion(alton, watercressLine, 320),
            new FeaturedDestinationSuggestion(paris, louvre, 1000),
            new FeaturedDestinationSuggestion(paris, eiffelTower, 5000),
            new FeaturedDestinationSuggestion(alton, flowerFarm, 5300)
        ),
        recommendations.recommendationsFor(Set.of(paris, alton))
    );
}
```

Example 16.6 [interfaces-to-funs.0:src/test/java/travelator/recommendations/RecommendationsTests.java]

Introduce Functions

Before we start moving from interfaces to functions, we'll convert `Recommendations` to Kotlin. This is the class that currently expresses its dependencies with interfaces, and Kotlin function types are less clunky than Java's.

Converting to Kotlin and applying the refactorings introduced in Chapters 10 and 13 gives:

```
class Recommendations(
    private val featuredDestinations: FeaturedDestinations,
    private val distanceCalculator: DistanceCalculator
) {
    fun recommendationsFor(
        journey: Set<Location>
    ): List<FeaturedDestinationSuggestion> =
        journey
            .flatMap { location -> recommendationsFor(location) }
            .deduplicated()
            .sortedBy { it.distanceMeters }

    fun recommendationsFor(
        location: Location
    ): List<FeaturedDestinationSuggestion> =
        featuredDestinations.findCloseTo(location)
            .map { featuredDestination ->
                FeaturedDestinationSuggestion(
                    location,
                    featuredDestination,
                    distanceCalculator.distanceInMetersBetween(
                        location,
                        featuredDestination.location
                    )
                )
            }
}

private fun List<FeaturedDestinationSuggestion>.deduplicated() =
    groupBy { it.suggestion }
        .values
        .map { suggestionsWithSameDestination ->
            suggestionsWithSameDestination.closestToJourneyLocation()
        }

private fun List<FeaturedDestinationSuggestion>.closestToJourneyLocation() =
    minByOrNull { it.distanceMeters } ?: error("Unexpected empty group")
```

Example 16.7 [interfaces-to-funs.3:src/main/java/travelator/recommendations/Recommendations.kt]

To see how the internals of `Recommendations` would use a function rather than the interface, without having to change its interface yet, we can add a property initialized from an interface method. Let's add a property for `featuredDestinations::findCloseTo`, calling it `destinationFinder`:

```
class Recommendations(
    private val featuredDestinations: FeaturedDestinations,
    private val distanceCalculator: DistanceCalculator
) {
    private val destinationFinder: ❶
```

```
        (Location) -> List<FeaturedDestination> =
        featuredDestinations::findCloseTo

    ...

    fun recommendationsFor(
        location: Location
    ): List<FeaturedDestinationSuggestion> =
        destinationFinder(location) ❷
            .map { featuredDestination ->
                FeaturedDestinationSuggestion(
                    location,
                    featuredDestination,
                    distanceCalculator.distanceInMetersBetween(
                        location,
                        featuredDestination.location
                    )
                )
            }
}
```

Example 16.8 [interfaces-to-funs.4:src/main/java/travelator/recommendations/Recommendations.kt]

❶ Extract a function from the interface.

❷ Use it in place of the method.

This passes the tests, so we are on to something. It feels like there should be a refactoring to move `destinationFinder` into the constructor, but we haven't found anything better than cutting the definition and pasting where we want it:

```
class Recommendations(
    private val featuredDestinations: FeaturedDestinations,
    private val distanceCalculator: DistanceCalculator,
    private val destinationFinder:
        (Location) -> List<FeaturedDestination> =
        featuredDestinations::findCloseTo
) {
```

Example 16.9 [interfaces-to-funs.5:src/main/java/travelator/recommendations/Recommendations.kt]

This is, once again, the *expand* in "Expand-and-Contract Refactoring" on page 44. Unfortunately, Java doesn't understand the defaulted parameter, so we have to fix up the call sites to add the function argument. It doesn't really matter, because this is what we want really anyway:

```
private final Recommendations recommendations = new Recommendations(
    featuredDestinations,
    distanceCalculator,
    featuredDestinations::findCloseTo
);
```

Example 16.10 [interfaces-to-funs.5:src/test/java/travelator/recommendations/RecommendationsTests.java]

Now nothing in `Recommendations` uses the `featuredDestinations` property, so we can remove it (contract):

```
class Recommendations(
    private val distanceCalculator: DistanceCalculator,
    private val destinationFinder: (Location) -> List<FeaturedDestination>
) {
```

Example 16.11 [interfaces-to-funs.6:src/main/java/travelator/recommendations/Recommendations.kt]

The places in our code that create `Recommendations` now look like this:

```
private final Recommendations recommendations = new Recommendations(
    distanceCalculator,
    featuredDestinations::findCloseTo
);
```

Example 16.12 [interfaces-to-funs.6:src/test/java/travelator/recommendations/RecommendationsTests.java]

If you're used to refactoring tests with mocks, it may surprise you that the tests have continued to pass through this refactoring. We can reason that they *should* pass—the effect of calling the function bound to `featuredDestinations::findCloseTo` is still to invoke the method on the mocked interface—but our reasoning is so often proved wrong by running the tests that we don't count our chickens.

We do like a single basket though, so let's do the same thing with the `distanceCalculator`, this time in a fell swoop, whatever that is:

```
class Recommendations(
    private val destinationFinder: (Location) -> List<FeaturedDestination>,
    private val distanceInMetersBetween: (Location, Location) -> Int
) {
    ...
    fun recommendationsFor(
        location: Location
    ): List<FeaturedDestinationSuggestion> =
        destinationFinder(location)
            .map { featuredDestination ->
                FeaturedDestinationSuggestion(
                    location,
                    featuredDestination,
                    distanceInMetersBetween( ❶
                        location,
                        featuredDestination.location
                    )
                )
            }
}
```

Example 16.13 [interfaces-to-funs.7:src/main/java/travelator/recommendations/Recommendations.kt]

❶ Calling the new function

The constructor invocations are now:

```
private final Recommendations recommendations = new Recommendations(
    featuredDestinations::findCloseTo,
    distanceCalculator::distanceInMetersBetween
);
```

Example 16.14 [interfaces-to-funs.7:src/test/java/travelator/recommendations/RecommendationsTests.java]

Note that a little thought around what to call functional variables can go a long way to making them seem natural in use, although that does sometimes make them a little cryptic where they are defined.

Again the tests still pass, giving us confidence that our production code will see the transformation the same way. It's particularly nice that we have shown that we can simultaneously cross a method/function boundary and a Java/Kotlin boundary. Maybe this interop will work out OK after all!

Moving On

We want our code to be simple and flexible. To this end, libraries need to hide implementation details from client code, and we want to be able to substitute one implementation of some functionality with another.

In OO, we hide configuration and implementation inside classes and express substitutable functionality with interfaces. In functional programming, functions take both roles. We might see the function as more fundamental, but we can view an object as a collection of functions, and a function as an object with a single method. Both Kotlin and Java allow us to move between realms at the boundaries between implementations and clients, but Kotlin's native function type syntax encourages the use of function types rather than interfaces. This allows even more decoupling than defining our own interfaces and should be our default approach.

We continue refactoring this example, and examining this relationship, in Chapter 17, *Mocks to Maps*.

CHAPTER 17
Mocks to Maps

Mocks are a common technique to decouple object-oriented code from its production dependencies. Are better solutions available in Kotlin?

This is a short bonus chapter, following on from Chapter 16. In that chapter, we saw that our tests used mocks because they had to implement two multimethod interfaces, even though most of those methods were not used. We left the refactoring, having replaced dependencies on multimethod interfaces with a dependency on just the two operations that were actually required to perform the task. The tests, though, still mock the whole interface, and then pass a reference to the required methods to the subject under test (`Recommendations`):

```
public class RecommendationsTests {

    private final DistanceCalculator distanceCalculator =
        mock(DistanceCalculator.class);
    private final FeaturedDestinations featuredDestinations =
        mock(FeaturedDestinations.class);
    private final Recommendations recommendations = new Recommendations(
        featuredDestinations::findCloseTo,
        distanceCalculator::distanceInMetersBetween
    );
    ...
}
```

Example 17.1 [interfaces-to-funs.7:src/test/java/travelator/recommendations/RecommendationsTests.java]

The tests abstract the mocking behind methods `givenFeaturedDestinationsFor` and `givenADistanceBetween`:

```
@Test
public void returns_recommendations_for_single_location() {
    givenFeaturedDestinationsFor(paris,
        List.of(
```

```
            eiffelTower,
            louvre
        ));
    givenADistanceBetween(paris, eiffelTower, 5000);
    givenADistanceBetween(paris, louvre, 1000);

    assertEquals(
        List.of(
            new FeaturedDestinationSuggestion(paris, louvre, 1000),
            new FeaturedDestinationSuggestion(paris, eiffelTower, 5000)
        ),
        recommendations.recommendationsFor(Set.of(paris))
    );
}
```

Example 17.2 [interfaces-to-funs.7:src/test/java/travelator/recommendations/RecommendationsTests.java]

Here is the implementation of `givenADistanceBetween`:

```
private void givenADistanceBetween(
    Location location,
    FeaturedDestination destination,
    int result
) {
    when(
        distanceCalculator.distanceInMetersBetween(
            location,
            destination.getLocation())
    ).thenReturn(result);
}
```

Example 17.3 [interfaces-to-funs.7:src/test/java/travelator/recommendations/RecommendationsTests.java]

Mock-Induced Test Damage

David Heinemeier Hansson coined the term test-induced design damage (*https://oreil.ly/8vgJU*) to refer to harm caused to systems in the name of testability. In practice, your authors don't recognize this as much of a problem; we find that systems are usually *improved* by the decoupling required to test them well. We *do* often see tests ruined by mocks though, so much so that mocking has fallen out of favor in our circles.

The problem is that, as well as implementing interfaces, mock frameworks allow us to specify the expected invocations of their methods and what should be returned in those cases. Often, though, expected calls and their results don't make for a human-readable description, as we'll see if we look at the inlined version of the last expectations:

```
when(featuredDestinations.findCloseTo(paris))
    .thenReturn(List.of(
        eiffelTower,
        louvre
```

```
        ));
    when(distanceCalculator.distanceInMetersBetween(
        paris, eiffelTower.getLocation())
    ).thenReturn(5000);
    when(distanceCalculator.distanceInMetersBetween(
        paris, louvre.getLocation())
    ).thenReturn(1000);

    when(featuredDestinations.findCloseTo(alton))
        .thenReturn(List.of(
            flowerFarm,
            watercressLine
        ));
    when(distanceCalculator.distanceInMetersBetween(
        alton, flowerFarm.getLocation())
    ).thenReturn(5300);
    when(distanceCalculator.distanceInMetersBetween(
        alton, watercressLine.getLocation())
    ).thenReturn(320);
```

Example 17.4 [interfaces-to-funs.1:src/test/java/travelator/recommendations/RecommendationsTests.java]

Defining methods like `givenADistanceBetween` allows us to express the relationship between the mock expectations and our test: they can hide the *how* to expose the *why*. In practice, though, very few developers take this step, leading to cryptic tests that are blamed on the use of mocking.

Nat is keen to point out that the mocks that he and Steve Freeman wrote about in *Growing Object-Oriented Software Guided by Tests* were never supposed to be used to implement query functionality like `findCloseTo` and `distanceInMetersBetween`, but only methods that change state. Duncan doesn't remember noticing that, and is personally not against using mocks in this way, because they are still a nice way to specify what we expect of collaborators when practicing outside-in test-driven development, whether reading-from or writing-to. In the end, maybe it doesn't matter, because in both of our experiences, most Java codebases have mocks that are used in this way, and most Kotlin codebases would be better off without them.

For now though, we are still mocking, but our previous refactoring has resulted in our passing narrow interfaces (the function types) to the code under test. Now that we don't need to implement uncalled methods, do we still need the mocks? Let's see where pulling that thread takes us.

Replacing Mocks with Maps

Before we go on, we'll convert the tests to Kotlin, because it has better support for function types. We could stay in Java, but then we would have to work out which of the Java function types (`Function`, `BiFunction`, etc.) expresses the operations. And we'd still have Java.

The automated conversion is quite smooth, although for some reason the converter created lambdas rather than using method references in the `Recommendations` constructor call that we have to replace by hand, leaving the setup as:

```
class RecommendationsTests {
    private val distanceCalculator = mock(DistanceCalculator::class.java)
    private val featuredDestinations = mock(FeaturedDestinations::class.java)

    private val recommendations = Recommendations(
        featuredDestinations::findCloseTo,
        distanceCalculator::distanceInMetersBetween
    )
    ...
```

Example 17.5 [mocks-to-maps.0:src/test/java/travelator/recommendations/RecommendationsTests.kt]

We could use Kotlin reified types to avoid those `::class.java` arguments, but we're moving away from mocks, not toward them, so we resist.

The term `when` is a keyword in Kotlin, but the converter is smart enough to quote it where required:

```
private fun givenFeaturedDestinationsFor(
    location: Location,
    result: List<FeaturedDestination>
) {
    Mockito.`when`(featuredDestinations.findCloseTo(location))
        .thenReturn(result)
}
```

Example 17.6 [mocks-to-maps.0:src/test/java/travelator/recommendations/RecommendationsTests.kt]

To see how to remove the mocking, it helps to view a function type as a mapping between its input parameters (as a tuple) and its result. So `destinationFinder` is a mapping between a single `Location` and a `List<FeaturedDestination>`, and `distanceInMetersBetween` is a mapping between `Pair<Location, Location>` and `Int`. The `Map` data structure is our way of expressing a set of mappings—the name isn't accidental. So we can fake a function by populating a `Map` with parameter keys and result values, and replacing the function call with a lookup of the supplied parameters. You may have used this trick to cache the result of expensive calculations. Here, we won't cache, but seed the `Map` with the parameters and result that we expect to see.

Taking the `destinationFinder` case first, we'll create a property to hold the `Map`, `featuredDestinations`:

```
private val featuredDestinations =
    mutableMapOf<Location, List<FeaturedDestination>>()
        .withDefault { emptyList() }
```

Example 17.7 [mocks-to-maps.1:src/test/java/travelator/recommendations/RecommendationsTests.kt]

`givenFeaturedDestinationsFor` can populate the `destinationLookup` `Map` rather than setting expectations on a mock:

```
private fun givenFeaturedDestinationsFor(
    location: Location,
    destinations: List<FeaturedDestination>
) {
    featuredDestinations[location] = destinations.toList()
}
```

Example 17.8 [mocks-to-maps.1:src/test/java/travelator/recommendations/RecommendationsTests.kt]

If we make `Recommendations` read out of the `featuredDestinations` `Map`, we have passing tests:

```
private val recommendations =
    Recommendations(
        featuredDestinations::getValue,
        distanceCalculator::distanceInMetersBetween
    )
```

Example 17.9 [mocks-to-maps.1:src/test/java/travelator/recommendations/RecommendationsTests.kt]

`getValue` is an extension on `Map`. It acts like `get` but respects the defaults set up by the `Map.withDefault` (in this case to return an `emptyList()`) and, hence, does not return a nullable result.

It won't surprise you when we do the same for `distanceInMetersBetween`, removing all our dependency on Mockito:

```
class RecommendationsTests {

    private val featuredDestinations =
        mutableMapOf<Location, List<FeaturedDestination>>()
            .withDefault { emptyList() }
    private val distanceInMetersBetween =
        mutableMapOf<Pair<Location, Location>, Int>()
            .withDefault { -1 }

    private val recommendations =
        Recommendations(
            featuredDestinations::getValue,
            { l1, l2 -> distanceInMetersBetween.getValue(l1 to l2) }
        )
```

```
    ...
}
```

Example 17.10 [mocks-to-maps.2:src/test/java/travelator/recommendations/RecommendationsTests.kt]

```
private fun givenADistanceFrom(
    location: Location,
    destination: FeaturedDestination,
    distanceInMeters: Int
) {
    distanceInMetersBetween[location to destination.location] =
        distanceInMeters
}
```

Example 17.11 [mocks-to-maps.2:src/test/java/travelator/recommendations/RecommendationsTests.kt]

It might take a couple of passes to see how that works; these are the details that mocking frameworks hide for us. You can safely ignore them and come back here if you ever execute this refactoring yourself.

Having to use a lambda rather than a method reference in the `Recommendations` constructor invocation is a bit irritating. We can tidy that up with a local `getValue` extension function. Did we mention how much we like extension functions?

```
private fun <K1, K2, V> Map<Pair<K1, K2>, V>.getValue(k1: K1, k2: K2) =
    getValue(k1 to k2)
```

Example 17.12 [mocks-to-maps.3:src/test/java/travelator/recommendations/RecommendationsTests.kt]

This lets us say:

```
private val recommendations =
    Recommendations(
        featuredDestinations::getValue,
        distanceInMetersBetween::getValue
    )
```

Example 17.13 [mocks-to-maps.3:src/test/java/travelator/recommendations/RecommendationsTests.kt]

Oh, and we can improve the readability of the test methods with some judicious parameter naming and helper methods. Previously, we had plain function calls:

```
@Test
fun deduplicates_using_smallest_distance() {
    givenFeaturedDestinationsFor(
        alton,
        flowerFarm, watercressLine
    )
    givenFeaturedDestinationsFor(
        froyle,
        flowerFarm, watercressLine
    )
    givenADistanceFrom(alton, flowerFarm, 5300)
    givenADistanceFrom(alton, watercressLine, 320)
    givenADistanceFrom(froyle, flowerFarm, 0)
```

```
    givenADistanceFrom(froyle, watercressLine, 6300)
    assertEquals(
        listOf(
            FeaturedDestinationSuggestion(froyle, flowerFarm, 0),
            FeaturedDestinationSuggestion(alton, watercressLine, 320)
        ),
        recommendations.recommendationsFor(setOf(alton, froyle))
    )
}
```

Example 17.14 [mocks-to-maps.3:src/test/java/travelator/recommendations/RecommendationsTests.kt]

A little effort yields:

```
@Test
fun deduplicates_using_smallest_distance() {
    givenFeaturedDestinationsFor(alton, of(flowerFarm, watercressLine))
    givenADistanceFrom(alton, to = flowerFarm, of = 5300)
    givenADistanceFrom(alton, to = watercressLine, of = 320)

    givenFeaturedDestinationsFor(froyle, of(flowerFarm, watercressLine))
    givenADistanceFrom(froyle, to = flowerFarm, of = 0)
    givenADistanceFrom(froyle, to = watercressLine, of = 6300)

    assertEquals(
        listOf(
            FeaturedDestinationSuggestion(froyle, flowerFarm, 0),
            FeaturedDestinationSuggestion(alton, watercressLine, 320)
        ),
        recommendations.recommendationsFor(setOf(alton, froyle))
    )
}
```

Example 17.15 [mocks-to-maps.4:src/test/java/travelator/recommendations/RecommendationsTests.kt]

Sometimes defining a tiny local function like `of` can go a long way to letting our brains just read code rather than spending effort interpreting it:

```
private fun of(vararg destination: FeaturedDestination)
    = destination.toList()
```

Example 17.16 [mocks-to-maps.4:src/test/java/travelator/recommendations/RecommendationsTests.kt]

Faking in Kotlin

There will be times, even in Kotlin, when we want to implement just some of an interface's methods for testing. On the JVM, we can combine dynamic proxies with anonymous objects, delegation, and selective overriding to write the following:

```
inline fun <reified T> fake(): T =
    Proxy.newProxyInstance(
        T::class.java.classLoader,
        arrayOf(T::class.java)
    ) { _, _, _ ->
        TODO("not implemented")
    } as T


val sentEmails = mutableListOf<Email>()
val testCollaborator: EmailSystem =
    object : EmailSystem by fake() {
        override fun send(email: Email) {
            sentEmails.add(email)
        }
    }
```

Have We Really Weaned Off Mocks, Though?

Ah, now that is a good question!

In some ways, we have just implemented a poor imitation of a mocking framework: we have no parameter matchers, no way of failing if a method isn't called, and no way of expressing execution order.

Looked at another way though, we have implemented the recommendation engine's dependencies as two maps. `Recommendations.recommendationsFor` is beginning to look like a simple calculation ("Calculations" on page 78). The result of that calculation depends on the `journey` parameter and on the contents of those maps that enable us to look up featured destinations and distances. We know that in reality *when* we call `recommendationsFor` does matter; it is really an action ("Actions" on page 79). The distance between locations probably won't change over time, but which destinations we find around a location will as we add or remove them from whatever database they are held in. In our tests, though, the distinction is moot, and we could treat `recommendationsFor` as a calculation in much the same way as we saw with `InMemoryTrips` in Chapter 7. Calculations are easier to test than actions—we just check that a given input returns a given output—so let's pull on this thread.

At the moment, *when* we call `recommendationsFor` in the tests matters too, because the result will depend on the contents of the `featuredDestinations` and `distanceInMetersBetween` maps. These are initially empty, and are populated by calls to `givenFeaturedDestinationsFor` and `givenADistanceFrom`. That's a time sensitivity right there. What we need is some way to convert an action to a calculation, and we can do that by manipulating scope.

In Chapter 16, we saw that we can view methods as functions with some of their arguments partially applied by capturing them as fields. In tests, we can reverse this process. We can write a function that creates the object from its dependencies once for each invocation. If we call the populated object the *subject* of the tests, we can create it from the test state like this:

```
private fun subjectFor(
    featuredDestinations: Map<Location, List<FeaturedDestination>>,
    distances: Map<Pair<Location, Location>, Int>
): Recommendations {
    val destinationsLookup = featuredDestinations.withDefault { emptyList() }
    val distanceLookup = distances.withDefault { -1 }
    return Recommendations(destinationsLookup::getValue, distanceLookup::getValue)
}
```

Example 17.17 [mocks-to-maps.5:src/test/java/travelator/recommendations/RecommendationsTests.kt]

Here we create a new instance of `Recommendations` every call so that it can capture immutable maps representing the state of the system.

Now we can write a `resultFor` function that uses `subjectFor`:

```
private fun resultFor(
    featuredDestinations: Map<Location, List<FeaturedDestination>>,
    distances: Map<Pair<Location, Location>, Int>,
    locations: Set<Location>
): List<FeaturedDestinationSuggestion> {
    val subject = subjectFor(featuredDestinations, distances)
    return subject.recommendationsFor(locations)
}
```

Example 17.18 [mocks-to-maps.5:src/test/java/travelator/recommendations/RecommendationsTests.kt]

Outside of the scope of the `resultFor` function, there is no time sensitivity, so it is effectively a calculation.

Now that we have a simple mapping of input to output (`resultFor`), we can write simple tests that call it. Each test can just specify the input parameters and check that the result is as expected, with no need for state in the test at all.

Every test can then be of the form:

```
private fun check(
    featuredDestinations: Map<Location, List<FeaturedDestination>>,
    distances: Map<Pair<Location, Location>, Int>,
```

```
        recommendations: Set<Location>,
        shouldReturn: List<FeaturedDestinationSuggestion>
    ) {
        assertEquals(
            shouldReturn,
            resultFor(featuredDestinations, distances, recommendations)
        )
    }
```

Example 17.19 [mocks-to-maps.5:src/test/java/travelator/recommendations/RecommendationsTests.kt]

This gives a pleasing simplicity to the previously confusing tests:

```
class RecommendationsTests {
    companion object {
        val distances = mapOf(
            (paris to eiffelTower.location) to 5000,
            (paris to louvre.location) to 1000,
            (alton to flowerFarm.location) to 5300,
            (alton to watercressLine.location) to 320,
            (froyle to flowerFarm.location) to 0,
            (froyle to watercressLine.location) to 6300
        )
    }

    ...

    @Test
    fun returns_no_recommendations_when_no_featured() {
        check(
            featuredDestinations = emptyMap(),
            distances = distances,
            recommendations = setOf(paris),
            shouldReturn = emptyList()
        )
    }

    ...

    @Test
    fun returns_recommendations_for_multi_location() {
        check(
            featuredDestinations = mapOf(
                paris to listOf(eiffelTower, louvre),
                alton to listOf(flowerFarm, watercressLine),
            ),
            distances = distances,
            recommendations = setOf(paris, alton),
            shouldReturn = listOf(
                FeaturedDestinationSuggestion(alton, watercressLine, 320),
                FeaturedDestinationSuggestion(paris, louvre, 1000),
                FeaturedDestinationSuggestion(paris, eiffelTower, 5000),
                FeaturedDestinationSuggestion(alton, flowerFarm, 5300)
```

```
            )
        )
    }
    ...
}
```

Example 17.20 [mocks-to-maps.5:src/test/java/travelator/recommendations/RecommendationsTests.kt]

It's instructive to compare this with an original test:

```
@Test
public void returns_recommendations_for_multi_location() {
    givenFeaturedDestinationsFor(paris,
        List.of(
            eiffelTower,
            louvre
        ));
    givenADistanceBetween(paris, eiffelTower, 5000);
    givenADistanceBetween(paris, louvre, 1000);

    givenFeaturedDestinationsFor(alton,
        List.of(
            flowerFarm,
            watercressLine
        ));
    givenADistanceBetween(alton, flowerFarm, 5300);
    givenADistanceBetween(alton, watercressLine, 320);

    assertEquals(
        List.of(
            new FeaturedDestinationSuggestion(alton, watercressLine, 320),
            new FeaturedDestinationSuggestion(paris, louvre, 1000),
            new FeaturedDestinationSuggestion(paris, eiffelTower, 5000),
            new FeaturedDestinationSuggestion(alton, flowerFarm, 5300)
        ),
        recommendations.recommendationsFor(Set.of(paris, alton))
    );
}
```

Example 17.21 [interfaces-to-funs.0:src/test/java/travelator/recommendations/RecommendationsTests.java]

Admittedly, this is Java, and broken up a bit by the `givenADistanceBetween` calls, but you can see how this refactoring has migrated our tests from woolly functions that may or may not have a common structure to a clear testing of inputs against outputs.

Moving On

Mocks have their place in software, and outside-in test-driven development (TDD) can certainly improve our designs by allowing us to prototype how to distribute functionality between collaborating objects without having to commit to complete implementations. However, they have a habit of masking design problems by allowing us to test designs expressed as object interactions that would be better seen as data flows.

In this example, we've seen how focusing on data can simplify our tests, especially where we are only reading values. In Chapter 20, *Performing I/O to Passing Data*, we explore how we can apply this technique to writing as well.

CHAPTER 18

Open to Sealed Classes

Our systems are composed of types and operations, nouns and verbs. In Java, nouns are expressed as classes and interfaces, verbs as methods; but Kotlin adds sealed class hierarchies and freestanding functions. What do they bring to the party?

Change is a constant challenge in designing software. The more people use our software, the more they think of things they want it to do. To support new use cases, we need to add new functions that work with existing data types, and new data types that work with existing functions. If our design is well aligned with the way the software has to evolve, we can add new features by adding new code and making few, localized changes to our existing code. If it isn't well aligned, we will have to change many functions when we add a new data type, or change many data types when we need to add a function.

We feel this tension between the variability of data types and of functions most keenly in the core entities of our domain model. For example, the traveler's itinerary is a core entity of our Travelator application. Many features of the application present views of, alter the contents of, or calculate information about itineraries. It's no surprise then that many of the feature requests from our users affect our `Itinerary` type. Our travelers want to include more kinds of things in their itineraries: not just journeys and accommodation, as we saw in Chapter 10, but now restaurant bookings and attractions along the route. They also want to do more things with their itineraries. In Chapter 14, we saw how we estimate their cost, but our customers also want to compare them by cost, time, or comfort, view them on a map, import them into their calendar, share them with their friends...their imagination is endless.

When we last looked at the `Itinerary` class in Chapter 14, we were modeling an itinerary as a data class, with a property for the route and another for the accommodation required along the route:

```
data class Itinerary(
    val id: Id<Itinerary>,
    val route: Route,
    val accommodations: List<Accommodation> = emptyList()
) {
    ...
}
```

Example 18.1 [accumulator.17:src/main/java/travelator/itinerary/Itinerary.kt]

Since then, we have added more features to the application and, hence, more types of items to the itinerary. We found it increasingly cumbersome to hold each type of itinerary item in a separate collection, because too much of our code involved combining those collections or applying the same filters and transforms to separate collections. So we decided that an `Itinerary` would maintain a single collection of `ItineraryItem` rather than keep each type of item in a separate collection:

```
data class Itinerary(
    val id: Id<Itinerary>,
    val items: List<ItineraryItem>
) : Iterable<ItineraryItem> by items
```

Example 18.2 [open-to-sealed.0:src/main/java/travelator/itinerary/Itinerary.kt]

`ItineraryItem` is an interface, implemented by the concrete item types we saw before: `Journey` and `Accommodation` and new types `RestaurantBooking` and `Attraction`:

```
interface ItineraryItem {
    val id: Id<ItineraryItem>
    val description: String
    val costs: List<Money>
    val mapOverlay: MapOverlay
    ... and other methods
}
```

Example 18.3 [open-to-sealed.0:src/main/java/travelator/itinerary/ItineraryItem.kt]

Operations on `Itinerary` don't depend on the concrete type of its items. For example, to display the itinerary on a map, we create a `MapOverlay` that will be rendered on top of map tiles on the frontend. The overlay for an `Itinerary` is the group of the overlays for all the items it contains. The `Itinerary` class and its clients don't know, or need to know, how each item represents itself as a map overlay.

```
val Itinerary.mapOverlay
    get() = OverlayGroup(
        id = id,
        elements = items.map { it.mapOverlay })
```

Example 18.4 [open-to-sealed.0:src/main/java/travelator/itinerary/Itinerary.kt]

This polymorphism makes it very easy to add new types of `ItineraryItem` to the system without having to change the parts of the application that use the `Itinerary` type.

For a while now, though, we haven't had to do that. Recently, we find that most of the new functionality we add to Travelator involves adding new operations to `Itinerary` and `ItineraryItem` rather than new types of `ItineraryItem`. Changes to the `ItineraryItem` interface and its implementations are a common source of merge conflicts between team members who are working on different features. With every new feature, the `ItineraryItem` gets larger. It seems to attract behavior to support distantly related parts of the application, with properties to support rendering, cost estimation, ranking by comfort, maps drawing, and more hidden beyond that `...and other methods`. Paradoxically, in the core of our application, object-oriented polymorphism is *increasing* coupling!

Object-oriented polymorphism enables variability of data types with an infrequently changing set of operations. For a while, that was what our codebase needed, but now that it has stabilized, we need the opposite: variability of operations applied to an infrequently changing set of data types.

If we were writing in Java (at least up to Java 16), there is no language feature to help us cope with variability in this dimension. Java's principal feature to support variability is object-oriented polymorphism, and that doesn't help when operations change more frequently than the set of data types.

We could use the double dispatch (*https://oreil.ly/8m2HL*) pattern, but it involves a lot of boilerplate code and, because it does not play well with checked exceptions, is not widely used in Java. Instead, Java programmers often resort to runtime type checks, using the `instanceof` and downcast operators to run different code for different classes of object:

```
if (item instanceof Journey) {
    var journey = (Journey) item;
    return ...
} else if (item instanceof Accommodation) {
    var accommodation = (Accommodation) item;
    return ...
} else if (item instanceof RestaurantBooking) {
    var restaurant = (RestaurantBooking) item;
    return ...
} else {
    throw new IllegalStateException("should never happen");
}
```

Example 18.5 [open-to-sealed.0:src/main/java/travelator/itinerary/ItineraryItems.java]

That `IllegalStateException` shows that this approach is risky. Whereas the compiler can type check our calls to polymorphic methods, our hand-coded runtime type checks and casts are explicitly circumventing compile-time checks. The type checker cannot tell whether our casts are correct or our conditional statement is *exhaustive*: whether it applies to all possible subclasses. If returning a value from the method, we have to write an `else` clause to return a dummy value or throw an exception, even if we have branches for every subclass of ItineraryItem, and the else clause "cannot possibly be executed™."

Even if we cover all the subtypes of ItineraryItem when we write the code, if we later add new types, we have to find all such code and update it. It turns out that we didn't do that here, so if we add an Attraction to an Itinerary, this code will fail with an IllegalArgumentException. OO solves this problem, but we circumvented the solution because we were tired of having to update lots of classes when we add an operation.

Type checking and downcasting are possible in Kotlin, too, and carry the same overheads and risks. However, Kotlin has another mechanism for organizing classes and behavior that makes runtime type checks safe and convenient: *sealed classes*. A sealed class is an abstract class with a fixed set of direct subclasses. We must define the sealed class and its subclasses in the same compilation unit and package; the compiler prevents us from extending the sealed class elsewhere. Thanks to this restriction, runtime type checks on sealed class hierarchies do not have the same problem as runtime type checks in Java. The static type checker can guarantee that when expressions that perform runtime type checks for a subtype of a sealed class cover all possible cases and only the possible cases.

When Statements Are Not Checked for Exhaustiveness

The compiler checks when expressions for exhaustiveness but does not check when *statements*; when becomes a statement if the value of the entire when expression is not used. You can force the compiler to check for exhaustiveness by using the result of the when, even though it is of type Unit.

If the when is the only statement in the body of a function, you can refactor the function to single-expression form. If when is the last statement in a multistatement function, you can explicitly use its value with the return keyword. When the when is in the middle of the function body, extracting it to its own function might make sense.

When none of those options apply, you can use the following utility function to force an exhaustiveness check:

```
val <T> T.exhaustive get() = this
```

When used like this, it will prevent compilation when when is not exhaustive:

```
when (instanceOfSealedClass) {
    is SubclassA -> println("A")
    is SubclassB -> println("B")
}.exhaustive
```

Compared to polymorphic methods, sealed classes and `when` expressions make it easy to add new operations that apply to a fixed type hierarchy, although we still have to change all those operations if we add a new type to that hierarchy. At this point the compiler will help us by checking that all those operations cover all possible types in the hierarchy.

Polymorphism or Sealed Classes?

Some languages have mechanisms that let us vary types *and* operations without modifying existing code. Haskell has type classes, Scala has implicit parameters, Rust has traits, Swift has protocols, and Clojure and Common Lisp have polymorphic functions that dispatch on the classes of multiple arguments.

Kotlin doesn't have any equivalent. When we're designing in Kotlin, we have to choose between object-oriented polymorphism or sealed classes based on the dimension—types or operations—we expect to vary most frequently as the program evolves. Object-oriented polymorphism is preferable when the set of data types varies more frequently than the set of operations on those data types, and sealed class hierarchies when the set of operations varies more frequently than the set of data types they apply to.

Only Typecast Down a Sealed Class Hierarchy

Only use typecasts to cast from the root of a sealed class hierarchy to one of the children in an exhaustive `when` expression. Otherwise, it is risky to cast away from the static type. The actual class used to implement a value may have operations that violate the constraints expressed by its static type.

For example, as we saw in Chapter 6, the static type `List` prevents mutation, but Kotlin's higher-order functions return lists that can be mutated if you downcast from `List` to `MutableList`. A function that downcasts a list argument from `List` to `MutableList` and mutates it is likely to introduce bugs in code, because it violates the expectations of its callers. It could introduce aliasing errors that are very hard to find, because the possibility of spooky action at a distance is not explicit in the type declarations of the function's signature. If a future version of the Kotlin standard library returned immutable lists from its higher-order functions, the function would continue to compile successfully but crash at runtime.

Just because you *can* cast from a super type to a subtype doesn't mean you are intended to. The possibility is likely to be a mere implementation detail. A sealed class hierarchy signals that downcasting is intended, supported, and made safe by the compiler's exhaustiveness checks.

Converting an Interface to a Sealed Class

We're about to add another feature that involves itineraries and itinerary items: making the `Itinerary` appear in the traveler's calendar app. We don't want to add more methods to the already bloated `ItineraryItem` interface and couple the core classes of our application's domain to the needs of another peripheral module. It's time to bite the bullet and convert `ItineraryItem` from an interface of polymorphic methods to a sealed class hierarchy and freestanding functions, and move those freestanding functions into the modules that use them.

Kotlin 1.4 was current when we wrote this, so we have to define a sealed class and its direct subclasses in the same file. Our first step, then, is to use the IDE's "Move Class" refactoring to move the implementations of `ItineraryItem` into the same file as the interface. Once we've done that, we can turn the interface and its implementations into a sealed class hierarchy. IntelliJ does not have an automated refactoring for this, so we have to do it by manually editing the class definitions. At least moving all the classes into the same file has made the task easier:

```
sealed class ItineraryItem { ❶
    abstract val id: Id<ItineraryItem> ❷
    abstract val description: String
    abstract val costs: List<Money>
    abstract val mapOverlay: MapOverlay
    ... and other methods
}

data class Accommodation(
    override val id: Id<Accommodation>,
    val location: Location,
    val checkInFrom: ZonedDateTime,
    val checkOutBefore: ZonedDateTime,
    val pricePerNight: Money
) : ItineraryItem() { ❸
    val nights = Period.between(
        checkInFrom.toLocalDate(),
        checkOutBefore.toLocalDate()
    ).days
    val totalPrice: Money = pricePerNight * nights

    override val description
        get() = "$nights nights at ${location.userReadableName}"
    override val costs
        get() = listOf(totalPrice)
    override val mapOverlay
        get() = PointOverlay(
            id = id,
            position = location.position,
            text = location.userReadableName,
            icon = StandardIcons.HOTEL
```

```
        )

    ... and other methods
}

... and other subclasses
```

Example 18.6 [open-to-sealed.2:src/main/java/travelator/itinerary/ItineraryItem.kt]

❶ We declare `ItineraryItem` as a `sealed class` instead of an `interface`.

❷ Because it is now a class, we have to explicitly mark its methods as `abstract`. If the interface had any methods with a default implementation, we would have had to declare them as `open` so that subclasses could still override them.

❸ We replace the declaration of the interface in the concrete item classes with a call to the superclass constructor.

Kotlin 1.5 (released as we completed this book) supports sealed *interfaces*, which make this refactoring easier. It's unnecessary to move the subclasses into the same file or to call the constructor.

`ItineraryItem` is now a sealed class. Its operations are still polymorphic methods, but we can add *new* operations without changing the `ItineraryItem` classes, by writing extension functions that use a `when` expression to safely dispatch on the concrete item type.

First we'll write the extension functions that we need to translate an `Itinerary` to a calendar. When we're done, we'll continue refactoring to make the other operations on `ItineraryItem` work the same way:

```
fun ItineraryItem.toCalendarEvent(): CalendarEvent? = when (this) {
    is Accommodation -> CalendarEvent(
        start = checkInFrom,
        end = checkOutBefore,
        description = description,
        alarms = listOf(
            Alarm(checkInFrom, "Check in open"),
            Alarm(checkOutBefore.minusHours(1), "Check out")
        )
    )
    is Attraction -> null
    is Journey -> CalendarEvent(
        start = departureTime,
        end = arrivalTime,
        description = description,
        location = departsFrom,
```

```
            alarms = listOf(
                Alarm(departureTime.minusHours(1)))
        )
        is RestaurantBooking -> CalendarEvent(
            start = time,
            description= description,
            location = location,
            alarms = listOf(
                Alarm(time.minusHours(1)))
        )
}
```

Example 18.7 [open-to-sealed.3:src/main/java/travelator/calendar/ItineraryToCalendar.kt]

Now, let's refactor the rest of the `ItineraryItem` methods from being polymorphic methods defined on the (now sealed) class, to extension functions that use `when` expressions to switch on the type of item. We'll walk through the process with the `mapOverlay` property.

When we Alt-Enter on the definition of `mapOverlay` in `ItineraryItem`, the context menu includes the action "Convert member to extension". Can it really be that easy? Unfortunately, no. At the time of writing, the IDE action only gets us part of the way there and leaves us with code that does not compile:

```
sealed class ItineraryItem {
    abstract val id: Id<ItineraryItem>
    abstract val description: String
    abstract val costs: List<Money> ❶
    ... and other methods
}

val ItineraryItem.mapOverlay: MapOverlay ❷
    get() = TODO("Not yet implemented")

data class Accommodation(
    override val id: Id<Accommodation>,
    val location: Location,
    val checkInFrom: ZonedDateTime,
    val checkOutBefore: ZonedDateTime,
    val pricePerNight: Money
) : ItineraryItem() {
    val nights = Period.between(
        checkInFrom.toLocalDate(),
        checkOutBefore.toLocalDate()
    ).days
    val totalPrice: Money = pricePerNight * nights

    override val description
        get() = "$nights nights at ${location.userReadableName}"
    override val costs
        get() = listOf(totalPrice)
    override val mapOverlay ❸
```

```
        get() = PointOverlay(
            id = id,
            position = location.position,
            text = location.userReadableName,
            icon = StandardIcons.HOTEL
        )

    ... and other methods
}
```

Example 18.8 [open-to-sealed.4:src/main/java/travelator/itinerary/ItineraryItem.kt]

❶ The IDE removed the `mapOverlay` method from the `ItineraryItem` class...

❷ ...and replaced it with an extension function. Unfortunately, the extension function only contains a `TODO` that throws `UnsupportedOperationException`.

❸ The IDE left `override` modifiers on the `mapOverlay` properties in the subclasses, which no longer have a method in the superclass to override.

We can get the code compiling again by removing the `override` modifiers in the subclasses. Then we'll make the code actually work by implementing the body of an extension function as a `when` expression that switches on the type of `ItineraryItem` and calls the now monomorphic `mapOverlay` getter on each concrete class:

```
val ItineraryItem.mapOverlay: MapOverlay get() = when (this) {
    is Accommodation -> mapOverlay
    is Attraction -> mapOverlay
    is Journey -> mapOverlay
    is RestaurantBooking -> mapOverlay
}
```

Example 18.9 [open-to-sealed.5:src/main/java/travelator/itinerary/ItineraryItem.kt]

The `when` expression will not compile until we have covered all the subclasses of `ItineraryItem`. IntelliJ also highlights each read of the subclass `mapOverlay` properties to show that the compiler's flow-sensitive typing is smart casting the implicit `this` reference from `ItineraryItem` to the correct subclass.

Now the point of this refactor was to prevent every implementation of `ItineraryItem` from having to know about map overlays. At present each still does, because each has its own `mapOverlay` property—the one that was originally overriding the property in the interface:

```
data class Accommodation(
...
) : ItineraryItem() {
    ...
    val mapOverlay
        get() = PointOverlay(
            id = id,
```

```
            position = location.position,
            text = location.userReadableName,
            icon = StandardIcons.HOTEL
        )
    ...
```

Example 18.10 [open-to-sealed.5:src/main/java/travelator/itinerary/ItineraryItem.kt]

We can solve this problem by converting the `mapOverlay` properties with "Convert member to extension":

```
data class Accommodation(
...
) : ItineraryItem() {
    ...
}

val Accommodation.mapOverlay
    get() = PointOverlay(
        id = id,
        position = location.position,
        text = location.userReadableName,
        icon = StandardIcons.HOTEL
    )
```

Example 18.11 [open-to-sealed.6:src/main/java/travelator/itinerary/ItineraryItem.kt]

Now `ItineraryItem.mapOverlay` doesn't appear to have changed at all:

```
val ItineraryItem.mapOverlay: MapOverlay get() = when (this) {
    is Accommodation -> mapOverlay
    is Attraction -> mapOverlay
    is Journey -> mapOverlay
    is RestaurantBooking -> mapOverlay
}
```

Example 18.12 [open-to-sealed.6:src/main/java/travelator/itinerary/ItineraryItem.kt]

Look closer, though (well, hover in IntelliJ), and we can see that those property accesses are now extension properties, not method calls—`Accommodation` and so on no longer depend on `MapOverlay`. And now that `ItineraryItem.mapOverlay` and all the subclass properties are extensions, they don't need to be defined in the same file as the sealed classes. We can move them to the module or package where they are used, and they won't clutter our core domain abstraction:

```
package travelator.geo

import travelator.itinerary.*

val ItineraryItem.mapOverlay: MapOverlay get() = when (this) {
    is Accommodation -> mapOverlay
    is Attraction -> mapOverlay
    is Journey -> mapOverlay
    is RestaurantBooking -> mapOverlay
```

```
}

private val Accommodation.mapOverlay
    get() = PointOverlay(
        id = id,
        position = location.position,
        text = location.userReadableName,
        icon = StandardIcons.HOTEL
    )

 ... Attraction.mapOverlay etc
```

Example 18.13 [open-to-sealed.7:src/main/java/travelator/geo/ItineraryToMapOverlay.kt]

We can do the same with the other members of `ItineraryItem`, until the sealed class declares only the fundamental properties of the type. For `ItineraryItem` at the moment, only the `id` property is truly fundamental: declaring `id` as an abstract property on the sealed class forces every subclass to have an identifier.

Of the other properties, some are clearly there just to support specific features of the application, like `mapOverlay` and `toCalendar`. Others, like `description`, are in a gray area: they support many features of the application, but are not a fundamental property of an `ItineraryItem`. For example, each subtype derives its description from its fundamental properties. Nat prefers to define properties like these as extensions, while Duncan prefers to define them as members of the class. Nat is writing this example, so we'll make `description` an extension:

```
val ItineraryItem.description: String
    get() = when (this) {
        is Accommodation ->
            "$nights nights at ${location.userReadableName}"
        is Attraction ->
            location.userReadableName
        is Journey ->
            "${departsFrom.userReadableName} " +
                "to ${arrivesAt.userReadableName} " +
                "by ${travelMethod.userReadableName}"
        is RestaurantBooking -> location.userReadableName
    }
```

Example 18.14 [open-to-sealed.8:src/main/java/travelator/itinerary/ItineraryDescription.kt]

You'll have to make your own judgment call in your own code. That leaves the sealed `ItineraryItem` class declaring only the `id` property and its subclasses declaring their fundamental properties. The whole hierarchy looks like this:

```
sealed class ItineraryItem {
    abstract val id: Id<ItineraryItem>
}

data class Accommodation(
    override val id: Id<Accommodation>,
```

```
    val location: Location,
    val checkInFrom: ZonedDateTime,
    val checkOutBefore: ZonedDateTime,
    val pricePerNight: Money
) : ItineraryItem() {
    val nights = Period.between(
        checkInFrom.toLocalDate(),
        checkOutBefore.toLocalDate()
    ).days
    val totalPrice: Money = pricePerNight * nights
}

data class Attraction(
    override val id: Id<Attraction>,
    val location: Location,
    val notes: String
) : ItineraryItem()

data class Journey(
    override val id: Id<Journey>,
    val travelMethod: TravelMethod,
    val departsFrom: Location,
    val departureTime: ZonedDateTime,
    val arrivesAt: Location,
    val arrivalTime: ZonedDateTime,
    val price: Money,
    val path: List<Position>,
    ... and other fields
) : ItineraryItem()

data class RestaurantBooking(
    override val id: Id<RestaurantBooking>,
    val location: Location,
    val time: ZonedDateTime
) : ItineraryItem()
```

Example 18.15 [open-to-sealed.8:src/main/java/travelator/itinerary/ItineraryItem.kt]

Our `ItineraryItem` model is now a sealed class hierarchy of pure data classes. The operations needed by the features of our application are all extension functions in the modules for those features. Only the `id` property remains as a polymorphic `val`, because it is a fundamental property of the type that is not specific to any one feature of the application.

Moving On

As our software evolves, we have to add new data types and new operations to our system. In Kotlin, as in Java, object-oriented polymorphism lets us easily add new data types without changing the code of existing functions. We can also use sealed classes and safe runtime type checks to easily add new functions over existing data types without changing the code that defines those types. Which we choose depends on what we expect to vary most frequently as the code evolves: data types or operations. Managing variability in Kotlin involves mastering when to apply these two mechanisms to our domain models.

If our bet turns out to have been wrong, we must refactor from one to the other. When all the code is in a single codebase, Kotlin and IntelliJ make refactoring between the two forms straightforward. This chapter described going from the kind of object-oriented polymorphism we'd write in Java to Kotlin's sealed classes. Going the other way involves refactoring steps described in Martin Fowler's *Refactoring: Improving the Design of Existing Code*, such as "Replace Conditional with Polymorphism," so we won't cover it in this book.

CHAPTER 19

Throwing to Returning

Java uses checked and unchecked exceptions to represent and handle errors. Kotlin supports exceptions, but doesn't build checked exceptions into the language in the same way. Why did Kotlin reject Java's approach, and what should we use instead?

You don't have program computers for long to discover that things go wrong…

…in *so many* ways.

Early in their careers, your authors tended to gloss over errors. We often still do, at least early in a project. As the system grows, though, we learn how failures affect the application and start to add code to cope—at first piecemeal, later with some strategy informed by experience. In this respect our error handling evolves in the same way as other aspects of our software design. Sometimes we design up front, making use of our experience of similar systems; other times we allow the writing of the software to teach us what it needs.

In the absence of a more deliberate strategy, most systems default to raising exceptions when something goes wrong, and catching and logging those exceptions at some outer level. Command-line utilities will just exit in this case, hopefully having provided enough information for the user to correct the problem and try again. A server app, or a GUI with an event loop, will usually abort only the current interaction and get on with the next.

Often this is just a poor experience for our users, but sometimes the error will corrupt the persistent state of the system, so correcting the initial problem and retrying does not work. This is the source of the sage advice to "turn it off and on again." Our systems mainly start in a safe state, so that after a restart a retry should succeed. If not, well, you've probably been in a situation where the only solution has been to reinstall the operating system—the ultimate way of removing corrupted persistent state.

Rebooting the Internet

Duncan had a problem where the integration between his Nest thermostat and IfThisThenThat was not working. IFTTT was receiving notifications when the Nest entered home mode, but not away mode. The great AWS outage of February 28, 2017 mysteriously fixed the problem. It turns out that all it required was a reboot of the internet.

If errors are not well managed, but despite this the system becomes successful, diagnosing and fixing corruption due to errors can expand to fill all the team's time. This is not a great place for a software project to be. Ask us how we know!

So we don't want errors because they annoy our users and may result in corruption that takes a lot of effort to fix, if we can fix it at all. What sort of errors do we see?

Programs can go wrong for many reasons. When we say *program*, we also mean functions, methods, procedures—any code that we invoke. And when we say *go wrong*, we mean fail to do the job that we expected them to do.

Reasons for this failure include:

- Sometimes programs need to talk to other systems and that communication fails in some way.
- Often we don't give software the correct input it needs to do its job.
- Apparently some programmers make errors: even instructing their computers to dereference null references or read past the ends of collections!
- The environment that we are running in fails for some reason; for example, it might run out of memory or not be able to load a class.

There are failures that don't fit into these categories, but most do.

That doesn't seem to be too long a list, and yet as an industry we don't have a great reputation for reliability. Error handling just seems to be hard. Why is that?

Well, for a start we often don't know whether an operation can fail and, if so, how it can fail. If we do know, then knowledge about how to handle an error may be in code a long way from where the problem is detected. Then the code that detects an error, and the code that recovers from it, are hard to isolate from the happy path and so are hard to test. Combine these with the tendency for errors to leave our system in unrecoverable states, and we end up with a situation where most developers would rather hope for the best than take on the hard work and still get it wrong.

Hard work *and* error-prone? Weren't computers supposed to free us from tasks like these, taking on the drudge work, so that we can focus on the fun creative stuff? Yes they were, so we will focus on error handling through the lens of how our programming language can make things safer and easier for programmers.

Error Handling Before Exceptions

Most error handling these days is based on exceptions, but other techniques have been used and are still applicable in some circumstances. We'll look at the pros and cons of those techniques first. The cons will show us why exceptions now dominate; the pros may give us options when exceptions aren't appropriate.

Ignoring errors
: We can ignore errors. Either the failing routine does nothing to bring them to the attention of the caller, or the caller doesn't bother to check.

  This may lead to corruption of persistent data and silent failure to do the job, so in most cases we need to aim higher.

Just crashing
: Some programs just exit when an error is detected.

  Combined with a supervisor to restart on error and careful coding to prevent corruption of persistent state, this is a battle-tested strategy that may be appropriate. Throwing an exception to abort an operation is the application of this technique to a procedure rather than to a whole program.

Returning a special value
: Returning a special value to signify an error can be a useful technique. For example, a function can return `-1` instead of an index when an item is not found in a list.

  This technique cannot be used when all return values are valid results for a function. It can also be dangerous, because the caller has to know (and remember) the convention. If we try to calculate the distance between two items in a list by subtracting their indices, when one of them is not found and returns -1, our calculation will be incorrect unless we explicitly handle the special case. We can't lean on the type checker to help us avoid errors.

  A special case of returning a special value is returning null on error. This is quite dangerous in most languages, because if the caller doesn't explicitly check for null, then using the result will throw a `NullPointerException`, which may be worse than the initial problem. In Kotlin, though, the type checker forces callers to deal with null, making this a safe and effective technique.

Setting a global flag
: One problem with returning special values is that they make it hard to signal which of several possible errors occurred. To solve this we can combine the special value with setting a global variable. When the special value is detected, the caller can read `errno`, for example, to establish what the problem was.

  This technique was popular in C but was largely superseded by exception-based error handling.

Returning a status code
: Another technique from the days before exceptions is returning a status code. This is possible when a function either returns no value (it is entirely side effect) or returns a value in another way, often by mutating a parameter passed by reference.

Invoking a special function
: Invoking a special function when an error occurs is sometimes a good strategy. Usually the error function is passed as a parameter to the invoked function. If a problem is detected, the error function is invoked with a value representing the error as a parameter. Sometimes the error function can signal by its return value if the failed operation should be retried or aborted. Another technique is for the error function to provide the value that should be returned by the invoked function.

  This technique is an example of the strategy pattern applied to error handling. Even when exceptions are available, it is a useful tool in niche situations.

Error Handling with Exceptions

All these techniques suffer from the drawback that the calling code is able, to a greater or lesser extent, to ignore that an error occurred.

Exceptions solve this problem. The operation automatically aborts on error, and the caller explicitly handles the exception. If the caller does not handle it, the exception propagates further down the call stack until something does, and if nothing handles the exception, the thread terminates.

Java and Checked Exceptions

Exceptions were relatively new when Java was released, and the language designers decided to innovate in this area. They made the exceptions that a method could throw part of its signature. This way, callers could know that, for example, a method might fail because the network resource that it was reading was no longer available. If a method declared that it could fail in this way, then every caller of that method would either have to deal with the failure (by specifying in a `catch` block how it should be handled) or declare that it, too, was liable to fail with the same exception. This ensures that the programmer takes account of the possibility of these errors. Such exceptions are called *checked exceptions*, because the compiler checks that they are handled (or redeclared to be thrown by the calling method).

Checked exceptions were designed for when the programmer might reasonably be able to find a way to recover: retrying a database write or reopening a socket, for example. The language designers identified two other types: errors and runtime exceptions.

Errors
: Subclasses of `java.lang.Error` are reserved for failures so severe that the JVM can no longer guarantee the correct functioning of the runtime. Maybe a class cannot be loaded, or the system runs out of memory. These conditions can happen at any point in the execution of a program, and so could cause any function to fail. Because any method could fail in this way, there is no value in including them in every method signature, so `Errors` do not have to be declared.

Runtime Exceptions
: Subclasses of `RuntimeException` represent other errors. The intention was that these would be reserved for problems caused by programmer mistakes, such as accessing a null reference or trying to read outside the bounds of a collection. In both these cases the programmer could have been more careful. Again though, every piece of code is subject to programmer error, so `RuntimeExceptions` are also exempted from having to be declared.

This scheme forces developers to deal with operations that can fail due to I/O errors or other things that are out of their control (the checked exceptions), allowing defensive programming where it is economical. At the other extreme, if an `Error` is thrown, the best default approach is exit the process as quickly as possible, before any more damage can be done to persistent state.

`RuntimeExceptions` are a middle ground. If they represent a programmer error, we should probably assume that we have just proved that we don't really know what is going on in our program and abort the current operation or whole application. Otherwise, we might try to recover, especially if our system has been designed to limit the damage that can be done to persistent state.

Your authors both really liked checked exceptions, but it seems they were in the minority, because checked exceptions fell out of favor in Java over the years. Checked exceptions were hampered from the start by the odd decision to make the unchecked `RuntimeException` a subclass of the otherwise checked `Exception`, so that code that wanted to handle all checked exceptions found itself catching unchecked ones as well, hiding programming errors. They were also not helped by the fact that the Java APIs used them inconsistently. Take extracting data from a string for example: the `URL` constructor `URL(String)` throws the *checked* `MalformedURLException`, while `Integer.parseInt(String)` throws the *unchecked* `NumberFormatException`.

> ## How Should parseInt Fail?
>
> This is an interesting case and shows why error handling is so hard.
>
> Looking through our strategies, `parseInt` can't return a special integer value, because all the ints are valid results. It could return `null` as a boxed `Integer`, but having to box and unbox for this, a really fundamental low-level operation that will be used in performance critical code, is undesirable, especially on the JVMs of the mid-1990s.
>
> Invoking an error function would similarly involve inefficient ceremony, so we are left with throwing an exception. Should that exception be checked or unchecked?
>
> The language designers decided that `parseInt` should throw `NumberFormatException` and that `NumberFormatException` should be an `IllegalArgumentException`, which is a `RuntimeException` and so unchecked.
>
> Those are both reasonable decisions in isolation. In combination, though, they lead to `parseInt` not forcing its callers to consider that it might fail, as they would if it declared a checked exception.
>
> We suspect that the JVM programmers were very used to parsing integers from strings in C (where there are no exceptions), using the `atoi` function, which helpfully returns `0` if it cannot succeed. They would have considered not planning for this failure to be a programmer error rather than a failure of the function itself. Your authors, though, would appreciate being reminded of the possibility of failure and would have specified a checked exception.

Confusion over what type of exception to use multiplied, and it wasn't long before the default was that the only checked exceptions that most Java libraries declared were `IOException`s. Even then, database libraries such as Hibernate, which were definitely talking over the network and definitely subject to `IOException`s, would throw only `RuntimeException`s.

Once a good proportion of the code that you call just uses unchecked exceptions, the game is up. You can't rely on checked exceptions to warn you about how a function might fail. Instead, you are reduced to some tactical defensive programming and the age-old technique of putting it into production, seeing what errors you log, and adding code to handle those you don't like the look of.

The final nail in the coffin of checked exceptions was the introduction of lambdas in Java 8. The decision was taken not to declare an exception type in the signature of the functional interfaces introduced to support lambdas (`Producer`, `Consumer`, etc.), so these cannot propagate checked exceptions. This wasn't an insurmountable problem, but to be fair, your authors would probably have given up there too. The net result, though, is that the old standard Java API declares checked exceptions (in particular, `IOException`) that the new standard API (in particular streams) forces developers to deny.

Kotlin and Exceptions

Kotlin has exceptions, because it runs on the JVM, and exceptions are built into the platform. It does not treat checked exceptions specially though, because Java had already lost that fight, and, as with Java, they are hard to reconcile with higher-order functions. Kotlin is able to largely ignore checked exceptions because they are not a feature of the JVM but, rather, of the Java compiler. The compiler does record in the bytecode what checked exceptions a method declares (to be able to check them), but the JVM itself does not care.

The result is that Kotlin programs are by default no better or worse than most Java programs when it comes to error handling.

An exception (lowercase e) to this is that, as we observed earlier, Kotlin can use `null` to indicate an error, safe in the knowledge that callers will have to take the possibility of `null` into consideration. An example of this is the `<T> Iterable<T>.firstOrNull(): T?` in the runtime. Tellingly, though, the runtime also defines `first()`, which throws `NoSuchElementException` if the collection is empty.

Beyond Exceptions: Functional Error Handling

Statically typed functional programming languages often reject exceptions in favor of another error handling technique based on *Either Types*. We'll see what an Either Type is shortly, but why don't functional programmers like exceptions?

A distinguishing feature of functional programming is *referential transparency*. When an expression is referentially transparent, we can safely replace it with the result of its evaluation. So if we write:

```
val secondsIn24hours = 60 * 60 * 24
```

then we can replace `60 * 60` with `3600` or `60 * 24` with `1440` without affecting the results. In fact, the compiler may decide to replace the whole expression with `86400` for us, and (unless we examine the bytecode or use a debugger) we will be none the wiser.

In contrast:

```
secondsIn(today())
```

is not referentially transparent, because `today()` will yield a different result than it did yesterday, and any day may have a leap second applied. As a result, the value of `secondsIn(today())` may differ depending on when we call it, and we can't just substitute the same value for the expression every time we use it.

This is the same concept as we saw in Chapter 7. "Calculations" on page 78 are referentially transparent; "Actions" on page 79 are not.

Why should we care? Because referential transparency makes it a lot easier to reason about the behavior of a program, which in turn leads to fewer errors and more opportunities to refactor and optimize. If we want these things (and at the very least we don't want more errors and fewer opportunities), then we should strive for referential transparency.

What does this have to do with error handling? Let's return to our `Integer.parseInt(String)` example and see. For a given valid input, `parseInt` will always return the same value, so it could be referentially transparent. In the cases where the `String` doesn't represent an integer, though, `parseInt` throws an exception rather than returning a result. We can't replace the result of the function invocation with an exception, because the type of the expression is `Int`, and an `Exception` isn't an `Int`. Exceptions break referential transparency.

If instead of using exceptions we returned to the old trick of using a special value to represent errors, we would have referential transparency, because that error value can replace the expression. In Kotlin, `null` would be great here, so we could define `parseInt` to return `Int?`. But what if we needed to know which was the first character that wasn't a digit? We can convey that information in an exception but not in a return type of `Int?`.

Can we find a way for our function to return *either* the `Int`, or the way that it failed?

The answer, as they say, is in the question. We define a type `Either`, which can hold one of two types, but only one at a time:

```
sealed class Either<out L, out R>

data class Left<out L>(val l: L) : Either<L, Nothing>()

data class Right<out R>(val r: R) : Either<Nothing, R>()
```

In Kotlin, sealed classes (Chapter 18) are excellent for this, because we can define our own subtypes but know that no one else can.

When `Either` is used for error handling, the convention is that `Right` is used for a result, `Left` for an error. If we stick to this convention, we could define:

```
fun parseInt(s: String): Either<String, Int> = try {
    Right(Integer.parseInt(s))
} catch (exception: Exception) {
    Left(exception.message ?: "No message")
}
```

How would we use this? As we saw in Chapter 18, `when` expressions and smart casting work really nicely to let us write things like:

```
val result: Either<String, Int> = parseInt(readLine() ?: "")
when (result) {
    is Right -> println("Your number was ${result.r}")
    is Left -> println("I couldn't read your number because ${result.l}")
}
```

By returning an `Either`, we force our clients to deal with the fact that we may have failed. This gives some of the advantages of checked exceptions in a functional form. To embrace this style, we make all functions that in Java we would have declared to throw a checked exception return an `Either`. The callers then either unwrap the success and act on it or pass on any failure:

```
fun doubleString(s: String): Either<String, Int> {
    val result: Either<String, Int> = parseInt(s)
    return when (result) {
        is Right -> Right(2 * result.r)
        is Left -> result
    }
}
```

Although using `when` to unwrap an `Either` is logical, it is also verbose. This particular pattern occurs so much that we define `map` to be:

```
inline fun <L, R1, R2> Either<L, R1>.map(f: (R1) -> R2): Either<L, R2> =
    when (this) {
        is Right -> Right(f(this.r))
        is Left -> this
    }
```

This allows us to write the previous function as:

```
fun doubleString(s: String): Either<String, Int> = parseInt(s).map { 2 * it }
```

Why is that function called `map` and not `invokeUnlessLeft`? Well, if you squint you may be able to see that it is kind of the same thing as `List.map`. It applies a function to the contents of a container, returning the result in another container. In the case of `Either`, `map` applies the function only if it is a `Right` (nonerror); otherwise, it passes `Left`s on unchanged.

Practice that squinting, because we are now going to define:

```
inline fun <L, R1, R2> Either<L, R1>.flatMap(
    f: (R1) -> Either<L, R2>
): Either<L, R2> =
    when (this) {
        is Right -> f(this.r)
        is Left -> this
    }
```

This unpacks our value and uses it to invoke a function that in turn might fail (as it returns `Either`). What can we do with that? Well, let's say we want to read from a `Reader` and print double the result. We can define a wrapper for `readLine` that returns an `Either` rather than failing with an exception:

```
fun BufferedReader.eitherReadLine(): Either<String, String> =
    try {
        val line = this.readLine()
        if (line == null)
            Left("No more lines")
        else
            Right(line)
    } catch (x: IOException) {
        Left(x.message ?: "No message")
    }
```

This lets us combine `eitherReadLine` and `doubleString` with `flatMap`:

```
fun doubleNextLine(reader: BufferedReader): Either<String, Int> =
    reader.eitherReadLine().flatMap { doubleString(it) }
```

This code will return a `Left` with the failure if `eitherReadLine` fails; otherwise, it will return the result of `doubleString`, which may itself be either a `Left` for failure or a `Right` with the final `Int` result. In this way a chain of `map` and/or `flatMap` calls acts like a series of expressions, which might throw an exception; the first failure aborts the rest of the computation.

If you come from an object-oriented background, this style does take some getting used to. In our experience no amount of reading helps; you just have to knuckle down and start writing code this way until it becomes less strange. We'll share your pain by pairing with you in the worked example later.

Error Handling in Kotlin

Now that we know the error handling options open to us, which should we use in our Kotlin projects, and how do we migrate our Java code?

As usual, it depends.

Using nullable types to represent failure is very effective, provided that you don't need to convey any information about the reason for failure.

You won't be fired for using exceptions as your default strategy. The lack of type checking makes it hard to communicate what code is subject to what failure, though, which in turn makes it hard to build reliable systems. Adding insult to this injury, you will lose the benefits of referential transparency, making it harder to refactor and fix your unreliable system.

Our preference is to return an `Either` type from those operations that would have thrown a checked exception in Java, either because of I/O problems, or because, like `parseInt`, they cannot give a result for all inputs. This allows us to reserve the use of exceptions for more pernicious problems. `Errors` are still appropriate for unrecoverable program errors: in this case we should design our systems so that the program exits and is restarted by some other process. `RuntimeExceptions` are still good for signaling when we have made an error as programmers: `IndexOutOfBounds` and the like. If we have carefully designed our system, it should be able to survive these issues and process other inputs that do not run into the same problem.

Which `Either` type should you choose? The built-in Kotlin `Result` type is, at the time of writing, a frustrating placeholder which just teases and gets in the way. It is designed for coroutines, is restricted to an `Exception` (actually `Throwable`) as its error value, and IntelliJ moans if you use it as a property type. This would be reasonable if it wasn't published in the `kotlin` package. It is, though, so if you try to use a more useful type called `Result`, you get strange error messages until you remember that the compiler is assuming that `Result` refers to the `kotlin.Result` type that you aren't supposed to use.

Plenty of other result types are available, but for this book we will use Result4k (*https://oreil.ly/F5Y4M*), not coincidentally written by Nat. Compared to the generic `Either` type we introduced earlier, Result4k defines `Result<SuccessType, FailureType>`, with subtypes `Success` and `Failure` rather than `Left` and `Right`. Because it is specialized for representing errors, Result4k reverses the `Either` convention by having the success type as the first of the generic parameters. It can also offer operations, such as `onFailure` and `recover`, that would not make sense on `Either`. We'll see some of these operations as we refactor.

Refactoring Exceptions to Errors

Now that we know the error handling options available to us, let's refactor some Java code to Kotlin, converting the error handling as we go.

There is an HTTP endpoint in Travelator that allows the client app to register a `Customer`:

```
public class CustomerRegistrationHandler {

    private final IRegisterCustomers registration;
    private final ObjectMapper objectMapper = new ObjectMapper();

    public CustomerRegistrationHandler(IRegisterCustomers registration) {
        this.registration = registration;
    }

    public Response handle(Request request) {
```

```
        try {
            RegistrationData data = objectMapper.readValue(
                request.getBody(),
                RegistrationData.class
            );
            Customer customer = registration.register(data);
            return new Response(HTTP_CREATED,
                objectMapper.writeValueAsString(customer)
            );
        } catch (JsonProcessingException x) {
            return new Response(HTTP_BAD_REQUEST);
        } catch (ExcludedException x) {
            return new Response(HTTP_FORBIDDEN);
        } catch (DuplicateException x) {
            return new Response(HTTP_CONFLICT);
        } catch (Exception x) {
            return new Response(HTTP_INTERNAL_ERROR);
        }
    }
}
```

Example 19.1 [errors.0:src/main/java/travelator/handlers/CustomerRegistrationHandler.java]

`CustomerRegistrationHandler`'s job is to extract data from the request body, pass it to `registration` for processing, and return a response with either a JSON representation of a `Customer` or a suitable error status code.

> ### HTTP
>
> We'd rather not tie our example code to a particular Java HTTP framework, so we have abstracted incoming calls behind a simple function that takes a `Request` and returns a `Response`.
>
> HTTP status codes are another example of a result type. The HTTP protocol returns 4xx errors when a request is unsuccessful because the request was wrong in some way, 5xx errors when a request couldn't be processed for server-related reasons; 2xx status codes are success cases; and 1xx and 3xx codes are used to signal an ongoing interaction.
>
> If we value the ability to correctly handle different types of error, we should take care to map error types in our application to and from status codes correctly when designing systems that communicate over HTTP.

`CustomerRegistration` implements the business rules, which is that potential customers should be vetted against an `ExclusionList`. We don't want to allow known undesirables to register and abuse our services, so we reject them at this point:

```java
public class CustomerRegistration implements IRegisterCustomers {

    private final ExclusionList exclusionList;
    private final Customers customers;

    public CustomerRegistration(
        Customers customers,
        ExclusionList exclusionList
    ) {
        this.exclusionList = exclusionList;
        this.customers = customers;
    }

    public Customer register(RegistrationData data)
        throws ExcludedException, DuplicateException {
        if (exclusionList.exclude(data)) {
            throw new ExcludedException();
        } else {
            return customers.add(data.name, data.email);
        }
    }
}
```

Example 19.2 [errors.0:src/main/java/travelator/CustomerRegistration.java]

Look at the `throws` clause of `register`. It tells us that the method can fail because of the explicit exclusion, but also that `customers.add` can fail with a `DuplicateException`. Here is the `Customers` interface:

```java
public interface Customers {

    Customer add(String name, String email) throws DuplicateException;

    Optional<Customer> find(String id);
}
```

Example 19.3 [errors.0:src/main/java/travelator/Customers.java]

Finally, `Customer` is another value type. Here it is after conversion to Kotlin:

```kotlin
data class Customer(
    val id: String,
    val name: String,
    val email: String
)
```

Example 19.4 [errors.1:src/main/java/travelator/Customer.kt]

This is typical of your authors' Java style. It expresses the things that might reasonably go wrong as the checked `ExcludedException` and `DuplicateException`, and these are all caught at the top level in `handle`, where they are reported to the caller, in this case as HTTP status codes. Your style might be to use unchecked exceptions, in which case this code would be similar but without the exceptions as part of the method signatures.

One thing we don't see is any checked exception related to failures to persist a `Customer` in `Customers::add`. This method will be talking across the network to a database, but our query code is evidently swallowing `IOException` at some point and raising a `RuntimeException` in its place. These will propagate out of `CustomerRegistration::register`, be caught at the top level of `CustomerRegistrationHandler`, and passed back to clients as `HTTP_INTERNAL_ERROR` (500). It's a shame that we aren't logging any information about those stray `RuntimeExceptions`, because they might reveal systematic connection issues or be hiding a frequent `NullPointerException` in some lower-level code. Someone should probably address that, but in the meantime at least we have a shorter example to show in this book.

Our Conversion Strategy

If we were just to convert this code to Kotlin, we would lose the advantages of checked exceptions to tell us what could go wrong and show where we are handling those problems. So as we convert, we will replace exception-based error handling with a functional alternative using Result4k.

In this example, we'll start at the lowest level and work our way up, keeping higher levels working until the predictable error cases (those that are currently expressed as checked exceptions) no longer use exceptions. At the same time, we have to be mindful that pretty much any instruction in the JVM can fail, so we need to defend against these runtime issues.

Starting at the Bottom

If we convert `Customers` to Kotlin, we get:

```
interface Customers {

    @Throws(DuplicateException::class) ❶
    fun add(name: String, email: String): Customer

    fun find(id: String): Optional<Customer>
}
```

Example 19.5 [errors.3:src/main/java/travelator/Customers.kt]

❶ Although Kotlin doesn't have checked exceptions, the `@Throws` annotation allows interop with Java code by adding the exception to the method's signature in the bytecode. Without it, a Java implementation of `Customers` that does throw `DuplicateException` cannot implement the method. Worse, Java code that calls the method on the interface would not be able to catch the exception or declare that it is passed on, because it is a compile error for Java code to handle a checked exception that the compiler cannot see is possible.

Our strategy is to add to our interface a version of `Customers::add` that, instead of throwing an exception, returns `Result<Customer, DuplicateException>`. If we were starting from scratch, we wouldn't use `DuplicateException` as the error type, but here it lets us interoperate with Java easily. We are going to keep the current throwy version around for now so that we don't break existing callers. Then we will convert those callers to use the `Result` version and then remove the old version when we can. That's right, it's our old friend "Expand-and-Contract Refactoring" on page 44.

What should we call the method that works like `Customers::add` but returns a `Result`? We can't name it `add` too, because both have the same parameters, so we call it `addToo` for now. If the new method delegates to `add`, we can make it a default method so that it is available to all implementations:

```
interface Customers {

    @Throws(DuplicateException::class)
    fun add(name: String, email: String): Customer

    fun addToo(name:String, email:String)
        : Result<Customer, DuplicateException> =
        try {
            Success(add(name, email))
        } catch (x: DuplicateException) {
            Failure(x)
        }

    fun find(id: String): Optional<Customer>
}
```

Example 19.6 [errors.5:src/main/java/travelator/Customers.kt]

Naming

It's a bit irritating that we can't name the new method `add` as well, but the JVM won't allow methods that differ only on return type to have the same name.

If we can't think of a good enough name in these sorts of situations, we err on the side of using a bad one. In all likelihood we'll come up with a better name later, and the bad name will reduce the risk that we settle for not good enough.

In this case, it really shouldn't matter, because we know that by the end of this refactor we will have deleted the original method and can steal its name once it is gone.

Now that we have both exception and result versions of the method, we can migrate the callers of the exception version. Although we can use Result4k from Java, it's a lot more convenient from Kotlin. So let's take `CustomerRegistration` (the caller of `add`):

```
public class CustomerRegistration implements IRegisterCustomers {

    private final ExclusionList exclusionList;
    private final Customers customers;

    public CustomerRegistration(
        Customers customers,
        ExclusionList exclusionList
    ) {
        this.exclusionList = exclusionList;
        this.customers = customers;
    }

    public Customer register(RegistrationData data)
        throws ExcludedException, DuplicateException {
        if (exclusionList.exclude(data)) {
            throw new ExcludedException();
        } else {
            return customers.add(data.name, data.email);
        }
    }
}
```

Example 19.7 [errors.5:src/main/java/travelator/CustomerRegistration.java]

Converting this to Kotlin gives:

```
class CustomerRegistration(
    private val customers: Customers,
    private val exclusionList: ExclusionList
) : IRegisterCustomers {

    @Throws(ExcludedException::class, DuplicateException::class)
    override fun register(data: RegistrationData): Customer {
        return if (exclusionList.exclude(data)) {
            throw ExcludedException()
        } else {
            customers.add(data.name, data.email)
        }
    }

}
```

Example 19.8 [errors.6:src/main/java/travelator/CustomerRegistration.kt]

That `customers.add` expression is the one that can throw `DuplicateException`. We're going to replace it with a call to `addToo` but keeping the behavior the same. So we pull out `result` as a local:

```
@Throws(ExcludedException::class, DuplicateException::class)
override fun register(data: RegistrationData): Customer {
    return if (exclusionList.exclude(data)) {
        throw ExcludedException()
    } else {
        val result = customers.add(data.name, data.email)
        result
    }
}
```

Example 19.9 [errors.7:src/main/java/travelator/CustomerRegistration.kt]

If we now call `addToo` instead, it will no longer throw, but the exception will be returned in the `Result`. This won't compile yet:

```
@Throws(ExcludedException::class, DuplicateException::class)
override fun register(data: RegistrationData): Customer {
    return if (exclusionList.exclude(data)) {
        throw ExcludedException()
    } else {
        val result: Result<Customer, DuplicateException> =
            customers.addToo(data.name, data.email)
        result ❶
    }
}
```

Example 19.10 [errors.8:src/main/java/travelator/CustomerRegistration.kt]

❶ `Type mismatch. Required: Customer Found: Result<Customer, DuplicateException>`

We have a `Result`, so we need to unpack it. When it is `Success`, we want to return the wrapped value; when `Failure`, throw the wrapped `DuplicateException` (to keep the current behavior of `register`):

```
@Throws(ExcludedException::class, DuplicateException::class)
override fun register(data: RegistrationData): Customer {
    return if (exclusionList.exclude(data)) {
        throw ExcludedException()
    } else {
        val result: Result<Customer, DuplicateException> =
            customers.addToo(data.name, data.email)
        when (result) {
            is Success<Customer> ->
                result.value
            is Failure<DuplicateException> ->
                throw result.reason
        }
    }
}
```

Example 19.11 [errors.9:src/main/java/travelator/CustomerRegistration.kt]

As it happens, where the error type is an `Exception`, Result4k has a function to shortcut this case: `Result::orThrow`:

```
@Throws(ExcludedException::class, DuplicateException::class)
override fun register(data: RegistrationData): Customer {
    return if (exclusionList.exclude(data)) {
        throw ExcludedException()
    } else {
        val result: Result<Customer, DuplicateException> =
            customers.addToo(data.name, data.email)
        result.orThrow()
    }
}
```

Example 19.12 [errors.10:src/main/java/travelator/CustomerRegistration.kt]

Now we can inline to get back to a shorter form:

```
@Throws(ExcludedException::class, DuplicateException::class)
override fun register(data: RegistrationData): Customer {
    return if (exclusionList.exclude(data)) {
        throw ExcludedException()
    } else {
        customers.addToo(data.name, data.email).orThrow()
    }
}
```

Example 19.13 [errors.11:src/main/java/travelator/CustomerRegistration.kt]

Finally, that nesting is too confusing for comfort, so let's simplify it by using "Replace 'if' with 'when'", "Replace return with 'when' expression", and "Remove braces from all 'when' entries". Alt-Enter all the things!

```
@Throws(ExcludedException::class, DuplicateException::class)
override fun register(data: RegistrationData): Customer {
    when {
        exclusionList.exclude(data) -> throw ExcludedException()
        else -> return customers.addToo(data.name, data.email).orThrow()
    }
}
```

Example 19.14 [errors.12:src/main/java/travelator/CustomerRegistration.kt]

Splendid. We've replaced one of the uses of exceptions with a result type; let's have a little rest.

Contract

Ready to go again? Good.

We now have to choose whether to proceed depth- or breadth-first. Depth-first would address the caller of `CustomerRegistration::register`; breadth-first would first fix up the other callers of `Customers::add` so that we can remove it. As it happens, our example code has no other callers of `add`, so breadth-first isn't an option, and we can get on with the contract phase of expand and contract.

We currently have two implementations of Customers::add. One is the production implementation that talks to the database, the other a test implementation. Our code now calls them via the default implementation of Customers::addToo that we added to the interface. We want to delete the add implementations, so we need to implement addToo directly. Let's look at the (not thread-safe) test version:

```
public class InMemoryCustomers implements Customers {

    private final List<Customer> list = new ArrayList<>();
    private int id = 0;

    @Override
    public Customer add(String name, String email) throws DuplicateException {
        if (list.stream().anyMatch( item -> item.getEmail().equals(email)))
            throw new DuplicateException(
                "customer with email " + email + " already exists"
            );
        int newId = id++;
        Customer result = new Customer(Integer.toString(newId), name, email);
        list.add(result);
        return result;
    }

    @Override
    public Optional<Customer> find(String id) {
        return list.stream()
            .filter(customer -> customer.getId().equals(id))
            .findFirst();
    }

    // for test
    public void add(Customer customer) {
        list.add(customer);
    }

    public int size() {
        return list.size();
    }
}
```

Example 19.15 [errors.12:src/test/java/travelator/InMemoryCustomers.java]

The easiest way to implement addToo here is probably just to duplicate add and fix it up, returning Failure where we had thrown and Success for the happy path:

```
@SuppressWarnings("unchecked")
@Override
public Result<Customer, DuplicateException> addToo(
    String name, String email
) {
    if (list.stream().anyMatch( item -> item.getEmail().equals(email)))
        return new Failure<>(
```

```
                new DuplicateException(
                    "customer with email " + email + " already exists"
                )
            );
        int newId = id++;
        Customer result = new Customer(Integer.toString(newId), name, email);
        list.add(result);
        return new Success<Customer>(result);
    }
```

Example 19.16 [errors.13:src/test/java/travelator/InMemoryCustomers.java]

We can also use this strategy to add `addToo` to our production implementations of `Customers`; we'll skip the details. Once we are done, we can delete the unused `add` from the implementations and the interface and then rename `addToo` to `add`, leaving us with:

```
interface Customers {

    fun add(name:String, email:String): Result<Customer, DuplicateException>

    fun find(id: String): Optional<Customer>
}
```

Example 19.17 [errors.14:src/main/java/travelator/Customers.kt]

The clients of `Customers` are now back to calling `add`, albeit the version returning a `Result` rather than declaring checked exceptions:

```
class CustomerRegistration(
    private val customers: Customers,
    private val exclusionList: ExclusionList
) : IRegisterCustomers {

    @Throws(ExcludedException::class, DuplicateException::class)
    override fun register(data: RegistrationData): Customer {
        when {
            exclusionList.exclude(data) -> throw ExcludedException()
            else -> return customers.add(data.name, data.email).orThrow()
        }
    }
}
```

Example 19.18 [errors.14:src/main/java/travelator/CustomerRegistration.kt]

We left `InMemoryCustomers` as Java really just to demonstrate that we could return Result4k types from our old code, but we can't resist the conversion, because the code now has a number of warnings of the type `Not annotated [X] overrides @NotNull [X]`.

After conversion, including moving from streams to Kotlin collection operations (Chapter 13), we have:

```
class InMemoryCustomers : Customers {

    private val list: MutableList<Customer> = ArrayList()
```

```
    private var id = 0

    override fun add(name: String, email: String)
        : Result<Customer, DuplicateException> =
        when {
            list.any { it.email == email } -> Failure(
                DuplicateException(
                    "customer with email $email already exists"
                )
            )
            else -> {
                val result = Customer(id++.toString(), name, email)
                list.add(result)
                Success(result)
            }
        }

    override fun find(id: String): Optional<Customer> =
        list.firstOrNull { it.id == id }.toOptional()

    // for test
    fun add(customer: Customer) {
        list.add(customer)
    }

    fun size(): Int = list.size
}
```

Example 19.19 [errors.15:src/test/java/travelator/InMemoryCustomers.kt]

Let's recap where we are now. `Customers` is now Kotlin, and `add` returns a `Result` instead of throwing `DuplicateException`:

```
interface Customers {

    fun add(name:String, email:String): Result<Customer, DuplicateException>

    fun find(id: String): Optional<Customer>
}
```

Example 19.20 [errors.15:src/main/java/travelator/Customers.kt]

`IRegisterCustomers` is still Java and still throws two types of exception:

```
public interface IRegisterCustomers {
    Customer register(RegistrationData data)
        throws ExcludedException, DuplicateException;
}
```

Example 19.21 [errors.15:src/main/java/travelator/IRegisterCustomers.java]

`CustomerRegistration` is now Kotlin and is where we now thunk between `Result.Error` and `DuplicateException`, using `orThrow`:

```
class CustomerRegistration(
    private val customers: Customers,
    private val exclusionList: ExclusionList
) : IRegisterCustomers {

    @Throws(ExcludedException::class, DuplicateException::class)
    override fun register(data: RegistrationData): Customer {
        when {
            exclusionList.exclude(data) -> throw ExcludedException()
            else -> return customers.add(data.name, data.email).orThrow()
        }
    }
}
```

Example 19.22 [errors.15:src/main/java/travelator/CustomerRegistration.kt]

We have converted a whole layer of our interaction to use a result type and can move out to the next.

Stepping Out

If we are to follow the same pattern with `IRegisterCustomers::register` as we did with `Customers`—providing a default implementation of an adapter between exception-throwing and error-returning—we will have to address the issue of how to express the result of a function that can fail for two reasons. That's because `register` is currently declaring that it throws both `ExcludedException` and `DuplicateException` checked exceptions. In code, we want something like `Result<Customer, Either<ExcludedException, DuplicateException>>`.

We *could* use a generic `Either` type, but that only gets us so far as a strategy. Unlike Java, where the order that we declare exceptions doesn't matter, `Either<ExcludedException, DuplicateException>` is not the same thing as `Either<DuplicateException, ExcludedException>`. The `Either` is at best really confusing and will get even worse if we ever have more than two exceptions: `OneOf<ExcludedException, DuplicateException, SomeOtherProblem>` is just horrible.

Another option is to move up to the common superclass of the two exceptions and declare the return type as `Result<Customer, Exception>`. This fails the communication test: we can't look at the signature and gain any clues about what types of errors we are expecting.

Instead, our best strategy here is not to try to express the error in terms of existing types, but to map to a new type.

As *exception* and *error* are all overloaded terms, we've chosen `RegistrationProblem`, with subtypes of `Excluded` (which carries no additional information and so can be an `object`), and `Duplicate` (which carries any message from the original `DuplicateException`):

```
sealed class RegistrationProblem

object Excluded : RegistrationProblem()

data class Duplicate(
    val message: String?
) : RegistrationProblem()
```

Example 19.23 [errors.16:src/main/java/travelator/IRegisterCustomers.kt]

By making `RegistrationProblem` a sealed class, we know at compile time what subclasses can exist and, hence, what errors have to be handled—very much like the checked exception signature of a method.

We can use this `RegistrationProblem` when we follow the pattern from earlier, adding a default implementation of `registerToo` to the interface that returns `Result<Customer, RegistrationProblem>`:

```
interface IRegisterCustomers {

    @Throws(ExcludedException::class, DuplicateException::class)
    fun register(data: RegistrationData): Customer

    fun registerToo(data: RegistrationData):
        Result<Customer, RegistrationProblem> =
        try {
            Success(register(data))
        } catch (x: ExcludedException) {
            Failure(Excluded)
        } catch (x: DuplicateException) {
            Failure(Duplicate(x.message))
        }
}
```

Example 19.24 [errors.16:src/main/java/travelator/IRegisterCustomers.kt]

Now we can migrate callers of `register` to `registerToo`. We'll start with `CustomerRegistrationHandler`, converting it to Kotlin first:

```
class CustomerRegistrationHandler(
    private val registration: IRegisterCustomers
) {
    private val objectMapper = ObjectMapper()

    fun handle(request: Request): Response {
        return try {
            val data = objectMapper.readValue(
                request.body,
                RegistrationData::class.java
            )
            val customer = registration.register(data)
            Response(
                HTTP_CREATED,
```

```
                objectMapper.writeValueAsString(customer)
            )
        } catch (x: JsonProcessingException) {
            Response(HTTP_BAD_REQUEST)
        } catch (x: ExcludedException) {
            Response(HTTP_FORBIDDEN)
        } catch (x: DuplicateException) {
            Response(HTTP_CONFLICT)
        } catch (x: Exception) {
            Response(HTTP_INTERNAL_ERROR)
        }
    }
}
```

Example 19.25 [errors.17:src/main/java/travelator/handlers/CustomerRegistrationHandler.kt]

Now, as we did before, we swap to calling the new method (`registerToo`) instead of the old one (`register`) and interpret the return type with a `when` expression:

```
class CustomerRegistrationHandler(
    private val registration: IRegisterCustomers
) {
    private val objectMapper = ObjectMapper()

    fun handle(request: Request): Response {
        return try {
            val data = objectMapper.readValue(
                request.body,
                RegistrationData::class.java
            )
            val customerResult = registration.registerToo(data)
            when (customerResult) {
                is Success -> Response(
                    HTTP_CREATED,
                    objectMapper.writeValueAsString(customerResult.value)
                )
                is Failure -> customerResult.reason.toResponse()

            }
        } catch (x: JsonProcessingException) {
            Response(HTTP_BAD_REQUEST)
        } catch (x: ExcludedException) {
            Response(HTTP_FORBIDDEN)
        } catch (x: DuplicateException) {
            Response(HTTP_CONFLICT)
        } catch (x: Exception) {
            Response(HTTP_INTERNAL_ERROR)
        }
    }
}

private fun RegistrationProblem.toResponse() = when (this) {
    is Duplicate -> Response(HTTP_CONFLICT)
```

```
        is Excluded -> Response(HTTP_FORBIDDEN)
    }
```

Example 19.26 [errors.18:src/main/java/travelator/handlers/CustomerRegistrationHandler.kt]

Finally, we can remove the unnecessary exception cases and simplify the error case with `map` and `recover`. `Result::recover` is a Result4k extension function that unwraps the result if it is `Success`, otherwise returning the result of mapping the failure's `reason`:

```
fun handle(request: Request): Response =
    try {
        val data = objectMapper.readValue(
            request.body,
            RegistrationData::class.java
        )
        registration.registerToo(data)
            .map { value ->
                Response(
                    HTTP_CREATED,
                    objectMapper.writeValueAsString(value)
                )
            }
            .recover { reason -> reason.toResponse() }
    } catch (x: JsonProcessingException) {
        Response(HTTP_BAD_REQUEST)
    } catch (x: Exception) {
        Response(HTTP_INTERNAL_ERROR)
    }
```

Example 19.27 [errors.19:src/main/java/travelator/handlers/CustomerRegistrationHandler.kt]

Note that this code is still not exception-free. First, the `ObjectMapper` can still throw `JSONProcessingException`. That is the reality of Java (and frankly most Kotlin) APIs, but the code is safe and communicates well, because the throwing and catching are in the same method. Second, we still have to consider other `RuntimeExceptions` that could be thrown from anywhere: `NullPointerException` and so on. These could have crossed function boundaries and leaked up to here, where the buck stops at the top-level catch-all, which returns `HTTP_INTERNAL_ERROR`. The reality is that we can still have *unexpected* exceptions, but the *expected* failure cases are now expressed by `Results` and communicated in our code.

More Fixup

We can now confess that the `RegistrationHandlerTests` got broken a few steps ago. Ordinarily we would have fixed them straightaway, but that would have interrupted our explanation.

The problem is that the tests are mock tests, which expect calls to `IRegister.register`, but we are now calling `registerToo`. For example:

```
public class CustomerRegistrationHandlerTests {

    final IRegisterCustomers registration =
        mock(IRegisterCustomers.class);
    final CustomerRegistrationHandler handler =
        new CustomerRegistrationHandler(registration);

    final String fredBody = toJson(
        "{ 'name' : 'fred', 'email' : 'fred@bedrock.com' }"
    );
    final RegistrationData fredData =
        new RegistrationData("fred", "fred@bedrock.com");

    @Test
    public void returns_Created_with_body_on_success()
        throws DuplicateException, ExcludedException {
        when(registration.register(fredData))
            .thenReturn(
                new Customer("0", fredData.name, fredData.email)
            );

        String expectedBody = toJson(
            "{'id':'0','name':'fred','email':'fred@bedrock.com'}"
        );
        assertEquals(
            new Response(HTTP_CREATED, expectedBody),
            handler.handle(new Request(fredBody))
        );
    }

    @Test
    public void returns_Conflict_for_duplicate()
        throws DuplicateException, ExcludedException {

        when(registration.register(fredData))
            .thenThrow(
                new DuplicateException("deliberate")
            );

        assertEquals(
            new Response(HTTP_CONFLICT),
            handler.handle(new Request(fredBody))
        );
    }
    ...

    private String toJson(String jsonIsh) {
        return jsonIsh.replace('\'', '"');
    }
}
```

Example 19.28 [errors.20:src/test/java/travelator/handlers/CustomerRegistrationHandlerTests.java]

To fix the tests, we need to change the call from `register`, returning `Customer` or throwing, to `registerToo`, returning `Result<Customer, RegistrationProblem>`:

```
@Test
public void returns_Created_with_body_on_success() {

    when(registration.registerToo(fredData))
        .thenReturn(new Success<>(
            new Customer("0", fredData.name, fredData.email)
        ));

    String expectedBody = toJson(
        "{'id':'0','name':'fred','email':'fred@bedrock.com'}"
    );
    assertEquals(
        new Response(HTTP_CREATED, expectedBody),
        handler.handle(new Request(fredBody))
    );
}

@Test
public void returns_Conflict_for_duplicate() {

    when(registration.registerToo(fredData))
        .thenReturn(new Failure<>(
            new Duplicate("deliberate")
        ));

    assertEquals(
        new Response(HTTP_CONFLICT),
        handler.handle(new Request(fredBody))
    );
}
    ...
```

Example 19.29 [errors.21:src/test/java/travelator/handlers/CustomerRegistrationHandlerTests.java]

The tests are actually simplified, because instead of having to choose `thenReturn` or `thenThrow`, we are now always mocking with `thenReturn`, with `Success` or `Failure`, respectively.

Now that our tests are passing again, we can return to production code and implement `CustomerRegistration::registerToo` directly. In lieu of any cleverer idea, we do this by duplicating the `register` method and fettling the error handling. We do this using `Result::mapFailure` (part of Result4k) to convert `DuplicateException` to `Duplicate`:

```
class CustomerRegistration(
    private val customers: Customers,
    private val exclusionList: ExclusionList
) : IRegisterCustomers {
```

```
    @Throws(ExcludedException::class, DuplicateException::class)
    override fun register(data: RegistrationData): Customer {
        when {
            exclusionList.exclude(data) -> throw ExcludedException()
            else -> return customers.add(data.name, data.email).orThrow()
        }
    }

    override fun registerToo(
        data: RegistrationData
    ): Result<Customer, RegistrationProblem> {
        return when {
            exclusionList.exclude(data) -> Failure(Excluded)
            else -> customers.add(data.name, data.email)
                .mapFailure { exception: DuplicateException -> ❶
                    Duplicate(exception.message)
                }
        }
    }
}
```

Example 19.30 [errors.22:src/main/java/travelator/CustomerRegistration.kt]

❶ Note that we explicitly specify the type of the lambda parameter in `mapFailure`. As we will see later, this way if we change the return type of `add` to have a different failure type, the compiler will force us to change how we handle it.

There are two problems with this. First, `registerToo` has no test code, and second, we have the duplicate logic caused by our duplicating `register` to create `registerToo`. We can fix both by implementing `register` in terms of `registerToo`—the opposite of what we did in `Customers`:

```
class CustomerRegistration(
    private val customers: Customers,
    private val exclusionList: ExclusionList
) : IRegisterCustomers {

    @Throws(ExcludedException::class, DuplicateException::class)
    override fun register(data: RegistrationData): Customer =
        registerToo(data).recover { error ->  ❶
            when (error) {
                is Excluded -> throw ExcludedException()
                is Duplicate -> throw DuplicateException(error.message)
            }
    }

    override fun registerToo(
        data: RegistrationData
    ): Result<Customer, RegistrationProblem> {
        return when {
            exclusionList.exclude(data) -> Failure(Excluded)
            else -> customers.add(data.name, data.email)
```

```
                .mapFailure { exception: DuplicateException ->
                    Duplicate(exception.message)
                }
        }
    }
}
```

Example 19.31 [errors.23:src/main/java/travelator/CustomerRegistration.kt]

❶ Delegate to `registerToo` and process `Error` type.

Now our `CustomerRegistrationTests`, which work in terms of `register`, will be testing `registerToo` for us:

```
public class CustomerRegistrationTests {

    InMemoryCustomers customers = new InMemoryCustomers();
    Set<String> excluded = Set.of(
        "cruella@hellhall.co.uk"
    );
    CustomerRegistration registration = new CustomerRegistration(customers,
        (registrationData) -> excluded.contains(registrationData.email)
    );

    @Test
    public void adds_a_customer_when_not_excluded()
        throws DuplicateException, ExcludedException {
        assertEquals(Optional.empty(), customers.find("0"));

        Customer added = registration.register(
            new RegistrationData("fred flintstone", "fred@bedrock.com")
        );
        assertEquals(
            new Customer("0", "fred flintstone", "fred@bedrock.com"),
            added
        );
        assertEquals(added, customers.find("0").orElseThrow());
    }

    @Test
    public void throws_DuplicateException_when_email_address_exists() {
        customers.add(new Customer("0", "fred flintstone", "fred@bedrock.com"));
        assertEquals(1, customers.size());

        assertThrows(DuplicateException.class,
            () -> registration.register(
                new RegistrationData("another name", "fred@bedrock.com")
            )
        );
        assertEquals(1, customers.size());
    }
```

```
    ...
}
```

Example 19.32 [errors.23:src/test/java/travelator/CustomerRegistrationTests.java]

This would be a good way to keep both `register` and `registerToo` while we migrate away from Java and exceptions to Kotlin and an error type. In this case, though, the tests are actually the last callers of `register`, so let's convert them to call `registerToo`. We could take the time to show how to use Result4k in Java, but we're all pretty tired of this example now, so we'll convert the tests to Kotlin and then have them call `register` with the immortal words, "Here's one I made earlier":

```
@Test
fun `adds a customer when not excluded`() {
    assertEquals(Optional.empty<Any>(), customers.find("0"))
    val added = registration.registerToo(
        RegistrationData("fred flintstone", "fred@bedrock.com")
    ).valueOrNull()
    assertEquals(
        Customer("0", "fred flintstone", "fred@bedrock.com"),
        added
    )
    assertEquals(added, customers.find("0").orElseThrow())
}

@Test
fun `returns Duplicate when email address exists`() {
    customers.add(Customer("0", "fred flintstone", "fred@bedrock.com"))
    assertEquals(1, customers.size())
    val failure = registration.registerToo(
        RegistrationData("another name", "fred@bedrock.com")
    ).failureOrNull()
    assertEquals(
        Duplicate("customer with email fred@bedrock.com already exists"),
        failure
    )
    assertEquals(1, customers.size())
}

    ...
```

Example 19.33 [errors.24:src/test/java/travelator/CustomerRegistrationTests.kt]

Now that we have no callers of `register`, we can finally remove it and rename `registerToo` to `register`, ending up with exception-free Kotlin:

```
interface IRegisterCustomers {
    fun register(data: RegistrationData):
        Result<Customer, RegistrationProblem>
}

sealed class RegistrationProblem
```

```
object Excluded : RegistrationProblem()

data class Duplicate(
    val message: String?
) : RegistrationProblem()
```

Example 19.34 [errors.25:src/main/java/travelator/IRegisterCustomers.kt]

```
interface Customers {

    fun add(name:String, email:String): Result<Customer, DuplicateException>

    fun find(id: String): Optional<Customer>
}
```

Example 19.35 [errors.25:src/main/java/travelator/Customers.kt]

Hmm, not quite exception-free because of that `DuplicateException`. It is not actually *thrown* from anywhere anymore, just created and put into a `Failure`. We can fix this either by renaming the class to `DuplicateCustomerProblem` and stop it from extending `Exception`, or reuse the existing `Duplicate` subclass of `RegistrationProblem`. Which is better?

Layers

If we think in terms of layers, `Customers` is in a lower layer than `Registration`, which depends on it. So `Customers` should not depend on the higher-level `RegistrationProblem`. We could try to invert the dependency so that the `Duplicate` subclass of `RegistrationProblem` is a subtype (or even just the same type) of `DuplicateCustomerProblem` declared in the repository layer. That would work here, but is a bit of a dead-end if `Customers::add` ever needs to declare another way that it might fail. If, for example, we want to show in our result that database communications might fail, we can't (well, shouldn't) make that a subtype of `DuplicateCustomerProblem`. So we will be back to the problem of expressing more than one error type in a single result.

Let's chase that through. If `Customers::add` needs to declare more than one way that it can fail—our previous `DuplicateCustomerProblem` and our new `DatabaseCustomerProblem`—we introduce a sealed `CustomersProblem` as the error type and make the two known problems its only subclasses:

```
interface Customers {

    fun add(name:String, email:String): Result<Customer, CustomersProblem>

    fun find(id: String): Optional<Customer>
}

sealed class CustomersProblem

data class DuplicateCustomerProblem(val message: String): CustomersProblem()
```

```
data class DatabaseCustomerProblem(val message: String): CustomersProblem()
```

Example 19.36 [errors.27:src/main/java/travelator/Customers.kt]

`CustomerRegistration` was calling `Customers::add` and handling just `DuplicateCustomerProblem` in `mapFailure`:

```
class CustomerRegistration(
    private val customers: Customers,
    private val exclusionList: ExclusionList
) : IRegisterCustomers {

    override fun register(
        data: RegistrationData
    ): Result<Customer, RegistrationProblem> {
        return when {
            exclusionList.exclude(data) -> Failure(Excluded)
            else -> customers.add(data.name, data.email)
                .mapFailure { duplicate: DuplicateCustomerProblem ->
                    Duplicate(duplicate.message)
                }
        }
    }
}
```

Example 19.37 [errors.26:src/main/java/travelator/CustomerRegistration.kt]

This no longer compiles, because the type of the failure is now the `CustomersProblem` base class. You can see that we are getting the advantages of checked exceptions: code is communicating the ways in which it can fail and forcing us to deal with the cases.

Now that `Customers::add` admits that it can fail in a new and interesting way, `register` is also forced to handle the truth. It decides to pass the knowledge on to its callers (well OK, we decide for it) by adding a new `DatabaseProblem` subtype of the existing `RegistrationProblem` sealed class:

```
sealed class RegistrationProblem

object Excluded : RegistrationProblem()

data class Duplicate(val message: String) : RegistrationProblem()

data class DatabaseProblem(val message: String) : RegistrationProblem()
```

Example 19.38 [errors.27:src/main/java/travelator/IRegisterCustomers.kt]

Now we can fix `register` by converting between the ways that `add` can fail (`DuplicateCustomerProblem` and `DatabaseCustomerProblem`) and the ways that `register` can fail (`Duplicate` and `DatabaseProblem`, respectively). This now makes the choice of `mapFailure` clear:

```
override fun register(
    data: RegistrationData
): Result<Customer, RegistrationProblem> {
    return when {
        exclusionList.exclude(data) -> Failure(Excluded)
        else -> customers.add(data.name, data.email)
            .mapFailure { problem: CustomersProblem ->
                when (problem) {
                    is DuplicateCustomerProblem ->
                        Duplicate(problem.message)
                    is DatabaseCustomerProblem ->
                        DatabaseProblem(problem.message)
                }
            }
    }
}
```

Example 19.39 [errors.27:src/main/java/travelator/CustomerRegistration.kt]

Finally, because we've added to the `RegistrationProblem` sealed hierarchy, the compiler now forces us to consider the `DatabaseProblem` in the next layer up by failing to compile `CustomerRegistrationHandler`:

```
private fun RegistrationProblem.toResponse() = when (this) {
    is Duplicate -> Response(HTTP_CONFLICT)
    is Excluded -> Response(HTTP_FORBIDDEN)
    is DatabaseProblem -> Response(HTTP_INTERNAL_ERROR) ❶
}
```

Example 19.40 [errors.27:src/main/java/travelator/handlers/CustomerRegistrationHandler.kt]

❶ We have to add a case for `DatabaseProblem` to get the `when` expression to compile.

Because the `CustomerRegistrationHandler` is the entry point for this interaction, our work is now done.

Moving On

This has been a long chapter, but its length is in proportion to its importance.

Your Java project may already have declared exception bankruptcy, with no systematic use of checked exceptions. In this case, Kotlin's policy of treating everything as an unchecked exception will be fine.

If you do lean on checked exceptions and want to translate to Kotlin, or want to raise your error handling game as part of the conversion, then using a result type is the best strategy. Where an operation can fail in multiple ways, we can use sealed classes to enumerate the failure modes, at the expense of not being able to propagate the same type through multiple layers. When we have multiple layers, things return to being tedious, but at least they are not very error prone.

We could (and maybe should) write a whole book on error handling, but in the meantime you can follow Duncan's journey down the rabbit hole on his blog (*https://oreil.ly/kfvAn*). As well as the material covered here, this shows how to reduce the number of functions that are subject to failure because they are partial functions (*https://oreil.ly/8RoO4*).

Reducing the number of our functions that can fail is important, because code that is subject to error is very similar to the actions that we saw in Chapter 7, *Actions to Calculations*. Actions pollute their callers: by default, code that calls an action becomes an action. In the same way, code that calls code that is subject to failure is itself subject to failure. We can mitigate the effects of both actions and errors by moving them as close as we can to the entry points to our system, so that they taint the least code.

We touched briefly in this chapter on making our code robust to errors when they occur. Actions are a problem here too, because they affect the state of our system. State can be corrupted when two things need to be updated, and the first action writes, but the second doesn't because an error happened before it was invoked. A rigorous focus on the difference between actions and calculations is the key to making robust software.

We will return to error handling in Chapter 21, *Exceptions to Values*.

CHAPTER 20

Performing I/O to Passing Data

Input and output are problematic in code. Our program is subject to errors talking to the outside world when files disappear or network sockets fail. I/O is also an action and so limits our ability to reason with and refactor our code. How can we limit the scope of the problems that I/O causes?

Now that earlier chapters have built some foundations, we're going to up the pace here, going straight into refactoring and learning lessons as we go.

Listening to Tests

In Chapter 10, we looked at some Java code that produced a report for marketing. When we left the code, we had introduced extension functions to the `HighValueCustomersReport`, giving us:

```
@Throws(IOException::class)
fun generate(reader: Reader, writer: Writer) {
    val valuableCustomers = reader
        .readLines()
        .toValuableCustomers()
        .sortedBy(CustomerData::score)
    writer.appendLine("ID\tName\tSpend")
    for (customerData in valuableCustomers) {
        writer.appendLine(customerData.outputLine)
    }
    writer.append(valuableCustomers.summarised())
}

private fun List<String>.toValuableCustomers() = withoutHeader()
    .map(String::toCustomerData)
    .filter { it.score >= 10 }

private fun List<String>.withoutHeader() = drop(1)
```

```
private fun List<CustomerData>.summarised(): String =
    sumByDouble { it.spend }.let { total ->
        "\tTOTAL\t${total.toMoneyString()}"
    }
```

Example 20.1 [io-to-data.0:src/main/java/travelator/marketing/HighValueCustomersReport.kt]

Here are the tests after conversion to Kotlin:

```
class HighValueCustomersReportTests {

    @Test
    fun test() {
        check(
            inputLines = listOf(
                "ID\tFirstName\tLastName\tScore\tSpend",
                "1\tFred\tFlintstone\t11\t1000.00",
                "4\tBetty\tRubble\t10\t2000.00",
                "2\tBarney\tRubble\t0\t20.00",
                "3\tWilma\tFlintstone\t9\t0.00"
            ),
            expectedLines = listOf(
                "ID\tName\tSpend",
                "4\tRUBBLE, Betty\t2000.00",
                "1\tFLINTSTONE, Fred\t1000.00",
                "\tTOTAL\t3000.00"
            )
        )
    }

    ...
    private fun check(
        inputLines: List<String>,
        expectedLines: List<String>
    ) {
        val output = StringWriter()
        generate(
            StringReader(inputLines.joinToString("\n")),
            output
        )
        assertEquals(expectedLines.joinToString("\n"), output.toString())
    }
}
```

Example 20.2 [io-to-data.1:src/test/java/travelator/marketing/HighValueCustomersReportTests.kt]

We didn't really look at the tests in Chapter 10, but if we do now, what stands out in the light of your authors' obsession with actions and calculations (Chapter 7)? In particular, look at that `check` function.

`check` is evidently not a calculation ("Calculations" on page 78), because it works entirely by throwing an exception instead of returning a value. What if we look at it this way though?

```
private fun check(
    inputLines: List<String>,
    expectedLines: List<String>
) {
    val output = StringWriter()
    val reader = StringReader(inputLines.joinToString("\n"))
    generate(reader, output)
    val outputLines = output.toString().lines()

    assertEquals(expectedLines, outputLines)
}
```

Example 20.3 [io-to-data.2:src/test/java/travelator/marketing/HighValueCustomersReportTests.kt]

This is for all intents and purposes the same code, but now we can see that we have a calculation, taking `inputLines` and yielding `outputLines`, before we go on to the assertion. Even though `generate` is an action, relying on the side effects of reading and writing to and from its parameters, we can convert it to a calculation by limiting the scope of its side effects to local variables.

If we stop for a moment and listen, we can hear the tests talking to us. They are saying, "Look, that report generation is fundamentally a calculation: it converts a `List<String>` to a `List<String>`. We know it does, because that's what we are checking."

So the tests are telling us that the fundamental signature of `generate` is `generate(lines: List<String>): List<String>`. If *this* was the signature, then it would not have to declare that it throws `IOException` either, because all the I/O would happen outside the function. I/O has to happen somewhere, but, in common with other actions, the closer to the entry points of our system we can move it, the more we can deal in nice easy calculations.

Shall we refactor toward this goal? You're right, that was a rhetorical question.

I/O to Data

As the first stage in our refactor, let's try to wean `generate` off its `reader` parameter. The code is currently:

```
@Throws(IOException::class)
fun generate(reader: Reader, writer: Writer) {
    val valuableCustomers = reader
        .readLines()
        .toValuableCustomers()
        .sortedBy(CustomerData::score)
    writer.appendLine("ID\tName\tSpend")
```

```
        for (customerData in valuableCustomers) {
            writer.appendLine(customerData.outputLine)
        }
        writer.append(valuableCustomers.summarised())
    }
```

Example 20.4 [io-to-data.3:src/main/java/travelator/marketing/HighValueCustomersReport.kt]

We can convert `generate` to read from a `List` by invoking "Introduce parameter" on the `reader.readLines()` expression, naming the parameter `lines`. Because the expression is the only use of the existing `reader` parameter, IntelliJ removes `reader` for us:

```
@Throws(IOException::class)
fun generate(writer: Writer, lines: List<String>) {
    val valuableCustomers = lines
        .toValuableCustomers()
        .sortedBy(CustomerData::score)
    writer.appendLine("ID\tName\tSpend")
    for (customerData in valuableCustomers) {
        writer.appendLine(customerData.outputLine)
    }
    writer.append(valuableCustomers.summarised())
}
```

Example 20.5 [io-to-data.4:src/main/java/travelator/marketing/HighValueCustomersReport.kt]

The refactoring has moved the `readLines()` out into the callers; here is the result in test:

```
private fun check(
    inputLines: List<String>,
    expectedLines: List<String>
) {
    val output = StringWriter()
    val reader = StringReader(inputLines.joinToString("\n"))
    generate(output, reader.readLines())
    val outputLines = output.toString().lines()

    assertEquals(expectedLines, outputLines)
}
```

Example 20.6 [io-to-data.4:src/test/java/travelator/marketing/HighValueCustomersReportTests.kt]

This now shouts what the test was whispering all along. We were having to create a `StringReader` from a list of lines just to parse the lines back out in `generate`. Now that the steps are in the same place in the test, we can elide them to remove the `Reader`:

```
private fun check(
    inputLines: List<String>,
    expectedLines: List<String>
) {
    val output = StringWriter()
    generate(output, inputLines)
    val outputLines = output.toString().lines()
```

```
        assertEquals(expectedLines, outputLines)
    }
```

Example 20.7 [io-to-data.5:src/test/java/travelator/marketing/HighValueCustomersReportTests.kt]

We are now reading from a `List`. Let's go back and look at how to return a `List` too, rather than modifying the `Writer`. Here is the code:

```
writer.appendLine("ID\tName\tSpend")
for (customerData in valuableCustomers) {
    writer.appendLine(customerData.outputLine)
}
writer.append(valuableCustomers.summarised())
```

Example 20.8 [io-to-data.5:src/main/java/travelator/marketing/HighValueCustomersReport.kt]

Instead of thinking imperatively about the ways that we want to mutate `Writer`, let's think in terms of the data that we want written and create that:

```
val resultLines = listOf("ID\tName\tSpend") +
    valuableCustomers.map(CustomerData::outputLine) +
    valuableCustomers.summarised()
```

Example 20.9 [io-to-data.6:src/main/java/travelator/marketing/HighValueCustomersReport.kt]

Then we can write it in one lump to `writer`:

```
@Throws(IOException::class)
fun generate(writer: Writer, lines: List<String>) {
    val valuableCustomers = lines
        .toValuableCustomers()
        .sortedBy(CustomerData::score)
    val resultLines = listOf("ID\tName\tSpend") +
        valuableCustomers.map(CustomerData::outputLine) +
        valuableCustomers.summarised()
    writer.append(resultLines.joinToString("\n"))
}
```

Example 20.10 [io-to-data.6:src/main/java/travelator/marketing/HighValueCustomersReport.kt]

This function is now two statements that make up a calculation, and a final action taking the result of the calculation. If we now "Extract function" with the calculation lines, making it public and calling it `generate` too, we get the following:

```
@Throws(IOException::class)
fun generate(writer: Writer, lines: List<String>) {
    val resultLines = generate(lines)
    writer.append(resultLines.joinToString("\n"))
}

fun generate(lines: List<String>): List<String> {
    val valuableCustomers = lines
        .toValuableCustomers()
        .sortedBy(CustomerData::score)
```

```
        val resultLines = listOf("ID\tName\tSpend") +
            valuableCustomers.map(CustomerData::outputLine) +
            valuableCustomers.summarised()
        return resultLines
    }
```

Example 20.11 [io-to-data.7:src/main/java/travelator/marketing/HighValueCustomersReport.kt]

Inlining both vestigial `resultLines` gives:

```
@Throws(IOException::class)
fun generate(writer: Writer, lines: List<String>) {
    writer.append(generate(lines).joinToString("\n"))
}

fun generate(lines: List<String>): List<String> {
    val valuableCustomers = lines
        .toValuableCustomers()
        .sortedBy(CustomerData::score)
    return listOf("ID\tName\tSpend") +
        valuableCustomers.map(CustomerData::outputLine) +
        valuableCustomers.summarised()
}
```

Example 20.12 [io-to-data.8:src/main/java/travelator/marketing/HighValueCustomersReport.kt]

One more inline then, this time of the old `generate` function. That replaces its invocation in client code, leaving this in the test:

```
private fun check(
    inputLines: List<String>,
    expectedLines: List<String>
) {
    val output = StringWriter()
    output.append(generate(inputLines).joinToString("\n"))
    val outputLines = output.toString().lines()

    assertEquals(expectedLines, outputLines)
}
```

Example 20.13 [io-to-data.9:src/test/java/travelator/marketing/HighValueCustomersReportTests.kt]

This refactor has moved the action part of `generate` out a level, leaving the nice pure calculation bits in its place. Another way of looking at this is that our original `Writer` was an accumulating object, which we have replaced with a transformation, as we saw in Chapter 14. Our tests didn't really want to be testing an action anyway, so they again have redundant I/O, which we can simplify to the form we were aiming for:

```
private fun check(
    inputLines: List<String>,
    expectedLines: List<String>
) {
```

```
        assertEquals(expectedLines, generate(inputLines))
    }
```

Example 20.14 [io-to-data.10:src/test/java/travelator/marketing/HighValueCustomersReportTests.kt]

Let's take stock of our new `generate`:

```
fun generate(lines: List<String>): List<String> {
    val valuableCustomers = lines
        .toValuableCustomers()
        .sortedBy(CustomerData::score)
    return listOf("ID\tName\tSpend") +
        valuableCustomers.map(CustomerData::outputLine) +
        valuableCustomers.summarised()
}

private fun List<String>.toValuableCustomers() = withoutHeader()
    .map(String::toCustomerData)
    .filter { it.score >= 10 }

private fun List<String>.withoutHeader() = drop(1)
```

Example 20.15 [io-to-data.11:src/main/java/travelator/marketing/HighValueCustomersReport.kt]

Now that `generate` is doing so much less, it isn't clear that the function `toValuableCustomers()` is worthwhile. Looking at it afresh, we see that it is working at mixed levels, converting and filtering. Let's try inlining it:

```
fun generate(lines: List<String>): List<String> {
    val valuableCustomers = lines
        .withoutHeader()
        .map(String::toCustomerData)
        .filter { it.score >= 10 }
        .sortedBy(CustomerData::score)
    return listOf("ID\tName\tSpend") +
        valuableCustomers.map(CustomerData::outputLine) +
        valuableCustomers.summarised()
}
```

Example 20.16 [io-to-data.12:src/main/java/travelator/marketing/HighValueCustomersReport.kt]

That's better. The local variable `valuableCustomers` does a good job of telling us what the expression means, and the list operations spell out the implementation in place. This function is a case where a single-expression function (Chapter 9) would probably make things worse, so we'll leave it in two parts. We'll also continue to resist the temptation to make it an extension function, `List<String>.toReport()`, at least for now.

Refactoring for Readability

Refactoring for readability is often this way. We might extract a function to make something more readable in context, but when the context changes, the function we extracted makes things worse. Time is also a context. Sometimes something that we felt was quite expressive when we wrote it turns out to be less so when we read it back later, or could now be improved because we have internalized new idioms.

Efficient Writing

We're quite pleased with this refactor. It has simplified our tests and the production code, and we have moved from mixing I/O and logic to a simpler calculation with no side effects.

For a while, all is fine in production too, but with the easing of COVID-19 travel restrictions, Travelator becomes the roaring success that we all knew it would be. Eventually, though, the lovely people in marketing start complaining that the report generation is failing with an `OutOfMemoryError`. Could we look into it?

(Apart from running out of memory, we have had two other issues with errors in this code in living memory. Both these times, the input file turned out to have been malformed, but marketing sit next door and just call us over to help if these occur. They feed us cake in these cases, so we're hardly incentivized to do a better job of error handling for now (but see Chapter 21). If we can fix the `OutOfMemoryError` quickly, we think we saw some crumpets...)

We haven't bothered you with the details so far, but there is a `main` method that invokes our report. It is designed to be invoked with shell redirection, reading from a file piped as the standard input and writing to a file collected from the standard output. This way, our process doesn't have to read filenames from the command line:

```
fun main() {
    InputStreamReader(System.`in`).use { reader ->
        OutputStreamWriter(System.out).use { writer ->
            generate(reader, writer)
        }
    }
}
```

Example 20.17 [io-to-data.0:src/main/java/travelator/marketing/HighValueCustomersMain.kt]

When we refactored `generate` to work with `List`s rather than a `Reader` and `Writer`, IntelliJ automatically updated `main` to yield:

```
fun main() {
    System.`in`.reader().use { reader ->
```

```
            System.out.writer().use { writer ->
                writer.append(
                    generate(
                        reader.readLines()
                    ).joinToString("\n")
                )
            }
        }
    }
```

Example 20.18 [io-to-data.9:src/main/java/travelator/marketing/HighValueCustomersMain.kt]

Ah, there's our problem. We're reading the whole of the input into memory (`readLines()`), processing it, and then creating the entire output in memory (`joinToString()`) before writing it back out.

We sometimes run into problems like these with functional decomposition. In this case the original `Reader` and `Writer` code did not have this issue, so we have brought it on ourselves in the name of good style. We could quickly revert our changes and go and see whether there are any crumpets left, or we could find a more functional solution.

Let's go back to `generate` and see what leeway we have:

```
fun generate(lines: List<String>): List<String> {
    val valuableCustomers = lines
        .withoutHeader()
        .map(String::toCustomerData)
        .filter { it.score >= 10 }
        .sortedBy(CustomerData::score)
    return listOf("ID\tName\tSpend") +
        valuableCustomers.map(CustomerData::outputLine) +
        valuableCustomers.summarised()
}
```

Example 20.19 [io-to-data.12:src/main/java/travelator/marketing/HighValueCustomersReport.kt]

Concentrating on the output for now, we can see that we are building a `List` of the lines of the output; `main` then takes each `String` in the result and creates one giant one with `joinToString()`. At this point both the individual output lines and their conglomerate will be taking up memory. To avoid running out of memory, we'll need to defer the creation of the intermediate collections, and, as we saw in Chapter 13, `Sequence`s are designed for just that.

We can convert `generate` to return a `Sequence` methodically or quickly. For once, we'll choose quickly and just replace `listOf` with `sequenceOf` in our `return` expression:

```
fun generate(lines: List<String>): Sequence<String> {
    val valuableCustomers = lines
        .withoutHeader()
        .map(String::toCustomerData)
        .filter { it.score >= 10 }
```

```
        .sortedBy(CustomerData::score)
    return sequenceOf("ID\tName\tSpend") +
        valuableCustomers.map(CustomerData::outputLine) +
        valuableCustomers.summarised()
}
```

Example 20.20 [io-to-data.13:src/main/java/travelator/marketing/HighValueCustomersReport.kt]

Now we will only be creating the output lines one at a time when the `Sequence` is iterated; each line can be disposed of quickly rather than hanging around until we have written the whole file.

The tests have to change to convert the returned `Sequence` to a `List`:

```
private fun check(
    inputLines: List<String>,
    expectedLines: List<String>
) {
    assertEquals(
        expectedLines,
        generate(inputLines).toList()
    )
}
```

Example 20.21 [io-to-data.13:src/test/java/travelator/marketing/HighValueCustomersReportTests.kt]

Interestingly, though, `main` does not:

```
fun main() {
    System.`in`.reader().use { reader ->
        System.out.writer().use { writer ->
            writer.append(
                generate(
                    reader.readLines()
                ).joinToString("\n")
            )
        }
    }
}
```

Example 20.22 [io-to-data.13:src/main/java/travelator/marketing/HighValueCustomersMain.kt]

`main` needs to be *recompiled* now that `generate` returns a `Sequence` rather than a `List`, but its *source* doesn't need to be changed. This is because there are extension functions `joinToString()` defined on both `Iterable` and `Sequence`, both returning `String`.

It might not *need* to change, but unless `main` *does* change, we are still creating one large string of all the output before writing it in one operation. To avoid that, we need to get imperative again and write each output line individually, as our original `generate` had done:

```
fun main() {
    System.`in`.reader().use { reader ->
        System.out.writer().use { writer ->
```

```
            generate(
                reader.readLines()
            ).forEach { line ->
                writer.appendLine(line)
            }
        }
    }
}
```

Example 20.23 [io-to-data.14:src/main/java/travelator/marketing/HighValueCustomersMain.kt]

The pedantic reader (don't worry, you're among friends) will have spotted that this behavior is subtly different from the `joinToString("\n")` version. We're quietly confident that a trailing newline won't break anything, so we press on.

We can always pretend we aren't looping by hiding the iteration inside a `Writer::appendLines` extension function that we assumed the Kotlin standard library would define, but doesn't seem to:

```
fun main() {
    System.`in`.reader().use { reader ->
        System.out.writer().use { writer ->
            writer.appendLines(
                generate(reader.readLines())
            )
        }
    }
}

fun Writer.appendLines(lines: Sequence<CharSequence>): Writer {
    return this.also {
        lines.forEach(this::appendLine)
    }
}
```

Example 20.24 [io-to-data.15:src/main/java/travelator/marketing/HighValueCustomersMain.kt]

Note that although the definition of `Writer::appendLines` is a single expression, we agreed in Chapter 9 to use the long form where functions are actions, and `appendLines` is definitely that.

Now that we are here, we realize that we could have postponed our memory crisis by just iterating over the original result `List` in `main`, writing each line individually, as we are doing now with the `Sequence`. This solution will use even less memory, though, so we'll commit it, having bought ourselves lots of headroom with few changes and earned our crumpets. Is there any butter?

Efficient Reading

We would be remiss if we didn't finish the job and pretend that we also need to save memory on reading too. Let's look at `generate` again:

```
fun generate(lines: List<String>): Sequence<String> {
    val valuableCustomers = lines
        .withoutHeader()
        .map(String::toCustomerData)
        .filter { it.score >= 10 }
        .sortedBy(CustomerData::score)
    return sequenceOf("ID\tName\tSpend") +
        valuableCustomers.map(CustomerData::outputLine) +
        valuableCustomers.summarised()
}
```

Example 20.25 [io-to-data.15:src/main/java/travelator/marketing/HighValueCustomersReport.kt]

The pipeline of operations that builds `valuableCustomers` will build intermediate `Lists`: one for each stage, and each taking up memory. Every line in the input is going to be in memory at once, along with a `CustomerData` object for every line.

We can avoid the intermediate collections by reading from a `Sequence`, although that will bring a few problems of its own. We can see this if we change the code in `generate` to convert the `lines` to a `Sequence` and fix up the methods that did take `List`:

```
fun generate(lines: List<String>): Sequence<String> {
    val valuableCustomers: Sequence<CustomerData> = lines
        .asSequence()
        .withoutHeader()
        .map(String::toCustomerData)
        .filter { it.score >= 10 }
        .sortedBy(CustomerData::score)
    return sequenceOf("ID\tName\tSpend") +
        valuableCustomers.map(CustomerData::outputLine) +
        valuableCustomers.summarised()
}

private fun Sequence<String>.withoutHeader() = drop(1)

private fun Sequence<CustomerData>.summarised(): String =
    sumByDouble { it.spend }.let { total ->
        "\tTOTAL\t${total.toMoneyString()}"
    }
```

Example 20.26 [io-to-data.16:src/main/java/travelator/marketing/HighValueCustomersReport.kt]

This passes the unit tests. Are we done? Is this another rhetorical question?

We'll cut to the chase and say that the issue is that we end up iterating over `valuableCustomers` twice, once *before* we return from `generate` in that `sumByDouble`, and again *after* we return, when our callers iterate over the returned `Sequence` to print the report. If we iterate over a `Sequence` twice, we do all the work of creating the `Sequence` twice, in this case: removing the header and mapping and filtering and sorting twice. Worse, when we try to use the code in production, passing a `Sequence` reading standard input, we won't be able to iterate over that twice, giving an `IllegalStateException`. As we saw in Chapter 13, instances of `Sequence` differ in ways that aren't expressed in the type system, and they also carry hidden state. Iterating over a `Sequence` looks like iterating over a `List` but will change the `Sequence` itself by consuming its contents.

We can show that we are abusing this `Sequence` by adding a `.constrainOnce()` call:

```
val valuableCustomers: Sequence<CustomerData> = lines
    .asSequence()
    .constrainOnce()
    .withoutHeader()
    .map(String::toCustomerData)
    .filter { it.score >= 10 }
    .sortedBy(CustomerData::score)
```

Example 20.27 [io-to-data.17:src/main/java/travelator/marketing/HighValueCustomersReport.kt]

This will cause our tests to fail with an `IllegalStateException`. The simplest fix is to resolve the `Sequence` with a `.toList()` call:

```
val valuableCustomers: List<CustomerData> = lines
    .asSequence()
    .constrainOnce()
    .withoutHeader()
    .map(String::toCustomerData)
    .filter { it.score >= 10 }
    .sortedBy(CustomerData::score)
    .toList()
```

Example 20.28 [io-to-data.18:src/main/java/travelator/marketing/HighValueCustomersReport.kt]

This terminates the sequence (and hence ultimately reads the whole file) in that statement, but at least we run the pipeline only once, and the memory for each line can be discarded as soon as it is parsed `toCustomerData`. We will in fact have to read through the whole input in this function anyway, because `Sequence.sortedBy` needs to read every item to perform the sort—it may return a `Sequence`, but it isn't lazy.

Now we can replay the "Introduce parameter" refactoring we used at the beginning of this chapter. There we converted a `Reader` parameter into a `List`; now we convert the `List` to a `Sequence`. The parameter we introduce is the expression `lines.asSequence().constrainOnce()`:

```
fun generate(lines: Sequence<String>): Sequence<String> {
    val valuableCustomers = lines
        .withoutHeader()
        .map(String::toCustomerData)
        .filter { it.score >= 10 }
```

```
            .sortedBy(CustomerData::score)
            .toList()
    return sequenceOf("ID\tName\tSpend") +
            valuableCustomers.map(CustomerData::outputLine) +
            valuableCustomers.summarised()
}

private fun List<CustomerData>.summarised(): String =
    sumByDouble { it.spend }.let { total ->
        "\tTOTAL\t${total.toMoneyString()}"
    }
```

Example 20.29 [io-to-data.19:src/main/java/travelator/marketing/HighValueCustomersReport.kt]

The refactoring pulls the conversion of the `List` to the `Sequence` up into the tests:

```
private fun check(
    inputLines: List<String>,
    expectedLines: List<String>
) {
    assertEquals(
        expectedLines,
        generate(
            inputLines.asSequence().constrainOnce()
        ).toList()
    )
}
```

Example 20.30 [io-to-data.19:src/test/java/travelator/marketing/HighValueCustomersReportTests.kt]

It also pulls it up into `main`:

```
fun main() {
    System.`in`.reader().use { reader ->
        System.out.writer().use { writer ->
            writer.appendLines(
                generate(
                    reader.readLines().asSequence().constrainOnce()
                )
            )
        }
    }
}
```

Example 20.31 [io-to-data.19:src/main/java/travelator/marketing/HighValueCustomersMain.kt]

This is where we are really able to save memory. Instead of reading all the lines at once and converting to a `Sequence`, we can get a `Sequence` from the `Reader` with `buffered().lineSequence()`:

```
fun main() {
    System.`in`.reader().use { reader ->
        System.out.writer().use { writer ->
            writer.appendLines(
                generate(
```

```
                        reader.buffered().lineSequence()
                    )
                )
            }
        }
    }
```

Example 20.32 [io-to-data.20:src/main/java/travelator/marketing/HighValueCustomersMain.kt]

Now `generate` will be pulling the lines into memory one by one as it executes its pipeline. We're now really quite efficient in our use of memory and run pleasingly quickly. Can we resist one last tinker? How much nicer would `main` read with more extension functions?

```
fun main() {
    System.`in`.reader().use { reader ->
        System.out.writer().use { writer ->
            reader
                .asLineSequence()
                .toHighValueCustomerReport()
                .writeTo(writer)
        }
    }
}
```

Example 20.33 [io-to-data.21:src/main/java/travelator/marketing/HighValueCustomersMain.kt]

Which finally answers the question we posed back at the end of Chapter 10: yes, we do end up with report generation as an extension function. We love it when a plan comes together:

```
fun Sequence<String>.toHighValueCustomerReport(): Sequence<String> {
    val valuableCustomers = this
        .withoutHeader()
        .map(String::toCustomerData)
        .filter { it.score >= 10 }
        .sortedBy(CustomerData::score)
        .toList()
    return sequenceOf("ID\tName\tSpend") +
        valuableCustomers.map(CustomerData::outputLine) +
        valuableCustomers.summarised()
}
```

Example 20.34 [io-to-data.21:src/main/java/travelator/marketing/HighValueCustomersReport.kt]

Moving On

This refactoring was motivated by a desire to simplify our code. By moving I/O to the entry point of our program, the inner workings can be calculations rather than actions. They can also abdicate responsibility for I/O errors. That was all well and good, but calculations take and return values, and forming a value of the entire contents of large files is sometimes too much for even today's computers.

To solve this problem, we resorted to converting our `Lists` to `Sequences`. Sequences have state and are not values, but with a little care we can treat them like lazy values—lazy in that they don't require or return all their contents up front, but can read or supply them on demand. They aren't as simple as lists, but their compatible Kotlin API allows something of the best of both worlds.

Our original `Reader` to `Writer` version of `generate` had to worry about I/O errors, whereas the `List` to `List` version moved all I/O to its callers. The `Sequence` version is in a middle ground. It doesn't worry about I/O errors because they are hidden from it by the `Sequence` abstractions wrapping the `Reader` and `Writer`. That doesn't mean that they can't happen, just that `generate` isn't responsible for them. We'll take a break to see whether our colleagues in marketing have any more batter-based rewards before addressing that topic in Chapter 21, *Exceptions to Values*.

CHAPTER 21

Exceptions to Values

In Chapter 19 we looked at error-handling strategies for Kotlin, and how to refactor from exceptions in Java to more functional techniques. The truth is that most code ignores errors in the hope that they won't happen. Can we do better?

Someone new in marketing has taken to tweaking the spreadsheet that we last saw in Chapter 20—the one that generates the high-value customer scores. We don't know what they are doing in detail, but they keep on exporting files that break our parsing and then asking us to explain what a stack trace is. It's getting a bit embarrassing on both sides of the relationship, so the cake has begun to dry up. Could there be any more incentive?

Well yes, there could. We've also been asked to write an unattended job so that marketing can save the file onto a server, and *we* will automatically write the summarized version. Without a person in the loop to interpret those stack traces, it looks like we'll have to find a way to report errors properly.

Identifying What Can Go Wrong

Here's the code as we left it:

```
fun Sequence<String>.toHighValueCustomerReport(): Sequence<String> {
    val valuableCustomers = this
        .withoutHeader()
        .map(String::toCustomerData)
        .filter { it.score >= 10 }
        .sortedBy(CustomerData::score)
        .toList()
    return sequenceOf("ID\tName\tSpend") +
        valuableCustomers.map(CustomerData::outputLine) +
        valuableCustomers.summarised()
}
```

```
private fun List<CustomerData>.summarised(): String =
    sumByDouble { it.spend }.let { total ->
        "\tTOTAL\t${total.toMoneyString()}"
    }

private fun Sequence<String>.withoutHeader() = drop(1)

internal fun String.toCustomerData(): CustomerData =
    split("\t").let { parts ->
        CustomerData(
            id = parts[0],
            givenName = parts[1],
            familyName = parts[2],
            score = parts[3].toInt(),
            spend = if (parts.size == 4) 0.0 else parts[4].toDouble()
        )
    }

private val CustomerData.outputLine: String
    get() = "$id\t$marketingName\t${spend.toMoneyString()}"

private fun Double.toMoneyString() = this.formattedAs("%#.2f")

private fun Any?.formattedAs(format: String) = String.format(format, this)

private val CustomerData.marketingName: String
    get() = "${familyName.toUpperCase()}, $givenName"
```

Example 21.1 [exceptions-to-values.0:src/main/java/travelator/marketing/HighValueCustomersReport.kt]

If we're to do a thorough job of error handling, the first thing we have to do is establish what might go wrong. As we saw in Chapter 19, in Kotlin we don't have checked exceptions to give us clues, but these were so badly used in most Java code that in this respect there isn't much of a difference between the languages. Unless code has been written to communicate the ways that it can fail, we'll have to rely on examination, intuition, and experience to work it out. In this case, experience tells us that the failures we actually get are due to missing fields, so we can concentrate there, but we should still do due diligence on all aspects of the code. Let's work our way up the functions from the bottom of the listing, looking for potential errors.

`CustomerData.marketingName` looks benign:

```
private val CustomerData.marketingName: String
    get() = "${familyName.toUpperCase()}, $givenName"
```

Example 21.2 [exceptions-to-values.0:src/main/java/travelator/marketing/HighValueCustomersReport.kt]

If `CustomerData` were implemented in Java, we might find `familyName` resolving to `null` and, hence, throwing when we try `toUpperCase()`, but in Kotlin it can't, so it won't. As with all code, the function is subject to subclasses of `Error` (such as `OutOfMemoryError`) being thrown, but it should be generally safe. From here on we'll count throwing `Error` as extraordinary and not consider it in our analysis.

Now `formattedAs`:

```
private fun Any?.formattedAs(format: String) = String.format(format, this)
```

Example 21.3 [exceptions-to-values.0:src/main/java/travelator/marketing/HighValueCustomersReport.kt]

`String.format(format, this)` is implemented as `java.lang.String::format`, which is documented to throw `IllegalFormatException` if the `format` is not compatible with its other input. This is a partial function (*https://oreil.ly/ErpGo*): one that only returns a result for some of the possible values of its parameters. In this case, it can return a result for all values of `Double`, but only when we use very specific values of `format`. Luckily, we are only feeding it one particular `format`, the value `%#.2f`, which we know works, so this and its only caller, `Double.toMoneyString()`, should not fail. If they do fail, it's because our analysis is incorrect (or its assumptions are no longer true), and runtime errors are a reasonable way of signaling this programmer error.

Next we have:

```
private val CustomerData.outputLine: String
    get() = "$id\t$marketingName\t${spend.toMoneyString()}"
```

Example 21.4 [exceptions-to-values.0:src/main/java/travelator/marketing/HighValueCustomersReport.kt]

This only calls code that we have just reasoned shouldn't fail, so by the transitive property of failure, it should also be safe.

Note this has been easy so far because these functions are all calculations ("Calculations" on page 78). They don't depend on any external state, so we can reason about them just by looking at them.

So far so good, now `String.toCustomerData()`:

```
internal fun String.toCustomerData(): CustomerData =
    split("\t").let { parts ->
        CustomerData(
            id = parts[0],
            givenName = parts[1],
            familyName = parts[2],
            score = parts[3].toInt(),
            spend = if (parts.size == 4) 0.0 else parts[4].toDouble()
        )
    }
```

Example 21.5 [exceptions-to-values.0:src/main/java/travelator/marketing/HighValueCustomersReport.kt]

OK, this is another partial function: almost no values of the `String` receiver will lead to this function being able to return a result. Luckily, almost all the ones that we are getting in practice are OK, which is why error handling is only now becoming a priority. What could go wrong though?

Starting from the top of the function, `String.split` may behave oddly if we pass it an empty delimiter, but we aren't. Then we may not have enough parts, so that `parts[n]` throws `IndexOutOfBoundsException`. Finally, `parts[3]` may not represent an `Int`, or `parts[4]` may not represent a `Double`, both of which will throw `NumberFormatException`.

Having established that `toCustomerData` can fail if passed a `String` that doesn't meet our format specification, what should we do about it? At the moment, all the ways that it can fail result in an exception being thrown, the program being aborted with an unfriendly error message, and marketing calling us over. Which leads to two follow-on questions: "Should we abort?" and "How can we improve the error message so that marketing can interpret it?"

As we saw in Chapter 19, we shouldn't use exceptions to abort on predictable errors. The lack of checked exceptions in Kotlin (and their lack of use in Java) means that if we do, we lose the opportunity to communicate that the code is susceptible to failure. The callers of our code then have to do what we are currently doing: reason with every line of code in an implementation. Even after then, the implementation might change, silently invalidating the findings.

If we aren't to throw an exception, then the cheapest change (provided our callers are all Kotlin) is to return `null` when we fail. Client code will then be forced to consider the `null` case and act accordingly. For example:

```
internal fun String.toCustomerData(): CustomerData? =
    split("\t").let { parts ->
        if (parts.size < 4)
            null
        else
            CustomerData(
                id = parts[0],
                givenName = parts[1],
                familyName = parts[2],
                score = parts[3].toInt(),
                spend = if (parts.size == 4) 0.0 else parts[4].toDouble()
            )
    }
```

Example 21.6 [exceptions-to-values.1:src/main/java/travelator/marketing/HighValueCustomersReport.kt]

We could have chosen to simply wrap the whole implementation in a `try` block and return `null` from the `catch`, but here we have been more proactive than reactive. This means that the code will still throw if the relevant fields cannot be converted to `Int` or `Double`. We'll get to that.

This change breaks `toHighValueCustomerReport`, which is now forced to consider the possibility of failure:

```
fun Sequence<String>.toHighValueCustomerReport(): Sequence<String> {
    val valuableCustomers = this
        .withoutHeader()
```

```
        .map(String::toCustomerData)
        .filter { it.score >= 10 } ❶
        .sortedBy(CustomerData::score)
        .toList()
    return sequenceOf("ID\tName\tSpend") +
        valuableCustomers.map(CustomerData::outputLine) +
        valuableCustomers.summarised()
}
```

Example 21.7 [exceptions-to-values.1:src/main/java/travelator/marketing/HighValueCustomersReport.kt]

❶ Doesn't compile because `it` is nullable.

Now if we want to just ignore badly formed input lines, we can get everything running again with `filterNotNull`:

```
fun Sequence<String>.toHighValueCustomerReport(): Sequence<String> {
    val valuableCustomers = this
        .withoutHeader()
        .map(String::toCustomerData)
        .filterNotNull()
        .filter { it.score >= 10 }
        .sortedBy(CustomerData::score)
        .toList()
    return sequenceOf("ID\tName\tSpend") +
        valuableCustomers.map(CustomerData::outputLine) +
        valuableCustomers.summarised()
}
```

Example 21.8 [exceptions-to-values.2:src/main/java/travelator/marketing/HighValueCustomersReport.kt]

We don't have any tests to support this, and we really should write some, but for now we'll proceed without a safety net because this is an exploratory spike solution. From here, we can use `null` to represent the other ways that we know `toCustomerData` can fail:

```
internal fun String.toCustomerData(): CustomerData? =
    split("\t").let { parts ->
        if (parts.size < 4)
            return null
        val score = parts[3].toIntOrNull() ?:
            return null
        val spend = if (parts.size == 4) 0.0 else parts[4].toDoubleOrNull() ?:
            return null
        CustomerData(
            id = parts[0],
            givenName = parts[1],
            familyName = parts[2],
            score = score,
            spend = spend
        )
    }
```

Example 21.9 [exceptions-to-values.3:src/main/java/travelator/marketing/HighValueCustomersReport.kt]

Note that the Kotlin standard library has helped us out by providing `String::toSomethingOrNull` functions with just this error-handling convention. Now that this code represents all reasonable errors with `null`, we can go back to `toHighValueCustomerReport` and work out what to do with them instead of pretending that they haven't happened (pronounced `filterNotNull`).

We could abort on the first error, but it seems worth the extra effort to collect all the problem lines and report them somehow. *Somehow* is a bit vague, but funnily enough it has a type: `(String) -> Unit` in this case. Which is to say, we can delegate the what-to-do to a function that accepts the errant line and doesn't affect the result. We allude to this technique in "Error Handling Before Exceptions" on page 283. To illustrate this, let's add a test:

```
@Test
fun `calls back on parsing error`() {
    val lines = listOf(
        "ID\tFirstName\tLastName\tScore\tSpend",
        "INVALID LINE",
        "1\tFred\tFlintstone\t11\t1000.00",
    )

    val errorCollector = mutableListOf<String>()
    val result = lines
        .asSequence()
        .constrainOnce()
        .toHighValueCustomerReport { badLine -> ❶
            errorCollector += badLine
        }
        .toList()

    assertEquals(
        listOf(
            "ID\tName\tSpend",
            "1\tFLINTSTONE, Fred\t1000.00",
            "\tTOTAL\t1000.00"
        ),
        result
    )
    assertEquals(
        listOf("INVALID LINE"),
        errorCollector
    )
}
```

Example 21.10 [exceptions-to-values.4:src/test/java/travelator/marketing/HighValueCustomersReportTests.kt]

❶ This lambda implements `onErrorLine` in the next sample.

Let's implement that with the simplest thing that could possibly work:

```kotlin
fun Sequence<String>.toHighValueCustomerReport(
    onErrorLine: (String) -> Unit = {}
): Sequence<String> {
    val valuableCustomers = this
        .withoutHeader()
        .map { line ->
            val customerData = line.toCustomerData()
            if (customerData == null)
                onErrorLine(line)
            customerData
        }
        .filterNotNull()
        .filter { it.score >= 10 }
        .sortedBy(CustomerData::score)
        .toList()
    return sequenceOf("ID\tName\tSpend") +
        valuableCustomers.map(CustomerData::outputLine) +
        valuableCustomers.summarised()
}
```

Example 21.11 [exceptions-to-values.4:src/main/java/travelator/marketing/HighValueCustomersReport.kt]

This is still filtering out error lines, but only after passing them off to `onErrorLine`, which can decide what to do. In `main`, we'll use it to print errors to `System.err` and then abort:

```kotlin
fun main() {
    System.`in`.reader().use { reader ->
        System.out.writer().use { writer ->
            val errorLines = mutableListOf<String>()
            val reportLines = reader
                .asLineSequence()
                .toHighValueCustomerReport {
                    errorLines += it
                }
            if (errorLines.isNotEmpty()) {
                System.err.writer().use { error ->
                    error.appendLine("Lines with errors")
                    errorLines.asSequence().writeTo(error)
                }
                exitProcess(-1)
            } else {
                reportLines.writeTo(writer)
            }
        }
    }
}
```

Example 21.12 [exceptions-to-values.4:src/main/java/travelator/marketing/HighValueCustomersMain.kt]

This is one of the few places in this book where we have fallen back on a mutable `List`. Why here? For example, we could have changed `toHighValueCustomerReport` to return `Pair<Sequence<String>, List<String>>`, where the second of the pairs is the errors. The main advantage of this scheme is that it allows the caller to abort early by throwing an exception in `onErrorLine`. For maximum flexibility, we could even have an error-handling strategy with signature `(String) -> CustomerData?` so that the caller could supply a substitute, allowing recovery from errors in any particular line.

In Chapter 20, we went out of our way to convert `toHighValueCustomerReport` from an action to a calculation. We then relaxed the purity a little by reading and writing from and to a `Sequence`. Here we have introduced an error-handling function returning `Unit`, a sure sign that we have introduced an action. Provided that action's scope is confined to error handling, and any side effects are, as in this `main`, restricted to local variables, this is another reasonable compromise. This is an expedient error-handling solution that is flexible and communicates well, but pure it isn't.

Representing Errors

Now that we are communicating *that* our parsing can fail (by returning a nullable type), and *where* it has failed (with a callback passing the line), can we better communicate *why* it has failed?

Returning a result type rather than a nullable type allows us to specify what failure modes there are and provide details when they happen. Let's change `String.toCustomerData()` to return a `Result` rather than nullable:

```
internal fun String.toCustomerData(): Result<CustomerData, ParseFailure> =
    split("\t").let { parts ->
        if (parts.size < 4)
            return Failure(NotEnoughFieldsFailure(this))
        val score = parts[3].toIntOrNull() ?:
            return Failure(ScoreIsNotAnIntFailure(this))
        val spend = if (parts.size == 4) 0.0 else parts[4].toDoubleOrNull() ?:
            return Failure(SpendIsNotADoubleFailure(this))
        Success(
            CustomerData(
                id = parts[0],
                givenName = parts[1],
                familyName = parts[2],
                score = score,
                spend = spend
            )
        )
    }
```

Example 21.13 [exceptions-to-values.5:src/main/java/travelator/marketing/HighValueCustomersReport.kt]

As we did in Chapter 19, we create a sealed class to represent why parsing failed:

```
sealed class ParseFailure(open val line: String)
data class NotEnoughFieldsFailure(override val line: String) :
    ParseFailure(line)
data class ScoreIsNotAnIntFailure(override val line: String) :
```

```
    ParseFailure(line)
data class SpendIsNotADoubleFailure(override val line: String) :
    ParseFailure(line)
```

Example 21.14 [exceptions-to-values.5:src/main/java/travelator/marketing/HighValueCustomersReport.kt]

To be honest, this is overkill in this situation (a single data class carrying the failing line and a string reason would do here), but we are exemplifying excellence in error engineering. We can fix up the callers of `toCustomerData` by invoking `onErrorLine` with the data held in the `ParseFailure` and then yielding `null` when we have an `Error`. This passes the current tests:

```
fun Sequence<String>.toHighValueCustomerReport(
    onErrorLine: (String) -> Unit = {}
): Sequence<String> {
    val valuableCustomers = this
        .withoutHeader()
        .map { line ->
            line.toCustomerData().recover {
                onErrorLine(line)
                null
            }
        }
        .filterNotNull()
        .filter { it.score >= 10 }
        .sortedBy(CustomerData::score)
        .toList()
    return sequenceOf("ID\tName\tSpend") +
        valuableCustomers.map(CustomerData::outputLine) +
        valuableCustomers.summarised()
}
```

Example 21.15 [exceptions-to-values.5:src/main/java/travelator/marketing/HighValueCustomersReport.kt]

What we really want, though, is to expose the `ParseFailure`. Let's change the test first to collect the `ParseFailures` instead of lines with errors:

```
val errorCollector = mutableListOf<ParseFailure>()
val result = lines
    .asSequence()
    .constrainOnce()
    .toHighValueCustomerReport { badLine ->
        errorCollector += badLine
    }
    .toList()
assertEquals(
    listOf(NotEnoughFieldsFailure("INVALID LINE")),
    errorCollector
)
```

Example 21.16 [exceptions-to-values.6:src/test/java/travelator/marketing/HighValueCustomersReportTests.kt]

Now we can change `onErrorLine` to take the failure:

```
fun Sequence<String>.toHighValueCustomerReport(
    onErrorLine: (ParseFailure) -> Unit = {}
): Sequence<String> {
    val valuableCustomers = this
        .withoutHeader()
        .map { line ->
            line.toCustomerData().recover {
                onErrorLine(it)
                null
            }
        }
        .filterNotNull()
        .filter { it.score >= 10 }
        .sortedBy(CustomerData::score)
        .toList()
    return sequenceOf("ID\tName\tSpend") +
        valuableCustomers.map(CustomerData::outputLine) +
        valuableCustomers.summarised()
}
```

Example 21.17 [exceptions-to-values.6:src/main/java/travelator/marketing/HighValueCustomersReport.kt]

This lets `main` report the reason and the line:

```
if (errorLines.isNotEmpty()) {
    System.err.writer().use { error ->
        error.appendLine("Lines with errors")
        errorLines.asSequence().map { parseFailure ->
            "${parseFailure::class.simpleName} in ${parseFailure.line}"
        }.writeTo(error)
    }
    exitProcess(-1)
} else {
    reportLines.writeTo(writer)
}
```

Example 21.18 [exceptions-to-values.6:src/main/java/travelator/marketing/HighValueCustomersMain.kt]

We might not have used the runtime type of the `ParseFailure` to process errors differently, but we have used its name in the error message, so we are at least getting some value from our little sealed class hierarchy. If the resulting error messages aren't enough to allow marketing to fix their input, then we can use a `when` expression on the sealed class to differentiate between the types of failure, as we saw in "Layers" on page 311.

At this point, everything is compiling and our tests pass, so all is good in this little part of the world at least. Had we had more client code calling this API, or our changes were to ripple through more layers of code, we might have picked a more sophisticated refactoring strategy than changing code in one file and fixing the broken things. Often, though, it isn't worth the effort when we can get the code compiling and passing the tests in a couple of minutes at most. If we do find out that we have bitten off more than we can chew, it's easy to revert and take a more considered approach.

Now that the tests are passing, we should go back and make sure everything is as tidy and expressive as it can be. In particular, we did the quickest thing we could to get everything to work again in `toHighValueCustomerReport`:

```
fun Sequence<String>.toHighValueCustomerReport(
    onErrorLine: (ParseFailure) -> Unit = {}
): Sequence<String> {
    val valuableCustomers = this
        .withoutHeader()
        .map { line ->
            line.toCustomerData().recover {
                onErrorLine(it)
                null
            }
        }
        .filterNotNull()
        .filter { it.score >= 10 }
        .sortedBy(CustomerData::score)
        .toList()
    return sequenceOf("ID\tName\tSpend") +
        valuableCustomers.map(CustomerData::outputLine) +
        valuableCustomers.summarised()
}
```

Example 21.19 [exceptions-to-values.6:src/main/java/travelator/marketing/HighValueCustomersReport.kt]

There's something about yielding `null` from the `recover` block and then skipping these with `filterNotNull` that is a little unsatisfactory. It doesn't communicate how it works directly, and gets in the way of the happy path. We would like to be able to find a nicer formulation of the `valuableCustomers` expression, but the truth is that everything else is a bit worse in your authors' eyes. If you do find a nice simple way, then please let us know.

Similarly, the early returns in `toCustomerData` look a bit ugly:

```
internal fun String.toCustomerData(): Result<CustomerData, ParseFailure> =
    split("\t").let { parts ->
        if (parts.size < 4)
            return Failure(NotEnoughFieldsFailure(this))
        val score = parts[3].toIntOrNull() ?:
            return Failure(ScoreIsNotAnIntFailure(this))
        val spend = if (parts.size == 4) 0.0 else parts[4].toDoubleOrNull() ?:
            return Failure(SpendIsNotADoubleFailure(this))
        Success(
            CustomerData(
                id = parts[0],
                givenName = parts[1],
                familyName = parts[2],
                score = score,
```

```
                spend = spend
            )
        )
    }
```

Example 21.20 [exceptions-to-values.6:src/main/java/travelator/marketing/HighValueCustomersReport.kt]

"Proper" functional error handling would not return early, but use a `flatMap` chain. Readers of a nervous disposition may wish to look away:

```
internal fun String.toCustomerData(): Result<CustomerData, ParseFailure> =
    split("\t").let { parts ->
        parts
            .takeUnless { it.size < 4 }
            .asResultOr { NotEnoughFieldsFailure(this) }
            .flatMap { parts ->
                parts[3].toIntOrNull()
                    .asResultOr { ScoreIsNotAnIntFailure(this) }
                    .flatMap { score: Int ->
                        (if (parts.size == 4) 0.0
                        else parts[4].toDoubleOrNull())
                            .asResultOr { SpendIsNotADoubleFailure(this) }
                            .flatMap { spend ->
                                Success(
                                    CustomerData(
                                        id = parts[0],
                                        givenName = parts[1],
                                        familyName = parts[2],
                                        score = score,
                                        spend = spend
                                    )
                                )
                            }
                    }
            }
    }
```

Example 21.21 [exceptions-to-values.7:src/main/java/travelator/marketing/HighValueCustomersReport.kt]

Your authors like a single expression even more than most people, but not if this is the `Result` (pun intended). We could obviously simplify here by introducing more functions (`asResultOr ... flatMap` looks like it is a concept trying to get out, for example). Some other result libraries would let us abuse coroutines or exceptions to get the same effect as the previous early returns, but without better language support to avoid the indent-per-statement, the grain of Kotlin favors early returns in these cases. We haven't addressed it specifically in this book, but the fact that lambdas can be compiled inline and so support returns from their enclosing function encourages us to use imperative code in situations like this. For us then, the early returns will do.

Finally, returning to `main` on our final check before check-in:

```
fun main() {
    System.`in`.reader().use { reader ->
        System.out.writer().use { writer ->
            val errorLines = mutableListOf<ParseFailure>()
            val reportLines = reader
                .asLineSequence()
                .toHighValueCustomerReport {
                    errorLines += it
                }
            if (errorLines.isNotEmpty()) {
                System.err.writer().use { error ->
                    error.appendLine("Lines with errors")
                    errorLines.asSequence().map { parseFailure ->
                        "${parseFailure::class.simpleName} in ${parseFailure.line}"
                    }.writeTo(error)
                }
                exitProcess(-1)
            } else {
                reportLines.writeTo(writer)
            }
        }
    }
}
```

Example 21.22 [exceptions-to-values.6:src/main/java/travelator/marketing/HighValueCustomersMain.kt]

Those three levels of nested `use` obfuscate the actual structure, and that `exitProcess` from deep in the bowels of the function is also a bit iffy. We can define our own `using` overload to address the former and pass out an exit code to solve the latter (an example of using data rather than control flow to address errors). We can extract an extension function to print the errors too:

```
fun main() {
    val statusCode = using(
        System.`in`.reader(),
        System.out.writer(),
        System.err.writer()
    ) { reader, writer, error ->
        val errorLines = mutableListOf<ParseFailure>()
        val reportLines = reader
            .asLineSequence()
            .toHighValueCustomerReport {
                errorLines += it
            }
        if (errorLines.isEmpty()) {
            reportLines.writeTo(writer)
            0
        } else {
            errorLines.writeTo(error)
            -1
        }
    }
```

```
        exitProcess(statusCode)
    }

    inline fun <A : Closeable, B : Closeable, C : Closeable, R> using(
        a: A,
        b: B,
        c: C,
        block: (A, B, C) -> R
    ): R =
        a.use {
            b.use {
                c.use {
                    block(a, b, c)
                }
            }
        }

    private fun List<ParseFailure>.writeTo(error: OutputStreamWriter) {
        error.appendLine("Lines with errors")
        asSequence().map { parseFailure ->
            "${parseFailure::class.simpleName} in ${parseFailure.line}"
        }.writeTo(error)
    }
```

Example 21.23 [exceptions-to-values.8:src/main/java/travelator/marketing/HighValueCustomersMain.kt]

What About I/O?

That's very nearly good enough. Before we go, though, we should think about I/O errors. Since we introduced `Lists` and then `Sequences`, our report generation code does not have to worry about writing failing, because it is the calling code's responsibility to iterate over the result lines and actually perform the write. The `main` function in this case makes the reasonable assumption that `System.out` will always be there, but when we implement the unattended job that motivated this refactor, we will have to deal with the possibility that the file or network socket may disappear even if it was open when we started.

There is a similar situation reading. We are now iterating over each `String` in a `Sequence`. In the test code, these are in memory, but in production they are being fetched from a file (via `System.in`). So our `Sequence` operations are subject to failure with `IOExceptions` that the report generation is blissfully unaware of.

There is little that `toHighValueCustomerReport()` can or should do in these cases. There is no practical way of recovering from I/O errors once we have started reading here—aborting the whole operation is the sensible thing to do. Helpfully, now the onus is entirely on the caller (in this case `main`). `toHighValueCustomerReport` signals the errors that it knows about (failure to parse) and how they are represented (subclasses of `ParseFailure`) through its `onErrorLine` parameter. `IOExceptions` are not its responsibility. It is `main` that is passing an I/O-backed `Sequence` into `toHighValueCustomerReport`, so `main` should be aware that `toHighValueCustomerReport` can therefore fail with an `IOException` and deal with it accordingly. Let's add that code:

```
fun main() {
    val statusCode = try {
        using(
            System.`in`.reader(),
            System.out.writer(),
            System.err.writer()
        ) { reader, writer, error ->
            val errorLines = mutableListOf<ParseFailure>()
            val reportLines = reader
                .asLineSequence()
                .toHighValueCustomerReport {
                    errorLines += it
                }
            if (errorLines.isEmpty()) {
                reportLines.writeTo(writer)
                0
            } else {
                errorLines.writeTo(error)
                -1
            }
        }
    } catch (x: IOException) {
        System.err.println("IO error processing report ${x.message}")
        -1
    }
    exitProcess(statusCode)
}
```

Example 21.24 [exceptions-to-values.9:src/main/java/travelator/marketing/HighValueCustomersMain.kt]

This is perhaps overkill for this application, but it shows the pattern of catching and dealing with the exceptions that we *expect* (printing a relatively friendly message for `IOException`) but allowing all others to leak and quit the application. If we follow the strategy from Chapter 19, *unexpected* exceptions are either unrecoverable environment errors or programmer errors. In both cases, the default JVM behavior of quitting the process after printing a stack trace gives us a fighting chance of diagnosing the issue. When we convert this to an unattended server job, we will similarly process expected errors in our top-level handler function. We might abort on `IOException` or retry the whole interaction if we think the problem may be transient. We know that retrying won't help with parse errors, so we will have to log these and/or send notifications somewhere. Unexpected errors in handler functions are normally allowed to leak to generic exception-handling code, which will log them and send an internal server error status before returning the thread to its pool.

Moving On

Very often in engineering, we have to make compromises. In particular, attempts to make one thing simpler often complicate another. I/O complicates our software in two ways. It is an action, so we can't just ignore whether or when it happens as we refactor; and it is subject to errors, which we have to deal with if we want a robust system. These errors may be simple environmental failures to read or write, or because the things that we are reading don't meet our expectations—when the marketing file ends badly formatted, for example.

Both actions and errors taint their callers, and the solution in both cases is the same: move the code closer to the entry points so that it taints less of our system. This, then, is an area where, rather than having to compromise, we can kill two birds with one stone. By moving I/O to the outside of our systems, we can reduce the ways that both actions and errors complicate our code.

CHAPTER 22

Classes to Functions

Object-oriented programmers are adept at solving problems by creating types. Functional programmers tend to augment existing types with functions. How far can we go without defining new types?

In Chapter 15, *Encapsulated Collections to Type Aliases*, we saw the advantages of working with raw collections, and in Chapter 16, *Interfaces to Functions*, we looked at using built-in function types rather than creating new ones. In this chapter, we'll apply the lessons we've learned to write some Kotlin from scratch.

Even in these days of REST APIs and webhooks, much of automatic business-to-business communication is in the form of tabular text data exchanged by Secure File Transfer Protocol (SFTP). Travelator has to import data for campsite locations, points of interest, unsettled bills, and more, all in regular rows and columns, with different column separators, and with and without a header naming the columns for the remaining rows. In Chapter 20, we saw that one team had created its own parser; in other places, we use the tried-and-trusted Apache Commons CSV library (*https://oreil.ly/jnI4h*). Honestly, for most uses, we would still use Commons CSV, because it works out of the box, is nicely configurable for special cases, and plays really well with Kotlin.

Today though we're going to see what a clean-room Kotlin parser would look like. When we're done, we'll compare what we come up with to the Commons CSV functionality so that we can see how the grains of Java and Kotlin lead to different APIs and implementations.

An Acceptance Test

As you might have been able to tell from the preceding chapters, the Travelator developers are Extreme Programmers (*Extreme Programming Explained: Embrace Change*). We write code test first, starting with a high-level acceptance test. We're working on a table reader, so we create a class `TableReaderAcceptanceTests` with a stub method and check that it runs:

```
class TableReaderAcceptanceTests {
    @Test
    fun test() {
    }
}
```

Example 22.1 [table-reader.1:src/test/java/travelator/tablereader/TableReaderAcceptanceTests.kt]

It does run (it even passes!), so now we can start coding proper.

Part of the acceptance test's job is to help us decide what our interface should look like. Having parsed a few files in our time, we know that what we almost always want to do is read a file and return a list of values of some domain type, one for each (non-header) row. Let's sketch that as our test, with `Measurement` as our domain type:

```
class TableReaderAcceptanceTests {
    data class Measurement(
        val t: Double,
        val x: Double,
        val y: Double,
    )

    @Test
    fun `acceptance test`() {
        val input = listOf(
            "time,x,y",
            "0.0,  1,  1",
            "0.1,1.1,1.2",
            "0.2,1.2,1.4",
        )
        val expected = listOf(
            Measurement(0.0, 1.0, 1.0),
            Measurement(0.1, 1.1, 1.2),
            Measurement(0.2, 1.2, 1.4)
        )
        assertEquals(
            expected,
            someFunction(input)
        )
    }

    private fun someFunction(input: List<String>): List<Measurement> {
        TODO("Not yet implemented")
```

```
    }
}
```

Example 22.2 [table-reader.2:src/test/java/travelator/tablereader/TableReaderAcceptanceTests.kt]

Here `Measurement` is a value type that represents the data that we want to extract from each row of the table. In Java, we would probably start by creating a `TableReader` class, but we can see from the test that reading a table is simply a calculation: a mapping of the input lines to a list of the data that we want ("Calculations" on page 78). So we'll default to using a top-level `someFunction` until we are forced to do something more complicated.

We can imagine all sorts of magic ways that our API could implement `someFunction`, but unless it has some special knowledge of the `Measurement` type (and libraries don't have knowledge of *our* types, that's the wrong way around), we will have to tell it how to map from some representation of a row to a `Measurement`.

That's twice we've used the word *map*. Maybe *map* holds the key? (An accidental pun, that one.) What if `someFunction` looked like this?

```
private fun someFunction(input: List<String>): List<Measurement> =
    readTable(input) ❶
        .map { record -> ❷ ❸
        Measurement(
            record["time"].toDouble(), ❹
            record["x"].toDouble(), ❹
            record["y"].toDouble(), ❹
        )
    }
```

Example 22.3 [table-reader.3:src/test/java/travelator/tablereader/TableReaderAcceptanceTests.kt]

❶ `readTable` is our table reading API entry point

❷ It returns something that has a `map` implementation.

❸ `record` is our representation of a row in the table.

❹ We can index into `record` by field name, yielding a `String` that we can convert to other types.

This doesn't compile, because we don't have `readTable` yet, but if we Alt-Enter on the error, IntelliJ will create the function for us:

```
private fun readTable(input: List<String>): Any {
    TODO("Not yet implemented")
}
```

Example 22.4 [table-reader.3:src/test/java/travelator/tablereader/TableReaderAcceptanceTests.kt]

We haven't given IntelliJ enough clues about the return type of `readTable`, so it chose `Any`, and so `someFunction` still doesn't compile. What type could we return to fix that? Well, if we return a `List` from `readTable`, then `map` is an operation on `List`. And if that `List` contained `Map<String, String>`, our `record` variable would be `Map<String, String>`, so we could call `record["time"]`, and so on. The only issue is that `Map.get` returns a nullable value. That's close enough—let's take account of it in `someFunction` by raising errors if `get` returns `null`:

```
private fun someFunction(input: List<String>): List<Measurement> =
    readTable(input).map { record ->
        Measurement(
            record["time"]?.toDoubleOrNull() ?: error("in time"),
            record["x"]?.toDoubleOrNull() ?: error("in x"),
            record["y"]?.toDoubleOrNull() ?: error("in y"),
        )
    }

fun readTable(input: List<String>): List<Map<String, String>> {
    TODO("Not yet implemented")
}
```

Example 22.5 [table-reader.4:src/test/java/travelator/tablereader/TableReaderAcceptanceTests.kt]

This compiles, although obviously the `TODO` fails the test. (You might ask why we are taking such a cavalier attitude toward errors compared to our forensic Chapter 21. The answer is that this is just test code: the API of `Map.get` is forcing us to consider what to do in the case of errors, and our test is choosing to throw.)

We put our client hats on to write the acceptance tests, and these tests have shown that we can at least use a function with the signature of `readTable` to convert lines to a list of `Measurement`. Now that we have a plausible API, we can move the definition of `readTable` into *src/main/travelator/tablereader/table-reading.kt*:

```
fun readTable(input: List<String>): List<Map<String, String>> {
    TODO("Not yet implemented")
}
```

Example 22.6 [table-reader.5:src/main/java/travelator/tablereader/table-reading.kt]

Finally in this first stage, we can inline `someFunction` to give our acceptance test:

```
@Disabled
@Test
fun `acceptance test`() {
    val input = listOf(
        "time,x,y",
        "0.0,  1,  1",
        "0.1,1.1,1.2",
        "0.2,1.2,1.4",
    )
    val expected = listOf(
        Measurement(0.0, 1.0, 1.0),
```

```
            Measurement(0.1, 1.1, 1.2),
            Measurement(0.2, 1.2, 1.4)
        )
        assertEquals(
            expected,
            readTable(input).map { record ->
                Measurement(
                    t = record["time"]?.toDoubleOrNull() ?: error("in time"),
                    x = record["x"]?.toDoubleOrNull() ?: error("in x"),
                    y = record["y"]?.toDoubleOrNull() ?: error("in y"),
                )
            }
        )
    }
```

Example 22.7 [table-reader.5:src/test/java/travelator/tablereader/TableReaderAcceptanceTests.kt]

Note that we have disabled the test because it will be some time before we get it running. That's OK with acceptance tests. We don't expect to get them to pass quickly, more tell us when we are done. For now, it has done its job, helping us sketch a simple API that we can now implement.

Before we do go on, let's reflect on the fact that we have managed to define the interface to our parser without defining any new types, instead using `List` and `Map` of `String`. By using standard types, we know that we have rich Kotlin APIs to supply the `List` that we are reading from, and to interpret the `List` of `Map`s that we are returning.

Unit Testing

Now that we have an interface to implement, we can park the acceptance test and write a minimal unit test. What is minimal? We like to start with empty: what should happen if we read an empty file?

```
class TableReaderTests {
    @Test
    fun `empty list returns empty list`() {
        val input: List<String> = emptyList()
        val expectedResult: List<Map<String, String>> = emptyList()
        assertEquals(
            expectedResult,
            readTable(input)
        )
    }
}
```

Example 22.8 [table-reader.6:src/test/java/travelator/tablereader/TableReaderTests.kt]

The simplest way to get this to pass is to hard-code the result in `readTable`:

```
fun readTable(input: List<String>): List<Map<String, String>> {
    return emptyList()
}
```

Example 22.9 [table-reader.7:src/main/java/travelator/tablereader/table-reading.kt]

This passes. It may seem trivial, but it's always a good idea to have a test for empty input. The more complicated our algorithm, the more likely it is to fail in this case. It's a poor parser that always returns an empty result, though, so let's crack on. Following TDD (*Test-Driven Development By Example*), we need to add a failing test first to give us a reason to change the implementation. We choose to add the case of reading a table with no header and one line of data.

Why this rather than a header and one line of data? To be honest, this is just the first thing that came to mind; maybe if we were actually pairing at this point, you would have suggested using a header row. Our choice leaves us having to decide how to name the columns, and we decide to use the `String` representation of their index, `"0"` for the first column, `"1"` for the second, and so on; this feels like the simplest way that we can generate a `String` key:

```
@Test
fun `empty list returns empty list`() {
    assertEquals(
        emptyList<Map<String, String>>(),
        readTable(emptyList())
    )
}

@Test
fun `one line of input with default field names`() {
    assertEquals(
        listOf(
            mapOf("0" to "field0", "1" to "field1")
        ),
        readTable(listOf(
            "field0,field1"
        ))
    )
}
```

Example 22.10 [table-reader.8:src/test/java/travelator/tablereader/TableReaderTests.kt]

We *could* instead have made `readTable` return `<Map<Int, String>>` when we don't have a header row. If you have some spare time, that might be a path worth following to see where it leads.

Back in our current predicament, we have a failing test, and we can be clever or we can be quick. We choose quick, to get the test passing straightaway by hardcoding the result again:

```
fun readTable(lines: List<String>): List<Map<String, String>> {
    return if (lines.isEmpty())
        emptyList()
    else listOf(
        mapOf("0" to "field0", "1" to "field1")
    )
}
```

Example 22.11 [table-reader.8:src/main/java/travelator/tablereader/table-reading.kt]

Now that our tests are passing, we can simplify the implementation by noticing that we want a line in the output for every line in the input. `Iterable::map` will do this, allowing us to remove the `if` expression:

```
fun readTable(lines: List<String>): List<Map<String, String>> {
    return lines.map {
        mapOf("0" to "field0", "1" to "field1")
    }
}
```

Example 22.12 [table-reader.9:src/main/java/travelator/tablereader/table-reading.kt]

This continues to pass the tests and would now work for more lines (of identical data)! It's only a stepping-stone though, allowing us to extract the lambda as a function:

```
fun readTable(lines: List<String>): List<Map<String, String>> {
    return lines.map(::parseLine)
}

private fun parseLine(line: String) = mapOf("0" to "field0", "1" to "field1")
```

Example 22.13 [table-reader.10:src/main/java/travelator/tablereader/table-reading.kt]

Now we'll start removing the hard-coded values by splitting the pairs into `keys` and `values`:

```
private fun parseLine(line: String): Map<String, String> {
    val keys = listOf("0", "1")
    val values = listOf("field0", "field1")
    return keys.zip(values).toMap()
}
```

Example 22.14 [table-reader.11:src/main/java/travelator/tablereader/table-reading.kt]

We're still resolutely cheating, but we can now see the pattern in the `keys` and generate these from the `values`:

```
private fun parseLine(line: String): Map<String, String> {
    val values = listOf("field0", "field1")
    val keys = values.indices.map(Int::toString)
    return keys.zip(values).toMap()
}
```

Example 22.15 [table-reader.12:src/main/java/travelator/tablereader/table-reading.kt]

For the values, we can split the line around the commas:

```
private fun parseLine(line: String): Map<String, String> {
    val values = line.split(",")
    val keys = values.indices.map(Int::toString)
    return keys.zip(values).toMap()
}
```

Example 22.16 [table-reader.13:src/main/java/travelator/tablereader/table-reading.kt]

Success: we have removed the hard-coded keys and values, and the tests still pass. Because we used `lines.map` in `readTable`, we believe the function will work for any numbers of lines, but it would be good to have a test to confirm that.

We make a note to add it, because something is bothering us that we'd like to look at first. If you are as old as your authors (or younger and gifted) you may have developed spidey senses for code, and they may be tingling when you look at that `split`. What will happen if we try to split an empty line? For that matter, what should `readTable` return when fed an empty line?

Discussing it, we come to the conclusion that an empty line should yield an empty `Map`. That feels clean, so we write a test to both document our decision and check that it works:

```
@Test
fun `empty line returns empty map`() {
    assertEquals(
        listOf(
            emptyMap<String, String>()
        ),
        readTable(listOf(
            ""
        ))
    )
}
```

Example 22.17 [table-reader.14:src/test/java/travelator/tablereader/TableReaderTests.kt]

Aha!

```
org.opentest4j.AssertionFailedError:
Expected :[{}]
Actual   :[{0=}]
```

After a little investigation, we discover that calling `split` on an empty `String` returns a `List` of a single empty `String`. Maybe that makes sense in other circumstances. Maybe, but it messes up our algorithm, so we have to work around it with a special case in `parseLine`:

```
private fun parseLine(line: String): Map<String, String> {
    val values = if (line.isEmpty()) emptyList() else line.split(",")
    val keys = values.indices.map(Int::toString)
```

```
    return keys.zip(values).toMap()
}
```

Example 22.18 [table-reader.14:src/main/java/travelator/tablereader/table-reading.kt]

That gets the tests passing but muddies the waters of the `parseLine` function. So we extract the muddy line to a function called `splitFields`:

```
private fun parseLine(line: String): Map<String, String> {
    val values = splitFields(line)
    val keys = values.indices.map(Int::toString)
    return keys.zip(values).toMap()
}

private fun splitFields(line: String): List<String> =
    if (line.isEmpty()) emptyList() else line.split(",")
```

Example 22.19 [table-reader.15:src/main/java/travelator/tablereader/table-reading.kt]

If we make `splitFields` an extension function and introduce a `separators` parameter, we get the function we always really wanted `split` to be:

```
private fun parseLine(line: String): Map<String, String> {
    val values = line.splitFields(",")
    val keys = values.indices.map(Int::toString)
    return keys.zip(values).toMap()
}

private fun String.splitFields(separators: String): List<String> =
    if (isEmpty()) emptyList() else split(separators)
```

Example 22.20 [table-reader.16:src/main/java/travelator/tablereader/table-reading.kt]

So far, we have gotten the code working with an empty input and then an input of a single line. If we had written an imperative solution, we might now have to add a loop to handle more input, but `map` has our back, because it will always return as many items as we give it. We believe that `readTable` should work for all the numbers known to programmers: 0, 1, and infinity (well, OK, 2^{31} - 1 rather than actual infinity).

"Trust but verify" they say though, so we add a test:

```
@Test
fun `two lines of input with default field names`() {
    assertEquals(
        listOf(
            mapOf("0" to "row0field0", "1" to "row0field1"),
            mapOf("0" to "row1field0", "1" to "row1field1")
        ),
        readTable(listOf(
            "row0field0,row0field1",
            "row1field0,row1field1"
        ))
```

```
    )
}
```

Example 22.21 [table-reader.17:src/test/java/travelator/tablereader/TableReaderTests.kt]

It passes, and we reason that `(0, 1, 2)` is close enough to `(0, 1, 2147483647)` that we are done for now. This seems like a good place to check in, make a fresh coffee, and dispose of the last one before getting back to work.

Headers

Ready to go again? OK, what about a header line?

First, how should our API know to expect one? We could add a flag to `readTable` to tell it that our data has a header, or we can add another function. Generally we prefer a different function for different functionality, so let's add a function named `readTableWithHeader`.

As with `readTable`, we first add a test that calls the function that we wish we had:

```
@Test
fun `takes headers from header line`() {
    assertEquals(
        listOf(
            mapOf("H0" to "field0", "H1" to "field1")
        ),
        readTableWithHeader(
            listOf(
                "H0,H1",
                "field0,field1"
            )
        )
    )
}
```

Example 22.22 [table-reader.18:src/test/java/travelator/tablereader/TableReaderTests.kt]

Alt-Enter on the compilation error at `readTableWithHeader` and IntelliJ will create it for us. Then we can name the parameters and delegate to our original function for now:

```
fun readTableWithHeader(lines: List<String>): List<Map<String, String>> {
    return readTable(lines)
}

fun readTable(lines: List<String>): List<Map<String, String>> {
    return lines.map(::parseLine)
}
```

Example 22.23 [table-reader.18:src/main/java/travelator/tablereader/table-reading.kt]

This compiles but fails the tests, as we expect:

```
org.opentest4j.AssertionFailedError:
Expected :[{H0=field0, H1=field1}]
Actual   :[{0=H0, 1=H1}, {0=field0, 1=field1}]
```

To get the tests to pass, we could hard-code the result as before, but this time we're going to modify the code to make room for the functionality. When we say *make room*, what we are aiming for is code that does the current thing (using `Int::toString` field names) and which we are able to *augment* rather than modify to support the new functionality. The new feature will then be an addition *rather* than a modification (the open–closed principle (*https://oreil.ly/MwO5l*)).

Currently, the field name information is buried in `parseLine`:

```
private fun parseLine(line: String): Map<String, String> {
    val values = line.splitFields(",")
    val keys = values.indices.map(Int::toString)
    return keys.zip(values).toMap()
}
```

Example 22.24 [table-reader.18:src/main/java/travelator/tablereader/table-reading.kt]

We're going to pull it out from here to a place where we can use the header line to supply it.

`Int::toString` is our current mapping from index to key. Let's prepare to make this configurable by introducing a variable named `headerProvider`:

```
private fun parseLine(line: String): Map<String, String> {
    val values = line.splitFields(",")
    val headerProvider: (Int) -> String = Int::toString
    val keys = values.indices.map(headerProvider)
    return keys.zip(values).toMap()
}
```

Example 22.25 [table-reader.19:src/main/java/travelator/tablereader/table-reading.kt]

This still passes our tests, except for the new `takes headers from header line`, which is still failing. We shouldn't really be refactoring with a failing test, because every time we run the tests, we will have to check that any failure is actually the one we expect. So we `@Disabled` it for now to only run tests for completed features while we are refactoring.

"Introduce Parameter" on the `headerProvider` line and naming it `headerProvider` will allow us to support different behaviors:

```
private fun parseLine(
    line: String,
    headerProvider: (Int) -> String
): Map<String, String> {
    val values = line.splitFields(",")
    val keys = values.indices.map(headerProvider)
```

```
    return keys.zip(values).toMap()
}
```

Example 22.26 [table-reader.20:src/main/java/travelator/tablereader/table-reading.kt]

Unfortunately, IntelliJ currently fails to make this refactor work, breaking `readTable`:

```
fun readTableWithHeader(lines: List<String>): List<Map<String, String>> {
    return readTable(lines)
}

fun readTable(lines: List<String>): List<Map<String, String>> {
    return lines.map(::parseLine) ❶
}
```

Example 22.27 [table-reader.20:src/main/java/travelator/tablereader/table-reading.kt]

❶ We could use the function reference when `parseLine` only had one parameter. Now it needs two arguments, but `map` can only supply one.

"Replace function reference with lambda" *before* the refactor would have made everything work now, but we'll fail forward by expanding the lambda now and adding `Int::toString` as the `headerProvider` to get things compiling again:

```
fun readTableWithHeader(lines: List<String>): List<Map<String, String>> {
    return readTable(lines)
}

fun readTable(lines: List<String>): List<Map<String, String>> {
    return lines.map { parseLine(it, Int::toString) }
}
```

Example 22.28 [table-reader.21:src/main/java/travelator/tablereader/table-reading.kt]

All our tests still pass, so we're quietly confident that we haven't broken anything.

Where are we going with this? Our plan is to have the new `readTableWithHeader` read the header line to create a `headerProvider` to pass to `parseLine`. Sitting between `readTableWithHeader` and `parseLine` is the call to our old `readTable`, so it needs a `headerProvider` parameter too, so that it can relay the value. So it's "Introduce Parameter" (with "Introduce Default Value") again, this time on `Int::toString` in `readTable`:

```
fun readTableWithHeader(lines: List<String>): List<Map<String, String>> {
    return readTable(lines)
}

fun readTable(
    lines: List<String>,
    headerProvider: KFunction1<Int, String> = Int::toString ❶
): List<Map<String, String>> {
    return lines.map { parseLine(it, headerProvider) }
}
```

Example 22.29 [table-reader.22:src/main/java/travelator/tablereader/table-reading.kt]

❶ Doesn't compile: `Unresolved reference: KFunction1`

It's hard to say why IntelliJ (at the time of writing) sometimes uses function types and sometimes `KFunctionN` types when refactoring. It would be nice if it was consistent, or at least generated code that compiled. We'll fix this one by translating the `KFunction1` to an `(Int) -> String` by hand and hold just a little grudge for this second failed refactor in a row:

```
fun readTableWithHeader(lines: List<String>): List<Map<String, String>> {
    return readTable(lines)
}

fun readTable(
    lines: List<String>,
    headerProvider: (Int) -> String = Int::toString
): List<Map<String, String>> {
    return lines.map { parseLine(it, headerProvider) }
}
```

Example 22.30 [table-reader.23:src/main/java/travelator/tablereader/table-reading.kt]

On the plus side, because the `headerProvider` parameter has a default value, our tests are unchanged and continue to pass.

Now we're in a position to parse the header line; `readTableWithHeader` will need to read the header, create a `headerProvider` (an `(Int) -> String` remember), and then delegate to `readTable`. It needs to split the lines into the header (`Iterable.first()`) and the rest (`Iterable.drop(1)`). `Iterable.first` will fail if there are no lines, so we make a note to add a test for this case. As for converting the header line into a `headerProvider`, we'll pretend that we have a function to do that called `headerProviderFrom(String)`:

```
fun readTableWithHeader(lines: List<String>): List<Map<String, String>> {
    return readTable(
        lines.drop(1),
        headerProviderFrom(lines.first())
    )
}
```

Example 22.31 [table-reader.24:src/main/java/travelator/tablereader/table-reading.kt]

Alt-Enter on the new function's invocation allows us to create it, giving:

```
fun headerProviderFrom(header: String): (Int) -> String {
    TODO("Not yet implemented")
}
```

Example 22.32 [table-reader.24:src/main/java/travelator/tablereader/table-reading.kt]

This is a function that needs to return a function type. We can implement the return value with a lambda that takes an `Int` index and returns a `String`. The `String` we need to return is the header field at that index. We can use our `splitFields` again here:

```
private fun headerProviderFrom(header: String): (Int) -> String {
    val headers = header.splitFields(",")
    return { index -> headers[index] }
}
```

Example 22.33 [table-reader.25:src/main/java/travelator/tablereader/table-reading.kt]

We've taken care to split the `header` outside the lambda; otherwise, it will happen for every other row of the table. Our tests still pass, and if we're right, so will the test for `readTableWithHeader` that we disabled previously. Let's un-`@Disabled` it:

```
@Test
fun `takes headers from header line`() {
    assertEquals(
        listOf(
            mapOf("H0" to "field0", "H1" to "field1")
        ),
        readTableWithHeader(
            listOf(
                "H0,H1",
                "field0,field1"
            )
        )
    )
}
```

Example 22.34 [table-reader.26:src/test/java/travelator/tablereader/TableReaderTests.kt]

This passes, hooray! We are about to say that we're done for now, until we look down at our to-do list and remember that we predicted `readTableWithHeader` should fail given an empty input. So we write a test asserting the desired behavior, which is to return an empty `List`:

```
@Test
fun `readTableWithHeader on empty list returns empty list`() {
    assertEquals(
        emptyList<String>(),
        readTableWithHeader(
            emptyList()
        )
    )
}
```

Example 22.35 [table-reader.26:src/test/java/travelator/tablereader/TableReaderTests.kt]

As we thought, this fails with `java.util.NoSuchElementException: List is empty.`, because `readTableWithHeader` is trying to call `lines.first()` on an empty `List`:

```
fun readTableWithHeader(lines: List<String>): List<Map<String, String>> {
    return readTable(
        lines.drop(1),
        headerProviderFrom(lines.first())
```

```
    )
}
```

Example 22.36 [table-reader.25:src/main/java/travelator/tablereader/table-reading.kt]

Our irritation at not being finished is mitigated by being right about there being a problem! The simplest fix is to split our function into two definitions, with a `when` to choose between them. This passes all the tests and empties our to-do list. Here, then, is our public API:

```
fun readTableWithHeader(
    lines: List<String>
): List<Map<String, String>> =
    when {
        lines.isEmpty() -> emptyList()
        else -> readTable(
            lines.drop(1),
            headerProviderFrom(lines.first())
        )
    }

fun readTable(
    lines: List<String>,
    headerProvider: (Int) -> String = Int::toString
): List<Map<String, String>> =
    lines.map { parseLine(it, headerProvider) }
```

Example 22.37 [table-reader.26:src/main/java/travelator/tablereader/table-reading.kt]

This is nice. Our clients now can read with or without a header row. But wait! Looking at the code, we realize that if they want to specify their own field names for `readTable`, they can do this by overriding the default `headerProvider` in `readTable`. We have a feature for free! Let's write a test to demonstrate it:

```
@Test
fun `can specify header names when there is no header row`() {
    val headers = listOf("apple", "banana")
    assertEquals(
        listOf(
            mapOf(
                "apple" to "field0",
                "banana" to "field1",
            )
        ),
        readTable(
            listOf("field0,field1"),
            headers::get
        )
    )
}
```

Example 22.38 [table-reader.27:src/test/java/travelator/tablereader/TableReaderTests.kt]

See how easy it is to convert from a `List<String>` to our header provider function `(Int) -> String` with the method reference `headers::get`? This is an interesting way to view collections. We can view:

Type	as function type	by
`List<T>`	`(index: Int) -> T`	`List.get(index)`
`Set<T>`	`(item: T) -> Boolean`	`Set.contains(item)`
`Map<K, V>`	`(key: K) -> V?`	`Map.get(key)`

If we are able to express a dependency as one of these function types, then our clients, and our tests, can use standard collections to provide an implementation.

Now that we have implemented reading a table with a header, we are in a position to try running our acceptance test. This was:

```
@Disabled
@Test
fun `acceptance test`() {
    val input = listOf(
        "time,x,y",
        "0.0,  1,  1",
        "0.1,1.1,1.2",
        "0.2,1.2,1.4",
    )
    val expected = listOf(
        Measurement(0.0, 1.0, 1.0),
        Measurement(0.1, 1.1, 1.2),
        Measurement(0.2, 1.2, 1.4)
    )
    assertEquals(
        expected,
        readTable(input).map { record ->
            Measurement(
                t = record["time"]?.toDoubleOrNull() ?: error("in time"),
                x = record["x"]?.toDoubleOrNull() ?: error("in x"),
                y = record["y"]?.toDoubleOrNull() ?: error("in y"),
            )
        }
    )
}
```

Example 22.39 [table-reader.26:src/test/java/travelator/tablereader/TableReaderAcceptanceTests.kt]

The function that we thought we would call `readTable` when we wrote the test turns out to be `readTableWithHeader`, so we make the change and run the test:

```
assertEquals(
    expected,
    readTableWithHeader(input).map { record ->
        Measurement(
```

```
            t = record["time"]?.toDoubleOrNull() ?: error("in time"),
            x = record["x"]?.toDoubleOrNull() ?: error("in x"),
            y = record["y"]?.toDoubleOrNull() ?: error("in y"),
        )
    }
```

Example 22.40 [table-reader.27:src/test/java/travelator/tablereader/TableReaderAcceptanceTests.kt]

It passes, and we ride the little dopamine hit to check in the code and take a coffee break.

Different Field Separators

Returning from coffee, we make a quick survey of the different places in Travelator that read tables. Interestingly, we only have one use case that reads classic "comma", "separated","variables" (with the quotes), but several need to use a semicolon as the field separator. It seems that some French SQL Server export job is using semicolons and then saving the file with a *.CSV* extension; maybe the *C* is for çemicolon? We'll address reading those next, but try to find an interface that will work with more complicated quoting and escaping rules. To add flexibility, we need to identify an abstraction, as we did with the `headerProvider` previously. What is the abstraction here?

Looking at the code, we see that the header and body parsing both call `splitFields`:

```
private fun headerProviderFrom(header: String): (Int) -> String {
    val headers = header.splitFields(",")
    return { index -> headers[index] }
}

private fun parseLine(
    line: String,
    headerProvider: (Int) -> String
): Map<String, String> {
    val values = line.splitFields(",")
    val keys = values.indices.map(headerProvider)
    return keys.zip(values).toMap()
}

private fun String.splitFields(separators: String): List<String> =
    if (isEmpty()) emptyList() else split(separators)
```

Example 22.41 [table-reader.28:src/main/java/travelator/tablereader/table-reading.kt]

Neither the header parsing nor the body parsing really want to depend on the details of how the splitting should happen, so let's abstract that behind a function `(String) -> List<String>`. Why that signature rather than just parameterizing the character?

That's an interesting question, thank you for asking it. Introducing a `separators` parameter to `parseLine` and `headerProviderFrom`, and eventually their callers `readTable` and `readTableWithHeader`, would be the simplest thing that we could do. We get a lot more flexibility from using a function type, though, because we can hide all the details of separating, quoting, and escaping behind that signature. In pre-lambda Java, the benefit of the flexibility wouldn't have been worth the cost of introducing and implementing a SAM interface, at least not until we really needed all that control. With lambdas in Java, the equation feels more balanced but probably not natural for most Java programmers. In Kotlin, designed from the outset with function types as part of the language, we use them even more readily. As soon as we need to parameterize an aspect of our code, it is natural to ask whether a function would provide more value than, erm, a simple value.

Let's start in `parseLine`. To extract the current splitting implementation, we can select `line.splitFields(",")` and "Introduce Functional Parameter", choosing the parameter name `splitter`:

```
fun readTable(
    lines: List<String>,
    headerProvider: (Int) -> String = Int::toString
): List<Map<String, String>> =
    lines.map {
        parseLine(it, headerProvider) { line -> ❶
            line.splitFields(",")
        }
    }

...

private fun parseLine(
    line: String,
    headerProvider: (Int) -> String,
    splitter: (String) -> List<String>, ❷
): Map<String, String> {
    val values = splitter(line)
    val keys = values.indices.map(headerProvider)
    return keys.zip(values).toMap()
}
```

Example 22.42 [table-reader.29:src/main/java/travelator/tablereader/table-reading.kt]

❶ This lambda…

❷ …implements the splitter.

We could continue this process, extracting the splitter lambda to the top level. Our lives will be made a bit easier, though, if we have a global value for the splitter, so we select the lambda in `readTable` and "Introduce Variable" named `splitOnComma`:

```
fun readTable(
    lines: List<String>,
    headerProvider: (Int) -> String = Int::toString
): List<Map<String, String>> =
```

```
    lines.map {
        val splitOnComma: (String) -> List<String> = { line ->
            line.splitFields(",")
        }
        parseLine(it, headerProvider, splitOnComma)
    }
```

Example 22.43 [table-reader.30:src/main/java/travelator/tablereader/table-reading.kt]

Now we can cut the `val` from the function and move it to the top level. It feels like there should be an automated refactor for this, but nothing works at the time of writing:

```
fun readTable(
    lines: List<String>,
    headerProvider: (Int) -> String = Int::toString
): List<Map<String, String>> =
    lines.map {
        parseLine(it, headerProvider, splitOnComma)
    }

val splitOnComma: (String) -> List<String> = { line ->
    line.splitFields(",")
}
```

Example 22.44 [table-reader.31:src/main/java/travelator/tablereader/table-reading.kt]

Now that `splitOnComma` is a global property, we can conveniently use it as a default. We select the reference to it in `readTable` and then "Introduce Parameter", with "Introduce default value", calling the new parameter `splitter`. This yields:

```
fun readTable(
    lines: List<String>,
    headerProvider: (Int) -> String = Int::toString,
    splitter: (String) -> List<String> = splitOnComma
): List<Map<String, String>> =
    lines.map {
        parseLine(it, headerProvider, splitter)
    }

val splitOnComma: (String) -> List<String> = { line ->
    line.splitFields(",")
}
```

Example 22.45 [table-reader.32:src/main/java/travelator/tablereader/table-reading.kt]

Because of the default value, we haven't had to change any of the clients, and the tests continue to pass. As it stands, `readTable` is now using the supplied `splitter`, but `headerProviderFrom` is not:

```
private fun headerProviderFrom(header: String): (Int) -> String {
    val headers = header.splitFields(",")
```

```
        return { index -> headers[index] }
    }
```

Example 22.46 [table-reader.32:src/main/java/travelator/tablereader/table-reading.kt]

Introducing a functional parameter for `header.splitFields(...)` yields:

```
fun readTableWithHeader(
    lines: List<String>
): List<Map<String, String>> =
    when {
        lines.isEmpty() -> emptyList()
        else -> readTable(
            lines.drop(1),
            headerProviderFrom(lines.first()) { header -> ❶
                header.splitFields(",")
            }
        )
    }

...

val splitOnComma: (String) -> List<String> = { line ->
    line.splitFields(",")
}

private fun headerProviderFrom(
    header: String,
    splitter: (String) -> List<String> ❷
): (Int) -> String {
    val headers = splitter(header)
    return { index -> headers[index] }
}
```

Example 22.47 [table-reader.33:src/main/java/travelator/tablereader/table-reading.kt]

❶ This lambda…

❷ …implements the splitter.

Now the lambda in `readTableWithHeader` is the same code as `splitOnComma`, so we use that instead:

```
fun readTableWithHeader(
    lines: List<String>
): List<Map<String, String>> =
    when {
        lines.isEmpty() -> emptyList()
        else -> readTable(
            lines.drop(1),
            headerProviderFrom(lines.first(), splitOnComma)
        )
    }
```

```
...

val splitOnComma: (String) -> List<String> = { line ->
    line.splitFields(",")
}
```

Example 22.48 [table-reader.34:src/main/java/travelator/tablereader/table-reading.kt]

You can see the pattern here. Now we make a parameter from the `splitOnComma` reference, again with a default to avoid breaking existing clients:

```
fun readTableWithHeader(
    lines: List<String>,
    splitter: (String) -> List<String> = splitOnComma
): List<Map<String, String>> =
    when {
        lines.isEmpty() -> emptyList()
        else -> readTable(
            lines.drop(1),
            headerProviderFrom(lines.first(), splitter)
        )
    }
```

Example 22.49 [table-reader.35:src/main/java/travelator/tablereader/table-reading.kt]

Finally, in `readTableWithHeader`, we are calling `readTable` without providing a `splitter`, so it will use its default (`splitOnComma`). We don't want this, so we pass the parameter down. The header and body should be using the same splitter, so we pass it from `readTableWithHeader` to the inner `readTable`:

```
fun readTableWithHeader(
    lines: List<String>,
    splitter: (String) -> List<String> = splitOnComma
): List<Map<String, String>> =
    when {
        lines.isEmpty() -> emptyList()
        else -> readTable(
            lines.drop(1),
            headerProviderFrom(lines.first(), splitter),
            splitter ❶
        )
    }

fun readTable(
    lines: List<String>,
    headerProvider: (Int) -> String = Int::toString,
    splitter: (String) -> List<String> = splitOnComma
): List<Map<String, String>> =
    lines.map {
        parseLine(it, headerProvider, splitter)
    }
```

Example 22.50 [table-reader.36:src/main/java/travelator/tablereader/table-reading.kt]

❶ Pass on the `splitter`.

Some test-driven developers might insist on a failing test to show the need for that last step. We certainly should write a test to demonstrate the use of the splitter, but before we do, let's make it more convenient to make one. Here is `splitOnComma`:

```
val splitOnComma: (String) -> List<String> = { line ->
    line.splitFields(",")
}
```

Example 22.51 [table-reader.36:src/main/java/travelator/tablereader/table-reading.kt]

It would be nice to be able to create splitters without having to define a lambda every time. That way, our French clients could call `readTable` with, for example, `splitter = splitOn(";")`. The `splitOn` function would take the separators and return a value of function type `(String) -> List<String>`. We could try to extract this function from our current `splitOnComma` lambda, but the refactoring is tedious, so instead let's just define the function and call it:

```
fun splitOn(
    separators: String
): (String) -> List<String> = { line: String ->
    line.splitFields(separators)
}

val splitOnComma: (String) -> List<String> = splitOn(",")
val splitOnTab: (String) -> List<String> = splitOn("\t")
```

Example 22.52 [table-reader.37:src/main/java/travelator/tablereader/table-reading.kt]

You can see that we have taken the opportunity to define a `splitOnTab`, too, so that we can use it in the new test we promised ourselves that we would write:

```
@Test
fun `can specify splitter`() {
    assertEquals(
        listOf(
            mapOf(
                "header1" to "field0",
                "header2" to "field1",
            )
        ),
        readTableWithHeader(
            listOf(
                "header1\theader2",
                "field0\tfield1"
            ),
            splitOnTab
        )
    )
}
```

Example 22.53 [table-reader.38:src/test/java/travelator/tablereader/TableReaderTests.kt]

This passes, giving us both reassurance and documentation. Let's check it in and take a break for a few minutes before coming back to take stock.

Sequences

We now have the basics of a table parser, and we haven't introduced any new types beyond those in the standard Kotlin runtime. This is often the way with a more functional approach. The grain of Kotlin is to leverage the rich abstractions provided by the standard library, where Java programs are more likely to define new types. As we saw in Chapter 6 and Chapter 15, one reason for the difference is that Kotlin allows us to treat collections as values, which makes them more safely composable than Java's mutable objects. We are able to define an API that takes and returns collection types without worrying about aliasing.

Value types may make for APIs composed of predictable calculations, but they can bring their own problems. Our naïve API suffers from the same issue as we saw in Chapter 20: it works on a `List<String>` loaded into memory and produces a `List<Map<String, String>>` also in memory. Even discounting the cost of the data structures, the memory footprint of `readTable` is twice the number of bytes of the input, which is (probably) twice the size of a UTF-8 encoded file containing the data. To process large files, it would be nice to work in terms of sequences rather than in terms of lists, since if-necessary sequences can keep only one item in each stage of a pipeline in memory at a time.

As we saw in Chapter 13, we can convert a `Sequence` to a `List` and back (with some caveats) very easily, so we could implement `Sequence` functions by delegating to our existing `List` API. This wouldn't reduce our memory footprint though, so instead we'll write the `Sequence` versions and delegate the `List` versions to them. If we're clever, we can test through the convenient `List` API, thus getting two sets of tests for the price of one.

`readTable` currently looks like this:

```
fun readTable(
    lines: List<String>,
    headerProvider: (Int) -> String = Int::toString,
    splitter: (String) -> List<String> = splitOnComma
): List<Map<String, String>> =
    lines.map {
        parseLine(it, headerProvider, splitter)
    }
```

Example 22.54 [table-reader.39:src/main/java/travelator/tablereader/table-reading.kt]

We can try out our plan by converting to and from `Sequence` in the middle of the pipeline:

```
fun readTable(
    lines: List<String>,
    headerProvider: (Int) -> String = Int::toString,
    splitter: (String) -> List<String> = splitOnComma
): List<Map<String, String>> =
    lines
        .asSequence()
        .map {
            parseLine(it, headerProvider, splitter)
        }
        .toList()
```

Example 22.55 [table-reader.40:src/main/java/travelator/tablereader/table-reading.kt]

That passes the tests, and they all funnel through this function, so that's reassuring. Now we can extract the inner workings into a function taking and returning a `Sequence`; this is extracting part of a chain as described in "Extracting Part of a Pipeline" on page 188:

```
fun readTable(
    lines: List<String>,
    headerProvider: (Int) -> String = Int::toString,
    splitter: (String) -> List<String> = splitOnComma
): List<Map<String, String>> =
    readTable(
        lines.asSequence(),
        headerProvider,
        splitter
    ).toList()

fun readTable(
    lines: Sequence<String>,
    headerProvider: (Int) -> String = Int::toString,
    splitter: (String) -> List<String> = splitOnComma
) = lines.map {
        parseLine(it, headerProvider, splitter)
    }
```

Example 22.56 [table-reader.41:src/main/java/travelator/tablereader/table-reading.kt]

This gives us a `Sequence` version of `readTable` that the `List` version calls, and the `List` version is well tested. Now for the outer `readTableWithHeader`. It looks like this:

```
fun readTableWithHeader(
    lines: List<String>,
    splitter: (String) -> List<String> = splitOnComma
): List<Map<String, String>> =
    when {
        lines.isEmpty() -> emptyList()
        else -> readTable(
            lines.drop(1),
            headerProviderFrom(lines.first(), splitter),
            splitter
```

```
    )
}
```

Example 22.57 [table-reader.42:src/main/java/travelator/tablereader/table-reading.kt]

Currently, `readTableWithHeader` is delegating to the `List` version of `readTable`. If we want to produce a `Sequence` version (and we do), it should call the `Sequence` version of `readTable`, so we inline the call here to give:

```
fun readTableWithHeader(
    lines: List<String>,
    splitter: (String) -> List<String> = splitOnComma
): List<Map<String, String>> =
    when {
        lines.isEmpty() -> emptyList()
        else -> readTable(
            lines.drop(1).asSequence(),
            headerProviderFrom(lines.first(), splitter),
            splitter
        ).toList()
    }
```

Example 22.58 [table-reader.43:src/main/java/travelator/tablereader/table-reading.kt]

Now, by hand, create a `linesAsSequence` as a variable and use it in place of `lines`. This nearly works:

```
fun readTableWithHeader(
    lines: List<String>,
    splitter: (String) -> List<String> = splitOnComma
): List<Map<String, String>> {
    val linesAsSequence = lines.asSequence()
    return when {
        linesAsSequence.isEmpty() -> emptySequence() ❶
        else -> {
            readTable(
                linesAsSequence.drop(1),
                headerProviderFrom(linesAsSequence.first(), splitter),
                splitter
            )
        }
    }.toList()
}
```

Example 22.59 [table-reader.44:src/main/java/travelator/tablereader/table-reading.kt]

❶ Doesn't compile because there is no `Sequence<T>.isEmpty()`.

How do we tell if a `Sequence` is empty? `linesAsSequence.firstOrNull() == null` does the trick:

```
fun readTableWithHeader(
    lines: List<String>,
    splitter: (String) -> List<String> = splitOnComma
```

```
): List<Map<String, String>> {
    val linesAsSequence = lines.asSequence()
    return when {
        linesAsSequence.firstOrNull() == null -> emptySequence()
        else -> {
            readTable(
                linesAsSequence.drop(1),
                headerProviderFrom(linesAsSequence.first(), splitter),
                splitter
            )
        }
    }.toList()
}
```

Example 22.60 [table-reader.45:src/main/java/travelator/tablereader/table-reading.kt]

This passes the tests, so we can again extract the expression between the `return` and `.toList()` as the function we are looking for. After extracting it and tidying up, we have the `Sequence` version of `readTableWithHeader`:

```
fun readTableWithHeader(
    lines: List<String>,
    splitter: (String) -> List<String> = splitOnComma
): List<Map<String, String>> =
    readTableWithHeader(
        lines.asSequence(),
        splitter
    ).toList()

fun readTableWithHeader(
    lines: Sequence<String>,
    splitter: (String) -> List<String> = splitOnComma
) = when {
    lines.firstOrNull() == null -> emptySequence()
    else -> {
        readTable(
            lines.drop(1),
            headerProviderFrom(lines.first(), splitter),
            splitter
        )
    }
}
```

Example 22.61 [table-reader.46:src/main/java/travelator/tablereader/table-reading.kt]

At this point, we have two versions of `readTable` and `readTableWithHeader`: a `List` and a `Sequence` version of each. Given how easy it is to convert a `List` argument to a `Sequence`, and a `Sequence` result to a `List`, maybe the `List` variants aren't paying their way? Let's just move their definitions into the tests while we don't have any production uses. That way, the tests can use them to stay simple, and the production code is kept minimal.

Here, then, is the entire public interface to our table parser:

```
fun readTableWithHeader(
    lines: Sequence<String>,
    splitter: (String) -> List<String> = splitOnComma
): Sequence<Map<String, String>> =
    when {
        lines.firstOrNull() == null -> emptySequence()
        else -> readTable(
            lines.drop(1),
            headerProviderFrom(lines.first(), splitter),
            splitter
        )
    }

fun readTable(
    lines: Sequence<String>,
    headerProvider: (Int) -> String = Int::toString,
    splitter: (String) -> List<String> = splitOnComma
): Sequence<Map<String, String>> =
    lines.map {
        parseLine(it, headerProvider, splitter)
    }

val splitOnComma: (String) -> List<String> = splitOn(",")
val splitOnTab: (String) -> List<String> = splitOn("\t")

fun splitOn(
    separators: String
) = { line: String ->
    line.splitFields(separators)
}
```

Example 22.62 [table-reader.47:src/main/java/travelator/tablereader/table-reading.kt]

This is supported by three utility functions:

```
private fun headerProviderFrom(
    header: String,
    splitter: (String) -> List<String>
): (Int) -> String {
    val headers = splitter(header)
    return { index -> headers[index] }
}

private fun parseLine(
    line: String,
    headerProvider: (Int) -> String,
    splitter: (String) -> List<String>,
): Map<String, String> {
    val values = splitter(line)
    val keys = values.indices.map(headerProvider)
    return keys.zip(values).toMap()
```

```
}

// Necessary because String.split returns a list of an empty string
// when called on an empty string.
private fun String.splitFields(separators: String): List<String> =
    if (isEmpty()) emptyList() else split(separators)
```

Example 22.63 [table-reader.47:src/main/java/travelator/tablereader/table-reading.kt]

When we looked back at the code, we realized that it wasn't clear *why* we needed `splitFields`, so we added a comment. It's often easier to do this in retrospect when we are trying to understand code we are returning to, rather than code we have just written. Apart from that, we think that the code is pretty self-explanatory. Sometimes we're wrong about that. If it takes us more than a glance to work out what is going on next time we read this code, we'll take the opportunity then to add more comments or, better, refactor to be more expressive.

Reading from a File

This seems a fine interface in the abstract, but the first time we come to use it in anger, we hit on a snag. Let's illustrate the problem with a test. This calls the `Sequence` version of `readTableWithHeader`:

```
@Test
fun `read from reader`() {
    val fileContents = """
        H0,H1
        row0field0,row0field1
        row1field0,row1field1
    """.trimIndent()
    StringReader(fileContents).useLines { lines ->
        val result = readTableWithHeader(lines).toList()
        assertEquals(
            listOf(
                mapOf("H0" to "row0field0", "H1" to "row0field1"),
                mapOf("H0" to "row1field0", "H1" to "row1field1")
            ),
            result
        )
    }
}
```

Example 22.64 [table-reader.48:src/test/java/travelator/tablereader/TableReaderTests.kt]

Can you see why this fails? What if we say that it fails with `java.lang.IllegalStateException: This sequence can be consumed only once.`?

Yes, once again ("Multiple Iterations" on page 173), `Sequence`s bite us because we didn't test both types—those that can and can't be consumed twice—as input:

```
fun readTableWithHeader(
    lines: Sequence<String>,
    splitter: (String) -> List<String> = splitOnComma
): Sequence<Map<String, String>> =
    when {
        lines.firstOrNull() == null -> emptySequence()
        else -> readTable(
            lines.drop(1),
            headerProviderFrom(lines.first(), splitter),
            splitter
        )
    }
```

Example 22.65 [table-reader.47:src/main/java/travelator/tablereader/table-reading.kt]

So `lines.firstOrNull()` consumes the sequence, and when reading from a `Reader` we can't just go back and start again in order to evaluate `lines.drop(1)` and `lines.first()`. Our unit tests were all starting from a `List` of all the file lines; those sequences *can* be consumed again, because they are held in memory.

To use our `Sequence` interface on data in files, we will either have to load it all into memory or find a way to fetch the first and rest of a `Sequence` without trying to read it twice. Given that we introduced the `Sequence` specifically to avoid loading all the data into memory at once, we choose the latter. All we need to do then is to check whether a `Sequence` has any items without consuming it. Can you see how?

Ah, that one was a trick question. To check, we *have* to call `iterator()` on the `Sequence`, which is the very thing that consumes it. We cannot see whether the `Sequence` is empty and then use it again later. Sometimes in logic though, when we can't do a thing that we want in isolation, we can do it and another thing that we want together. In this case, we don't just want to see whether the `Sequence` is empty; we want to split it into its head and tail if it isn't. We can achieve that wider goal by destructuring the `Sequence` with a function like this:

```
fun <T> Sequence<T>.destruct()
    : Pair<T, Sequence<T>>? {
    val iterator = this.iterator()
    return when {
        iterator.hasNext() ->
            iterator.next() to iterator.asSequence()
        else -> null
    }
}
```

Example 22.66 [table-reader.49:src/main/java/travelator/tablereader/table-reading.kt]

This `destruct` returns `null` if the `Sequence` is empty; otherwise, it returns a `Pair` of the head and the tail (where the tail may be an empty `Sequence`). It consumes the original (by calling `iterator()`) but provides a fresh `Sequence` to continue processing. We can use it to refactor `readTableWithHeader`, currently:

```
fun readTableWithHeader(
    lines: Sequence<String>,
    splitter: (String) -> List<String> = splitOnComma
): Sequence<Map<String, String>> =
    when {
        lines.firstOrNull() == null -> emptySequence()
        else -> readTable(
            lines.drop(1),
            headerProviderFrom(lines.first(), splitter),
            splitter
        )
    }
```

Example 22.67 [table-reader.48:src/main/java/travelator/tablereader/table-reading.kt]

It certainly isn't a trivial rearrangement, but we can transform this into:

```
fun readTableWithHeader(
    lines: Sequence<String>,
    splitter: (String) -> List<String> = splitOnComma
): Sequence<Map<String, String>> {
    val firstAndRest = lines.destruct()
    return when {
        firstAndRest == null -> emptySequence()
        else -> readTable(
            firstAndRest.second,
            headerProviderFrom(firstAndRest.first, splitter),
            splitter
        )
    }
}
```

Example 22.68 [table-reader.49:src/main/java/travelator/tablereader/table-reading.kt]

The new form passes all the tests, because it doesn't consume `lines` more than once. If it feels a little clunky, we can combine a `?.let`, destructuring, and an Elvis operator to give a single expression that you may or may not find acceptably terse. The result is this public API:

```
fun readTableWithHeader(
    lines: Sequence<String>,
    splitter: (String) -> List<String> = splitOnComma
): Sequence<Map<String, String>> =
    lines.destruct()?.let { (first, rest) ->
        readTable(
            rest,
            headerProviderFrom(first, splitter),
            splitter
        )
    } ?: emptySequence()

fun readTable(
    lines: Sequence<String>,
    headerProvider: (Int) -> String = Int::toString,
```

```
    splitter: (String) -> List<String> = splitOnComma
): Sequence<Map<String, String>> =
    lines.map {
        parseLine(it, headerProvider, splitter)
    }

val splitOnComma: (String) -> List<String> = splitOn(",")
val splitOnTab: (String) -> List<String> = splitOn("\t")

fun splitOn(
    separators: String
) = { line: String ->
    line.splitFields(separators)
}
```

Example 22.69 [table-reader.50:src/main/java/travelator/tablereader/table-reading.kt]

We are almost done, we promise.

The last step, now that the API has crystallized around two functions, is to take the opportunity to make the tests more expressive:

```
class TableReaderTests {
    @Test
    fun `empty input returns empty`() {
        checkReadTable(
            lines = emptyList(),
            shouldReturn = emptyList()
        )
    }

    @Test
    fun `one line of input with default field names`() {
        checkReadTable(
            lines = listOf("field0,field1"),
            shouldReturn = listOf(
                mapOf("0" to "field0", "1" to "field1")
            )
        )
    }

    ...
    @Test
    fun `can specify header names when there is no header row`() {
        val headers = listOf("apple", "banana")
        checkReadTable(
            lines = listOf("field0,field1"),
            withHeaderProvider = headers::get,
            shouldReturn = listOf(
                mapOf(
                    "apple" to "field0",
                    "banana" to "field1",
                )
```

```
            )
        )
    }

    @Test
    fun `readTableWithHeader takes headers from header line`() {
        checkReadTableWithHeader(
            lines = listOf(
                "H0,H1",
                "field0,field1"
            ),
            shouldReturn = listOf(
                mapOf("H0" to "field0", "H1" to "field1")
            )
        )
    }

    ...
}

private fun checkReadTable(
    lines: List<String>,
    withHeaderProvider: (Int) -> String = Int::toString,
    shouldReturn: List<Map<String, String>>,
) {
    assertEquals(
        shouldReturn,
        readTable(
            lines.asSequence().constrainOnce(),
            headerProvider = withHeaderProvider,
            splitter = splitOnComma
        ).toList()
    )
}

private fun checkReadTableWithHeader(
    lines: List<String>,
    withSplitter: (String) -> List<String> = splitOnComma,
    shouldReturn: List<Map<String, String>>,
) {
    assertEquals(
        shouldReturn,
        readTableWithHeader(
            lines.asSequence().constrainOnce(),
            splitter = withSplitter
        ).toList()
    )
}
```

Example 22.70 [table-reader.52:src/test/java/travelator/tablereader/TableReaderTests.kt]

This is an important step. As we saw in Chapter 17, finding the patterns in our tests and expressing them in functions (like `checkReadTable`) both help readers of the tests to see what the code is doing and can help us find gaps in our test coverage. For example, what is the behavior of our parser when there are more fields than headers or vice versa? The tests that we write for quick feedback while we are test-driving our implementation are unlikely to be optimally effective for communicating about the API, finding issues, or catching regressions if we return to the implementation and modify it. If we use TDD as a design technique, we mustn't forget to make sure that the final tests are fit for determining correctness, adding documentation, and preventing regression.

Comparison with Commons CSV

We started this chapter by saying that in most real-world situations, we would reach for Apache Commons CSV rather than rolling our own parser. Before we finish the chapter, let's compare our API with that of the Commons equivalent.

The most common use case for a table parser is to read a file with known columns, translating each row into some data class. Here is how we do that with our parser:

```
@Test
fun example() {
    reader.useLines { lines ->
        val measurements: Sequence<Measurement> =
            readTableWithHeader(lines, splitOnComma)
                .map { record ->
                    Measurement(
                        t = record["time"]?.toDoubleOrNull()
                            ?: error("in time"),
                        x = record["x"]?.toDoubleOrNull()
                            ?: error("in x"),
                        y = record["y"]?.toDoubleOrNull()
                            ?: error("in y"),
                    )
                }
        assertEquals(
            expected,
            measurements.toList()
        )
    }
}
```

Example 22.71 [table-reader.53:src/test/java/travelator/tablereader/CsvExampleTests.kt]

Real-world code would probably need more error handling (we see how in Chapter 21), but this shows the basic use case. We use the Kotlin `Reader.useLines` extension function to produce a `Sequence<String>`, which our parser transforms into a `Sequence<Map<String, String>>`. We can `map` over the `Map`s, indexing by field name to extract the data we need and transform it to the type (`Measurement`) that we actually want. This design didn't happen by accident—it was the decisions that we made at the very start, albeit with `List` rather than with `Sequence` at the time.

Here is the Commons CSV version:

```
@Test
fun `commons csv`() {
    reader.use { reader ->
        val parser = CSVParser.parse(
            reader,
            CSVFormat.DEFAULT.withFirstRecordAsHeader()
        )
        val measurements: Sequence<Measurement> = parser
            .asSequence()
            .map { record ->
                Measurement(
                    t = record["time"]?.toDoubleOrNull()
                        ?: error("in time"),
                    x = record["x"]?.toDoubleOrNull()
                        ?: error("in x"),
                    y = record["y"]?.toDoubleOrNull()
                        ?: error("in y"),
                )
            }
        assertEquals(
            expected,
            measurements.toList()
        )
    }
}
```

Example 22.72 [table-reader.53:src/test/java/travelator/tablereader/CsvExampleTests.kt]

It too has a static function entry point, `CSVParser.parse`, which also takes configuration about the table format (in this case, `CSVFormat.DEFAULT.withFirstRecordAsHeader()`; in ours, `splitOnComma`). We have two functions to differentiate between files with or without headers; the Apache API rolls this into the `CSVFormat`.

The Commons `parse` takes a `Reader` though, rather than our `Sequence<String>`. This allows it to handle record separators other than newline, and cope with having new lines in the middle of fields, but leads to a proliferation of `parse` methods. There are variants taking `Path`, `File`, `InputStream`, `String`, and `URL`. The developers probably felt these were necessary because Java provides so little support for converting between these types of sources and disposing of them safely. The `CSVParser` returned by the `parse` static method has a lot of code to manage resources. Our API delegates these to the workings of `Sequence` and Kotlin life cycle functions like `use` and `useLines`.

On the subject of lines, you have to read between them in the code example to see it, but `CSVParser` implements `Iterable<CSVRecord>`. This is a clever design choice, because it allows Java developers to use a `for` statement to loop over the records, and Kotlin developers to convert to a `Sequence` with `.asSequence`. In fact, the Kotlin usability is due to the design of the Kotlin standard library, which builds on the same `Iterable` abstraction that the Apache developers also leverage.

Moving on, the code to create an individual `Measurement` looks identical in both examples:

```
.map { record ->
    Measurement(
        t = record["time"]?.toDoubleOrNull()
            ?: error("in time"),
        x = record["x"]?.toDoubleOrNull()
            ?: error("in x"),
        y = record["y"]?.toDoubleOrNull()
            ?: error("in y"),
    )
}
```

Example 22.73 [table-reader.53:src/test/java/travelator/tablereader/CsvExampleTests.kt]

Although the type of `record` in our parser is `Map<String, String>`, in the Commons case it is `CSVRecord`. `CSVRecord` has a `get(String)` method, which is how `record["time"]` and so on are resolved. It also has methods: `get(int)` to retrieve a field by index, where we could use `Map.values.get(Int)`; `size()` rather than `Map.size()`; and `isSet(String)` to substitute for `Map.hasKey(String)`.

Basically, `CSVRecord` is having to reproduce the `Map` interface by hand rather than just *being* a `Map`. Why? Because, as we discussed in Chapter 6, the Java `Map` interface is mutable, and mutation makes no sense in the context of reading fields from a file; mutations certainly aren't going to be written back to the source. When programming in Java, we find ourselves having to create new types to solve problems, where in Kotlin we can express ourselves in standard types and then enjoy the richness of the Kotlin API on those types.

One area in which the Commons CSV library Excels™ is its provision of ready-made parser defaults. These are expressed as constants in the `CSVFormat` class. We've seen `CSVFormat.DEFAULT`, but there are many others, including `CSVFormat.EXCEL`. Armed with a `CSVFormat`, you can pass it to the `CSVParser.parse` method as we saw, or use it directly, for example, `CSVFormat.EXCEL.parse(reader)`. Can we provide this facility without defining new types in our API? How about using `splitOnComma` as if it was our configuration:

```
@Test
fun `configuration example`() {
    reader.use { reader ->
        val measurements = splitOnComma.readTableWithHeader(reader)
            .map { record ->
                Measurement(
                    t = record["time"]?.toDoubleOrNull()
                        ?: error("in time"),
                    x = record["x"]?.toDoubleOrNull()
                        ?: error("in x"),
                    y = record["y"]?.toDoubleOrNull()
                        ?: error("in y"),
```

```
                )
            }
        assertEquals(
            expected,
            measurements.toList()
        )
    }
}
```

Example 22.74 [table-reader.54:src/test/java/travelator/tablereader/CsvExampleTests.kt]

We can achieve this by defining `splitOnComma.readTableWithHeader(reader)` as an extension function on the function type:

```
fun ((String) -> List<String>).readTableWithHeader(
    reader: StringReader
): Sequence<Map<String, String>> =
    readTableWithHeader(reader.buffered().lineSequence(), this)
```

Example 22.75 [table-reader.54:src/main/java/travelator/tablereader/table-reading.kt]

In reality, `CSVFormat` represents a whole package of strategies for escaping rules, what to do with blank lines, and so on, not just how to split a line. When our parser grows these facilities, then we will probably want to create a data class to collect them. Until that point, we have been able to progress using just the built-in types and Kotlin language features.

There is another useful feature that the Commons interface provides that ours doesn't, and that we will finally need to create a type to implement. Commons CSV has `CSVParser.getHeaderNames` to provide access to the header information. Can we add this facility without modifying our current API, or at least requiring changes to our client code?

For many inputs, we could just call `Map.keys` on the first of the output `Sequence`, but this won't work if the table has no data rows, only a header. To return header information *and* the parsed records, we could return a `Pair<List<String>, Sequence<Map<String, String>>`, but this will force our current clients to discard the first of the pair. Instead, we can return a type `Table` that implements `Sequence<Map<String, String>>` but also has a header property. This way, all our current callers remain unchanged, but we can access `headers` when required:

```
@Test
fun `Table contains headers`() {
    val result: Table = readTableWithHeader(
        listOf(
            "H0,H1",
            "field0,field1"
        ).asSequence()
    )
    assertEquals(
        listOf("H0", "H1"),
```

```
            result.headers
        )
    }

    @Test
    fun `Table contains empty headers for empty input`() {
        assertEquals(
            emptyList<String>(),
            readTableWithHeader(emptySequence()).headers
        )
    }
```

Example 22.76 [table-reader.55:src/test/java/travelator/tablereader/TableReaderTests.kt]

We'll spare you the refactoring steps, but here is the implementation:

```
class Table(
    val headers: List<String>,
    val records: Sequence<Map<String, String>>
) : Sequence<Map<String, String>> by records

fun readTableWithHeader(
    lines: Sequence<String>,
    splitter: (String) -> List<String> = splitOnComma
): Table =
    lines.destruct()?.let { (first, rest) ->
        tableOf(splitter, first, rest)
    } ?: Table(emptyList(), emptySequence())

private fun tableOf(
    splitter: (String) -> List<String>,
    first: String,
    rest: Sequence<String>
): Table {
    val headers = splitter(first)
    val sequence = readTable(
        lines = rest,
        headerProvider = headers::get,
        splitter = splitter
    )
    return Table(headers, sequence)
}
```

Example 22.77 [table-reader.55:src/main/java/travelator/tablereader/table-reading.kt]

Moving On

In this final leg of our journey, we allowed ourselves the luxury of writing Kotlin from scratch rather than refactoring our existing Java. Even then, we started from the tests and then just copied the test data into our implementation and refactored from there. We can't write all code this way, but it does work well when our code is just calculations, and the more of it that is just calculations, the better our code works, too.

We saw the power of reusing built-in types in Chapter 15, *Encapsulated Collections to Type Aliases*, and Chapter 16, *Interfaces to Functions*, and defining APIs as extension functions in Chapter 10, *Functions to Extension Functions*. In this example, both collection and function types came together nicely, and we even managed to define an extension function on a function type! Where we would have had to define new classes to encapsulate Java's mutable collections, and methods to manipulate those collections, we passed Kotlin's immutable collections between our functions and wrote application-specific extensions on those collection types. Where we would have needed to define interfaces in Java, we used Kotlin's function types.

Again, not all problems can or should be solved this way, but your authors have found that while it is hard to make Java bend in this direction, Kotlin features combine to actively encourage this style. We shouldn't get hung up on not defining new types, but neither should we leap to solve every problem with a new class.

CHAPTER 23

Continuing the Journey

We've arrived at the end of the book. Thank you for coming on the journey. Your authors are privileged to have worked with, and learned from, many great developers, and now you are on that list. Even if you skipped a couple of chapters, or zoned out in the middle of the odd refactoring, it's been good to have someone to talk to. We can't pair on improving Travelator anymore, but what have we learned from our travels?

When O'Reilly asked us if we would like to write a book on Kotlin, we had to think about what we wanted to write and about what enough people might want to read. We knew that we had been on a journey adopting the language and that we are comfortable at the destination, but we also knew that our starting point was not that of the typical Java developer. We saw that most existing books taught Kotlin as if it were just another syntax for Java, one that could achieve more with less typing but didn't require a change in approach. That wasn't our experience; we found that Kotlin's sweet spot required more functional thinking than Java. Books on functional programming in Kotlin, though, seem to ask the reader to leave behind all that they know about programming with objects and join a new cult. We weren't comfortable with this either. Classes and objects are a humane way of expressing behavior, especially compared to many functional idioms. Why remove tools from our box when there is plenty of room? Can't we just have more tools and pick the right one for the job?

Grain

This thinking led Nat to come up with the metaphor that programming languages have a grain that influences the design of the programs we write in them. The grain makes certain design styles easy to apply and makes others arduous or risky.

The grain of Kotlin is different from that of Java. Java's grain favors mutable objects and reflection at the cost of composability and type safety. Compared to Java, Kotlin favors the transformation of immutable values and freestanding functions, and has a type system that is unobtrusive and helpful. Although it is easy to convert Java to Kotlin with IntelliJ, we end up with Java in Kotlin syntax rather than taking advantage of all that the new language could offer if we changed our thinking, too.

Java and Kotlin can coexist in the same codebase, and the interop boundary is almost seamless, but there are some risks when you pass information from the strictly typed world of Kotlin to the more loosely typed world of Java. With care, we find that we can transform code from idiomatic Java to idiomatic Kotlin in small, safe steps, using automated refactoring tools where possible and editing text as a last resort. We can also support the conventions of both languages at the same time when we must maintain Java code while we are converting code it depends on to Kotlin.

Functional Thinking

As we've seen in some of our history lessons, the grain of Java was formed in the 1990s, when we believed that object-oriented programming was the mythical silver bullet. When OO turned out not to solve all our problems, mainstream programming languages, and even Java itself, began to adopt ideas from functional programming. Kotlin was born from Java in this age, and, like our children are better equipped for the future than we are, Kotlin is more suited to modern programming than Java is.

What do we mean by functional thinking?

Our software is ultimately limited by our ability to understand it. Our understanding is in turn ultimately limited by the complexity of the software we have created, and a lot of that complexity arises over confusion about *when* things happen. Functional programmers have learned that the easiest way to tame that complexity is simply to have things *happen* a lot less. They call things happening an *effect*: a change that is observable in some scope.

Mutating a variable or a collection *inside* a function is an effect, but unless that variable is shared *outside* the function, it doesn't *affect* any other code. When the scope of an effect is local to a function, we don't have to consider it when reasoning about what our system does. As soon as we mutate shared state (a parameter to the function, perhaps, or a global variable, or a file or network socket), our local effect becomes an effect in whatever scope can see the shared thing, and that quickly increases complexity and makes understanding more difficult.

It isn't enough that a function doesn't *actually* mutate shared state. If there is a possibility that a function *could* mutate shared state, we have to examine the source of the function and, recursively, every function that it calls, to understand what our system does. Every piece of global mutable state makes every function suspect. Similarly, if we program in an environment in which every function can write to the database, we lose the ability to predict when such writes can occur and plan accordingly.

So functional programmers tame complexity by reducing mutation. Sometimes they program in languages (like Clojure and Haskell) that enforce controls on mutation. Otherwise, they work by convention. If we adopt these conventions in more general languages, we gain more ability to reason with our code. Kotlin chooses not to enforce the control of effects, but the language and its runtime come with some built-in conventions to nudge us in the right direction. Compared to Java, we have, for example, an immutable `val` declaration rather than an optional `final` modifier, read-only views of collections, and concise data classes to encourage copy-on-write rather than mutation. Many of this book's chapters describe more subtle conventions with the same aim: Chapter 5, *Beans to Values*, Chapter 6, *Java to Kotlin Collections*, Chapter 7, *Actions to Calculations*, Chapter 14, *Accumulating Objects to Transformations*, and Chapter 20, *Performing I/O to Passing Data*.

There is, of course, much more to functional programming than simply not mutating shared state. But if we just focus on solving problems without mutation (or where mutation is the point, we minimize its scope), our systems become easier to understand and change. Like "Don't repeat yourself" (*https://oreil.ly/HSaLs*) (aka "Once and only once" (*https://oreil.ly/5HKxy*)), assiduous application of a simple rule has profound effects. Both "Don't mutate shared state" and "Once and only once" share another property though—if we aren't careful, applying the rules can increase complexity faster than they reduce it. We need to learn techniques that allow us to manage mutation (and remove duplication, facilitate testing, and so on) without making our code even harder to understand, and to recognize these techniques for what they are when we see them. These techniques will tend to be different in different languages, environments, and domains, and are the craft of our profession.

If you research functional techniques, you will come across a lot of anti-object sentiment. This seems to be rooted in a perception that OO is all about mutable objects, but we shouldn't throw the message-passing baby out with the mutable bathwater. Although we can use OO to manage shared mutable state, in practice, these days we generally use objects to encapsulate immutable state, or to represent services and their dependencies. We saw in Chapter 16, *Interfaces to Functions*, that we can use both functions with closure, and classes with properties, to encapsulate data. Both can also hide code details and allow a client to work with different implementations. We need these points of inflection to build flexible, robust, and testable systems. Where in Java we traditionally reach for subclassing as a tool, Kotlin, with its default-closed classes, encourages a more compositional style. Instead of overriding a protected method, we have a function-typed property representing a strategy or a collaborator. We should favor this style but not be embarrassed to define class and subclass hierarchies where they simplify our implementation. Similarly, extension functions in Chapter 10, *Functions to Extension Functions*, are all very well, and they can work wonders to reduce coupling between disparate concerns in our codebases, but they are no substitute for polymorphic methods when that is what we need.

In the end, one of the attractions of programming is its combination of the human and the mathematical. Objects and classes are, to your authors at least, a more human way of modeling the world, and that is often a fine starting point. When we need rigor (which is often, but not as often as muggles might think), functional programming is there for us. We see no reason to have to choose one camp or the other when we can have two tents and move between them both, and Kotlin allows us to do that better than any other language we have found.

Simple Design

If complexity is the limiting factor in our software, and functional thinking is a tool for reducing complexity, how does that fit with other maxims—in particular, Kent Beck's Rules of Simple Design (*Extreme Programming Explained: Embrace Change*)? These have served us well for two decades, and say that a simple design:

- Passes the tests
- Reveals intention
- Has no duplication
- Has fewest elements

Of these, "reveals intention" is the most open to interpretation, so let's pull on that thread.

An intention is "an aim or plan": it implies change. It implies action. By differentiating between actions and calculations in our code, we show where we expect things to happen and where we don't: which things may be affected by other things and which things won't. When the majority of our code is in the form of calculations, we can be explicit about which functions are actions, better revealing our intent.

As we saw in Chapter 7, *Actions to Calculations*, and Chapter 20, *Performing I/O to Passing Data*, our main technique to disentangle calculations from actions is moving the actions out to the entry points of our interactions, so that they contaminate the least code. This is neither easy nor a panacea, but we find that it does produce designs that are simpler and code that is less complex.

Functional Programming and Textual Reasoning

When we finished this book, we realized—to our surprise—that we had not included any software design diagrams.

Partly, frankly, this was laziness. It's hard enough to manage the multiple versions of the example code as it passes through refactorings without having to worry about other views. But we also make it a habit to try to express ourselves in just the programming language that we have. If we can achieve enough comprehension in just the raw text, then in our day jobs, we won't be forced to switch contexts to view a diagram that may or may not be in sync with the code.

When we've written about object-oriented design, we've relied on diagrams to show the dynamic structure and behavior of the software and how changes to the source affect its dynamic behavior. In object-oriented software, that dynamic structure—the graph of objects and how messages flow between them—is largely implicit. This makes it hard to relate what you see in the source to what will happen at runtime, so visualization is a vital part of object-oriented programming. Through the 1980s and 1990s, software design luminaries created a variety of diagram notations to visualize object-oriented software. In the mid 1990s, the designers of the most popular notations, Grady Booch, Ivar Jacobson, and James Rumbaugh, combined their efforts into the *Unified Modeling Language* (UML).

The functional programming community doesn't have such a focus on diagrams and visualization. The goal of functional programming is *algebraic reasoning*: reasoning about the behavior of a program by manipulating its textual expressions. Referential transparency and static types allow us to reason about our programs solely by using the syntax of the source code. This results in a much closer correspondence between source code and runtime. As our code becomes more functional, we find that we can *read* our system's behavior without having to think hard about mechanisms that are not immediately apparent in the source and have to be visualized to be understood.

Refactoring

Along with the pragmatic functional programming, refactoring is the other key tenet of this book. Refactoring plays an important part in our professional lives because, if we don't know enough about the eventual form of our system to get its design right the first time, we will have to transform what we have into what we need. Your authors, at least, have never known enough about the eventual form of a system to get its design right the first time. Even those applications where we started with detailed requirements ended up very different from those specifications by the time they were delivered.

Late in a project and against schedule pressure is no time to learn how to refactor your code. Instead, we take every opportunity to practice refactoring. As we saw in Chapter 22, *Classes to Functions*, even when writing code from scratch we will often hard-code values to get a test to pass and then refactor to remove duplication between the tests and production code. We are always looking for new ways to get tests passing quickly and then refactor our way into code that looks like we planned it that way. Sometimes we discover a new automated refactoring built into IntelliJ; other times, we find a way to combine existing refactorings to achieve our aims.

When the scope of a change is small, we can get away with hand-editing a definition and then its uses to match, or sometimes, more usefully, the other way around. This becomes tedious and error prone when a change affects many files though, so practicing using the tools to achieve even small changes will equip us when faced with larger refactoring challenges. Where we do have a multistage refactor, or where we have to manually apply changes in multiple places, "Expand-and-Contract Refactoring" on page 44 allows us to keep the system building and working throughout the process. This is vital when a change may take multiple days or even weeks, because it allows us to continually merge our work with other changes in the system. Once you've thrown away a month of work because a big-bang merge at the end proved impossible, you come to appreciate the value of this technique and want to practice it even when it isn't strictly necessary.

We hope that the refactorings in this book expand your ambition. Your authors have been lucky enough to work with some world-class practitioners, the sort of people who tut if you cause a compile error during a refactoring. The transformations we have shown may not be optimal (and even if they were, the state of the art will change with tooling and language changes), but they are genuine, and they do reflect how we write and refactor code.

Refactoring and Functional Thinking

As we've seen on our tour, there is a relationship between functional thinking and refactoring. Refactoring is a rearrangement of our code, and where that code represents actions ("Actions" on page 79)—code that depends on when you run it—the rearrangement may change when actions run, and so the functioning of the software. In contrast, calculations ("Calculations" on page 78) are safe to rearrange but are ultimately impotent. (Without reading and writing, our code is simply generating heat.) Functional thinking encourages us to recognize and control actions and, by doing so, makes refactoring much safer.

Your authors learned this the hard way. We learned to refactor in the days of mutable objects, and introduced bugs when we failed to predict the consequences. This could have led us to abandon refactoring, but we still weren't clever enough to design our systems right in the first place. Instead, we discovered that a certain style of programming—object orientation but with immutable objects—was expressive and understandable, refactorable and safe. When we adopted that style in our Java code, it was often working against the grain, but despite this, it was much more productive than the alternatives. Discovering Kotlin, we realized that this is the sweet spot for us. Now we can use a modern language where functional thinking is part of the design, objects are still well-supported, and refactoring tooling is not an afterthought.

As Kent Beck put it: "Make the change easy, then make the easy change." Continually refactor so that every change you need to make is an easy change. Refactoring is the fundamental practice for tackling the inherent complexity of our software.

Safe travels.

Bibliography

Learning Kotlin

Bruce Eckel and Svetlana Isakova. *Atomic Kotlin*. Mindview. 2021. ISBN 978-0981872551.

Dawn Griffiths and David Griffiths. *Head First Kotlin*. O'Reilly Media, Inc. 2019. ISBN 978-1491996690.

Venkat Subramaniam. *Programming Kotlin*. Pragmatic Bookshelf. 2019. ISBN 978-1680506358.

Testing and Test-Driven Development

Kent Beck. *Test-Driven Development By Example*. Addision-Wesley Professional. 2002. ISBN 978-0321146533.

Steve Freeman and Nat Pryce. *Growing Object-Oriented Software Guided by Tests*. Addison-Wesley Professional. 2009. ISBN 978-0321503626.

Catalin Tudose. *JUnit in Action, Third Edition*. Manning Publications. 2021. ISBN 978-1617297045

Working with Legacy Code

Ola Ellnestam and Daniel Brolund. *The Mikado Method*. Manning Publications. 2014. ISBN 978-1617291210.

Michael Feathers. *Working Effectively with Legacy Code*. Prentice Hall. 2004. ISBN 978-0131177055.

Oscar Nierstrasz, Stéphane Ducasse, and Serge Demeyer. *Object-Oriented Reengineering Patterns*. Square Bracket Associates. 2009. ISBN 978-3952334126.

Software Design and Development

Kent Beck. *Extreme Programming Explained: Embrace Change*. Addison-Wesley Professional. 1999. ISBN 978-0201616415.

Martin Fowler. *Refactoring: Improving the Design of Existing Code*. Addison-Wesley Professional. 1999. ISBN 978-0201485677.

Martin Fowler. *Refactoring: Improving the Design of Existing Code*. 2nd edition. Addison-Wesley Professional. 2018. ISBN 978-0134757599.

Erich Gamma, Richard Helm, Ralph Johnson, and John Vlissides. *Design Patterns: Elements of Reusable Object-Oriented Software*. Addison-Wesley Professional. 1999. ISBN 978-0201633610.

Joshua Kerievsky. *Refactoring to Patterns*. Addison-Wesley Professional. 2004. ISBN 978-0321213358.

Eric Normand. *Grokking Simplicity: Taming Complex Software with Functional Thinking*. Manning Publications. 2021. ISBN 978-1617296208.

Java and the JVM

James Gosling, Bill Joy, Guy Steele, Gilad Bracha, and Alex Buckley. *The Java Language Specification, Java SE 8 Edition*. Addison-Wesley Professional. 2014. ISBN 978-0133900699.

Tim Lindholm, Frank Yellin, Gilad Bracha, and Alex Buckley. *The Java Virtual Machine Specification, Java SE 8 Edition*. Addison-Wesley Professional. 2014. ISBN 978-0133905908.

Index

Symbols

A

B

C

D

E

F

G

H

I

J

K

L

M

N

O

P

Q

R

W

X

About the Authors

Between them, **Nat Pryce** and **Duncan McGregor** have over five decades of professional experience in software development. They've written a lot of software in a lot of industries. They've also written a lot about writing software, written software to help them write about writing software, given talks about writing software, run workshops about writing software at conferences, and helped organize conferences about writing software.

A lot of the software they wrote they wrote in Java. Not all, but a lot. They are old enough to remember when Java was a breath of fresh air compared to C++. And now they find Kotlin to be a breath of fresh air compared to Java. So they've written a book about writing software with Kotlin (and wrote some software to help them write it).

Colophon

The animal on the cover of *Java to Kotlin* is a Hausa genet (*Genetta thierryi*), also known as Thierry's genet. Genets are small, cat-like creatures found in the forests, savannahs, and shrublands ranging from The Gambia to Cameroon. Their speed and agility make them difficult to observe in nature, but Hausa genets have been spotted in the rainforests of Sierra Leone, Ghana, and Côte d'Ivoire, the steppes of Senegal, and the woodlands of Guinea-Bissau.

Hausa genets are typically light brown with rusty to black spots on the body and stripes down the back. Large triangular ears and round eyes protrude from their long, angular face. Their tails are as long as the body and banded with dark rings. The different genet species all have similar markings, grow from 13–33 inches, and weigh anywhere between 4–40 pounds. Hausa genets are on the smaller end of this range in both size and weight. Because they have been so hard to study, we don't know much about their behavior or diet. Other species of genet are nocturnal and spend their days sleeping in burrows or hollow trees. By night, these opportunistic omnivores hunt for small mammals and reptiles, or forage for eggs, fruit, insects, and roots.

Hausa genets are rare, but they are classified as a species of "Least Concern" by the IUCN due to the variety of habitats and relatively wide range they occupy in West Africa. However, they have been trafficked for their skin or as pets in the past, and have been hunted as bushmeat. Many of the animals on O'Reilly covers are endangered; all of them are important to the world.

The cover illustration is by Karen Montgomery, based on a black and white engraving from Wood's *Animate Creation*. The cover fonts are Gilroy Semibold and Guardian Sans. The text font is Adobe Minion Pro; the heading font is Adobe Myriad Condensed; and the code font is Dalton Maag's Ubuntu Mono.

Milton Keynes UK
Ingram Content Group UK Ltd.
UKHW030107200923
428991UK00005B/15